Organizational Behaviour in Healthcare

Published in co-operation with the Society for Studies in Organizing Healthcare (SHOC), this series has two strands, the first of which consists of specially selected papers taken from the biennial conferences held by SHOC that present a cohesive and focused insight into issues within the field of organizational behaviour in healthcare.

The series also encourages proposals for monographs and edited collections to address the additional and emergent topics in the field of health policy, organization and management. Books within the series aim to advance scholarship on the application of social science theories, methods and concepts to the study of organizing and managing healthcare services and systems.

Providing a new platform for advanced and engaged scholarship, books in the series will advance the academic community by fostering a deep analysis on the challenges for healthcare organizations and management with an explicitly international and comparative focus.

All book proposals and manuscript submissions are single blind peer reviewed. All chapters in contributed volumes are double blind peer reviewed. For more information on Palgrave Macmillan's peer review policy please visit our website: https://www.palgrave.com/gp/book-authors/your-career/early-career-researcher-hub/peer-review-process

To submit a book proposal for inclusion in this series please contact Liz Barlow for further information: liz.barlow@palgrave.com. For information on the book proposal process please visit this website: https://www.palgrave.com/gp/book-authors/publishing-guidelines/submit-a-proposal

More information about this series at
https://link.springer.com/bookseries/14724

Justin Waring · Jean-Louis Denis ·
Anne Reff Pedersen · Tim Tenbensel
Editors

Organising Care in a Time of Covid-19

Implications for Leadership, Governance and Policy

palgrave
macmillan

Editors
Justin Waring
Health Services Management Centre
University of Birmingham
Birmingham, UK

Jean-Louis Denis
School of Public Health
Université de Montréal
Montréal, QC, Canada

Anne Reff Pedersen
Copenhagen Business School
Copenhagen, Denmark

Tim Tenbensel
University of Auckland
Auckland, New Zealand

ISSN 2662-1045 ISSN 2662-1053 (electronic)
Organizational Behaviour in Healthcare
ISBN 978-3-030-82695-6 ISBN 978-3-030-82696-3 (eBook)
https://doi.org/10.1007/978-3-030-82696-3

This Palgrave Macmillan imprint is published by the registered company Springer Nature Switzerland AG
The registered company address is: Gewerbestrasse 11, 6330 Cham, Switzerland

Contents

Notes on Contributors

Mathieu Albert is an Associate Professor in the Department of Psychiatry and the Institute of Health Policy, Management and Evaluation at the University of Toronto, and Senior Scientist at the Institute for Research in Education and the Wilson Centre at the University Health Network. His current work is located at the intersection of higher education and the sociology of science and knowledge. He has published in a wide range of disciplinary and interdisciplinary journals in social science and in medicine, including articles on interdisciplinarity, academic assessment criteria and boundary-making between scientific groups. He received the Sociology of Knowledge and Technology section best paper award in 2011 (American Sociological Association) for his paper entitled: *Boundary-Work in the Health Research Field: Biomedical and Clinician Scientists' Perceptions of Social Science Research*, and the 2001 Sheffield Prize awarded by the Canadian Society for the Study of Higher Education for his paper on funding agencies.

G. Ross Baker is a Professor in the Institute of Health Policy, Management and Evaluation at the University of Toronto. His research includes studies of patient safety, quality improvement, patient engagement and integrated care systems. Recent projects include an assessment of the impact of hospital characteristics, including safety culture on the incidence of adverse events in hospitals and studies of patient engagement in Canadian healthcare organisations.

Minal Bakhai is the National Clinical Director for Digital First Primary Care at NHS England and NHS improvement (NHSE/I) and a GP in a highly deprived area of London where she has spent the last 10 years focused on reducing health inequalities for her population. Minal is an expert advisor for the UK's National Institute for Health and Care Excellence (NICE) and chairs a number of forums, such as the national Digital Primary Care Clinical Leads Network. She also sits on the UK Cross Regulatory Group for Standards in Digital Healthcare.

Alongside being a GP, in her NHSE/I role, Minal has been developing a national shared learning system, driven by data and evidence, to inform policy and the implementation of digital interventions to improve outcomes for patients and staff in primary care. Minal has a strong focus on promoting user-centred design in digital health to mitigate against exclusion, improve the patient and staff experience, and strengthen clinical safety. During COVID-19, she led national clinical guidance for the inclusive and safe implementation of online and video consultation systems and digitally supported triage in primary care and a national evidence and support strategy to enable continuous service improvement.

Jenske Bal is a junior researcher at the Healthcare Governance department of ESHPM. She studied cultural anthropology and science and technology studies and is trained as a qualitative researcher. She is interested in topics on the verge of social science, humanities, healthcare and biology. For her master's thesis, she researched the practice of (re)writing infection prevention protocols in a Dutch academic hospital during the emerging corona crisis and continues to research the regional organisation of COVID care. She published on the management of uncertainty in COVID care in the journal *Health, Risk & Society*.

Roland Bal is Professor in and chair of the Department of Healthcare governance at ESHPM of the Erasmus University Rotterdam. Having a background in Science & Technology Studies, he is particularly interested in the ways in which infrastructures for the governance of healthcare are developed and the ways in which these constitute healthcare practices. Being interested in action-oriented forms of doing research, Bal has organised many partnerships with actors in healthcare, ranging from healthcare providers to regulators. He has worked extensively with the Dutch healthcare inspectorate on methods of supervision and with ZonMw, the main funder of health research in The Netherlands, on programme evaluation. From the start of the COVID crisis he leads an ethnographic study of pandemic decision-making. Recent publications have appeared in *Science, Technology & Human Values*, *Governance & Regulation*, and *BMJ Quality & Safety*, amongst others.

Mylaine Breton is an Associate Professor in Department of social science and medicine, Faculty of Medicine and Health Science, University of Sherbrooke, Researcher at Research Center Charles-Lemoyne Hospital. The research of Professor Breton aims at better understanding promising organisational innovations to improve primary healthcare accessibility and continuity such as the implementation of centralised waiting list for patients without a family physician and advanced access.

Emily Burn is a Research Fellow at the University of Birmingham. Working within the Health Services Management Centre (HSMC), she contributes to projects researching health policy and management, and other related fields. Prior to this, Emily was part of a research team exploring local authority social care market-shaping activities and the development and access of personalised care and support. Before joining the University of Birmingham, Emily held a number of research and policy positions across the health and social care sector.

Trishna Chauhan is a Ph.D. student at Warwick Business School. Her doctoral thesis uses a paradox lens to understand the processes and responses embedded with ongoing tensions. Her research interests include issues of identity, paradoxical tensions and collaboration between different occupational groups. The majority of her research focuses on healthcare services, with a particular interest in policy and organisational behaviour. Trishna's research is funded by the NIHR West Midlands.

Kath Checkland is a GP and health policy researcher. After an early career spent as a GP partner, she moved into academia with a Ph.D. exploring the effect of bureaucratic initiatives such as guidelines and quality incentives on GP practices. She leads a team of researchers at the University of Manchester whose work explores the development and impact of health policy in the UK. Working with colleagues from the University of Kent and the London School of Hygiene and Tropical Medicine, she is a Co-Director of the Policy Research Unit in Health and Care Systems and Commissioning, leading research commissioned by the Department of Health and Social Care to support policy in this area. Her work seeks to bring together knowledge of the day-to-day realities of NHS service organisation and delivery with a sociologically-informed understanding of the institutions, organisations and policy context that underpin and affect those services.

Charlotte Croft is an Associate Professor at Warwick Business School. Her research interests include issues of professional identity, leadership and collaboration in healthcare contexts. Her work has been widely published in world leading journals including the *Journal of Management Studies*, *Organization Studies*, *Human Relations* and *Public Administration*. Charlotte was previously an NIHR-funded Research Fellow exploring the absorptive capacity of Clinical Commissioning Groups during commissioning decisions. She was awarded her Ph.D. from Warwick Business School in 2012, and her doctoral thesis focused on the challenges of leadership for nurses in middle management positions. Charlotte has worked extensively into collaborative research and educational projects in Australia, and holds an honorary faculty position at Monash University, Melbourne. Prior to moving into academia, Charlotte worked as an Intensive Care Staff Nurse.

Jean-Louis Denis holds the Canada research chair (tier I) on Health System Design and Adaptation. He is Senior Scientist, Health System and Innovation, at the Research Center of the CHUM (CRCHUM), and Visiting Professor, Department of Management, King's College London. His current research looks at integration of care and services, healthcare reforms and health system transformation, medical compensation, professional leadership and clinical governance.

Bert de Graaff works as an Assistant Professor at the Healthcare Governance department of ESHPM at the Erasmus University Rotterdam. He is trained as a sociologist at the University of Amsterdam and is generally interested in questions on the sociology of risk and uncertainty and patient and client participation. Bert addresses these questions mainly using qualitative research methods, and often in close collaboration with healthcare practice, like the Dutch Health and Youth Care Inspectorate (IGJ) and as a coordinator of an Academic Collaboration with the Dutch National Healthcare Institute (ZIN). Recent empirical research focuses on understanding Dutch healthcare decision-making and the crisis-organisation during the COVID-19 pandemic in an ongoing ethnographic study.

Paul du Gay is Professor and Director of Research in the School of Business and Management, Royal Holloway, University of London, and

Professor in the Department of Organization (IOA), Copenhagen Business School. He is the author inter alia of *In Praise of Bureaucracy* (Sage) and co-author (with Signe Vikkelsø) of *For Formal Organization* (OUP). He is currently completing *For Public Service: State/Office/Ethics* (with Thomas Lopdrup Hjorth) for Routledge.

Martijn Felder is Assistant Professor at ESHPM of the Erasmus University Rotterdam. Trained as a social scientist, he obtained his Ph.D. degree at ESHPM studying the epistemological and political dimensions of policy experimentation in Dutch healthcare governance. Felder has strong interests in social theory and different conceptions of healthcare, politics and practice. He draws on current advances in the literature(s) on Professionalism and Science and Technology Studies—as well as Public Administration and Political Theory—to explore the diverse and intricate connections between professionalisation, rationalisation and politisation. Martijn typically uses qualitative research methods and currently studies the professionalisation of Dutch nursing, foregrounding the emotional, relational and political dimensions in the (re)organisation and (re)valuation of nursing work.

Rebecca Fisher is a Senior Policy Fellow at the Health Foundation where she leads policy work on primary care and general practice. This aims to analyse, understand and inform national policies on general practice in England. She is particularly interested in general practice performance (including how we can, do and should define 'good' performance in general practice), primary care and NHS reform, and increasing equity in primary care provision. Becks works two days a week as GP and is co-founder of Next Generation GP—a national programme aiming to energise engage and empower the next generation of GP leaders.

Richard Gleave is the Deputy Chief Executive at Public Health England and undertakes research at the Nuffield Department of Primary Care Sciences and the Department of Continuing Education at Oxford University. His current research is focused on how government organisations use evidence to influence public health policy and practice. Previously he has worked as a senior civil servant, NHS chief executive and academic and in 2008–2009 was a Harkness Fellow at Kaiser Permanente and University of California Berkeley.

Jonathan Hammond is a Research Fellow at The University of Manchester. A social scientist by background, his research focuses on the implementation and local enactment of national health policy in the English NHS, and he has a range of interests and expertise across governance, commissioning, innovation, inequalities and access to services. His research seeks to use social theory to understand how and why policy is enacted in particular ways in particular contexts. An expert in qualitative methods including ethnography and the use of observational methods in organisational research, he is currently working upon a national evaluation of Primary Care Networks. In addition, he was recently commissioned by the NIHR Policy Research Programme to lead a community-based participation project focused on exploring ways to bridge policy and practise in order to optimise access to general practice.

Karin Kee is a Ph.D. candidate at VU University Amsterdam, The Netherlands. Her research focuses on how collaboration between actors involved in integrated care initiatives and shared decision-making processes can be enhanced. In so doing, Karin focuses mainly on what is needed to ensure all stakeholders speak up and share their ideas, concerns and perspectives.

Sophie King-Hill is a Senior Fellow in the Health Services Management Centre at the University of Birmingham, where she teaches on the NHS Leadership Academy award in Senior Healthcare Leadership and the M.Sc. in Healthcare Leadership. She was previously a Senior Lecturer in Education and Inclusion at the University of Worcester, and also a regional tutor for the M.Ed. in Social, Emotional and Behavioural Difficulties with the School of Education at the University of Birmingham. She has worked extensively in the third sector with many diverse groups. Her research interests encompass policy implementation, transfer and success frameworks and evaluation strategies. She specialises in sexual behaviours and first point assessment in children and young people, sexual health, controversial issues and teenage parents.

Simon Kitto is a medical sociologist who has been working in health professions education research since 2002. He is a Professor at the University of Ottawa's *Department of Innovation in Medical Education* and is the Director of Research in the *Office of Continuing Professional Development*. Dr. Kitto's research focuses on the nature and role of continuing interprofessional education and practice as imbricated with patient safety, quality improvement and implementation science intervention design and practice. Simon is the current Editor-in-Chief of the *Journal of Continuing Education in the Health Professions.*

Jean Ledger is Senior Research Fellow at the Department of Applied Health Research, University College London. Her research focuses on the implementation and evaluation of policies, programmes and service innovations in healthcare settings. She has a special interest in mobilising evidence to inform practice, especially in the evolving field of digital health. During COVID-19, she supported the Digital First Primary Care programme at NHS England and NHS improvement (NHSE/I) with evaluation and research activities to better understand the impact of digital service delivery models in primary care, bringing together stakeholders to share findings and explore the real-world impacts of remote consultations and remote triage on staff and patients.

Louise Locock is Professor in Health Services Research in the Health Services Research Unit, University of Aberdeen, where she leads the Improving Experiences of Care theme. Before joining Aberdeen in 2017, she spent 14 years with the Health Experiences Research Group, Nuffield Department of Primary Care Health Sciences, University of Oxford, where she was Director of Applied Research. Louise is a qualitative social science researcher interested in personal experience of health and illness; patient-centred quality improvement and co-design; and patient and family involvement in research and care. A major recent focus of her work has been how we can better use different types of patient experience data to improve care.

Mirella Minkman is a Professor at Tilburg University/TIAS Business school. Her chair is about the innovation of the organisation and governance of integrated care and health services. Mirella's research focuses on the governance of networks, alliances of (local/regional/national) and collaborations including leadership, supervision and accountability arrangements in healthcare. She is the CEO (Chair of the Board) of Vilans, the national centre of expertise in long-term care and also a board member of the International Foundation of Integrated Care. She chairs the national committee on the innovation of governance in healthcare in The Netherlands.

Prof. Henk Nies is Director of Strategy and Development of Vilans, The Netherlands Centre of Expertise for Long-Term Care, and Professor of Organisation and Policy Development in Long-term Care at the Jo Visser Endowed Chair at the Vrije University of Amsterdam. Further, he is member of the Quality Council at the National Health Care Institute of The Netherlands. He was involved in many national innovation and improvement programmes in long-term care. His current field of interest is integrated care, quality management, quality of work, dignity in long-term care, as well as comparative research. He ran projects for the Dutch Government, Dutch Parliament, various stakeholders in The Netherlands, as well as the European Commission, OECD, WHO and the European Social Network.

Natalia Niño is an anthropologist with a master's and a doctorate degree in Science and Technology Studies from the University of Edinburgh. She has conducted qualitative research on infectious diseases, nutrition and disability. Her research focuses on the sociocultural aspects embedded in the production and use of metrics, classification systems and standardisation processes in the context of public health and global health.

John Øvretveit works as R&D officer for Stockholm healthcare system and as Professor of improvement, implementation and evaluation at the Karolinska Institute medical university Stockholm.

Previously he learned the value of thermal underwear at Nordic School of Public Health where he worked for 15 years. When establishing and running the quality improvement programme at Bergen Medical School, he was advised by his Norwegian family to buy the best rain wear at the North Atlantic fisherman store there. He served a frightening 12 years as a board director of the US Joint Commission International where he saw the best and worst of healthcare and serves as a board director of the global implementation society leading their implementation competencies committee. He has published over 400 scientific peer-reviewed articles and 12 books and is reviewer to 6 scientific journals and editor of one.

Kirstine Zinck Pedersen is Associate Professor at Department of Organization, Copenhagen Business School, Denmark. Her research attends to the organisational, practical and ethical implications of recent managerial and technological transformations of the public sector—and in particular to the constitutive effects of quality and safety reform in the healthcare sector. Methodologically, she often combines ethnographic investigation or historical analysis with an analytical interest in American pragmatism, classic organisation theory and sociological perspectives on professional work, frontline discretion and public office holding. Kirstine Zinck Pedersen is the author of *Organizing Patient Safety: Failsafe Fantasies and Pragmatic Practices* (Palgrave Macmillan, 2018).

Martin Powell is Professor of Health and Social Policy at the Health Services Management Centre, School of Social Policy, University of Birmingham. He has had research interests in the UK NHS for nearly 40 years and has published over 100 peer-reviewed articles, and books including *Evaluating the NHS* (1997). He has recently examined policy transfer and COVID-19 in the UK with Sophie King-Hill and Ian Greener.

Anne Reff Pedersen is Professor at Copenhagen Business School. Her main research interest is public organisation and innovation. She has an interest in organisational studies in particular how organisations effect people, work and time. People can be defined as the people working in organisations as local managers and professionals and their collaboration with users and other stakeholders. Work can be defined as work relations to create coordination or routines in organisations.

Hamish Robertson is a health geographer with a background in health and aged care. This included 20 years' experience in the Australian healthcare system. His Ph.D. was on the geography of Alzheimer's disease, applying geographic concepts and methods to the issue of rising chronic disease and the systemic complexities of population ageing. He is currently a Senior Lecturer in Health Services Management in the Faculty of Health at the University of Technology Sydney.

Paula Rowland is an Assistant Professor in the University of Toronto's Department of Occupational Science and Occupational Therapy (Temerty Faculty of Medicine) and the Institute of Health Policy, Management and Evaluation (Dalla Lana School of Public Health). She is a Scientist with the Post MD Program (University of Toronto), the Wilson Centre (University of Toronto and University Health Network) and The Institute for Education Research (University Health Network). Having completed a Ph.D. in Human and Organizational Systems in 2013, Paula's primary interest is in the future of healthcare work and education. Making connections between sociology of the professions, sociology of work and sociocultural learning theories, her current research examines relationships between power, learning and identity within the context of major change initiatives in health service organisations. Through her work, Paula explores intersections of professional practice, organisational change and institutionalised notions of expertise.

Olivier Saulpic is Professor in the Management Control Department at ESCP Business School and Co-Director of the Health Management Innovation Research Centre.

He conducts field-based research on performance measurement and management systems in the health sector: their design, their appropriation by individuals and their effects. His research has led him to interact with organisations in the context of intervention research projects. He also investigates the link between research and teaching.

He graduated with an engineering degree from Ecole Centrale Paris, holds an MBA from HEC, and a Doctorate degree in Economics from Ecole Polytechnique and a HDR degree (French Qualification for Ph.D. Supervisor) in management from Université d'Orléans. Before joining ESCP Business School, Professor Saulpic worked as a consultant in industrial organisation. He also worked for a venture capital company and then as head of the industrial department of a chemical company.

James Shaw is an Assistant Professor at the Department of Physical Therapy at University of Toronto. Jay's program of research addresses the implementation and ethical implications of innovations in health care, with a special focus on innovative models of community-focused integrated care, digital health technologies, and applications of AI in health care.

Judith Smith is Professor of Health Policy and Management, and Director of the Health Services Management Centre (HSMC) at the University of Birmingham. She is also Director of the Birmingham RAND and Cambridge (BRACE) Rapid Evaluation Centre funded for five years (2018–2023) by the National Institute for Health Research (NIHR). Her research focuses on the management and organisation of primary and integrated care, evaluation of new models of care and healthcare governance. Judith is also a Non-Executive Director of the Birmingham Women's and Children's NHS Foundation Trust, Deputy Director of the NIHR Health Services and Delivery Research Programme, and trustee and Deputy Chair of the board of Health Services Research UK.

Sharon Spooner worked for several years as an NHS GP before researching doctors' experiences of working in the UK NHS during a mid-career Ph.D. in Sociology and taking up a role as Clinical Lecturer at the University of Manchester. Her research focuses on the delivery of primary care with a particular interest in changes affecting the primary care workforce, applying theories of professionalism, identity and work-place routines to understand how GP practices accomplish their work. She has led projects exploring factors influencing junior doctors' career choices and the training experiences and career intentions of recently qualified GPs. Following a health policy shift towards increased employment in primary care of practitioners from different allied health professions, she recently completed a mixed methods study of how '*skill mix*' is being implemented and the health outcomes that are associated with the employment of different types of practitioner.

Carolyn Steele Gray is a Scientist at the Bridgepoint Collaboratory for Research and Innovation in the Lunenfeld-Tanenbaum Research Institute at Sinai Health System in Toronto, Canada. She is also an Assistant Professor at the Institute of Health Policy, Management and Evaluation at the University of Toronto. Her research programme focuses on the development, implementation and evaluation of digital health solutions used in models of integrated community-based primary healthcare.

Tim Tenbensel is an Associate Professor at the University of Auckland's School of Population Health. Since the late 1990s his research has focused on comparative health policy, New Zealand health policy, implementation, public policy and public management theory, and health services research. From 2005 to 2012, he served as a health policy editor for *Social Science & Medicine*. His substantive research topics include the implementation of emergency department waiting time targets, the restructuring of the New Zealand health system, and processes and systems of priority-setting. He is the co-editor (wth Kieke Okma) of *Health Reforms Across the World: The Experience of Twelve Small and Medium-Sized Nations with Changing Their Healthcare Systems*, which was published in March 2020. He regularly contributes to international, comparative projects based on his New Zealand health policy expertise. His current research focuses on primary healthcare policy and health system improvement.

Maike V. Tietschert is Assistant Professor at the Organization Sciences department, Faculty of Social Sciences, Vrije Universiteit Amsterdam, The Netherlands and a 2017/2018 Harknessfellow. She studies teams, organisations and systems to understand how care can be organised in ways that promote the delivery of high-value, safe and patient-oriented care to patients with high need and focuses on issues related to integration, coordination, organisational culture and leadership.

Joanne Travaglia is a medical sociologist with a background in health services research. She is Professor of Health Services Management and Director of the Centre for Health Services Management in the School of Public Health, University of Technology Sydney. After her original training as a social worker, she has worked in the health, welfare and higher education fields since 1980. She has a lifelong commitment to bringing to light, and addressing, the sociocultural and economic factors by which individuals and groups are made more vulnerable to harm.

Simon Turner is a member of Faculty in the School of Management, University of Los Andes, Colombia. Prior to joining Los Andes, Simon was Senior Lecturer in Health Policy and Organisation at the University of Manchester. He has held postdoctoral research positions at University College London, King's College London, London School of Hygiene & Tropical Medicine and University of Cambridge. His research interests lie in the application of social science theory and methods to the study of the organisation and improvement of public services, particularly healthcare. Simon holds a Ph.D. in economic geography from the University of Durham and undergraduate and masters degrees in human geography from the University of Birmingham. He is principal investigator of a nationally-funded study on the coordination of change in response to COVID-19 within the Colombian health system.

Ana María Ulloa obtained her doctorate in Anthropology from the New School for Social Research. Her research lies at the intersection of anthropology of food and the senses and science and technology studies. She has focused on the study of science and industry relations in the case of artificial flavours. She has experience in qualitative research on health, nutrition and infectious diseases.

Vivian Valencia Godoy is a researcher at the School of Management in the Universidad de los Andes. She holds a degree in Finance and International Trade and a master's degree in international business from the University of Greenwich. Through governmental advisory roles, she has expertise in designing and implementing social development projects so as to improve the quality of life of communities in areas such as health, education and sanitation. Her research interests lie in studying organisational processes and its effects in building partnerships amongst governmental bodies and other sectors in social development projects, as well as their impact and influence on decision-making processes and delivery in public policy.

Iris Wallenburg is Associate Professor at the Erasmus School of Health Policy & Management (ESHPM) of the Erasmus University Rotterdam. Trained as a nurse and health policy scientist, she studies policy reforms in complex healthcare systems, using a practice-based research approach. She is interested in how local practices (e.g. patient care, healthcare demands in specific geographical areas) are related to professional issues and healthcare policies. In her research, she focuses on the enactment of new governance arrangements, like the application of technology, statistical models and the professionalisation of new professional roles. Current projects include regional collaboration in healthcare for older persons, the values and valuation of nurses and nursing work, and the impact of COVID-19 on healthcare policymaking, professional work and patient care. She has widely published, recently in *Sociology of Health & Illness, Public Administration, Safety Science and BMJ Quality & Safety.*

Dr. Paul Wankah is a Ph.D. candidate at Université de Sherbrooke in Québec, Canada. He is also a Lecturer in the Department of Gerontology at Université de Sherbrooke. His research focuses on understanding the conditions for implementing integrated community-based primary healthcare models for older adults.

Justin Waring is Professor of Medical Sociology and Healthcare Organisation at the Health Services Management Centre, University of Birmingham. His research deals with the changing organisation and management of healthcare systems, and public services more broadly. His primary interest is to understand how new organisational forms and processes interact with institutionalised professional practices, cultures and identities, and how such institutional influences can both stimulate or stymie reform. He is interested in the application of social theory to different social, cultural and organisational contexts, as a means of both explaining social phenomena and extending theoretical rigour. The conceptual and theoretical foundations of his work involve making connections between medical and organisational sociology, sociology of the professions and public services management. He specialises in the use of ethnographic and mixed method research techniques.

Walter P. Wodchis is a Professor at the Institute of Health Policy, Management and Evaluation at the University of Toronto and Research Chair in Implementation and Evaluation Science at the Institute for Better Health, Trillium Health Partners in Canada. He has led a number of large-scale integrated care research and evaluation studies.

Philippe Zarlowski is Professor at ESCP Business School. His main research and teaching interests are in the fields of performance management and public management. In his research, he investigates the role of performance measurement, management technologies and accountability systems in policy implementation and organisational transformation, notably in the healthcare sector.

He was scientific director of the Deloitte Chair on Public service and managerial performance, in partnership with ENA (2013–2017) and co-editor in chief of the multidisciplinary journal Politiques et Management Public (2013–2018).

Before joining ESCP, Philippe Zarlowski was a Professor at ESSEC Business School. He also held positions at the universities of Tours and Paris Dauphine. He was a visiting researcher at Pompeu Fabra University in Barcelona and at SCANCOR research centre, Stanford University. He is a graduate of ESCP Business School, Paris School of Economics and Paris Dauphine University.

Nick Zonneveld is a health services/system researcher with a Master's in Public Administration from Erasmus University (2011). Nick currently is a Ph.D. candidate at Tilburg University/TIAS School for Business and Society and works at Vilans, Centre of Expertise in Long-Term Care in The Netherlands. Nick is involved in several (international) projects on the organisation and integration of health services in primary, social and long-term care. His research especially focuses on the 'softer' normative-cultural aspects.

List of Figures

List of Tables

CHAPTER 1

Introduction

Justin Waring, Jean-Louis Denis, Anne Reff Pedersen, and Tim Tenbensel

In December 2019, reports started to emerge from the Chinese city of Wuhan of a new viral pneumonia that resembled the Serious Acute Respiratory Syndrome (SARS) of the early 2000s. By January 2020, the viral pathogen was classified as a novel coronavirus (SARS-CoV-2) that causes the disease now known as COVID-19. By the end of January, the number of fatalities from COVID-19 were beginning to increase across

J. Waring (✉)
University of Birmingham, Birmingham, UK
e-mail: j.waring@bham.ac.uk

J.-L. Denis
Université de Montréal, Montréal, QC, Canada
e-mail: jean-louis.denis@umontreal.ca

A. R. Pedersen
Copenhagen Business School, Frederiksberg, Denmark
e-mail: arp.ioa@cbs.dk

T. Tenbensel
University of Auckland, Auckland, New Zealand
e-mail: t.tenbensel@auckland.ac.nz

J. Waring et al. (eds.), *Organising Care in a Time of Covid-19*, Organizational Behaviour in Healthcare,
https://doi.org/10.1007/978-3-030-82696-3_1

China and by February across Southeast Asia and beyond. By early March, the number of COVID-19 cases surpassed 100,000, with the disease spreading rapidly across Europe, especially in Italy, Spain and the UK. On 11th March, the World Health Organization (WHO) declared COVID-19 a pandemic with global reach and significance. At the time of writing of this introduction, the virus has spread to almost every region and territory on the planet, and there have been over 200million confirmed cases and more than 4million confirmed deaths.

Around the world, the COVID-19 pandemic has prompted radical transformations in health policy and the organisation of health and care services. Arguably one of the most significant and controversial policy responses has been the restrictions of social and economic life to limit the spread of the coronavirus. In nearly all countries, this has involved 'social distancing' or limiting the physical contact between people and communities; it has also included routine masking wearing in public spaces; restrictions on movement and travel; closure of schools, non-essential retail and hospitality; and widespread limits of civil liberties. The scale and pace of these 'lockdown' measures varied between regions and countries, with some going '*hard and fast*' to severely limit social activity and hence the spread of disease; whilst others went for a more staged '*slow and soft*' approach. The consequences of lockdown policies will be debated for years to come as analyst review data on whether and how they contained the 'waves' of infection and disease. The social and political consequences of such policies also vary. New Zealand is often singled out for adopting a '*hard and fast*' approach which not only seemed to contain disease, but also won plaudits for its Prime Minister Jacinda Ardern and her government (Wilson, 2020). In contrast, other liberal economies, notably the US and UK, adopted different approaches and not only saw significant numbers of COVID-19 deaths relative to their population size, but also significant criticism of their political leaders. It is noteworthy that the political response to COVID-19 has, in some countries, been complicated by the recent resurgence of right-wing populism, such as in the US and Brazil where mask wearing and social control measures are hotly disputed. The political and public debates that surround these policies are, it is often said, guided by the 'science', but in the case of a novel disease and rapidly changing global pandemic, this 'science' is often in short-supply. As such, when policymakers claim to be 'following the science' is it important to ask: whose science! Take for example, the former US President Donald Trump who regularly compared COVID-19 to influenza, recommended various un-tested therapies and interventions, and dismissed scientific experts who disagreed with his policy position.

In many countries, policymakers have also rushed to re-organise care services to meet the 'surge demand' and 'waves' of COVID-19 infection and disease. One prominent strategy has been the creation of emergency 'field' hospitals, seemingly drawing lessons from the military and past pandemics, such as Ebola. In the Chinese city of Wuhan, for example, two new hospitals (of 1000 and 1500 beds) were hastily constructed over a two-week period to isolate and treat the growing number of COVID-19 patients. Other nations have followed suit, with conference centres and sports centres being re-purposed as field hospitals. Notwithstanding the symbolic significance of such measures, healthcare services have responded in other ways, from suspending or pausing to re-profiling or re-purposing other routine services. As critical care beds have been overwhelmed with demand, hospital services have responded by re-purposing anaesthetic and surgical rooms for the treatment patients, with the inevitable postponement of routine surgical procedures. In other ways, the need to re-allocate clinical staff to COVID-19 care has created unprecedented backlogs in demand for other urgent care, especially for cancer care. In areas of essential non-COVID care, such as primary, maternity and mental health services, many new models of care have been developed to maintain levels of service provision whilst limiting the spread of diseases, especially through the use of digital technologies and remote consultations. However, the impact of the pandemic and lockdown restrictions of the mental health of people is now recognised as the next health crisis facing many countries around the world. And yet, the pandemic has seen marked declines in other sources of illness and death, such as road traffic accidents due to the reduce volume of vehicle use.

Such strategies signal important and sweeping changes in the organisation of *both* 'COVID' *and* 'non-COVID care, whilst asking more fundamental questions about the long-term organisation of care 'after COVID'. This includes, for example, unprecedented patterns and levels of funding; new ways of governing, managing and leading services; and the reconfiguration of clinical teams and frontline care delivery. In some contexts, COVID-19 has exposed the fragilities and vulnerabilities of long held ways of organising care, especially where services operate at the very brink of resource constraints or at near full capacity. In others, it has shown how services are organised to be more resilient and adaptive to unanticipated pressures and surge demand.

Although these unprecedented changes in the organisation and governance of health and care services have emerged in response to a particular challenge, there is every possibility that they will ask more fundamental and long-lasting questions, not only about how services might prepare for and deal with future pandemic-like events, but how nations should organise and govern services more broadly. One of the key challenges for the future is how (and whether) health systems can return from 'crisis mode' to more customary ways of organising and delivering care, or whether a 'new normal' of care organisation will become institutionalised. The COVID-19 pandemic might therefore represent a more fundamental watershed in the funding, organisation and delivery of health and care services, in which policymakers, professionals and citizens re-appraise their norms and expectations for care. Longer term, and when this present crisis abates, the relationship between the state, health professions and the public is likely to be the subject of significant re-appraisal. The post-crisis period may see, in some contexts, more authoritarian State policies continuing to regulate and govern economic recovery, whereas in other contexts political solutions may favour a minimalist State with a return to more market orientations to rebalance public finances.

The policy and organisational responses to COVID-19 are the primary focus on this collection. The COVID-19 pandemic presents a rare opportunity to examine empirically and theoretically how and why health systems adapt to such unusual and intense pressures. As described in this collection, these responses appear to unsettle long-established institutions of care, or at least reveal instances of institutional plasticity as established ways of working become stretched and re-fashioned. These changes also bring to the fore new questions about strategic leadership at local, regional, national and transnational level, especially the precarious relationships between political leadership, services leadership and the scientific community. They also transform the day-to-day realities of care work, such as new leadership and authority structures, the remaking of professional boundaries, or the emotional and psychological work of COVID-19 care.

A distinctive feature of this collection is the explicit engagement with organisational and social science theory to interpret the policy and organisational responses to COVID-19. These theories are drawn from multiple sources, including more prescriptive or functional perspectives of organisational change as well as more critical approaches to organisation and governance. In different and complementary ways, these shed light on the experiences of policymaking and service organisation in different national context (Australia, Canada, Colombia, Denmark, the Netherlands, Sweden, the UK), in different service areas (primary care, acute care, care of the elderly) and with different areas of focus (policymaking, organisation change, professional work, and governance). Looking across these contributions it is possible to detect both similarities and difference in policy and organisational response. There has been, for example, an almost isomorphic approach to the imposition of social distance, reconfiguration of acute care and the race for a vaccine, and yet, as described above, nations have taken distinct approaches in scale and pace, which do not always correspond to their prevailaing socio-political and cultural institutions. This collection brings together fourteen contributions authored by world-leading scholars to help us think through and reflect upon the policy and organisational responses to COVID-19. These are organised under the themes of 'Policy learning', 'Healthcare governance in hospital organisations', 'Professions and professional work', 'Technologies, governance and governmentalities' and 'Organising and organisational responses to COVID-19'.

Policy Learning

Across the world, but especially in liberal democracies, the pandemic has asked profound questions of policymakers and policymaking. As with other crisis events, political leaders are expected to provide direction to their people and, ultimately, find a way of assuring their safety and well-being. The rarity, complexity and uniqueness of crisis events makes it difficult for leaders to follow a pre-prepared 'playbook' and often decision-making takes place in the context of imperfect and changeable information, rapidly changing circumstances, limited resources and intense public scrutiny (Boin et al., 2013). That said, public health crises are a consistent feature of human history, and the experiences of the 'Spanish flu' of early twentieth century, SARS in the early 2000s and the recent outbreak of Ebola in West Africa all seemed to have influenced policies around containment and control. It is also the case that national policymakers have looked to global agencies, especially WHO, and each other for guidance on policy options. Some nations and transnational blocs have seemingly followed similar patterns for 'lockdowns' whilst others have tried to 'wait and see' before reaching a decision. It is important to look at the role of science and the scientific community in policymaking, especially specialist advisory bodies that have been brought to the centre of decision-making processes, but also where 'scientists' have disagreed on the interpretation of evidence and policy recommendations. The three chapters in this theme deal directly with these key policy issues, each revealing a different understanding of the role of learning, evidence and history in shaping policymaking.

Powell and King-Smith bring together key questions from 'crisis policy learning' literature (Boin et al., 2013) with more longstanding literature on policy transfer associated with Richard Rose, and Dolowitz and Marsh. They focus on how much was (and could be) learnt from history and from international experience and conclude that the UK experience highlights many barriers to policy learning. Lesson drawing from history, they argue, was significantly constrained by the fact that public officials, scientific advisors and politicians were initially (in February and early March 2020) looking in the wrong direction by basing their policy response on approaches and tools designed primarily for dealing with influenza. This is contrasted with more successful policy learning in East Asian countries that had experienced SARS and MERS over the past 20 years.

Whilst it may be expected that a crisis unfolding simultaneously across the world would provide ample opportunities for international policy learning, Powell and King-Smith focus on the factors that limited such learning in the UK and raise questions about the willingness of policymakers to look beyond their own backyard. Whilst some limitations, they argue, are due to inherent limitations to cross-national learning in crisis conditions, they also posit a more concerning explanation of 'UK exceptionalism', leaving open the question as to whether this exceptionalism pertains to scientific advisors, public officials or politicians, or all of the above. Their argument implicitly raises a deeper question as to whether and how the extent and nature of policy learning from the past and abroad varies between countries. The idea that there are also cultural limitations to policy learning opens up important new research questions that are not limited to the issue of pandemic responses. Powell and King-Smith's focus is primarily on the policy outcomes and consequences, from which they work backwards to explain how these problematic consequences were attributable to inherent and malleable limitations in the UK's capacity to learn.

The chapter by Richard Gleave complements Powell and King-Smith by delving further into the scientific advisory system in the UK. As a key participant in this system, Gleave (the Deputy Director of Public Health

England at the time) is well placed to map the multifaceted nature of the scientific advice-giving process. Drawing on complexity theory and institutional theory, as well as ideas of 'policy staging' (a dramaturgical metaphor), he paints a detailed picture of a de-centred and dispersed ecosystem of scientific advice that included official bodies, such as the UK Scientific Advisory Group for Emergencies (SAGE), as well as a multitude of quasi-public agencies and ad hoc policy actors 'outside' governmental processes; all of whom sought to influence public attitudes and policymaking through a range of media. His account profoundly challenges the contention that COVID-19 prompted a highly centralised and rational policymaking processes in which scientific evidence is collated and translated into policy decisions.

To develop his argument, Gleave uses a case study of advice on social distancing to illustrate the plural, contingent and path-dependent features of the UK's pandemic response. Viewed in this way, policy responses, and the scientific advice that feed into them, are the product of complex 'backstage' and 'sidestage' interactions and negotiations between agents that are hidden from public view, but as in any drama performance, it is still possible for actors to fluff their lines. As with Powell and King-Hill, the Gleave chapter demonstrates the fragility of UK policy processes and scientific advice in a pandemic, concluding that '(t)he three challenges of providing advice in a crisis (time, information and consequences) are in practice so exacting that the normative approach based on the principles of independence, role clarity and transparency is impossible to faithfully follow'. Far from representing a 'return to evidence-based policy', the COVID-19 pandemic acutely highlights the normative and practical limitations inherent in the ideal of a rationalist policy process.

In the third chapter in this section, Simon Turner, Ana Maria Ulloa, Vivian Valencia and Natalia Nino further develop the focus on learning from international experience and learning from history to examine a more localised policy and institutional response to COVID-19 in the Colombian capital, Bogota. Drawing on interviews with national and local health officials, their overall argument is that decentred networks of policy actors at the regional level, including insurers, health service managers and senior clinicians, demonstrated considerable agility and the capacity for ad hoc and continuous learning. Here the focus of learning is more on the practices of healthcare service providers and local public health officials, where learning from other countries is facilitated by international professional networks. In contrast to Powell and

King-Smith, Turner et al. suggest that the Colombian response to the pandemic drew positive lessons from earlier experience with the H1N1 influenza in 2009, as well as other, quite different regional epidemics such as dengue fever and Zika. They also take a broad interpretation of learning from history which is informed by Best et al.'s (2012) framework for understanding major system change in health care. In this framework, 'attending to history' involves learning from previous experiences of managing changes in local health systems. Like Gleave, these authors emphasise the highly pluralist environment in which pandemic responses developed in Bogota. However, the authors regard this as a significant strength of decision-making that facilitated necessary improvisation at the local level for dealing with the wide fluctuations of demand for critical care across waves of the pandemic. These improvisations were not centralised and, importantly, acknowledged the 'uncertainty' that characterised knowledge about the pandemic's progress and effects. In this sense, learning from history is not about learning specifically what to do and what not to do, rather it is about the process of learning itself, and the development of collective confidence at the local level to deal with both ambiguity and uncertainty.

Taken together, the three chapters offer different, but clearly linked levels of policy analysis, with Powell and King-Smith looking at policy learning at the historical and international level, Gleave deals with the relationship between scientific advice and policymaking at the national level, and Turner looks at the idea of learning at the sub-national regional level.

Healthcare Governance in Hospital Organisations

The COVID-19 pandemic presents significant and unprecedents dilemmas about how to govern and steer the organisation of healthcare services. This has been especially the case for hospitals which have, in most countries, become the symbolic battleground where clinicians fight tirelessly to maintain the life of COVID-19 patients, often where their own physical and mental health is put at risk. In these hospitals, the normal routines of hospital activity have been curtailed, visitors are prohibited, non-emergency care has been postponed, and hospital wards have been re-purposed as COVID wards. Three chapters in this collection describe how the governance of hospital organisation has changed during the pandemic. Rather than focusing on the relevance or merits of more prescriptive and instrumental crisis management frameworks, these chapters focus on the structures and social dynamics of hospital governance, especially the introduction of new guidelines, technologies and procedures that would normally be contested and protracted. The chapters show how new (and old) healthcare governance practices involving healthcare professionals and local hospital managers have been placed at the centre of this new governance configuration, to facilitate the management of patients and the delivery of care in this crisis situation. The classical literature of public governance shows how healthcare governance has evolved through the different traditions of public administration, new public management, network governance and even hybrid governance models (Ferlie et al., 2013), and in different ways, these chapters examine how the pandemic has brought about new or modified practices of hospital governance.

The Pedersen and du Gay chapter considers how rapid and flexible responses during the COVID-19 crisis were linked to classic bureaucratic features of hospital governance, such as clear lines of command, visible hierarchies, formalisation, authority based on expertise and office-holding, and a focus on the duties, purposes and ethics of office, as the driving force in making reorganisations happen. They build on an interview study of the emergency responses developed and introduced within a large Danish university hospital in the first months of the COVID-19 pandemic. In this chapter, they challenge the common critique of bureaucracy as being rule-bound, mechanistic and slow to respond to environmental change, by arguing instead that as an organisational form, bureaucracy is both capable of rule and response, and can be a precondition for flexibility and responsiveness. In Brown's (1974) analysis, bureaucratic formalisation was viewed as a supple and multifaceted organisational device enabling people and tasks to be deployed at complementary levels. Empirically, they show how the emergency response of Danish hospitals was a highly formalised and largely planned exercise, based on clear hierarchies and decision-making structures. But also, an exercise that allowed for flexible and situation-based decision-making not least through the division of labour and delegation of responsibility based on expertise. In short, the response was enabled, rather than constrained by bureaucracy. Thereby this chapter contributes to the knowledge of how not only new, but also old (or more classical) governance models and ideas from public administration have been of importance in steering hospital responses to the COVID-19 crisis.

This perspective is contrasted, and to some extent challenged, by the chapter from Wallenburg, de Graaff, Felder and Bal who similarly examine how hospitals, in this case in the Netherlands, steered, organised and delivered care during the first months of the COVID-19 outbreak. They build on an extensive ethnographic study in one Dutch university hospital and use the metaphor of 'dance' to show and how hospitals have engaged with the virus and its emerging consequences. In particular, the dance metaphor is used to explain the reconfiguration of vested hospital routines, socio-spatial interactions, and rhythms of organising care. The analogy of the dance is useful as it draws attention to the embodied and relational practices of collaborative action, 'connecting spaces and contexts and each other, "leading" and "following" and making sense of the spaces in-between' (Biehl, 2017). More concretely they demonstrate how hospitals have been engaged in finding situated solutions to emerging and often uncertain organisational and practical issues through improvising new strategies and routines. This chapter demonstrates how processes of innovation and improvisation have been important in hospital governance during the crisis.

Taken together, these two chapters unfold how both features of bureaucratic command and features of situated improvisation have contributed to the reorganisation and governance of hospitals from the start of the crises. The Saulpic and Zarlowski chapter is, in some way, a bridge between these two preceding chapters by describing the concrete governance practices of engaging healthcare professionals in managerial decision-making. Through their interviews with doctors and administrative managers in France, Saulpic and Zarlowski consider how the medicalisation of hospital governance during the pandemic has restored the role and power of the medical profession contra to the expansion of managerial powers witnessed in the pre-pandemic era. In particular, medical doctors (and arguably other clinical professionals) played a direct role in both hospital and departmental management during the pandemic, from which they have supported local experimentation, simplified reporting processes and changed activity-based funding arrangements. These new conditions support both a conceptualisation of hospitals in terms of 'organised professionalism' (Noordegraaf, 2011) and illustrate new forms of collective and distributed leadership (Baker & Denis, 2011). Thereby this chapter describes how hospital governance not only relates to old or new governance models, but also reflect the close relation between hospital governance and professionals. In many European countries' high degree of professional work and organisation has led to what one could call 'the professional governance model', where decision-making related to hybrid managerial and professional logics and values.

Together, these three chapters describe governance practices in hospital organisation witnessed during the COVID-19 crisis, showing how different types of governance have been used, they offer, in particular, a developed understanding of hospital governance during the crisis as the meeting point between centralised and formal policy guidelines and incremental informal, learning experiments, but also as a place where the crisis led to re-enforcing the collaboration between managerial levels and healthcare professionals.

Professions and Professionalism

Although health professions have tended to hold high levels of public esteem and trust, the COVID-19 pandemic has enhanced their public standing and reputation. They are widely portrayed as heroes working on the frontline of the pandemic response, struggling to care for the mounting tide of sick people, often in suboptimal conditions and where their own health and well-being is put at risk. Around the world, the work of these professionals has been acknowledgement and celebrated by politicians, news media and through public acts of recognition. At the same time, and as described above, the pandemic has brought about radical changes in the social organisation of professional work, which in many ways confounds over 40 years of social science research that has emphasised the institutional endurance of professional expertise, routines, boundaries and identities. Although the ecosystem of professional work is always dynamic and changeable, the longstanding picture has been for jurisdictions and hierarchies within the division of labour to be slow to change. Equally, professional identities are often regarded as relatively enduring, tied to long periods of socialisation that are sustained through communities of practices within relatively discrete technical networks. However, the pandemic has seen many health professionals suspend their own practices and assume new or extended roles as they have worked to support specialists dealing directly with COVID-19. It has also involved the rapid, and seemingly uncontested, implementation of new clinical routines and treatment guidelines based on emerging clinical research. And it has seen staffing ratios and team configurations radically changed as clinicians respond to the growing number of COVID patients. In clinical domains not directly involved in COVID care, such as primary, community, maternity and mental health services, it is also the case that working patterns have changed with the widespread introduce of remote working and tele-medicine. Many of the chapters in this collection deal with the changing social organisation of professional work, whether through the introduction of new technologies or new modes of organising.

Rowland's chapter deals directly with the impact of the pandemic on professional work organisation. Engaging with well-established sociological debates on the system of expert work (Abbott, 1988), the chapter examines how the redeployment of professionals and changes in the relationships between professionals, and between professionals and patients, signal potentially broader transformations in professional boundaries and jurisdictions. Drawing on Langley et al. (2019) they attend to the ongoing processual dynamics of boundary change through their empirical study within the Canadian care system during the initial wave of the pandemic. It highlights the role of government agencies in triggering rapid and unprecedent transformation through suspending, redeploying or re-purposing care services to meet the anticipated surge demand for COVID-19 care. Of note, the chapter presents a broader and more inclusive understanding of the 'system' of healthcare 'work' that is not limited to traditional professionals, but includes specialists from outside the care sector and, importantly, patients, carers and family members. It contrasts the dynamics of boundary work and the changing inter-connections between actors. Whilst policies have long advocated for the increased role of patients and carers in the organisation of work, the pandemic saw the rapid exclusion of such groups from care settings, largely on the grounds of infection control. At the same time, military experts and services were brought into the care sector to inform the rapid transformation of services. As such, the chapter demonstrates the continued relevance of understanding the inter-connections between the state, professions and the public, but also for the pandemic to present radical and unprecedented changes to these inter-connections.

In contrast, Smith at el. focus on changes experienced in primary care. Although not on the symbolic 'frontline' of the pandemic, primary care services needed to find new ways of organising professional practice to meet the growing demands for non-COVID care and, at the same time, to limit the further transmission of coronavirus in community settings. Their chapter makes connections between two distinct theoretical perspectives to interpret the experiences of General Practitioners (family doctors) in the English National Health Service (NHS). The first is the idea of punctuated equilibrium to account for the periods of relative stability interspersed with dramatic and radical change, and the second relates to the concept of identity transition to consider how professional identities changed during this period of instability. The chapter develops a narrative analysis from the reflective experiences of GPs working during the initial pandemic period of Spring 2020. It highlights sudden and unsettling changes in GP practice, from the widespread use of remote working and tele-medicine, the restructuring of physical spaces and the need for additional PPE. Such changes were experienced as three interconnected lines of uncertainty. The first uncertainty centred on the changes in clinical practice and the sense that the pandemic made it difficult for GPs to know how best to (remote) care for their patients with a consequent sense of disempowerment. The second related to the impact on professional identity and the sense of not being able to fulfil their professional obligations and responsibilities. And the third related to broader uncertainties about the future organisation and role of primary care. These uncertainties are interpreted as ontological insecurities (Waring & Bishop, 2011) that challenge the professional identities of GP, with some foreseeing a new form of medicine that no longer centred on a close relationship with patients, whilst others seeing GPs as the anchor of the care system in the post-pandemic period.

Dealing with the public image and professional identity of nurses, Croft and Chauhan suggest the pandemic has potentially transformed the public perception of nurses and nursing practice. They locate their chapter in established debates on contemporary professionalism, especially the view that professions and their organisational contexts are inherently and increasingly interdependent. At the same time, they note the perception of nurses has tended to be under-valued and limited to caring functions in support of doctors. Through exploring the nurses uses of social media during the pandemic, Croft and Chauhan consider how nurses' communications about their practices and identities have challenged common public stereotypes, setting out a new public image of nursing as being more technically complex, as hardworking, on 'the frontline' of the pandemic, and ultimately as a heroic saviour. Social media posts have also allowed nurses to express the emotional and physical demands of dealing with the pandemic, especially where they take on the burden of end-of-life care and working in a system pushed to the very limits. Again, this has enhanced the professional standing and identity of nursing in the wider society. This chapter highlights the possibility that the nursing profession might be under-valued or stereotyped, but through communicating their experiences of the pandemic nurses have made more obvious and explicit to the wider public their advanced clinical skills and competencies, their ability to work under extreme pressures and their integral contributions, not only to the organisation of pandemic care, but health care more broadly. All of which has enhanced their social, professional and political standing.

Together the chapters offer new insights into the changing social organisation of professional work. In different ways they speak to the fundamental change, perhaps break, in the relationship between health professions, the state and the public. In the main, health professionals have responded positively to profound changes in the organisation of their work that, under normal circumstances, would have been the focus of significant opposition and resistance. Further questions now need to be asked about whether these changes are here to stay, or whether the post-pandemic period will see elements of this '*pandemic professionalism*' becoming normalised and institutionalised. The post-pandemic period might see a return to less cordial modes of organising care as policymakers and services leaders seek to retain certain changes in the name of efficiency or innovation, whilst professional may seek to reclaim old or claim new jurisdictions based on their pandemic experiences.

Technologies, Governance, and Governmentalities

In time of crisis, politicians and public policy leaders are under immense pressures to bring about rapid solutions and maintain public confidence. They have to act promptly, to take major decisions in context of great uncertainties. Crisis is challenging and often renders established routines, and the foundations of social confidence, obsolete. In the end, governmental responses to the pandemic reveal as much about predominant policy frames than the ability of officials to learn and innovate in extreme context. Three chapters deal with technics and frames that have been mobilised within the context of the COVID-19 pandemic. As described above, governments around the world have taken unusual measures and decisions that have imposed significant constraints on population to limit the spread of disease and control the surge in cases, and hence demand on care services. Governments and political leaders have been able to exert unusual power and faced very little opposition, compared to the usual practices of liberal democracies. The meanings and implications of decisions and policies for the governance of health and society during and in the aftermath of the pandemic are the focus of the three chapters.

In their chapter, Checkland, Hammond & Spooner look at efforts in UK to protect the health of the population within the early stage of the pandemic. They focus their analysis on 'shielding' as a technology to manage differential risks within the UK population. They suggest that shielding has a strong affiliation with a broader policy frame, namely 'population health', where techniques of population segmentation according to health risks are used to design responses to the pandemic. Developing a critical interpretation of this approach, the authors explore the biases and potential consequences of population management for sub-groups with specific diseases or from specific age category. Population management is part of the arsenal associated with the governmentalisation project of the State in advanced liberal democracies, being associated with categorisation, risk attribution and discriminating within a population with the aim to protect or restore health. Whilst population health is generally considered as part of the progressive side of contemporary debates in health policy, population health can rely on set of concepts and tools that neglect to take into account the social determinants of health. In the end, the management of the population by governments may culminate in more inequalities and in making the more vulnerable segment of the population even more vulnerable and constrained. Shielding policies appear to be a form of depoliticised population health, and yet the practices of population management seem to take precedence over a critical assessment of how health status disparities result from prevailing inequities in society and how the pandemic reveals and amplifies such inequities. The authors suggest that centralisation of public health within the State may limit the ability to take into account the significance of the broader social context in the determination of health and within health policy.

Travaglia and Robertson are also interested in the social meaning and consequences of the State's and government's responses to the pandemic. As with Checkland and colleagues, they focus their analysis on the management of vulnerabilities within the population during the crisis. They build their analysis on an intriguing assumption: *All humans are vulnerable by virtue of our existence. But not all vulnerabilities pose the same risk….* Risks associated with situations of vulnerabilities are not inherent to one's own health condition, but are defined and amplified by

State policies to tame the pandemic. The authors identify two predominant rationalities that guide responses to the pandemic in advanced liberal democracies: the bio-medical logic and the economic logic. Both logics act as political rationalities in the determination of pandemic response strategies and implicitly attribute relative value to the life of individuals on the basis of economic actors or citizens. They argue that these two logics are broad frames used by political and public policy leaders to guide their decisions on *who may live and who must die*. The matter here is not about the intentionality of leaders in making moral choices, but more about systematic biases associated with these political rationalities that make things simultaneously governable and discriminatory. The metaphor of necropolitics (Mbembe, 2008) is used to characterise situations where various types of vulnerabilities culminate in differential risks including the long-term effects on health of COVID-19. Illustrations of necropolitic in the management of the pandemic are found in neglected groups, such as frail elderlies in long-term care settings, prisoners and homeless people. According to the authors, within any society, some groups will be less protected and less efforts will be made to protect their health despite their vulnerabilities. These two chapters advocate for the importance of taking a critical stance at responses that are developed by States and governments in situations of massive emergencies, showing that the policy responses to the pandemic are not rational or neutral, they are based on complex set of assumptions and values embedded in policy frames and in tools used to manage population.

In their chapter, Ledger and Bakhai take a very different route. They explore the growing plasticity of primary care organisations and practices within the context of the pandemic in UK. They rely, in a very astute way, on *Roger's diffusion of innovationtheory* to look at the dynamics of innovation within the atypical context of the COVID-19 pandemic. One of their main interests is to explore the relationship between time and the dissemination of innovations. The pandemic creates a context in which organisations, practitioners and the users of services become much more inclined to adopt innovations. Innovations, like tele-consultations and tele-health, are adopted and implemented much faster than usual. The adoption curve, at the heart of classical diffusionist theory of innovation, is compressed in reaction to massive emergencies. Based on Ledger and Bakhai analysis, one may ask if innovations, with perceived positive valence, have become a new political rationality that co-exist with population health management and economic in shaping responses to the pandemic. At first sight, these innovations appear very valuable for clinicians, health managers and patients or service users. They are contemplated for a long time and the pandemic creates a favourable context to spread old good ideas. One potential drawback with such rapid adoption and implementation of innovations is to neglect some of their potential negative consequences. For some groups of patients, tele-consultations may not respond to their needs. As well mentioned by the authors, attention must then be paid to the risk of confirming or expanding inequalities with such rapid innovation process. Practitioners, organisations and service users must be alert to the risks associated with pro-innovation biases.

Overall, these three chapters look at the pandemic as a revelatory of broad logics that guide States and governments to the unusual. The techniques and frames mobilised in the context of the pandemic are considered core elements of the governmentalisation project of States and society.

Organising and Organisational Responses to COVID-19

The literature on crisis management is replete with frameworks and models to inform both policy and organisational responses. These typically focus on linked stages or tasks that comprises the processes of managing through a crisis event. Common stages include: detection and diagnosis, developing control and response strategies, strategy implementation, appraisal and recovery. This literature is complemented through research on 'crisis' leadership, communication, business continuity and regulation, for example, further demonstrating the intersections between different organisational and management science perspectives. In contrast with more critical scholarship, this body of research explicitly seeks to offer guidance, often prescriptive guidance, to leaders and stakeholders about how best to respond to an unfolding crisis event. In other words, they contribute important social scientific insight to inform the strategic response to crises. In this vein, two chapters in this collection, Øvretveit and Steele-Gray & colleagues, focus their analysis on the production of knowledge to guide the development of effective organisational responses to the pandemic. Their main preoccupation is instrumental and they respond to a broad call to produce actionable knowledge in a context of high uncertainties. As such, they stand somewhat in contrast to the earlier chapters, by paying attention to the delivery side of health system where in the end, at least partly, policies will land. For these authors, knowledge serves the purpose of facilitating the design and implementation of effective organisational or individual responses to COVID-19.

Drawing on empirical observations, Øvretveit proposes and develops a 'response system' to maximise the contribution of organisational behaviour (OB) research to the healthcare sector. The proposed system, Rapid Impact Organisation Behaviour (RIOB) research, aims to direct and develop 'real-time' and 'in context' OB research to respond to the need of organisations and individuals facing unusual situations. The value added of the framework is based on the recognition that the crisis management literature pay little attention to processes of change and adaptation within organisations. For Øvretveit, healthcare organisations are for the most part not prepared to face long duration massive emergencies. He suggests the behavioural sciences have much insight to offer managers and clinicians on the ground as they face the challenges of the pandemic. The RIOB research response addresses in a very tangible manner the importance of a better connection between the dynamics of healthcare delivery in a pandemic context and the development of adequate policy responses. The contribution of behavioural research may, at first, appear to deal with small or trivial problems, like systematic hand washing in clinical context. But it is in these day-to-day behavioural procedures and tasks significant battles are engaged to limit the spread of COVID-19 often through simple and well-known solutions that are difficult to execute in a systematic way. The RIOB research response depends on the implementation of a set of methodological decisions and partnerships between practitioners and researchers. Social scientists involved in health services research appear well-equipped to support the development of RIOB research, and they may also contribute to broaden approaches by offering complementary theoretical refinements; for example, May and Finch's (2009) work on *Normalisation Process Theory* may support the development of RIOB.

The chapter by Steele-Gray & colleagues develops an additional framework for organisational health system change, the Rapid and Sustainable Transformation (or RAST) framework. Their aim is to offer guidance for the development of sustainable innovations in crisis context. One of the interesting aspects of their work is to link sustainability challenges with broader implications for health system transformation, whereby short-term innovations implemented during the COVID-19 pandemic may in the long run result in undesirable transformations for health systems. By combining literatures on sustainability with crisis management within a perspective on health system transformation, the authors offer guidance to assess empirically the potential of innovations that are generated in such short period of time. The focus of this chapter partly coincides with the one of Ledger and Bahkai, with its preoccupation to properly evaluate the lasting potential of innovations generated during the crisis. The RAST framework is structured around three interdependent phases of a crisis: pre-disaster context, during-disaster context and post-disaster context. Three empirical cases are presented to probe empirically the RAST framework. Overall, the chapter by Steele-Gray & colleagues offer a well-developed framework to guide the work of policy, managerial and clinical leaders in the context of the pandemic and in their attempt to innovate in a systematic way. The framework pays attention to the role of broader policy context that influence how innovations unfold across the different phases of a crisis.

Overall, these two chapters offer explicit guidance to support the work of individuals and organisations that are engaged in the battle against the pandemic. Whilst it is important to stay alert on the various dimensions and consequences of policies adopted in extreme context, these two chapters suggest that a more instrumental approach to problems may help people navigating the complex landscape of change and adaptation within health systems and organisations.

References

Abbott, A. (1988). *The system of profession*. University of Chicago Press.

Baker, G. R., & Denis, J. L. (2011). Medical leadership in health care systems: From professional authority to organizational leadership. *Public Money & Management, 31*(5), 355–362.

Best, A., Greenhalgh, T., Lewis, S., Saul, J. E., Carroll, S., & Bitz, J. (2012). Large system transformation in health care: A realist review. *The Milbank Quarterly, 90*(3), 421–456.

Biehl, B. (2017). *Dance and organisation: Integrating dance theory and methods into the study of management*. Routledge.

Boin, A., Kuipers, S., & Overdijk, W. (2013). Leadership in times of crisis: A framework for assessment. *International Review of Public Administration, 18*(1), 79–91.

Brown, W. (1974). *Organization*. Penguin.

Dolowitz, D., & Marsh, D. (1996). Who learns what from whom. *Political Studies, 44*, 343–357.

Ferlie, E., Fitzgerald, L., McGivern, G., Dopson, S., & Bennett, C. (2013). *Making wicked problems governable?: The case of managed networks in health care*. Oxford University Press.

Langley, A., Lindberg, K., Mørk, B. E., Nicolini, D., Raviola, E., & Walter, L. (2019). Boundary work among groups, occupations, and organizations: From cartography to process. *Academy of Management Annals, 13*(2), 704–736.

May, C., & Finch, T. (2009). Implementing, embedding, and integrating practices: An outline of normalization process theory. *Sociology, 43*(3), 535–554.

Mbembe, A. (2008). Necropolitics. In S. Morton & S. Bygrave (Eds.), *Foucault in an age of terror* (pp. 152–182). Palgrave Macmillan.

Noordegraaf, M. (2011). Risky business: How professionals and professional fields (must) deal with organizational issues. *Organization Studies, 32*(10), 1349–1371.

Roger, E. (2003). *Diffusion of innovation*. Free Press.

Rose, R. (1993). *Lesson-drawing in public policy. A guide to learning across time and space*. Chatham House Publishers.

Waring, J., & Bishop, S. (2011). Healthcare identities at the crossroads of service modernisation: The transfer of NHS clinicians to the independent sector? *Sociology of Health & Illness, 33*(5), 661–676.

Wilson, S. (2020). Pandemic leadership: Lessons from New Zealands approach to COVID-19. *Leadership, 16*(3), 279–293.

CHAPTER 2

Intra-Crisis Policy Transfer: The Case of COVID-19 in the UK

Martin Powell and Sophie King-Hill

Introduction

The literature on policy formulation highlights the importance of learning from abroad and policy transfer (e.g. Bennett & Howlett, 1992; Vagionaki & Trein, 2020) including health care policy (e.g. Ettelt et al., 2012; Klein, 1997). However, this often focuses on 'normal' rather than 'crisis' policymaking. This chapter brings together the literatures on learning and policy transfer with material on crisis learning in order to assess policy transfer in the COVID-19 Pandemic in the UK. A 'novel pandemic' such as COVID-19 has, by definition, no 'manual' or 'playbook'. In such a case, it is important to explore possible policy transfer, as sources of learning may come from the past (such as previous Pandemics) or from other nations (which experienced the pandemic earlier) (e.g. Dolowitz & Marsh, 1996, 2000; Rose, 1991).

M. Powell (✉) · S. King-Hill
University of Birmingham, Birmingham, UK
e-mail: m.powell@bham.ac.uk

J. Waring et al. (eds.), *Organising Care in a Time of Covid-19*, Organizational Behaviour in Healthcare,
https://doi.org/10.1007/978-3-030-82696-3_2

According to Dolowitz and Marsh (1996: 344), 'policy transfer, emulation and lesson drawing all refer to a process in which knowledge about policies, administrative arrangements, institutions etc. in one time and/or place is used in the development of policies, administrative arrangements and institutions in another time and/or place'. They continue that they do not consider that the difference in nomenclature is overly significant, but while Rose (1991, 1993) uses the terms 'policy transfer' and 'lesson drawing' interchangeably, they regard 'lesson drawing' as 'voluntary policy transfer', where political actors or decision makers in one country draw lessons from one or more other countries, which they then apply to their own political system. Some commutators (e.g. Benson and Jordan 2011) point to a large literature on a broad field of cognate terms such as policy transfer, lesson-drawing, policy diffusion and emulation, while others (e.g. Baker & Walker, 2019; Hadjiisky et al., 2017) discuss the broad literature in terms of 'pathways', 'songlines' or 'conversations'. According to Williams and Dzekova (2014), numerous scholars view cross-national policy transfer as a form of policy-oriented learning and lesson-drawing, where a lesson is 'a detailed cause-and-effect description of a set of actions that government can consider in the light of experience elsewhere' (Rose, 1993). They continue that the extensive literature on policy transfer and lesson-drawing recognises a number of problems associated with the process of extrapolating 'lessons' and best practices and applying them to different contexts.

We focus on a number of these problems. First, it has been argued that the policy transfer literature says little about learning or Evidence-based policymaking (EBPM) (e.g. Ingold & Monaghan, 2016). Second, the policy transfer literature focuses on 'normal' times, but there is little on policy transfer in a crisis, with its constituent elements of threat, uncertainty and urgency. The literature distinguishes learning across crises and learning within a crisis, or inter-crisis and inter-crisis management, and between 'routine' and 'non-routine' or 'less routine' crises (e.g. Moynihan, 2008, 2009). While there is some literature on inter-crisis learning from Pandemics (e.g. Stark, 2018), the material on intra-learning during Pandemics is limited (e.g. Baekkeskov, 2016; Baekkeskov and Robin 2014; Salajan et al. 2020).

The aim of the chapter is to explore the UK policy response to the COVID-19 crisis, with respect to the crisis and lesson-drawing literatures. From the crisis perspective, how do threat, uncertainty and urgency relate to policy transfer in a non-routine and intra-crisis situation? From the lesson-drawing perspective, to what extent did the UK look to learn from the past or from abroad; where did the UK look, and why; and what did the UK learn? Putting these two perspectives together, we focus on intra-crisis policy transfer (Powell & King-Hill, 2020).

The material is primarily drawn from 'scientific' (e.g. minutes of scientific advisory bodies such as the UK Scientific Advisory Group for Emergencies (SAGE); see, e.g., Cairney, 2020) and 'political' sources (e.g. government documents, Hansard Debates). It is analysed by Interpretative Content Analysis (Drisko & Maschi, 2016), using a deductive approach that focuses on both manifest and latent content. A deductive approach is useful if the general aim is to test a previous theory, and keywords are derived from the interest of researchers or review of literature. Content analysis (CA) may also be focused on manifest or latent content. Manifest CA involves analysing for the appearance of a particular word or content, while latent CA refers to the process of interpretation of content, or discovering underlying meanings of the words or the content. In addition to keywords, it drew on connotative codes, which are based not on explicit words but on the overall or symbolic meaning of phrases or passages.

Learning and Lesson-Drawing

Policy learning has long attracted attention of scholars in the field (Heikkila & Gerlak, 2013), and the analysis of learning has been a classic topic for many years (Vagionaki & Trein, 2020). A number of reviews of learning (e.g. Bennett & Howlett, 1992; Grin & Loeber, 2007; Heikkila & Gerlak, 2013; Vagionaki & Trein, 2020) discuss 'lesson-drawing' (Rose, 1991, 1993) and 'policy transfer' (Dolowitz & Marsh, 1996, 2000).

Richard Rose (1991, 1993) is known as the author who coined the concept 'lesson-drawing' for public policy. Rose (1991) states that lesson-drawing addresses the question: under what circumstances and to what extent can a programme that is effective in one place transfer to another. The critical analytic question is: Under what circumstances and to what extent would a programme now in effect elsewhere also work here?

Two of the leading authors in the field of policy transfer stress 'learning' and 'lessons' in their titles: '*Who learns what from whom*' (Dolowitz & Marsh, 1996) and '*Learning from abroad*' (Dolowitz & Marsh, 2000), but arguably say little about learning. More generally, it has been claimed that the lesson-drawing and policy transfer literatures do not consider learning in much detail (e.g. James & Lodge, 2003; Wolf & Baehler, 2018). Similarly, although the EBPM and policy transfer/translation literatures are concerned with similar themes, but have largely emerged separately (e.g. Legrand, 2012; Ingold and Monagan 2016). The few studies that link learning and transfer tend to be theoretical in nature and contain an implicit belief in policymaking as a rational process (e.g. Rose, 1993). There are still few studies that examine the 'type of learning' involved, what processes are involved in this learning and whether different learning processes are involved in the transfer of different types of information. While the policy transfer literature covers a large range of fields (e.g. Legrand, 2012; Vagionaki & Trein, 2020), there are few studies on crises and even fewer on Pandemics.

Learning and Crisis

The cross-national lesson-drawing literature (above) operates in 'normal' times, but how is it different in a crisis, with its constituent elements of threat, uncertainty and urgency (e.g. Boin et al., 2018; Moynihan, 2008, 2009). Moynihan (2008) considers that crises are characterised by high consequentiality, limited time, high political salience, uncertainty and ambiguity.

Boin et al (2013) consider that there are many reasons that we should not expect too much from crisis management. Similarly, according to Boin et al. (2018), crises create impossible conditions for those who seek to manage a response operation; they force first responders, public managers and political leaders to make urgent decisions while essential information about causes and consequences remains unavailable, unreliable or incomplete. It is broadly argued that lesson-drawing is one of the most underdeveloped aspects of crisis management (e.g. Boin et al., 2018). The literature distinguishes intra-crisis and inter-crisis management, and we know less about intra-crisis learning, which may be more difficult than, inter-crisis learning (Moynihan, 2008, 2009). It also differentiates between 'routine' and 'non-routine' or 'less routine' crises (Moynihan, 2008, 2009). In routine crises, standard procedures that work well in one setting can usually be applied to another, such as in forest fires or earthquakes. In such a setting, successful inter-crisis learning reduces the need for intra-crisis learning. However, less familiar crises with non-routine tasks are more difficult to manage. Crises contain barriers to learning. Moynihan (2009) sets out three key challenges to intra-crisis learning: a mismatch between information and task; cognitive limitations; and political barriers to learning.

There have been few studies of learning and crisis, especially epidemics and Pandemics. There have been a few studies on learning from crises. For example, Stark (2018) examined the post-crisis inquiry on the Canadian SARS outbreak of 2003. Hine (2010) provided an independent review of the UK response to the 2009 influenza pandemic. Baekkeskov (2016) focuses on the different response policies in the Netherlands and Denmark to the 2009 H1N1 'swine' influenza pandemic. More widely, he writes that nations such as the UK, Belgium, Sweden, Norway and Finland shared the Dutch strategy of ordering vaccines for everybody in 2009, while the USA and Germany shared the Danish strategy of ordering vaccines for groups. He notes that experts often play important roles in crisis responses. Baekkeskov and Robin (2014) claim that 'pandemic response is unique' because it was ruled by bureaucratised experts rather than by elected politicians. They argue that while natural disaster responses appear to follow a political logic, national pandemic vaccination policies follow a bureaucratic logic. However, pandemic vaccination policies diverge significantly between countries because expert judgements differ significantly.

The COVID-19 Pandemic in the UK

It is broadly agreed that the UK has fared badly in the COVID-19 Pandemic in terms of both process and outcomes. It has spent more money fighting coronavirus than almost all comparable countries but still languishes towards the bottom of league tables of economic performance in 2020 and deaths caused by the virus (Giles, 2020). As of 18 February 2021 (BBC, 2020), the UK has seen 118, 933 deaths within 28 days of a positive test result, 129,498 deaths certificate that mention COVID, and 116,326 deaths over and above the usual number at this time of year (so-called excess deaths). In international terms, the UK is fifth in the world for COVID-19 deaths per capita with 1753 deaths per million (Worldometers, 2021).

In terms of process, the UK response has been widely criticised with the All Party Parliamentary Group Interim Report on Coronavirus (APPG, 2020) stating that the UK 'should have been should have been much better prepared'. Scally et al (2020) reflected this stating that the UK's public health response to COVID-19 has been termed 'too little, too late, too flawed' and Richard Horton (2020), editor of The 'Lancet', has pointing to 'the COVID-19 Catastrophe', with the UK 'slow, complacent and flat-footed'. The UK has also been criticised in comparative accounts with other countries such as Germany and East Asia (see Horton, 2020).

In particular the UK has been criticised for its slow early response, notably in terms of failing to protect its borders (resulting in 18 million people travelling to the UK without relevant health screening or quarantine measures being in place), being slow to build up its stockpile of Personal Protective Equipment (PPE) (and exporting some PPE to China) and being slow to increase its testing capacity (APPG, 2020; Grey & MacAskill, 2020; Horton, 2020; Nickson et al., 2020).

The UK was also slow to 'lockdown'. On the 12th March Chris Whitty, the UK chief medical officer, announced that the intention of the interventions had shifted from trying to contain the disease to trying to slow its spread and that tracking every case would cease and the threat level was moved from moderate to high (Grey & MacAskill, 2020). Despite these stark warnings the UK government still did not impose school closures until 18th March and full lockdown until the 23rd March (Horton, 2020). This, according to Professor Neil Ferguson from Imperial College and SAGE member, doubled the death rate from 20,000 to 40,000. Nickson et al. (2020) assert that the decisions around this were slow and did not reflect the rigour of other countries.

One of the key failings related to the UK abandoning the international advice to test, track trace and isolate in March (Horton, 2020). While the UK subsequently increased its testing capacity, and eventually carried out some of the highest number of tests per capita in the world (16th in the world in December 2020), this happened much too late to contain the virus. Moreover, test results were returned too slowly, missing the vital 'golden time' for infected individuals to isolate. Finally, the number of people who isolated was low, partly due to lack of financial support (APPG, 2020; Nickson et al., 2020).

Another key area where deficiencies were evident is the failings in the supply and adequacy of PPE that was available for frontline staff, this was coupled with the minimal surge capacity of the NHS to deal with a national pandemic (Horton, 2020). The findings of the APPG (2020) report reflect this stating that the UK was not prepared with the 'the procurement, supply and distribution of PPE to the NHS and social care sector was delayed and poorly coordinated, with ineffective oversight' and PPE stocks had diminished after becoming a low priority due to many years of austerity.

The broadly centralised and privatised response has been criticised (e.g. APPG, 2020; Horton, 2020). Testing capacity was centralised, rather than allowing other organisations (such as universities) to assist. The tracking system was handed over to private companies such as Serco, which have been criticised in carrying out functions for government in the past, rather than to local public health teams. Similarly, PPE contracts were given to some companies with little or no experience in the field, with critics pointing out some close links to government ministers.

In addition to this was the lack of coordination of the protection of the most vulnerable within society. Many elderly patients were put into care homes directly from hospitals (Horton, 2020). This was coupled with unclear and often complex information given by the government on visiting care homes (APPG, 2020).

'Following the Science' in the UK

This section explores the science behind the UK response to the COVID-19 Pandemic. SAGE is the main venue to coordinate science advice to the UK government on COVID-19, including from NERVTAG (the New and Emerging Respiratory Virus Threats Advisory Group, reporting to PHE) and the SPI-M (Scientific Pandemic Influenza Group on Modelling) sub-groups on modelling (SPI-M) and behavioural public policy (SPI-B) which supply meeting papers to SAGE (Cairney, 2020; HMG, 2020). Cairney (2020) summarised SAGE's minutes (41 meetings, from 22 January to 11 June) and meeting/background papers (125 papers, estimated range 1–51 pages, median 4, not-peer-reviewed, often produced a day after a request). He points to the unusually high levels of uncertainty from the beginning, 'with the lack of solid evidence available to SAGE at each stage can only be appreciated fully if you read the minutes from 1 to 41'.

As Cairney (2020) stresses, following the science often means 'following our scientists'. Ministers and MPs in Parliament pointed to 'our world-leading scientists'. For example, for the Labour opposition, Jonathan Ashworth referred to 'our world-leading expertise at Public Health England and NHS England' (Hansard, 3 February). Health Secretary, Matt Hancock stated that Professor Chris Whitty, the chief medical officer, was one of the finest epidemiologists in the world (Hansard, 26 February), and that Public Health England has world-class expertise, from the past, in contact tracing (Hansard, 11 March). Ben Everitt (Con) argued that having a Professor of Epidemiology as Chief Medical Officer was 'literally the right man in the right job at the right time' (Hansard, 17 March).

Similarly, according to (Her Majesty's Government (HMG) (2020), the UK is a 'world leader in the field of outbreak modelling and data analytics'. The 'official' model (ICL, 2020; see Boseley 2020) claimed that an unmitigated epidemic would result in about 510,000 deaths, which could be reduced to between 8700 and 39,000 deaths with a full 'suppression strategy'. These very wide confidence intervals were also given by other models. For example, the University of Washington's Institute for Health Metrics and Evaluation (IHME, 2020) predicted that by August the UK could be looking at 66,314 deaths, which was an average taken from a large estimate range of between 14,572 and 219,211 deaths. However, the 'science' consists of a complex mix of material from the past and from abroad. The following sections focus on these two different sources of lessons.

Learning from the Past

The government *Action Plan* (HMG, 2020) claimed that the UK was well prepared for disease outbreaks, having responded to a wide range of infectious disease outbreaks in the recent past and having undertaken significant preparedness work for an '***influenza pandemic***' (our emphasis) for well over a decade, providing 'the basis for an effective response to COVID-19, which can be tailored as more specific information emerges about the virus'. It stated that there is similarity between COVID-19 and influenza (both are respiratory infections), but also some important differences. Consequently, contingency plans developed for pandemic influenza, and lessons learned from previous outbreaks, provide a useful starting point for the development of an effective response plan to COVID-19. That plan has been adapted, however, to take account of differences between the two diseases.

The *Action Plan* (HMG, 2020) noted the impact of some of the major respiratory virus Pandemics and epidemics in the last 100 years. It considered that experience of infectious disease outbreaks could be adapted for COVID-19. In the absence of clear information about COVID-19, some early NERVTAG and SAGE documents also used planning assumptions such as Case Fatality Rates from Pandemic Flu, which were updated as information from China, Italy and later the UK became available (e.g. SAGE, 2nd, 28 January; SAGE 4th, 4 February; Cairney, 2020).

After the 'swine flu' Pandemic of 2009–2010, the UK engaged in some inter-crisis learning (Hine, 2010). This was followed by a series of Pandemic influenza plans and guidance documents in 2011, 2013 and 2017 (Department of Health and Social Care, 2017), and a planning exercise in 2016 (below).

However, it has been claimed that the UK prepared from the wrong Pandemic (Britton, 2020; Dalton, 2021; Stubley, 2021). For example, former Health Secretary Jeremy Hunt has admitted the UK prepared for the wrong pandemic during his tenure by believing the next biggest threat would come from influenza. The National Risk Register in 2015 regarded the probability of a flu pandemic as high, but stated: 'The likelihood of a new disease spreading to the UK is low'. Exercise Cygnus of October 2016 aimed to test plans for a future 'worst-case-scenario' flu pandemic affecting up to half of the population, causing up to 400,000 excess deaths. However, Hunt argued that while these 'exhaustive pandemic preparations' were lauded by Johns Hopkins University as being the second-best-prepared country in the world (after the USA), we were 'sadly also part of a groupthink that said that the primary way that you respond to a pandemic is the flu pandemic playbook (with a focus on areas like vaccination and boosting hospital capacity), rather than the methods that you would use for SARS and MERS (surveillance and containment, community testing, contact tracing and isolation, and stockpiling personal protective equipment, and ventilators)'. He continued that this thinking was not unique to the UK and was shared in the USA and across Europe, but accounts for the 'stark difference in the effectiveness of our responses compared with countries in East Asia'.

Similarly, the former Chief Medical Officer, Dame Sally Davies, argued that the UK focused on the threat of pandemic influenza, and the country was therefore prepared for the 'wrong pandemic'. She said she questioned whether the country should rehearse for a coronavirus outbreak in 2015, but was told it would not 'reach us properly' by Public Health England officials. However, Public Health England denied this, adding: 'Dame Sally Davies participated in exercises which planned specifically for a MERS coronavirus scenario in the UK amongst other health threats'.

In short, nations that experienced previous Coronaviruses such as SARS and MERS exhibited inter-crisis learning. For example, Korea built an infrastructure after MERS in 2015 (Moon, 2020). An and Tang (2020) pointed out that many commentators attributed Asian polities' successes to aggressive and comprehensive policy instruments themselves or a culture that supports public cooperation and voluntary compliance, but less attention has been given to the institutional infrastructure they established before the COVID-19 pandemic. As there was limited inter-crisis learning in the UK (certainly with respect to Coronaviruses), this narrowed down the range of lessons from abroad (below) to 'short term fixes' as it was not possible to build up an infrastructure as part of intra-crisis learning.

Learning from Abroad

It is difficult to detect much influence from international groups in the urgency of a crisis situation, but two groups may be worth considering in more detail. First, supra-national organisations provided guidance (e.g. ECDC, 2020; OECD, 2020; WHO, 2020). It is noticeable that these organisations tended to discuss international experience. For example, before the end of March, OECD (2020) reported that data from Hubei (China) suggests that the implementation of a comprehensive package of containment and mitigation policies can be effective in suppressing the epidemic in the short term, but it is unclear whether the effect can last in the longer term. Similarly, ECDC (2020) noted that contact tracing was effective at helping to reduce the spread of the disease during the period of ongoing widespread transmission in China and South Korea and also discussed Singapore, Vietnam and New Zealand.

However, in a case of the 'dog that did not bark', neither the 'scientific' nor 'political' sources say much about supra-national organisations. For example, WHO is mentioned only a handful of times in HMG (2020). It was noted that on 30 January 2020, WHO declared the outbreak of COVID-19 a 'Public Health Emergency of International Concern' (PHEIC). Later it was stated that 'our response to COVID-19 is guided by the international situation, the advice of organisations such as the WHO, surveillance, data modelling based on the best available evidence and the recommendations of our expert bodies'. The WHO was mentioned some 30 times in Parliamentary Debates in the first half of 2020 (Hansard 2020), but very few of these could be described as 'lessons'.

Expert input from 'epistemic communities' should also be considered. As noted above, most governments, in a pandemic situation, claim to be following the science yet national approaches differ (e.g. Baekkeskov, 2016; Baekkeskov & Rubin, 2014; Salajan et al., 2020; Weible et al., 2020). A major debate in the UK was the extent to which the government 'followed the science', but this prompts further questions of which science and which scientists? (Cairney, 2020).

The government response and the scientific advice were heavily criticised, leading to the setting up of 'Independent SAGE' (www.independentSAGE.org) which, like the supra-national organisations (above) tended to feature more international evidence. For example, Independent SAGE (2020) noted statements that the government is learning from the experiences of other countries, but would wish to see more detailed evidence of how this learning is feeding into UK policies. It gave some examples of where it believed the UK could have learnt lessons: Korea (testing and digital app) and Greece (early partial and then full lockdown). In turn, Independent SAGE has been subject to critique (e.g. SMC, 2020). From an intra-crisis perspective, urgency meant that decisions needed to be made quickly, which narrowed the pool of actors to a small group of experts. All this leads to the counterfactual of to what extent the situation would have been different if different scientific advice had been followed. Many other nations appeared to have fared much better. Was this due to more closely following the advice or better advice?

While the long history of 'Non pharmaceutical interventions' (NPIs) such as 'quarantine' and 'lockdowns' was discussed in the media, there is little evidence that learning from the past featured much in political and scientific discussion. However, there did seem to be some attempt to learn from abroad for some other NPIs. While most nations had some form of social distancing, harshness, timing (and compliance) varied (e.g. Hale et al., 2020; Weible et al., 2020). SAGE (11th, 27 February) asked SPI-M to 'produce a narrative describing effects of interventions attempted in other countries, and develop illustrative scenarios showing the plausible impacts of combinations of interventions in the UK' for next SAGE meeting (Cairney, 2020) (although this did not seem to be discussed at the following meeting). Similarly, at the 14th Meeting on 10 March, it was noted: 'SAGE secretariat to consider how to provide a paper setting out where Italy, France, Germany and Spain are in terms of their epidemics and interventions (including efficacy of, and behavioural change related to, those interventions)'. Again, this appeared not to feature in future discussions.

It seems that there was more focus on learning from abroad when lessons were either geographically or institutionally closer. For example, the very successful lockdown in China did not seem to be discussed much. This is perhaps due to the feeling that while lockdowns may be a possible policy tool in authoritarian nations, they were not on the agenda for Western democratic nations. The 'negative' lesson of Italy seems to have been the main catalyst in changing this view. In the UK Parliament and media, the high death rates in Italy and concerns that its health system would be overwhelmed gave rise to the view that the UK was 'tracking' Italy, and that the Italian lockdown provided the signal that this was a policy tool for European nations. Matt Hancock pointed out that while there were 319 confirmed cases in the UK, Italy saw overnight 1,492 more cases and 102 more deaths, later adding that 'Italy is the epicentre of the European outbreak' (Hansard, 9 March). Hilary Benn (Labour) pointed out that two weeks ago Italy had the same number of confirmed cases as the UK, resulting in great pressure on intensive care units and hospitals (Hansard, 11 March). However, the UK would soon become Europe's 'negative lesson', with possibly the USA and the UK vying for this unwanted award in global terms.

Similarly, very limited notice seems to have taken place of the rapid closing of borders in distant nations such as Australia and New Zealand. However, the notion of the 'household bubble' seems to have its origins in New Zealand, and almost a year into the Pandemic the UK government has implemented the idea of 'hotel quarantine' for international travellers.

Few lessons from abroad featured in either scientific or political sources early on. As noted above, this tends to contrast with other sources (e.g. WHO, ECDC, OECD, Independent SAGE). At least for early sources, this might be partly explained by the lag period in determining 'what works'. For example, a paper for SAGE (19th, 26 March) stated that 'the impact of interventions will become apparent in around 3–4 weeks' (see also SAGE 22nd, 2 April; Cairney, 2020). However, infection and hospitalisation rates provide earlier signals than mortality figures.

While the experiences of other nations were often mentioned in Parliamentary Debates, they tended to be comparisons or analogies from abroad, rather than clear lessons. For example, simply pointing out the high mortality rate in the UK does not, in itself, provide anything more than a crude negative lesson that we are doing *something* wrong. 'Lessons' tended to consist of pointing out that particular nations that carried out particular interventions were doing better, making the assumptions that it was that particular intervention which was vital, and that the intervention was fungible.

Learning from the Past and from Abroad?

We have seen that there is fairly limited evidence of the UK learning from either the past or from abroad. There are perhaps three sets of reasons that may explain this. First, 'UK exceptionalism' may explain an unwillingness to learn. For example, according to English (2020), as COVID-19 ripped through Europe and the world, Britain's response to the pandemic showed that it was suffering from another dangerous disease: unshakeable belief in its own exceptionalism (cf the USA). Britain's belief in its own uniqueness meant that it was not possible to learn from others. For example, 'We talk about the different approach being taken by different countries, but the UK has to focus on what is right for our country at the right time... We need the right response for our culture and the way our people behave—not one transported from another country' (Alicia Kearns, Con, Hansard, 17 March).

Second, Rose (1991) pointed out that transfer was unlikely to involve situations of perfect fungibility or perfect blockage. Rose (1991) argued that the complexity of a programme affects its transferability; the more complex a policy or programme is the harder it will be to transfer, while Rose (1993) suggested six hypotheses on complexity. Some lessons may be complex rather than simple. For example, wearing masks is a simple policy tool (but see below), but a fully functioning 'Test, Trace and Isolate' system appears to be a more complex policy tool, involving many elements that need to fit together such as the availability of tests, the speed of getting results and the ability and willingness of the individual with a positive test to isolate. However, simple tools such as mask wearing may not be fully fungible as the willingness of the public to wear masks seems to be related to issues such as previous Pandemics, culture and ideology. UK politicians may have decided that tracking where infected patients visited through data mining of CCTV footage, credit card use and GPS information in Korea (Moon, 2020) was not feasible. An and Tang (2020) warn that to be effective, any policy instrument requires public cooperation and voluntary compliance, and that policy instruments that work in East Asia may not work well in other countries. More generally, Cao et al. (2020) claimed that nations with high levels of cultural tightness and government efficiency have slower virus growth and mortality rates compared with nations that have one of these factors or neither.

Third, if learning lessons from the past or from abroad is not simple in 'normal' times, it must be more difficult in crisis situations characterised by urgency, uncertainty and threat (Moynihan, 2008, 2009) or almost 'impossible conditions' (e.g. Boin et al., 2013). There was significant uncertainty in the scientific advice (Cairney, 2020). For example on the 3rd February, SPI-M-O asserted that there was not enough evidence to estimate a reasonable worst-case scenario (SPI-M-O, 2020). Moreover, the speed at which decisions had to be taken negated a straightforward lesson learning process of policy transfer. As Rose (1991) pointed out, the process of lesson-drawing begins with the scrutiny of other policies and the in-depth evaluation of whether they would work in the current situation. There was no time during an intra-crisis situation in the UK to set up the infrastructure that nations such as China or Korea had set up in an inter-crisis situation following SARS or MERS (An & Tang, 2020; Moon, 2020). Moreover, in terms of the crisis literature, while some East Asian nations (having experienced previous Coronaviruses) faced a more 'routine' crisis, Western nations faced a less routine crisis.

In conclusion, these factors together help to explain the limited degree of learning. Weible et al. (2020) point out that the novelty of COVID-19 may prevent learning opportunities from the past. 'Exceptional' nations such as the UK and the USA may be more resistant to learning from abroad. Finally, some complex and less fungible lessons, which may have made inter-crisis policy learning problematic, made learning in a non-routine, intra-crisis situation very difficult.

References

An, B. Y., & Tang, S.-Y. (2020). Lessons from COVID-19 responses in East Asia: Institutional infrastructure and enduring policy instruments. *American Review of Public Administration, 50*(6–7), 79–800.

All Party Parliamentary Action Group on Coronavirus. (2020). *Interim report on Coronavirus.* Accessed 4 December 2020. Available from: https://www.psl

hub.org/learn/coronavirus-covid19/data-and-statistics/all-party-parliamentary-group-on-coronavirus-interim-report-december-2020-r3704

Baekkeskov, E. (2016). Same threat, different responses: Experts steering politicians and stakeholders in 2009 H1N1 vaccination policy-making. *Public Administration, 94*(2), 299–315.

Baekkeskov, E., & Rubin, O. (2014). Why pandemic response is unique: Powerful experts and hands-off political leaders. *Disaster Prevention and Management, 23*(1), 81–93.

Baker, T., & Walker, C. (2019). Introduction: The centrality of arenas, agents and actions. In T. Baker & C. Walker (Eds.), *Public policy circulation* (pp. 2–24). Edward Elgar.

BBC. (2020). *Covid-19 in the UK: How many coronavirus cases are there in your area?* https://www.bbc.co.uk/news/uk-51768274. Accessed 18 February 2021.

Bennett, C., & Howlett, M. (1992). The lessons of learning: Reconciling theories of policy learning and policy change. *Policy Sciences, 25*, 275–294.

Boin, A., Kuipers, S., & Overdijk, W. (2013). Leadership in times of crisis: A framework for assessment. *International Review of Public Administration, 18*(1), 79–91.

Boin, A., 't Hart, P., & Kuipers, S. (2018). The crisis approach. In H. Rodríguez et al. (Eds.), *Handbook of disaster research* (pp. 23–38). Springer.

Boseley, S. (2020, April 8). Coronavirus: UK will have Europe's worst death toll, says study. *Guardian*. https://www.theguardian.com/world/2020/apr/07/uk-will-be-europes-worst-hit-by-coronavirus-study-predicts (Accessed 31 August 2021)

Brändström, A., Bynander, F., & 't Hart, P. (2004). Governing by looking back: Historical analogies and crisis management. *Public Administration, 82*(1), 191–210.

Britton, A. (2020, November 13). UK was prepared for 'wrong pandemic', former chief medical officer claims. *Independent*. https://www.independent.co.uk/news/uk/home-news/coronavirus-uk-prepared-for-wrong-pandemic-b1722321.html

Cairney, P. (2020). *COVID-19 policy in the UK: Did the UK Government 'follow the science'? Reflections on SAGE meetings*.

Cao, C., Li, N., & Liu, L. (2020). Do national cultures matter in the containment of COVID-19? *International Journal of Sociology and Social Policy, 40*(9/10), 939–961.

Dalton, J. (2021, February 11). We prepared for the wrong pandemic, admits former health secretary Jeremy Hunt. *Independent*. https://www.independent.co.uk/news/health/jeremy-hunt-wrong-flu-pandemic-covid-b1800583.html

Department of Health and Social Care. (2017). *Guidance: Pandemic flu*. Updated 24 November 2017. https://www.gov.uk/guidance/pandemic-flu

Dolowitz, D., & Marsh, D. (1996). Who learns what from whom. *Political Studies, 44*, 343–357.

Dolowitz, D., & Marsh, D. (2000). Learning from abroad: The role of policy transfer in contemporary policy making. *Governance, 13*(1), 5–24.

Drisko, J., & Maschi, T. (2016). *Content analysis*. Oxford University Press.

ECDC. (2020, April). Contact tracing for COVID-19: *Current evidence, options for scale-up and an assessment of resources needed*. ECDC: Solna.

English, O. (2020, May 5). *Cruel Britannia: Coronavirus lays waste to British exceptionalism*. https://www.politico.eu/article/cruel-britannia-coronavirus-lays-waste-to-british-exceptionalism/

Ettelt, S., Mays, N., & Nolte, E. (2012). Policy learning from abroad: Why it is more difficult than it seems. *Policy & Politics, 40*(4), 491–504.

Grey, S., & MacAskill, A. (2020, April 7). *Special Report: Johnson listened to his scientists about coronavirus—But they were slow to sound the alarm*. Reuters.

Giles, C. (2020, November 29). UK's high Covid spending delivers worse outcomes than peers. *Financial Times*. https://www.ft.com/content/1f52fd2b-7daf-418e-be8b-acc38f819b8d

Grin, J., & Loeber, A. (2007). Theories of policy learning: Agency, structure, and change. In F. Fischer, G. Miller, & M. Sidney (Eds.), *Handbook of public policy analysis. Theory, politics, and methods* (pp. 201–219). CRC Press.

Hadjiisky, M., Pal, L., & Walker, C. (2017). Introduction: Traversing the terrain of policy transfer: Theory, methods and overview. In M. Hadjiisky, L. Pal, & C. Walker (Eds.), *Public policy transfer micro-dynamics and macro-effects* (pp. 1–26). Edward Elgar.

Hale, T., Angrist, N., Kira, B., et al. (2020, May 25). *"Variation in government responses to COVID-19" Version 6.0* (Blavatnik School of Government Working Paper). Available from: www.bsg.ox.ac.uk/covidtracker

Heikkila, T., & Gerlak, A. (2013). Building a conceptual approach to collective learning: Lessons for public policy scholars. *Policy Studies Journal, 41*(4), 484–512.

Her Majesty's Government. (2020, March 20). *Coronavirus Action Plan*. TSO.

Hine, D. (2010). *The 2009 influenza pandemic: An independent review of the UK response to the 2009 influenza pandemic*. Cabinet Office.

Horton, R. (2020). *The COVID-19 catastrophe: What's gone wrong and how to stop it happening again*. Polity Press.

Imperial College London. (2020). *Report 9—Impact of non-pharmaceutical interventions (NPIs) to reduce COVID-19 mortality and healthcare demand*. Available from: https://www.imperial.ac.uk/mrc-global-infectious-disease-analysis/covid-19/report-9-impact-of-npis-on-covid-19/

Independent SAGE. (2020). *Final integrated find, test, trace, isolate, support (FTTIS) response to the pandemic* (Report 5).

Ingold, J., & Monaghan, M. (2016). Evidence translation: An exploration of policy makers' use of evidence. *Policy & Politics, 44*(2), 171–190.

Institute for Health Metrics and Evaluation. (2020). *COVID-19 projections*. Available from: https://covid19.healthdata.org/united-kingdom.

James, O., & Lodge, M. (2003). The limitations of 'policy transfer' and 'lesson drawing' for public policy research. *Political Studies Review, 1*, 179–183.

Klein, R. (1997). Learning from others: Shall the last be the first? *Journal of Health Politics, Policy and Law, 22*(5), 1267–1278.

Legrand, T. (2012). Overseas and over here: Policy transfer and evidence-based policymaking. *Policy Studies, 33*(4), 329–348.

Moon, M. J. (2020). Fighting COVID-19 with agility, transparency, and participation: Wicked policy problems and new governance challenges. *Public Administration Review*.

Moynihan, D. (2008). Learning under uncertainty: Networks in crisis management. *Public Administration Review, 68*(2), 350–361.

Moynihan, D. (2009). From intercrisis to intracrisis learning. *Journal of Contingencies and Crisis Management, 17*(3), 189–198.

Nickson, S. Thomas, A., & Mullens-Burgess, E. (2020). *Decision making in a crisis. First responses to the coronavirus pandemic*. Institute for Government.

OECD. (2020, March 24). *Flattening the COVID-19 peak: Containment and mitigation policies*. OECD.

Powell, M., & King-Hill, S. (2020) Intra-crisis learning and prospective policy transfer in the COVID-19 pandemic. *International Journal of Sociology and Social Policy, 40*(9/10), 877–892.

Rose, R. (1991). What Is lesson-drawing? *Journal of Public Policy, 11*(1), 3–30.

Rose, R. (1993). *Lesson-drawing in public policy. A guide to learning across time and space*. Chatham House Publishers.

Salajan, A., Tsolova, S., Ciotti, M., & Suk, J. E. (2020). To what extent does evidence support decision making during infectious disease outbreaks? A scoping literature review. *Evidence and Policy*, 1–23.

Scally, G., Jacobson, B., & Abbasi, K. (2020). The UK's public health response to COVID-19. Too little, too late, too flawed. *British Medical Journal*, 369:m1932. https://doi.org/10.1136/bmj.m1932

Science Media Centre. (2020). *Expert reaction to the Independent SAGE Report 7 on elimination of the virus from the UK*. https://www.independentsage.org/wp-content/uploads/2020/07/A-Better-Way-To-Go-FINAL-proof-copy-1.pdf

SPI-M-O. (2020). Consensus Statement on COVID-19, 3 February. https://assets.publishing.service.gov.uk/government/uploads/system/uploads/attach

ment_data/file/962824/s1073-spi-m-o-consensus-statement-030221.pdf. (Accessed 31 August 2021)

Stark, A. (2018). *Public inquiries, policy learning and threat of future crises*. Oxford University Press.

Stubley, P. (2021, February 14). Covid: UK failed to prepare for inevitable pandemic, says vaccine scientist. *Independent*. https://www.independent.co.uk/news/health/coronavirus-pandemic-warnings-uk-sarah-gilbert-vaccine-b1802015.html

Vagionaki, T., & Trein, P. (2020). Learning in political analysis. *Political Studies Review, 18*(2), 304–319.

Williams, C., & Dzhekova, R. (2014). Evaluating the cross-national transferability of policies: A conceptual framework. *Journal of Developmental Entrepreneurship, 19*(4), 1–18.

Weible, C., Nohrstedt, D., Cairney, P., et al. (2020). COVID-19 and the policy sciences: Initial reactions and perspectives. *Policy Sciences, 53*, 225–241.

WHO. (2020, March 22). *Critical preparedness, readiness and response actions for COVID-19*. WHO.

Wolf, A., & Baehler, K. (2018). Learning transferable lessons from single cases in comparative policy analysis. *Journal of Comparative Policy Analysis: Research and Practice, 20*(4), 420–434.

Worldometers. (2021). https://www.worldometers.info/coronavirus/. Last accessed 18 February 2021.

CHAPTER 3

Whose Science Did Government Follow? The Organisation of Scientific Advice to the UK Government in the First Wave of the COVID-19 Response

Richard Gleave

Introduction

In the early weeks of the COVID-19 pandemic, UK politicians frequently described their approach as following or being guided by the science (Newsnight, 2020) but rather than acting as a defensive shield, this rhetorical claim has become a stick used to beat the government. Constructivist social scientists (Dupre, 2020) and positivist bio-medical scientists (Ramakrishnan, 2020) have been united in explaining that science is too complicated, uncertain and contested to simply be "followed".

The formal basis for the provision of scientific advice to inform the UK Government's response during the first wave of COVID-19 was first set

R. Gleave (✉)
University of Oxford, Oxford, UK
e-mail: Richard.gleave@gtc.ox.ac.uk

J. Waring et al. (eds.), *Organising Care in a Time of Covid-19*, Organizational Behaviour in Healthcare,
https://doi.org/10.1007/978-3-030-82696-3_3

out a decade ago (GO-Science, 2010). This account of a rational, linear process provided through clear organisational structures should be seen as a purely normative description as the events of the first nine months of 2020 demonstrate that the reality was a more complicated process dominated by limited knowledge, involving multiple actors, challenged by informal, emergent approaches. Through two case studies on the range of advisory actors and the production of advice on social distancing, the concept of an *emergency scientific advisory system* is proposed as a more realistic analysis of the organising processes and organisational structures that have produced a diversity of scientific advice for policymakers and practitioners. Building on the literature about policy advisory systems, the paper concludes that there are important policy lessons from viewing the COVID-19 advisory system through three theoretically informed lenses (complexity theory, neo-institutional field theory and dramaturgical policy theory) to understand the dynamics of producing and providing scientific advice in a crisis.

The paper is informed by empirical data from a larger qualitative mixed methods case study of how Public Health England (PHE) used evidence to influence policy and practice between 2018 and 2020. PHE is the national public health agency and the author is its Deputy Chief Executive.

The data was collected through auto-ethnographic observation, elite interviews and document review. The auto-ethnographic approach uses observational participation (Alvesson, 2003) which provides a rare level of access and enables insights from discussions among elite participants about the provision of advice on public health measures as part of the wider government response. Anderson (2006)'s analytical approach to autoethnography and the use of structured reflectivity (Brannick & Coghlan, 2007) help address the challenges of ethics and subjectivity associated with insider research.

The Literature on Organising Scientific Advice in an Emergency

Although there has been a tsunami of commentaries and blogs in 2020 about scientific advice during COVID-19, the literature is mainly composed of government publications and a few peer-reviewed empirical studies on the provision of scientific advice in previous crises. This section uses the literature to create a framework for analysing the organisation of the provision of scientific advice.

How Does Government Describe the Organisation of Scientific Advice in an Emergency?

A decade ago the UK Government set out how it wanted scientific advice to be provided in an emergency (GO-Science, 2010, 2011, 2012) focused on the work of the Scientific Advisory Group on Emergencies (SAGE). The OECD (2018) described this system as "on the shelf" and relatively centralised compared to the dispersed, informal systems operating in Germany and the USA where bespoke structures are created to meet the requirements of each crisis.

The Government's model is guided by three principles of scientific advice of role clarity, transparency and independence. (GO-Science, 2010). It operates through a linear sequence of four stages (Fig. 3.1) centred around SAGE, an ad hoc group composed of invited scientists employed in government departments and arms-length agencies and in academic institutions, chaired by the Government Chief Scientific Advisor (GCSA), supported by the Chief Medical Officer (CMO). SAGE only meets when the Government's civil contingency committee (called COBR after the Cabinet Office Briefing Rooms where it meets) decides it needs scientific advice. It is supported by specially convened sub-committees, other standing scientific advisory committees (SACs) and government scientific staff and agencies, such as PHE, NHS England and the Environment Agency.

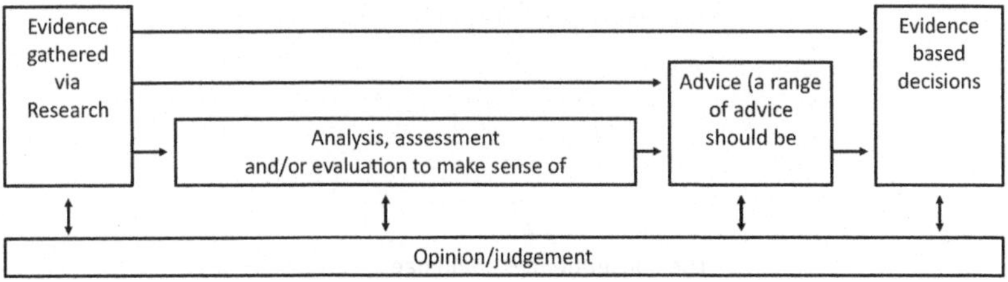

Fig. 3.1 The evidence-based decision-making process from "Enhancing SAGE guidance" (GO-Science, 2012) (*Note* The third box is incomplete in the original)

The Government has produced a normative description of how the scientific advisory system should operate in an emergency which is intuitively attractive but is not necessarily what will happen in practice. The model is similar to academic theories that describe policymaking through a series of phases, either in a line or often in a cycle, that have been popular since Lasswell (1956)'s model of seven functional stages. However, these have been criticised for being idealised, simplistic and prescriptive (Stone et al., 2001) and empirical studies show more complex *multi-centric policymaking* processes (Cairney et al., 2019).

What Does the Academic Literature Conclude About the Organisation of Scientific Advice in Crisis Situations?

This section reviews three strands of the existing academic literature that provide insights into the organisation of scientific advice in emergencies—the use of evidence in public health emergencies, the demands on advisors from crisis situations and the organisation of the provision of advice to policymakers. A framework for analysing the *emergency scientific advisory system* (Fig. 3.2) is proposed which combines the challenges of working in a crisis (in blue) and the organisation of advisory work (in red).

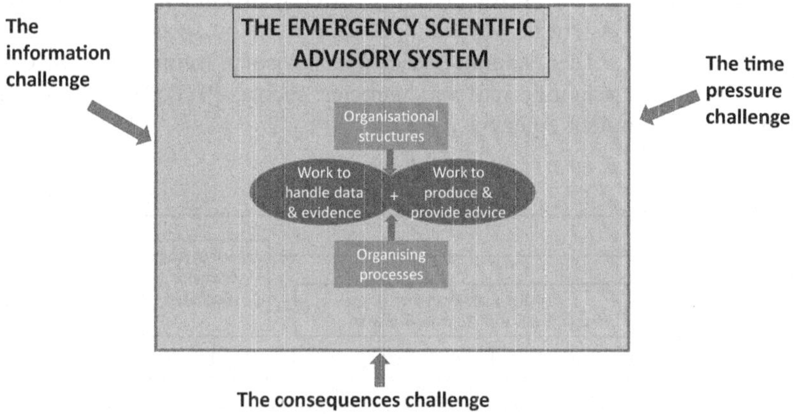

Fig. 3.2 The emergency scientific advisory system (1)—An initial framework

The Use of Evidence in Public Health Emergencies

Systematic reviews have demonstrated the complexity and situational variety of evidence-informed policymaking (Lawrence et al., 2019; Masood et al., 2019; Oliver et al., 2014; Orton et al., 2011), but none consider the pressures of an emergency. However, Salajan et al. (2020) looked at the use of knowledge in public health emergencies and concluded that "decision makers prioritise expert advice, epidemiological data and mathematical modelling data for risk characterisation and management, but tend to be challenged by scientific uncertainties, which allow for conflicting interpretations of evidence and for public criticism and contestation of decision-making processes" (p. 1). Although they did not explicitly consider the organisation of scientific advice, studies have shown how scientific advice from public health experts within national and international public health organisations shaped policy in the H1N1 response (Baekkeskov, 2020). The scientific advice sat alongside wider political and economic considerations leading the advisors to use sense-making skills to interpret ambiguous, uncertain information (Keller et al., 2012) and sometimes acting defensively not consistent with the evidence (Feufel et al., 2010).

The Demands on Scientific Advisors in a Public Health Crisis

Two distinctive strands in the academic literature on crises can be identified. Firstly the organisational and management literature has sought to identify the distinctive contemporaneous features of an emergency or crisis that impacts on leaders and decision-makers. Weick (1988) described crises as low probability, high impact events and systematic reviews of the organisational literature to produce largely consistent lists of the primary characteristics of a crisis situation (Bundy et al., 2017; Kovoor-Misra et al., 2001) describing the disruption, surprise, threat, time pressures, ambiguity and uncertainty that challenge leaders and organisations in their immediate response. The phrase "public health emergency" is widely used as a rhetorical claim (Blumenthal & Seervai, 2018) but it has a specific meaning in international law (WHO, 2005).

However, the political science academic tradition considers the consequences of a crisis, drawing on the original Greek where *krisis* is a decision or judgement leading to change. Thus a crisis becomes a *critical juncture* (Collier & Collier, 1991) creating uncertainty and instability resulting in major change from the pre-crisis trajectory. Hajer (2009) highlighted how crises act as ***moments of dislocation*** when the dominant discourse is challenged, disrupted and reframed.

The work of Boin and colleagues is widely referenced and their focus on the political, strategic dimensions of crisis leadership has some elements of both approaches. They have identified three core attributes of threat, uncertainty and urgency, to which the transnational aspect of most major crises was later added (Boin & Lodge, 2016; Rosenthal et al., 2001).

This chapter focuses on scientific advice in an emergency and both the event-focused and consequences-focused aspects of crises generate three challenges that put significant pressures on advisers.

- *The information challenge*—advisers face both gaps in the information that is required and different understandings of what data is available. Cairney (2018) highlighted the dual effect from uncertainty and ambiguity.
- *The consequences challenge*—the impact of advice given in crises is especially clear as it seeks to mitigate the immediate threat, while also considering the new opportunities that can arise.
- *The time-pressure challenge*—crises require not only the speeding-up of the normal advisory processes but also for new faster processes to be invented. Thus the usual deliberation and review of evidence are limited and advisors occupy positions much closer to decision-makers, putting pressure on their perceived (and actual) independence.

The Organisation of the Provision of Policy Advice

Scientific advice is produced by and through organisation. The cult of the personality focuses on individual advisors but advice is normally the product of a team composed of scientists with formal training and qualifications who produce evidence generated through systematic methodologies. Studying the organisation of scientific advice is about more than formal bodies that employ scientists and considers how individual and corporate actors work through organisational structures and organising processes (Weick, 1979). Organisation frames the work of actors but they have embedded agency (Battilana et al., 2009) as they modify and create new structures and design processes through their choices. This paper explores the role both of organisations as advisory actors and of the organisational context of individual advisors.

Theories of policymaking abound with organisational models—Cairney et al. (2014)'s review of policymaking has actors, institutions and networks/sub-systems as core elements of different theories. Although there are limited studies of the emergency situation, three are relevant to the organisation of scientific advice in COVID-19. Firstly Caplan's (1979) "two communities theory" separated researchers, who are knowledge-producers, from policymakers as knowledge-users. Studies have tended to focus either on the role of organisations that review the evidence, such as the Cochrane Collaborative, (Elvbakken & Hansen, 2018, Heywood et al., 2018) or on how experts use evidence when advising governments (Baekkeskov, 2016; Stevens, 2011). However, research has shown the model is too simple with extensive interaction and movement between the two groups (Lawrence et al., 2019; Newman et al., 2016) and the linear transfer of knowledge from research into policy is rare (Oliver et al., 2014). Although this model underpins the SAGE model, Pearce (2020) highlighted the problems that have resulted from the conflation of the two roles in the UK COVID-19 response with different perceptions of uncertainty.

Secondly many studies explore the role of *boundary organisations* (Guston, 2001) which bring together scientists and policymakers. They highlight the inherent tensions between influence/authority and independence/autonomy both for government scientific agencies (Boswell, 2018) which have often been created to *depoliticise* science and the arms-length *agentification* of advice (Pollitt et al., 2004), and for non-governmental organisations such as think tanks (Medvetz, 2012), who advocate on specific issues. These insights are relevant to the emergency situation even though the boundary organisation concept has not been used in empirical studies of crisis response.

Thirdly the concept of the *policyadvisory system* was proposed by Seymour-Ure (1987) and Halligan (1995) to describe the "interlocking set of actors and organizations with unique configurations in each sector and jurisdiction that provides recommendations for action to policy-makers" (Craft & Halligan, 2017: 49). Initially, it rather simplistically focused on the consequence of advisors being distant/close to decision-makers, and a distinction between technical, objective advice, such as from scientists, and political, partisan advice.

This paper develops the concept of a *scientific advisory system for emergencies*, building on two subsequent perspectives. Firstly a *second wave* (Craft & Wilder, 2017; Howlett, 2019) has emphasised a wider range of advisory actors, often international or outside public services, and the existence of an ideational compatibility between advisor and advisee/decision-maker. Secondly Parkhurst (2017) described effective institutionalised uses of evidence in policymaking in *evidence-advisory systems* ("the collection of structural bodies, rules and norms of practice which serve to govern the ways in which evidence informs policy decisions" (pp. 31–32), though Diamond (2020) highlighted the complexity and unpredictability of UK policy advisory systems.

Case Study 1: The Actors Who Provide Scientific Advice During COVID-19

This case study focuses on the diversity of advisory actors during the pandemic which contrasts with the Government's description of the organisation of scientific advice in an emergency that echoes Caplan's two communities model. This makes two assumptions, both of which are challenged by the experience of COVID-19. Firstly though the assumption that *scientistsadvise and ministers decide* has been supported by the GCSA and the Secretary of State (SoS), the reality is more complicated with Weible et al. (2020) highlighting how the greater prominence of scientific advisors obscures accountability for decisions. The GCSA described how "the ultimate decisions are a mixture of policy and timing, which are not in our control. Those are things that others have to make decisions around" (HoC, 2020b: Q1002) and the SoS said "I always argue that we are guided by the science, because you take into account the scientific evidence and then you also take into account everything else" (HoC, 2020b: Q1151).

Secondly the model implies a *homogenous community* of scientific advisors working through formal channels of advice, notably SAGE and associated SACs. However, during the pandemic, a variety of advisers have used both front-stage, public channels and informal, back-stage routes to provide recommendations to decision-makers. One of the SAGE members observed "actually what you got was other scientists making their views available both to government and directly to the public and the media of course getting involved, this all feeding back into the policymakers" (Yardley, 2020).

The academic literature uses a range of labels to describe different sorts of advisory body and Table 3.1 uses these terms to identify and categorise the main actors who have provided advice during the pandemic.

Table 3.1 A selection of advisory actors in the UK's COVID-19 response

Type of Actor	*Format*	*Comments on work in COVID-19*
Specialist or Scientific Advisory Committees (SACs) e.g. Scientific Advisory Group in Emergencies (SAGE) and sub-committees, Joint Committee on Vaccination and Immunisation (JCVI)	• Composed mainly of academics invited to join and government scientists; • Run by government; • Analyse evidence and provide recommendations;	• SAGE chaired by GCSA • SAGE initially criticised for lack of transparency and independence • Expansion in its membership during the response • Participants largely from bio-medical, environmental and behavioural science background
What Work's Centres e.g. National Institute for Health and Clinical Effectiveness (NICE) and Behavioural Insights Team (BIT)	• Mix of organisational forms (NICE is a government Arms-Length Body, BIT is a company spun-off from government, others are charities)	• Not had high profile role though NICE publications have been directed to NHS and social care • No clear alignment between SAGE and these organisations
Formal Individual Government Advisors e.g. Chief Medical Officer (CMO: Chris Whitty), Government Chief Scientific Adviser (GCSA: Sir Patrick Vallance) Also civil servants who provide policy advice that is not publicly visible	• Most government departments have chief scientific adviser • Individual leading scientists are sometimes given "tsar" roles alongside the formal CSA roles • Wider advice is provided by civil servants as a core part of their jobs and often this is informed or develops the scientific information • Government departments produce information for the public and specific sectors	• CMO and GCSA had very high profile roles during the pandemic • Played important role within SAGE and sub-committees • The less visible advice from civil servants to ministers has remained largely confidential • Government departments have produced the large quantities of formal government guidance on the Government website

(continued)

Table 3.1 (continued)

Type of Actor	*Format*	*Comments on work in COVID-19*
Government Scientific Regulators e.g. Health & Safety Executive (HSE) and Medicines and Healthcare products Agency Regulatory Agency (MHRA)	• Arms length—either government agencies or licensed by government to regulate specific areas • Employ scientists to assess and approve products or providers	• Specialist role in COVID-19 such as vaccine approval (MHRA) and role of PPE in workplace safety (HSE)
Government Research Institutes or Public Research Organisations e.g. Public Health England (PHE), Defence Science and Technology Laboratory (DSTL)	• Arms length—either government agencies or charities dependent on government funding • Employ scientists to work on government priorities • Focus on applied and translational work	• Multiple roles—scientific research, advice and policymaking, delivery functions • PHE criticised mainly for its delivery of services and its replacement by a new National Institute for Health Protection was announced in August 2020
Home nation advisory groups	• The devolved administrations have created their own scientific advisory groups to give them advice related to devolved responsibilities where they make key decisions	• Had very little publicity on the UK wide stage • Some have noted difference between some advisors approaches as more critical of UK policy and less critical of home nation policy
Government Planning Bureaux e.g. Joint Biosecurity Council (JBC)	• More common in Europe but remit is to produce forecasting information for government	• JBC is formally part of NHS Test and Trace which is part of DHSC created in May 2020 during the pandemic • Many of its products are co-produced with PHE

(continued)

To understand the role and influence of different advisers during the first wave of COVID-19, this list can be analysed using two variables as set out in Table 3.2.

Table 3.1 (continued)

Type of Actor	*Format*	*Comments on work in COVID-19*
Local Advisory Groups e.g. Scientific and Technical Advice Cells (STACs) and Directors of Public Health (DsPH)	• Established mechanisms for handling local health protection incidents and emergencies in which local agencies and local branches of national agencies come together	• The DsPH have become more vocal and providing distinct local advice as the national policy became more focused on local lockdowns
International Government Organisations e.g. World Health Organisation (WHO) and European Centre for Disease Control (ECDC)	• Based on governments agreeing to establish and fund an advisory agency with an international perspective	• Their role has been criticised, but their advice has been seen by many as a benchmark against which national advice can be compared
Academic Institutions e.g. Centre for Evidence-Based Medicine (CEBM) at Oxford University	• Run along conventional university lines of academic freedom • Largely funded by government directly and indirectly	• Successful in getting wide-spread publicity • Sometimes led to policy change though sometimes government has pushed back
Alternative sources of advice e.g. Independent SAGE and individual scientists	• Many individuals have had formal roles in the past or are members of formal committees but feel that they have a duty to speak out	• Independent SAGE—set up to mirror SAGE's format but identifies issues it believes are important and attracted considerable media attention for its advice • Individual scientists have become both commentators on government policy in the media and news stories in their own right

Institutional Legitimacy of Actors

Weible et al. (2020) noted how governments have used scientific advice to legitimise their policy but politicians' statements also legitimise the advisers. For organisational sociologists, legitimacy is an absence of questioning (Deephouse & Suchman, 2008) and comes from organisations aligning with social and political institutions ("the humanly devised constraints that structure political, economic, and social interaction...

Table 3.2 Analysis of the advisory actors in COVID-19 response in the UK

		Institutional Legitimacy of the Actor		
		Formal Legitimacy *Actor has a formal government role*	***Informal Legitimacy*** *Actor has informal government role*	***No Legitimacy*** *Actor has no or oppositional role*
Strategic Origin of the Advice	**Commissioned** *Topic of the advice is commissioned by the decision-makers to inform their work on the response*	• Individual Govt Advisers (CMO and GCSA) • Scientific Advisory Committees (SAGE and sub-committees) • Government Research Bodies and What Works Centres (PHE, NICE) • Government Planning Bureau (ONS, JBC)	• Research Funders (UKRI and NIHR) • Behavioural Insights Team • Local Directors of Public Health (DPHs)	None identified but "red teaming" approach has been adopted within government in other areas of the response
	Negotiated *Advisers and decision-makers discuss and agree the topic*			
	Volunteered *Topic of the advice is identified by the actor who thinks it is valuable to the response*	• Government Regulators (HSE)	• Academic institutions • Individual SAC members • Local DPHs	• Independent SAGE • Individual academics

both informal constraints … and formal rules" p. 97 (North, 1991). Institutional legitimacy is based largely on the formal authority granted to the advisor and though government can confer formal authority, Boswell et al. (2019) showed how public health advisory bodies located within government also needed informal legitimacy to a wider audience, including academia and the public while Dunlop (2014) highlighted that the authority which *certifies* policy communities of experts comes from both political and epistemic sources. Alongside the formal mechanisms, Cairney (2020) argued that science's influence on government policy during COVID-19 can be analysed by considering the informal "rules of the game" that advisors need to follow as shown in research about interest groups. One dimension of Table 3.2 categorises scientific advisors in the first wave of the pandemic into those with a formal government role; an informal role with government; and no formal role, even an anti-government role.

The most formal institutionalised source of advice is SAGE, though it has been publicly challenged for a lack of transparency and independence, which along with role clarity are the Government's three principles of scientific advice in an emergency (GO-Science, 2010). The initial lack of transparency about the membership and content of SAGE's advice was widely debated (Coker, 2020; Rutter, 2020) and the criticisms of the House of Commons Science and Technology Committee (Clark, 2020) led to minutes and papers of SAGE being published in June. This was in contrast to the work of existing SACs where minutes and attendance was routinely published and led to a perception of a lack of independence was shown in questions about appropriateness of Dominic Cummings, as a political advisor, attending SAGE (Carrell, 2020).

Although SAGE now has a clear national identity, it is a loose form of quasi-organisation structured around a handful of meetings when individuals come together. Most Scientific Advisory Committees have a stable membership meeting at regular intervals, but SAGE is a more fluid network of scientists convened only on specific issues rather than in a regular cycle of meetings. The pressures of an emergency response mean there is no time for organisational development work within the committee and the scientists' attendance is based on a model of goodwill without a contract or payment (GO-Science, 2012). The GCSA reflected that there needs to be a stable source of advice within the Government's operational machinery, though there are a range of views on whether this is best provided through committees or government agencies (HoC, 2021).

During 2020 SAGE has had to change the scale of its operations though the core model and remit remain unchanged. There were 67 meetings in ten months compared to 22 in nine months of H1N1 swine flu, the number of sub-committees increased from two to eight and an increase in participants from 24 (first five meetings) to 86 listed (all at 19 November 2020 [GO-Science, 2020]). The increase in participants has not led to a marked widening in academic expertise with mathematical modellers especially prominent and relatively little input from health protection practitioners. An interviewee observed that "SAGE sees itself purely to deliver the science as they see it – that's the only thing they see themselves there to do, deliver the evidence and its upto everyone else to do something about it".

The challenges to SAGE have enabled informal and oppositional actors to occupy the media stage, often taking an explicit "anti-government position". Both the creation of Independent SAGE (Independent-SAGE, 2020) with an explicit commitment to transparency and independence (Baker, 2020) and the public statements about anticipated government decisions from SAGE and SAC members have become a public-facing alternative source of advice designed to indirectly influence government policy (Campbell & Busha, 2020; Smyth, 2020). This is a marked contrast to business-as-usual, when most government scientific advisers choose not to use public channels, remaining "in the tent" and using informal back-stage routes to deliver their advice.

A further dynamic of the advisory machinery in COVID-19 has been the role of advice to decision-makers outside the Whitehall bubble. The devolved administrations have set up their own advisory groups and there has been a growing role for local advisors, notably Directors of Public Health in local authorities who had a formal statutory role but traditionally little national voice. The Government's emergency response arrangements have a role for local Scientific and Technical Committees (STACs) (GO-Science, 2010) but these have had a low profile as the early stages of the response were highly centralised (Atkinson et al., 2020). This echoes Hine (2012)'s conclusions on the H1N1 response in the formal Government review and a case study from Chambers et al. (2012). However, DPHs have played a greater role in advising local politicians (metro-mayors and council leaders) as key elements of testing and tracing service has focused on localities (de Gruchy, 2020).

Strategic Origin of the Advice

Advice during COVID has been both sought by decision-makers and provided unsolicited from both formal and informal advisors. Thus, the second variable in Table 3.2 is the origin of the need for advice where three types of requirement can be identified. The main distinction between advice commissioned by decision-makers and volunteered advice, based upon the advisers' assessment of relevance, is expanded as formal advisers can sometimes negotiate with decision-makers about the type of advice required.

An interviewee described the different routes: "every single academic in the country, including everybody who had never done any work on infectious diseases ... and it is the same as the private companies..they are all offering help but it is often not help but they are trying to increase the value for them in one way or another" and "how research has been commissioned not an open process, some academics benefit and there is a lot of anger about this".

Commissioning scientific advice is a skill and Parker (2013) has described the central role of *scientific integrators* who are government scientists that commission advice. SAGE has used both formal organisational arrangements to commission work, such as the NIHR-PHE Health Protection Research Units, notably the modelling and behavioural science units, and made ad hoc commissions from experts to meet specific needs.

The explicit formal commissions for advice within SAGE have been limited to bio-medical, environmental and psychological science as it has regarded issues covered by economic, implementation, social and political scientific advice as outside its remit, though occasionally experts from these fields have attended SAGE/SAC meetings. By contrast Germany has set up hybrid advisory committees (Krick, 2015) and Norway has independent advice on social science areas (Christensen, 2018).

Government has also received advice that it did not request and the OECD (2015) recognised the role of "academic institutions that provide policy relevant reports and advice that may or may not have been explicitly requested" (p. 5). The Oxford Centre for Evidence-Based Medicine (CEBM, 2020), which had 265 articles by 16 July, is an example of unsolicited but important advice that can change policy (Hugh, 2020).

The mediatisation of scientific advice has created an entrepreneurial role for some advisors to promote their recommendations consistent with Kingdon (1984)'s description of *policyentrepreneurs*.

Case Study 2: The Organisation of Social Distancing Advice

The frequent changes to the public guidance have been a dominant features of UK response. Even in the business-as-usual context, the organisation of scientific advice to the public is complicated and the evidence-base is often contested. This case study explores the provision of the advice on social distancing and shows the important role that organisation has in both framing the understanding of the issue and in the nature of the subsequent advice.

On 25 February 2020, PHE published the Government's formal position on "Guidance to assist professionals in advising the public" which was that people who had been "within 2 metres for 15 minutes or more" of a confirmed case of COVID should seek immediate healthcare assessment. However, the guideline became used for two other purposes—guidance to the public and businesses on a requirement about behaviours to reduce the risk of spread and the definition of what constitutes a "significant contact" for contact tracing. At this early stage, the public health perspective was undoubtedly the priority and inputs from other sectors were not influential.

2 m was at the longer range of distances being adopted in different countries and the WHO recommended at least 1 m (WHO, 2020). The advice sought to describe some form of relative risk in a simple memorable form, but it became known as a rule (Nuki, 2020) controversial because of its impact on socio-economic activity. Robert Dingwall, a sociologist member of NERVTAG, said the guidance "conjured out of nowhere" (BBC, 2020).

As the number of cases started to fall, the robustness of the scientific basis, especially its relative effectiveness to other distances and times in minimising the likelihood of transmission, was challenged with business leaders and politicians contributing as much as scientists. On 22 May, the House of Commons Science and Technology Committee questioned PHE, HSE and an environmental scientific academic on SAGE about the balance between health and economic factors (UK Parliament, 2020).

A WHO-funded systematic review and meta-analysis was published in The Lancet (Chu et al., 2020) on 1 June which concluded that distancing over 1 m or more was effective. There were significant differences in interpretation of the study in relation to the specific policy question of the relative risk associated with transmission at 1 m compared to 2 m. Public health professor Linda Bauld argued it supported 2 m (Siddique, 2020) while Dingwall said that there was a safety margin as it was very rare for virus particles to travel 1 m (Telegraph, 2020). Two professors of statistics highlighted flaws in the statistical calculation of the risk associated with different distances (Sample, 2020).

The formal route for advice to decision-makers was through SAGE where there were several discussions of the distancing issue. One of the features of the organisation of the advisory machinery in an emergency is that both standing and ad hoc committees report through SAGE rather than provide advice direct to ministers. Thus the original submission to SAGE came from NERVTAG on 13 March with the conclusion "1 metre is a minimum, 2 metres is precautionary" and "' >15 minutes' is therefore a pragmatic and possibly conservative threshold for the purposes of contact tracing" (NERVTAG, 2020: 1). Subsequently SAGE commissioned the Environmental and Modelling Group to provide evidence summaries as advice to policymakers about the distancing issue on several occasions. On 28 May, the advice was that the 2 m rule was "retained for public guidance" as it "is simple and is a good measure of the distance where the direct person-to-person transmission risk drops significantly" (SAGE, 2020a: 4) though it set out further work on control measures as these were likely to enable reduction in some situations. On 4 June it concluded that "2m separation should not be treated as an absolute rule" (SAGE, 2020b: 3), with the detailed paper saying "given the uncertainties about transmission and dose-response it is not possible to say with certainty what a safe distance of separation is, but best current evidence suggests that 1 m carries between 2 and 10 times the risk of 2m of separation", it recommended additional mitigation measures when 2 m could not be achieved (SAGE, 2020c: 1–2).

However, this formal route for advice did not happen in isolation as there was plenty of informal external scientific advice giving different opinions including abolishing the rule as it was not based on evidence (Heneghan et al., 2020), retaining it as there was no evidence it was yet safe to reduce distancing (Independent-SAGE, 2020) or developing alternatives to a simple rule to reflect different risks in specific situations (Qureshi et al., 2020).

Nor was the scientific and technical the only advice that is available to decision-makers There was also the advice from economic commentators alongside the lobbying of business leaders and MPs about the economic implications of not reducing to 1 m (Donnelly et al., 2020), though there were few public statements from academic economists.

In the context of the increasing public debate and lobbying, on 15 June the Government announced a review led by Simon Case, who had been appointed into the newly created role of Permanent Secretary for No. 10 on 21 May. It aimed to bring together scientific and non-scientific issues led by a civil servant rather than a scientific expert. The report drew on four key sources of information—the scientific evidence, the economic and social impacts, international comparisons and risk analysis by sector (UK Government, 2020a). However, the importance of clear communications for implementation and adoption is another dimension that is highlighted by behavioural scientists and communications experts (West, 2020) and the input from SPI-B on the issue is not explicitly recorded.

On 23rd June the Prime Minister announced the outcome changing the guidance on social distancing from being 2 m to "1m plus", meaning that "the Government recommends that you keep two metres away from people as a precaution or one metre when you can mitigate the risk by taking other precautions in this list" (UK Government, 2020b).

Discussion: Developing the Scientific Advisory System for Emergencies

The two case studies demonstrate that the experience of providing scientific during the first part of the response to COVID-19 in the UK is more complicated than the Government's 2010 model. The literature review informed the creation of a conceptual framework for an emergency scientific advisory system (ESAS). Using the findings from the case studies, the ESAS has been developed through the addition of three theoretically informed lenses that capture key features of the operation and organisation of the system (in green on Fig. 3.3). This section discusses the empirical data about the ESAS through these lenses—as a complex system, that is adapting to the emerging science of the novel virus and the political priorities; an institutional field, in which advisory organisations strive for legitimacy in providing their advice; and a stage on which the dramatic performance of scientific advice being given to policymakers plays out.

Complex Adaptive System

Complexity theory has been used by a number of academic commentators to describe the challenges facing policymakers, especially the uncertainty challenge. Rutter et al. (2020) argued that "Covid-19 is, *par excellence*, a complex problem in a complex system" while Greenhalgh (2020) asked whether a practice-based complex systems paradigm would have been more effective in informing the COVID-19 response than an evidence-based medicine one.

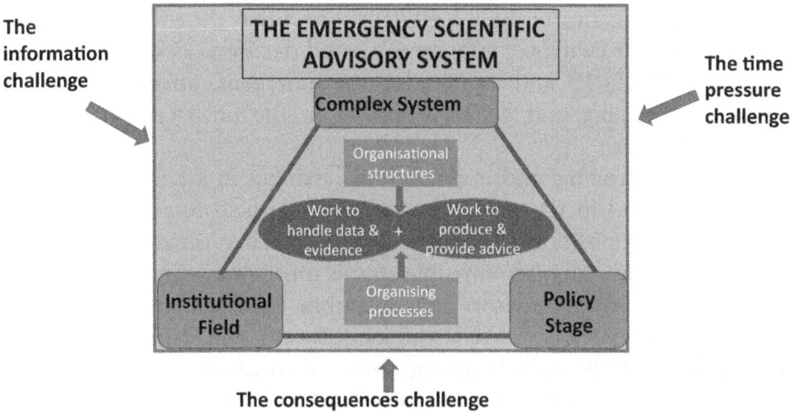

Fig. 3.3 The emergency scientific advisory system (2)—An expanded framework

Three insights from complex systems thinking align with the empirical observations. Firstly the interconnections between sub-systems are a key feature of complex adaptive systems. The scientific advisory system is one such sub-system, which can only be understood through its linkages with other sub-systems. Sturmberg and Martin (2020) described the interconnectedness between the sub-systems in COVID-19 pandemic that result from tensions between the *top-down causation* and *bottom-up emergence* which can be seen in the national-devolved administration-local tensions in the UK about the type and source of advice to decision-makers as the pandemic grew. Academic studies have shown the UK Government adopted a highly centralised approach to the response, leading to tensions over PPE, data, testing and tracing (Atkinson et al., 2020; Froud et al., 2020).

Secondly complex systems thinking highlights non-linear processes, including iterative, feedback loops, and Angeli and Montefusco (2020) showed how this perspective could help decision-makers make sense of the pandemic. Weick (1988) had described *enacted sensemaking* (acquiring information through action) as a core skill in managing an emergency and the non-linear perspective also applies to advisors and the social distancing case study showed how advice and decisions were interwoven as information and interpretations bounced between advisors and politicians. Lancaster et al. (2020) showed that the idealised descriptions which treat evidence, interventions and decisions as separate do not apply in COVID-19 and argued for the emergent, adaptive approach to evidence-making and decision-making in the uncertain situation of COVID-19.

Finally the dynamic and unpredictable changes in a complex adaptive system are found in the advisory work with leftfield interventions from informal and oppositional advisors. Their influence on decision-makers can be direct (though often invisible) but is more often mediated through an influence on other advisors and on public opinion. For example, the focus from Independent SAGE on schools and universities in summer 2020 influenced the agenda giving coverage to issues in advance of the work of the formal advisors being published or completed.

Institutional Field

The lens of neo-institutional theory focuses on the inter-organisational relationships between advisors in the pandemic. Scott's (2001) classic definition of a field as "a community of organizations that partakes in a common meaning system and whose participants interact more frequently and fatefully with one another than actors outside the field" (p. 56) highlights the alliances and tensions between advisors.

The research on *boundary organisations* shows that scientific advisors sit in at least two fields—the worlds of science and politics. Field theory explains that fields have different *institutional logics* ("material practices and symbolic constructions – which constitute its (the field's) organising principles" (Friedland & Alford, 1991: 232). The contrast between the scientific, academic logic and the political, decision-making logic can put advisors in uncomfortable positions. Formal advisors sit on the boundary combining the work of reviewing evidence to produce scientific advice and work that engages with decision-makers through the provision of the advice. However, oppositional advisors can remain within the scientific field and not necessarily engage with the political logics.

Acquiring and retaining legitimacy in both fields is an on-going tension highlighted by Boswell et al. (2019) in their comparative study of three public health agencies. The overall organisation of a crisis response needs to be legitimatised (Christensen et al., 2016) yet the time-pressure challenge gives advisors little opportunity to establish their legitimacy meaning they draw on pre-existing sources, if they exist. For example, criticism of PHE in the pandemic was partly linked to its work on non-communicable health risk factors as part of a *nanny state* approach (Sanderson, 2020), while the new entity of the JBC provided a new legitimacy for controversial ministerial decisions on local lockdowns.

Although organisational theorists stress the stability of fields, Bourdieu (1975) argued "the scientific field is the locus of a competitive struggle, in which the specific issue at stake is the monopoly of scientific authority" (p. 19). In COVID-19 a pattern of fluid alliances and arguments between advisors has emerged consistent with Weible et al.'s (2020) observation of the disruptive effect of the pandemic on the normally stable structure of policy networks resulting in the contestation of knowledge and evidence.

Policy Stage

Viewing the ESAS as a stage on which policy is made and implemented derives from dramaturgical theory, which has been widely used to analyse the provision of scientific advice (Hilgartner, 2000) and wider policymaking (Hajer, 2009). Van Dooren and Noordegraaf (2020) used this lens to consider the COVID-19 response in Holland and Belgium arguing controversially that science and its impact are not automatically privileged in the crisis and described the need for staging science to enable impact on the public.

The theatre of the Government daily briefings is a popular image ("the drama that is being played out daily in the only theatre that remains open – the political theatre of daily briefings" (Holmwood, 2020) though the dramaturgical perspective provides an analysis of the important dynamic of impression management. The distinction between the *front-stage* performance to the audience, the *back-stage* work of analysis and preparation, and the *off-stage* side-activity of covert influencing of the audience, provides insights into the discourse about a lack of transparency about SAGE's work and the decisions to set ambitious targets for testing and tracing which may not relate to scientific advice.

The decision to have scientific advisors and clinical leaders standing alongside ministers at these daily briefings was a visual symbol of the "following the science" message, though it also could communicate a lack of independence for scientific advisors and so later separate briefings were sometimes set up. This front-stage performance was the public-facing element of the wider organisation that also took place behind the scenes. On occasions the *scripting* of the performance did not go as planned, notably over comments about herd immunity and when scientists were asked about the need for everyone to follow lockdown rules.

Conclusions—Lessons for the Future

In November 2020, the Secretary of State refined his description of the Government's approach in COVID-19: "the difference between following the science and being guided by the science is that, if you are following the science, it implies an automaticity, as opposed to ministerial judgment, taking into account all of the effects based on the science. That is a truer reflection of what we do" (HoC, 2020a: Q505). At the same time, the BMJ carried an editorial arguing the Government had politicised, corrupted and supressed the science (Abbasi, 2020). The emergency scientific advisory system described in Fig. 3.3 provides a framework to both understand the diversity of views and prompt for policy learning by bringing together empirical and theoretical insights.

Although there will be further learning from the later stages of the response and from future publications about first wave, this paper concludes that there are early lessons about policy learning and the organisation of scientific advice from the first part of the pandemic.

The Prime Minister has agreed to a future inquiry (Smith, 2020) but the initial approach to learning has focused on important but "thin" technical lessons about specific services as the basis for preparing for the second wave, rather than the wider "thick" political learning (Howlett, 2012). Dunlop (2017) has warned of the pathologies of policy learning, and these are greater in a crisis. For example, Flinders (2020) anticipated the *blame game* as a reaction to the initial strategy of "following the science" which was a *blame avoidance or deflection* tactic of "hugging the experts". An early, though isolated comment was Therese Coffey, Work and Pensions Secretary saying in May "if the science was wrong, advice at the time was wrong, I'm not surprised if people will then think we then made a wrong decision" (Swinford et al., 2020). Some organisational structures have been especially susceptible to blame and organisational change and Hood's (2010) analysis highlighted executive agencies. In August, the Secretary of State for Health and Social Care announced the creation of a new organisation to be called the National Institute for Health Protection that combines PHE, NHS Test and Trace, including JBC (DHSC, 2020).

Alternative approaches to policymaking in the pandemic have been suggested. The former Cabinet Secretary, Lord O'Donnell, has suggested that SAGE and COBRA could be brought together into a single, more deliberative process. He referenced the National Security Council where the full range of advisors join the decision-makers to work through solutions for implementation (O'Donnell, 2020). Froud et al. (2020) proposed that government adopts a *care-ful approach* to policymaking in COVID-19, following their analysis of NHS capacity planning and the testing strategy. This would adopt the approach of multi-disciplinary teams managing chronic care, though there is little detail about how this would change the advisory processes and political behaviours.

Although there have been changes to the operation of the formal scientific advisory system during COVID-19, the relationship between the science and the policy remains contested and widely debated. In the second wave of the pandemic, the lockdown policy of non-pharmaceutical interventions has become even more controversial with open opposition from members of the political elite and the public. The three challenges of providing advice in a crisis (time, information and consequences) are in practice so exacting that the normative approach based on the principles of independence, role clarity and transparency is impossible to faithfully follow. Recognising the implications of the ESAS for both advisors and decision-makers suggests that a more deliberative and inclusive policy-making process could improve the understanding of the challenges of COVID-19, the trustworthiness of the policymaking processes and the effectiveness of the policy interventions on protecting and improving the public's health and well-being.

References

Abbasi, K. (2020). *Covid-19: Politicisation, "corruption," and suppression of science*. British Medical Journal Publishing Group.

Alvesson, M. (2003). Methodology for close up studies–struggling with closeness and closure. *Higher Education, 46*, 167–193.

Anderson, L. (2006). Analytic autoethnography. *Journal of Contemporary Ethnography, 35*, 373–395.

Angeli, F., & Montefusco, A. (2020). Sensemaking and learning during the Covid-19 pandemic: A complex adaptive systems perspective on policy decision-making. *World Development,* 136, 105106.

Atkinson, P., Gobat, N., Lant, S., Mableson, H., Pilbeam, C., Solomon, T., Tonkin-Crine, S., & Sheard, S. (2020). Understanding the policy dynamics of COVID-19 in the UK: early findings from interviews with policy makers and health care professionals. *Social Science & Medicine*, 113423.

Baekkeskov, E. (2016). Same threat, different responses: Experts steering politicians and stakeholders in 2009 H1N1 vaccination policy-making. *Public Administration, 94*, 299–315.

Baekkeskov, E. (2020). Pandemic preparedness and responses to the 2009 H1N1 influenza: Crisis management and public policy insights. *Oxford Research Encyclopedia of Politics.*

Baker, H. (2020). *Independent SAGE and their continued quest for transparency.* Available from: http://www.crassh.cam.ac.uk/blog/post/independent-sage-and-their-continued-quest-for-transparency

Battilana, J., Leca, B., & Boxenbaum, E. (2009). How actors change institutions: Towards a theory of institutional entrepreneurship. *Academy of Management Annals, 3*, 65–107.

BBC. (2020). Interview with Robert Dingwall. *Today Programme on 25 April 2020.* Radio 4: BBC.

Blumenthal, D., & Seervai, S. (2018). *Rising obesity in the United States is a public health crisis.* The Commonwealth Fund. Retrieved from https://www.commonwealthfund.org

Boin, A., & Lodge, M. (2016). Designing resilient institutions for transboundary crisis management: A time for public administration. *Public Administration, 94*, 289–298.

Boswell, J. (2018). Keeping expertise in its place: Understanding arm's-length bodies as boundary organisations. *Policy & Politics, 46*, 485–501.

Boswell, J., Cairney, P., & St. Denny, E. (2019). The politics of institutionalizing preventative health. *Social Science & Medicine.*

Bourdieu, P. (1975). The specificity of the scientific field and the social conditions of the progress of reason. *Information (international Social Science Council), 14*, 19–47.

Brannick, T., & Coghlan, D. (2007). In defense of being "native": The case for insider academic research. *Organizational Research Methods, 10*, 59–74.

Bundy, J., Pfarrer, M. D., Short, C. E., & Coombs, W. T. (2017). Crises and crisis management: Integration, interpretation, and research development. *Journal of Management, 43*, 1661–1692.

Cairney, P. (2018). *Policy in 500 words: uncertainty versus ambiguity* [Online]. Paul Cairney: Politics & Public Policy. Available: https://paulcairney.wordpress.com/2018/01/17/policy-in-500-words-uncertainty-versus-ambiguity/. Accessed 24 August 2020.

Cairney, P. (2020). The UK government's COVID-19 policy: what does 'guided by the science' mean in practice? *Frontiers in Frontiers in Political Science (The Politics of Expertise).*

Cairney, P., & Heikkila, T. (2014). A comparison of theories of the policy process. In *Theories of the policy process* (3rd ed.). Westview Press.

Cairney, P., Heikkila, T., & Wood, M. (2019). *Making policy in a complex world*. Cambridge University Press.

Campbell, L., & Busha, M. (2020). UK coronavirus: More scientists speak out against England lockdown easing—As it happened. *Guardian*.

Caplan, N. (1979). The two-communities theory and knowledge utilization. *American Behavioral Scientist, 22*, 459–470.

Carrell, S. (2020). Revealed: Cummings is on secret scientific advisory group for Covid-19. *The Guardian*.

CEBM. (2020). *Oxford COVID-19 Evidence Service* [Online]. Available: https://www.cebm.net/oxford-covid-19-evidence-service/. Accessed 24 August 2020.

Chambers, J., Barker, K., & Rouse, A. (2012). Reflections on the UK's approach to the 2009 swine flu pandemic: Conflicts between national government and the local management of the public health response. *Health & Place, 18*, 737–745.

Christensen, J. (2018). Economic knowledge and the scientization of policy advice. *Policy Sciences, 51*, 291–311.

Christensen, T., Lægreid, P., & Rykkja, L. H. (2016). Organizing for crisis management: Building governance capacity and legitimacy. *Public Administration Review, 76*, 887–897.

Chu, D. K., Akl, E. A., Duda, S., Solo, K., Yaacoub, S., Schünemann, H. J., El-Harakeh, A., Bognanni, A., Lotfi, T., & Loeb, M. (2020). Physical distancing, face masks, and eye protection to prevent person-to-person transmission of SARS-CoV-2 and COVID-19: A systematic review and meta-analysis. *The Lancet*.

Clark, G. (2020). *Letter to the Prime Minister on COVID-19 pandemic response*. H. O. C. S. A. T. Committee. UK Parliament website on 19 May 2020.

Coker, R. (2020). Coronavirus can only be beaten if groups such as Sage are transparent and accountable. *Guardian*.

Collier, R. B., & Collier, D. (1991). *Critical Junctures and historical legacies*.

Craft, J., & Halligan, J. (2017). Assessing 30 years of Westminster policy advisory system experience. *Policy Sciences, 50*, 47–62.

Craft, J., & Wilder, M. (2017). Catching a second wave: Context and compatibility in advisory system dynamics. *Policy Studies Journal, 45*, 215–239.

De Gruchy, J. (2020). A time for steady leadership, careful preparation and measured steps. *ADPH Presidential Blog* [Online]. Available from: https://www.adph.org.uk/2020/05/adph-presidential-blog-a-time-for-steady-leadership-careful-preparation-and-measured-steps/

Deephouse, D. L., & Suchman, M. (2008). Legitimacy in organizational institutionalism. In R. Greenwood, C. Oliver, T. B. Lawrence, & R. E. Meyer (Eds.), *The Sage handbook of organizational institutionalism*. Sage.

DHSC. (2020). *The future of public health, Speech by Secretary of State for Health and Social Care*. Department of Health and Social Care. Gov.UK website on 18 August 2020: UK Government.

Diamond, P. (2020). Polycentric governance and policy advice: Lessons from Whitehall policy advisory systems. *Policy & Politics*.

Donnelly, L., Hope, C., & Jones, A. (2020). Scientists say coronavirus two-metre rule can be relaxed. *Daily Telegraph*.

Dunlop, C. A. (2014). The possible experts: How epistemic communities negotiate barriers to knowledge use in ecosystems services policy. *Environment and Planning c: Government and Policy, 32*, 208–228.

Dunlop, C. A. (2017). Pathologies of policy learning: What are they and how do they contribute to policy failure? *Policy & Politics, 45*, 19–37.

Dupre, J. (2020). *Following the science in covid-19*. Available from: https://www.nuffieldbioethics.org/blog/following-the-science-in-the-covid-19-pandemic. Accessed 29 April 2020.

Elvbakken, K. T., & Hansen, H. F. (2018). Evidence producing organizations: Organizational translation of travelling evaluation ideas. *Evaluation*, 1356389018803965.

Feufel, M., Antes, G., & Gigerenzer, G. (2010). Competence in dealing with uncertainty: Lessons to learn from the influenza pandemic (H1N1) 2009. *Bundesgesundheitsblatt, Gesundheitsforschung, Gesundheitsschutz, 53*, 1283–1289.

Flinders, M. (2020). Democracy and the politics of Coronavirus: Trust, blame and understanding. *Parliamentary Affairs*.

Friedland, R., & Alford, R. R. (1991). Bringing society back in: Symbols, practices and institutional contradictions. In W. W. A. D. Powell & J. Paul (Eds.), *The new institutionalism in organizational analysis*. University of Chicago Press.

Froud, J., Haslam, C., Johal, S., Law, J. A., & Williams, K. I. (2020). *When systems fail: UK acute hospitals and public health after Covid-19*. Foundational Economics Collective website on 26th June 2020: Foundational Economics Collective.

GO-Science. (2010). *Principles of scientific advice to government*. B. E. I. A. Skills. UK.gov: UK Government.

GO-Science. (2011). *Code of practice for scientific advisory committees*. B. E. I. A. Skills. UK.Gov: UK Government.

GO-Science. (2012). *Enhancing SAGE guidance*. B. E. I. A. Skills. UK.GOV: UK Government.

GO-Science. (2020). *List of participants of SAGE and related sub-groups* [Online]. GOV.UK on 3 July 2020: UK Government. Available: https://www.gov.uk/government/publications/scientific-advisory-group-for-emergencies-sage-coronavirus-covid-19-response-membership/list-of-participants-of-sage-and-related-sub-groups. Accessed 24 August 2020.

Greenhalgh, T. (2020). Will COVID-19 be evidence-based medicine's nemesis? *PLoS Med, 17*(6).

Guston, D. H. (2001). Boundary organizations in environmental policy and science: an introduction. *Science Technology and Human Values.*

Hajer, M. A. (2009). *Authoritative governance: Policy making in the age of mediatization.* Oxford University Press.

Halligan, J. (1995). Policy advice and the public service. *Governance in a Changing Environment*, 138–172.

Heneghan, C., & Jefferson, T. (2020). There is no scientific evidence to support the disastrous two-metre rule. *Daily Telegraph.*

Heywood, P., Stephani, A. M., & Garner, P. (2018). The Cochrane Collaboration: Institutional analysis of a knowledge commons. *Evidence & Policy: A Journal of Research, Debate and Practice, 14*, 121–142.

Hilgartner, S. (2000). *Science on stage: Expert advice as public drama.* Stanford University Press.

Hine, D. (2012). Reflections on the UK's response to the 2009 swine flu pandemic: Conflicts between national government and the local management of the public health response. *Health & Place, 18*, 746–746.

HoC. (2020a). *Health and Social Care Committee Science and Technology Committee Oral evidence: Coronavirus: Lessons learnt, HC 877 on 24 November 2020.* HoC website.

HoC. (2020b). *UK science, research and technology capability and influence in global disease outbreaks, HC 136 oral evidence on 16 July 2020 witness Sir Patrick Vallance.* H. O. C. S. A. T. Committee. UK Parliament.

HoC, S. A. T. C. (2021). *The UK response to COVID-19: The use of scientific advice.* UK Parliament.

Holmwood, J. (2020). *Responding to covid-19—A failure of governance.* Available from: https://discoversociety.org/2020/04/02/responding-to-covid-19-a-failure-of-governance/

Hood, C. (2010). *The blame game: Spin, bureaucracy, and self-preservation in government.* Princeton University Press.

Howlett, M. (2012). The lessons of failure: Learning and blame avoidance in public policy-making. *International Political Science Review, 33*, 539–555.

Howlett, M. (2019). Comparing policy advisory systems beyond the OECD: Models, dynamics and the second-generation research agenda. *Policy Studies, 40*, 241–259.

Hugh, P. (2020). Coronavirus: England death count review reduces UK toll by 5,000. *BBC.*

Independent-SAGE. (2020). *Review of scientific evidence on 2m verses 1m rule social distancing* [Online]. Independent SAGE. Available: https://www.independentsage.org/review-of-scientific-evidence-on-2-metre-versus-1-metre-social-distancing/. Accessed.

Keller, A. C., Ansell, C. K., Reingold, A. L., Bourrier, M., Hunter, M. D., Burrowes, S., & Macphail, T. M. (2012). Improving pandemic response: A sensemaking perspective on the spring 2009 H1N1 pandemic. *Risk, Hazards & Crisis in Public Policy, 3*, 1–37.

Kingdon, J. W. (1984). *Agendas, alternatives, and public policies*. Little, Brown Boston.

Kovoor-Misra, S., Clair, J. A., & Bettenhausen, K. L. (2001). Clarifying the attributes of organizational crises. *Technological Forecasting and Social Change, 67*, 77–91.

Krick, E. (2015). Negotiated expertise in policy-making: How governments use hybrid advisory committees. *Science and Public Policy, 42*, 487–500.

Lancaster, K., Rhodes, T., & Rosengarten, M. (2020). Making evidence and policy in public health emergencies: Lessons from COVID-19 for adaptive evidence-making and intervention. *Evidence and Policy.*

Lasswell, H. D. (1956). *The decision process: Seven categories of functional analysis*. Bureau of Governmental Research, College of Business and Public Administration, University of Maryland.

Lawrence, L. M., Bishop, A., & Curran, J. (2019). Integrated knowledge translation with public health policy makers: A scoping review. *Healthcare Policy = Politiques de sante, 14*, 55–77.

Masood, S., Kothari, A., & Regan, S. (2019). The use of research in public health policy: A systematic review. *Evidence & Policy: A Journal of Research, Debate and Practice.*

Medvetz, T. (2012). Murky power: "Think tanks" as boundary organizations. In *Rethinking power in organizations, institutions, and markets*. Emerald Group Publishing Limited.

NERVTAG. (2020, March 12). *Paper for SAGE prepared by NERVTAG—Distance, time, handshakes*. SAGE. Gov.uk: UK Government.

Newman, J., Cherney, A., & Head, B. W. (2016). Do policy makers use academic research? Reexamining the "two communities" theory of research utilization. *Public Administration Review, 76*, 24–32.

Newsnight, B. (2020, May 7). Is the government really following the science? *BBC.* https://www.youtube.com/watch?v=kQrtd-WCjos

North, D. C. (1991). Institutions. *Journal of Economic Perspectives, 5*, 97–112.

Nuki, P. (2020). Little Britain: where the two-metre rule came from and why it is not actually a rule at all. *Daiy Telegraph.*

O'donnell, G. (2020). The Covid Tragedy: following the science or the sciences? *Annual Lecture 24 September 2020.* IFS Website: Institute of Fiscal Studies.

OECD. (2015). Scientific advice for policy making: The role and responsibility of expert bodies and individual scientists. T. A. I. P. P. OECD Science & N. 21. OECD Publishing.

OECD. (2018). *Scientific advice during crises: Facilitating transnational co-operation and exchange of information.* OECD Publishing.

Oliver, K., Innvar, S., Lorenc, T., Woodman, J., & Thomas, J. (2014). A systematic review of barriers to and facilitators of the use of evidence by policymakers. *BMC Health Services Research, 14*, 2.

Orton, L., Lloyd-Williams, F., Taylor-Robinson, D., O'flaherty, M., & Capewell, S. (2011). The use of research evidence in public health decision making processes: Systematic review. *PLoS ONE, 6*, e21704.

Parker, M. (2013). Making the most of scientists and engineers in government. In R. Doubleday & J. Wilsdon (Eds.), *Future directions in scientific advice in whitehall.* Centre for Science and Policy, Cambridge University

Parkhurst, J. (2017). *The politics of evidence: From evidence-based policy to the good governance of evidence.* Taylor & Francis.

Pearce, W. (2020). Trouble in the trough: How uncertainties were downplayed in the UK's science advice on Covid-19. *Humanities and Social Sciences Communications, 7*, 122.

Pollitt, C., Talbot, C., Caulfield, J., & Smullen, A. (2004). *Agencies: How governments do things through semi-autonomous organizations.* Springer.

Qureshi, Z., Jones, N., Temple, R., Larwood, J. P., Greenhalgh, T., & Bourouiba, L. (2020). *What is the evidence to support the 2-metre social distancing rule to reduce COVID-19 transmission?* Available from: https://www.cebm.net/covid-19/what-is-the-evidence-to-support-the-2-metre-social-distancing-rule-to-reduce-covid-19-transmission/.

Ramakrishnan, V. (2020). *Following the science.* Available from: https://royalsociety.org/blog/2020/05/following-the-science/

Rosenthal, U., Boin, R. A., & Comfort, L. K. (2001). The changing world of crises and crisis management. In U. Rosenthal, R. A. Boin, & L. K. Comfort (Eds.), *Managing crises: Threats, dilemmas, opportunities.* Charles C Thomas.

Rutter, H., Wolpert, M., & Greenhalgh, T. (2020). *Managing uncertainty in the covid-19 era.* Available from: https://blogs.bmj.com/bmj/2020/07/22/managing-uncertainty-in-the-covid-19-era/

Rutter, J. (2020). *More transparent scientific advice on coronavirus measures should help the government and the public.* Available from: https://www.instituteforgovernment.org.uk/blog/more-transparent-scientific-advice-coronavirus-help-government

SAGE. (2020a). *Environmental influence on transmission (28 May 2020 for Sage 29 and then updated).* S. E. A. M. Group. Gov.uk: UK Government.

SAGE. (2020b). *Minutes of the Fortieth Meeting on 4 June 2020 GOV.UK on 26 June 2020: UK Government*.

SAGE. (2020c). *Transmission of SARS-CoV-2 and Mitigating Measures (4 June 2020 for SAGE 40)*. EMG-SAGE. Gov.uk: UK Government.

Salajan, A., Tsolova, S., Ciotti, M., & Suk, J. E. (2020). To what extent does evidence support decision making during infectious disease outbreaks? A scoping literature review. *Evidence & Policy: A Journal of Research, Debate and Practice*.

Sample, I. (2020). Scientists report flaws in WHO-funded study on 2-metre distancing. *The Guardian*.

Sanderson, A. (2020). Public Health England was the bumbling nanny state at its worst. *Daily Express*.

Scott, W. R. (2001). *Institutions and organizations. Foundations for organizational science*.

Siddique, H. (2020). Risk of infection could double if 2 metre rule reduced study finds. *The Guardian*.

Smith, N. (2020). Coronavirus: PM promises future independent inquiry. *BBC*

Smyth, C. (2020). Boris Johnson's coronavirus adviser calls for a way out of lockdown. *The Times*.

Stevens, A. (2011). Telling policy stories: An ethnographic study of the use of evidence in policy-making in the UK. *Journal of Social Policy, 40*, 237–255.

Stone, D., Maxwell, S., & Keating, M. (2001). *Bridging research and policy: An international workshop funded by the UK Department for International Development Radcliffe House, Warwick University 16–17 July 2001*. Retrieved February 17, 2007.

Sturmberg, J. P., & Martin, C. M. (2020). COVID-19—How a pandemic reveals that everything is connected to everything else. *Journal of Evaluation in Clinical Practice*.

Swinford, S., & Whipple, T. (2020). Thérèse Coffey blames scientists for government mistakes over coronavirus. *The Sunday Times*.

Telegraph. (2020). Science behind two-metre rule 'does not consider economic devastation it brings'. *Daily Telegraph*.

UK Government. (2020a). *Review of two metre social distancing guidance* [Online]. UK Government website on 26 June 2020. Available: https://www.gov.uk/government/publications/review-of-two-metre-social-distancing-guidance/review-of-two-metre-social-distancing-guidance. Accessed 20 August 2020.

UK Government. (2020b). *Staying-safe-outside-your-home* [Online]. UK Government Website update of 24 June. Available: https://www.gov.uk/government/publications/staying-safe-outside-your-home/staying-safe-outside-your-home. Accessed 24 August 2020.

UK Parliament. (2020). *Oral evidence 22 May 2020: UK science, research and technology capability and influence in global disease outbreaks, HC 136*. H. O. C. S. T. Committee. UK Parliament.

Van Dooren, W., & Noordegraaf, M. (2020). Staging science: Authoritativeness and fragility of models and measurement in the COVID-19 crisis. *Public Administration Review*. https://doi.org/10.1111/puar.13219

Weible, C. M., Nohrstedt, D., Cairney, P., Carter, D. P., Crow, D. A., Durnová, A. P., Heikkila, T., Ingold, K., Mcconnell, A., & Stone, D. (2020). COVID-19 and the policy sciences: initial reactions and perspectives. *Policy Sciences*, 1–17.

Weick, K. E. (1979). *The social psychology of organizing*. McGraw-Hill Humanities.

Weick, K. E. (1988). Enacted sensemaking in crisis situations. *Journal of Management Studies, 25*, 305–317.

West, R. (2020). Should the Covid-19 lockdown 2m rule be dropped? BBC Radio 5's 'Your Call' (from 10 mins 57 secs) on 22 June 2020. *BBC*

WHO. (2005). *International health regulations* (3rd ed.). World Health Organisation.

WHO. (2020). *Coronavirus diseases (COVID-19) advice for the public* [Online]. WHO on 4 June 2020: World Health Organisation. Available: https://www.who.int/emergencies/diseases/novel-coronavirus-2019/advice-for-public. Accessed 24 August 2020.

Yardley, L. (2020). *Life sciences in a post-truth world: A COVID-19 case study*. You Tube on 4 December 2020: University of Bristol.

CHAPTER 4

Learning from History or Reacting to Events? Colombia's Navigation of Major System Change in Response to COVID-19

Simon Turner, Ana María Ulloa, Vivian Valencia Godoy, and Natalia Niño

Introduction

The concept of "major system change" (MSC) refers to coordinated changes within health systems, so change involving multiple organisations, and stakeholder interests, rather than more localised forms of change such as improvement work undertaken by an individual hospital (Turner et al., 2016a). This concept was chosen to analyse health system responses to COVID-19 because it resonates with the scale at which changes to health systems appear to be required to respond to COVID-19. For example, early evidence from Asian economies (Hong Kong, Singapore and Japan) coping with COVID-19 suggested that "integration of services in the health system and across other sectors amplifies the ability to absorb and adapt to shock" (Legido-Quigley et al., 2020:

S. Turner (✉) · A. M. Ulloa · V. Valencia Godoy · N. Niño
School of Management, University of Los Andes, Bogotá, Colombia
e-mail: s.turner@uniandes.edu.co

J. Waring et al. (eds.), *Organising Care in a Time of Covid-19*, Organizational Behaviour in Healthcare,
https://doi.org/10.1007/978-3-030-82696-3_4

849). The ability of health systems to identify and work across a variety of organisational boundaries, including national-local, centre-periphery, healthcare services and population health, and between provider entities, may influence their ability to adapt their services in response to COVID-19.

The purpose of this chapter is to explore organisational processes related to learning and implementing change influencing responses within Colombia to the health system challenges posed by COVID-19. It does on the basis of a qualitative study of the response to COVID-19 by various organisational actors, at the national level and within Colombia's capital city, Bogotá.

The findings are derived from a qualitative study of organisational responses to COVID-19 in Colombia, funded from May 2020 to March 2021. The study aimed to capture the experiences and perspectives of those involved in planning or delivering healthcare services as well as having an insight into the structure, functions and roles of the different stakeholders within and adjacent to the health system, at the national and local level. An appropriate method for analysing MSC is a case study approach (Yin, 2013), as such change involves multiple stakeholders working together across the context of a locality or wider geographical area. We drew on MSC theory, rather than alternatives such as historical institutionalism, because this was a newly established study that began in May 2020, meaning that we were not able to analyse Colombia's health system 'before' and 'after' the pandemic's arrival. If the study was already established and merely repurposed to study COVID-19, we may have drawn on historical institutionalism to analyse potential changes in social norms concerning orientations towards coordination (e.g. willingness to share knowledge and resources across organisational boundaries). However, with its emphasis on ongoing social processes of coordination, MSC allowed us to map emerging health system responses to COVID-19 in Colombia, while inquiring into actors' perceptions of the role of history in enacting such relations.

Between June and August 2020, 35 interviews and 42 documents were collected at the national level and in relation to Bogotá's health system. A range of stakeholders were interviewed including government stakeholders (advisers, middle and senior-level managers), national health delivery organisations, health insurance providers (public, private and mixed), NGOs, senior representatives from a variety of scientific associations and guilds, health planning authorities, directors of integrated networks of providers, healthcare providers (senior-level managers) from the public, mixed and private sectors, a variety of professional associations and expert advisers (e.g. professionals in an advisory capacity specialising in epidemiology and data scientists who experiment with possible scenarios to obtain useful data for decision-making). The interview transcripts and documentary evidence were analysed thematically using a combination of inductive and deductive coding (Bradley et al., 2007), with a particular emphasis on MSC. We focussed on the rule of 'attending to history'. The research team applied this concept to the data by dividing it into subcodes: the priority of local forms of learning and learning in relation to past change initiatives.

Conceptual Framework: History in MSC

MSC, or its synonym large system transformation, refers to "interventions aimed at coordinated, system-wide change affecting multiple organisations and care providers, with the goal of significant improvements in the efficiency of healthcare delivery, the quality of patient care, and population-level patient outcomes" (Best et al., 2012: 422). This definition highlights that decision-making on MSC requires agreement among multiple stakeholders, with potentially conflicting goals, and that it aims to produce a collective impact across a health system (i.e. planning and improving services for the benefit of patients across a whole metropolitan area, rather than for an individual provider's patients).

Best et al. (2012) suggest five "simple rules" or recommendations for guiding major system change processes (attend to history, combined top-down and bottom-up leadership, establish feedback loops, engage physicians and involve patients and families). The set of rules have been applied empirically to a number of service changes, including stroke service centralisation in the UK (Fulop et al., 2016; Turner et al., 2016b), while individual rules have been used to guide research on specific change topics, e.g. patient and public involvement in MSC (Djellouli et al., 2019; McKevitt et al., 2018). The exploration of the rules' relevance in different change contexts has resulted in suggested adaptations to the rules, for example, involving a range of stakeholders in system-level planning (Turner et al., 2016b) and utilising meso-level "clinical networks" as a middle ground between "top-down" and "bottom-up" leadership (Vindrola et al., 2020). Moreover, the need to both consider how politics and power are mobilised in MSC has been emphasised (Fraser et al.,

2017; Waring et al., 2018) and acknowledge the stakeholder perspectives from which such stories of change are told (Jones et al., 2019).

The particular challenges to health systems posed by COVID-19 raise questions about the relevance of current conceptualisations of MSC (Turner & Nino, 2020). For example, MSC has been studied predominantly in relation to longer-term planning of change, while responding to COVID-19 appears to have demanded rapid adaptations to health systems undertaken with high uncertainty, relative complexity and time pressure, all of which may be hallmarks of "crisis" decision-making ('t Hart et al., 1993). For instance, the importance of "proactive thinking" (Al-Dabbagh, 2020) in decision-making has been suggested in relation to the "crisis" presented by COVID-19. Moreover, health system leaders have had to grapple with the fluidity of the evidence base associated with COVID-19, while a more stable body of knowledge, and steadily developed case for change, has often been assumed in relation to MSC.

One of the rules or recommendations proposed by Best et al. (2012) for implementing MSC that may be problematic to apply to COVID-19 (given its seemingly unprecedented nature) is "attending to history". This rule suggests the need for leaders of change to learn from history by recognising that:

> past "failures," critical events, or near-misses (which are likely to reveal weaknesses in individuals, teams, or systems) should be viewed as opportunities for sensitive discussion and judicious planning for how similar situations might be avoided and/or managed if they recur. (Best et al., 2012: 439)

This chapter examines the relevance of aspects of this rule for navigating MSC in response to COVID-19: (1) the apparent priority of local forms of learning and (2) the nature of learning in relation to past change initiatives.

The Priority of Local Forms of Learning

The rule emphasises learning from "local histories"; however, given the global pandemic represented by COVID-19, it is important to also assess the relevance of non-local learning from other health systems internationally, including international scientific networks, especially given that cases of COVID-19 accelerated later in Latin America than Asia, Europe and North America.

Learning in Relation to Past Change Initiatives

The rule suggests the importance of learning from past change initiatives; however, given the unprecedented nature and widespread scale of the threat posed by COVID-19, it is critical to examine the potential role for, and potential challenges associated with, rapid or short-term learning during the response to the crisis.

This chapter explores the relevance of the rule "attending to history" using qualitative data on health system responses to COVID-19 within the Colombian health system. It does so by addressing the following research question: what is the relevance of the concept of learning from history in navigating MSC in response to the COVID-19 pandemic?

COVID-19 in Latin America and Colombia

Latin America was hit by the pandemic later than other regions. The first case of COVID-19 was reported in Brazil on 25 February 2020. Within weeks from this onset, countries across the region began early lockdown measures, closure of borders and started preparing to augment the capacity of their healthcare systems (Burki, 2020). The situation has not been the same for every Latin American country. Health systems across the region have shown different forms of adaptation as well as the implementation of varied policy measures (*The Economist*, 2020). Within Latin America, the capacity and competence of healthcare systems vary greatly, both between countries and within them (OECD, 2020; United Nations, 2020).

Despite early measures to control the spread of COVID-19 and having the advantage of witnessing how other countries across the world had responded to the pandemic and fared, Latin American countries felt particularly vulnerable given their antecedent poverty and inequality levels at the time of the crisis. According to the IMF, Latin America and the Caribbean (LATAM) is expected to be one of the regions worst affected by COVID-19 (Werner, 2020). The health systems in this region are fragile, and fragmentation and segmentation are considered to be among their ongoing challenges (Rodriguez-Morales et al., 2020). LATAM countries' health systems, compared to European or Asian countries, have significantly lower health expenditures, fewer hospital beds and health professional per 1000 inhabitants, and weaker disease surveillance systems (OECD, 2020). The virus has also highlighted racial and socioeconomic disparities in health across the globe and in the region (Belser, 2020). By June 2020, LATAM became the world's latest COVID-19 hotspot with the added burden of having resource-constrained health systems, high prevalence of chronic conditions and complex internal political dynamics (Pablos-Méndez et al., 2020). To lose jobs, informal and not, or protect health became the region's common conundrum.

In Colombia, the National Institute of Health confirmed the first case on 6 March 2020 from a young woman coming back from Milan, Italy. After that, early and preventive lockdowns were placed by local governments throughout Colombia, with Bogotá the first city to implement a lockdown on 20 March 2020. Relative to other countries, COVID-19 in Colombia has exhibited a slower but constant contagion pace. Yet, as the virus established itself in Colombia, it did so unequally and at different rates. Cases have steadily concentrated in dense urban centres such as Bogotá, Cali and Medellín. All departments have reported cases, but some municipalities (26%) were apparently free of COVID-19 by the end of July 2020 (de la Hoz-Restrepo et al., 2020). With the virus gaining contagion speed, Colombia's rate of testing and opportune diagnosis has been put to the test. It has also put the health system on 'red alert' despite the increase in ICUs' capacity. In July and August, Bogotá had occupancy rates around 80–90% which led local authorities to reinstate strict lockdowns by localities (Saludata, 2020). Figure 4.1 shows a timeline of events of Colombia's response to COVID-19.

The Colombian government responded quickly by instituting national measures with the objective of reducing the speed of contagion to prevent the collapse of the health system and increase its capacity (Cárdenas & Martínez, 2020). In contrast to other countries from the region such as Brazil and Mexico, Colombia's government made clear the importance of science and its reliance on evidence to manage the crisis and for decision-making (de la Hoz-Restrepo et al., 2020). Lessons learned from clinicians in Europe and the United States have reportedly been essential for the management of clinical aspects of COVID-19, and during the pandemic, scientific networks appear to have strengthened their collaboration (Apuzzo & Kirkpatrick, 2020). Colombia's previous experience with severe outbreaks of chikungunya (2015), Zika (2015, 2016) and dengue (seasonal) has reportedly prepared national scientific bodies, e.g.

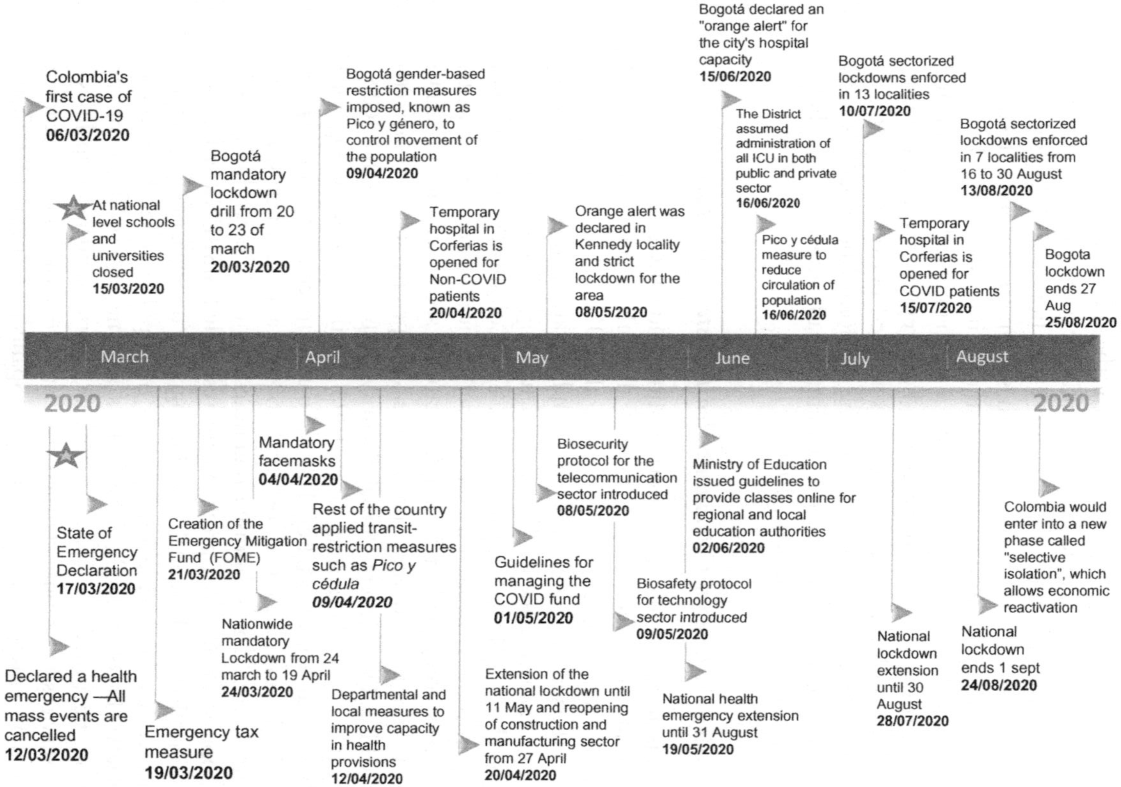

Fig. 4.1 Timeline of responses to COVID-19 in Colombia. Elaborated by authors (*Note* Bogotá level events above the line, national level below the line)

the National Institute of Health, and informed the responses of local health secretariats including their approach to public health surveillance.

However, despite the implementation of the measures established by national and local governments and healthcare organisations ready to spring into action, an increasing concern exists both for mortality rates and for the limited capacity of the health system to respond effectively to the needs of critically ill patients requiring intensive care. Tensions between national and local governments have hampered a coordinated response (Cárdenas and Martinez 2020). Each region is autonomous to base decisions on local needs; tension has accrued between the national government's strategies for re-opening the economy and Bogota's local government's insistence on not overloading already stretched healthcare infrastructures (Guillermoprieto, 2020).

Key Features of Colombia's Health System Structure

Colombia is an upper-middle-income country, and OECD member, with a social health insurance model, funded through general taxation and payroll deductible contributions (Ruiz et al., 2018). The country has a mixed health system where both public and private sectors participate in the insurance, management, delivery and funding of healthcare services (Guerrero et al., 2011). As shown in Fig. 4.2, Colombia's mixed system of care is governed through a complex set of healthcare arrangements. The system is composed of an ample sector of social security in health financed by public resources and a decreasing private sector (Guerrero et al., 2011). The General Social Security System for Health (SGSS) is the backbone of the system since 1993 when the country approved a health reform known as Ley 100. The reform created a mandatory universal health insurance with two types of insurance regimes: subsidised and contributory. The subsidised regime covers those individuals classified as poor according to a proxy means test called SISBEN (System for the identification of Potential Social Programs Beneficiaries); it targets the most vulnerable and poorer groups of population in the Colombian society (Escobar et al., 2009). This scheme covers 48,1% of the population, territorial entities (departments, districts and municipalities), contract services from publicly owned healthcare providers, also known as social state enterprises (ESE for their Spanish acronym) (Ministerio de Salud y Protección Social, 2020). The subsidised scheme is directed towards the health and welfare of poorer groups in Colombian society.

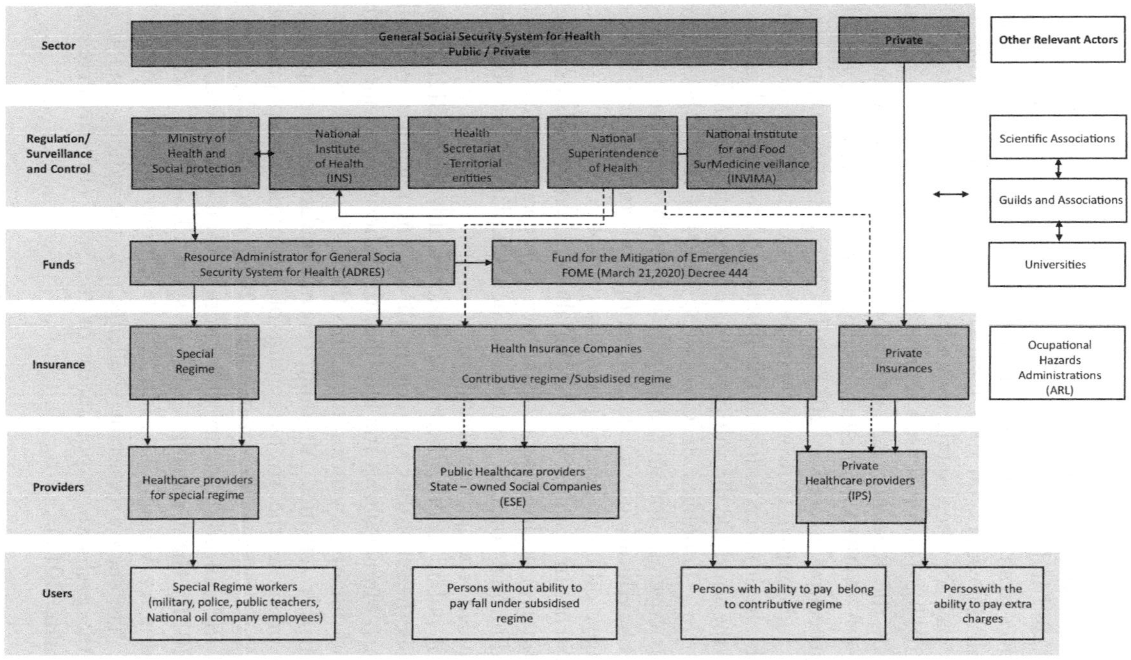

Fig. 4.2 Map of Colombian Health Care System with relevant stakeholders for responding to COVID-19. Adaptation made by authors based on the figure presented in Guerrero et al. (2011)

Barriers to access is a particular problem with the subsidised insurance system, as 70% of the total claims made come from this system (Orjuela et al., 2014).

In contrast, the contributory regime is for those with the ability to pay (wage earners and independent workers). Patients choose an insurer to purchase services from a network of public or private healthcare providers on their behalf. Providers, on their part, compete to deliver services to insurers who pay for their services (so-called 'managed competition') (Ruiz et al., 2018). The subsidised regime and the contributory regime are overseen by the Resource Administrator for General Social Security System in Health (ADRES), an entity ascribed to the Ministry of Health and Social Protection created in 2017 to be in charge of guaranteeing resource flow and control. However, in order to attend the needs of extra funding for the health sector during the pandemic, the national government created the fund for the mitigation of emergencies (FOME for its Spanish acronym) (República de Colombia, 2020). Finally, the system also comprises coverage for special populations such as military forces, the police, public education teachers and national oil company employees, all of whom have different benefit plans and do not pool their resources within the system. In combination to the above, there are also supplementary (voluntary) health insurances known as prepaid medicine, all of which offer additional coverage to the basic benefits plan. These plans are completely funded from private spending.

In terms of public health, there is a Basic Health Plan (BHP) that addresses public health issues and covers all citizens regardless of their insurance status. Municipalities and local health authorities provide health promotion and disease prevention programs through the BPH as well as other public health activities. Although recent regulatory developments in Colombia promote the strengthening of leadership for population health and system change (Franco-Giraldo, 2015; Vargas et al., 2016), and the need for multi-disciplinary and multi-sectoral care is recognised (Law 1438/2011), there remains a lack of system leadership and coordination (Rodríguez-Villamizar et al., 2016). Chronic underfunding of public health has been a constant challenge for the system, and it is taken to be the exclusive responsibility of the state (Riveros-Pérez & Amado-González, 2012).

Findings

Sources of Learning

Many of the stakeholders interviewed noted the importance of dealing with COVID-19 as a "third wave" geographically. However, as one interviewee stated, it was recognised that many countries were ill prepared to respond to COVID-19:

> We have to start by making certain clarities; one, no country in the world is prepared for this, no country in the world knew how to handle this. (Representative, National education organisation, SHA013)

Having learned about what had happened in Asia, Europe and the United States first, and being able to speak directly to colleagues abroad about their experience was a crucial aspect in how the local health system responded. Learning how other health systems organised themselves to absorb the shock caused by COVID-19 contributed to the effective coordination of local actors:

> I think that the relationship of the Health Secretariat with the private sector was facilitated because we have learned what had happened in Asia and Europe, so the private sector had all the will to collaborate and articulate with our actions. (Representative, Health planning organisation, Bogotá, SHB010)

Research about the COVID-19 situation in other countries was done at different organisational levels and on an ongoing basis. In the interviews with stakeholders representing the national and local governmental bodies, we found that international sources to learn about the virus and the disease were central, even considering their changing nature as it was the case with WHO's recommendations. However, in our interviews, we found that for hospitals and clinics, in particular, that direct learning from international peers became most relevant. Many stakeholders signalled a connection with peers in Spain, Italy or the United States via formal and informal meetings. But here more than research-based evidence, participants reported exchanging 'everyday' or practical experiences on the ground and clinical decisions about what worked and what did not. For this reason, webinars, seminars, meetings and private messages abounded at the beginning of the response in order for people to learn about the new virus and how it behaved in different countries.

> I would do one or two meetings every week through Teams, with a large group of hospitals in Spain, close to 25. We would meet with approximately 50 people from different hospitals in Colombia. People from different clinics and the Spaniards connected in real time, we met at 10:00 am, which was like 5:00 pm or 6:00 p.m. time in Spain, which is when they had already lowered the big hospital rush. (Representative, private health care provider, Bogotá, SHB015)

In the context of COVID-19, knowledge coming from experience acquired great relevance for various reasons: the evidence that is being built as the pandemic develops is still unstable, doctors and clinicians need to act under great amount of pressure and at the beginning with uncertainty and fear, a lot of actions take time to perform and adjust, and many clinics and hospitals wanted to know one another's "know-how" for thinking how best to adapt their internal operations and logistics.

> Epidemics are not to be followed but intervened. And to intervene, you have to look at what other people have described. For instance, we found that in Germany, it was useful to look at the oxygenation of the patient, so we set up schemes here for health insurance companies to follow. (Representative, association of Insurance Companies, SHA016)

Along with the importance of international scientific and non-scientific networks and their experience, from the beginning it became clear to many stakeholders that it was necessary to acknowledge local realities and resources as well as start producing local knowledge.

> We all have friends from abroad and people from Spain, Italy and the US were telling us how they did things. There was also all the literature from all over the world. But we had to sit and acknowledge that we needed to do things adapting to what we have. It was very hard at the beginning until local guidelines started appearing. (Representative, public health care provider, Bogotá, SHB001)

The need for gathering and producing real-time information about local realities (within the city or a single organisation) is commonly shared across stakeholders. Even though Colombia has a long tradition of epidemiological surveillance for different diseases, the characteristics of COVID-19 made necessary the consolidation of systems of information that could facilitate decision-making as fast as possible. The need for centralised information was also stressed by the fact that the disease was having a different behaviour in different territories of the country (diversity in terms of spread of contagion, availability and access to health services and health professionals and local strategies of leadership and public health strategies for disease prevention and control). In addition, given the unfamiliar nature of the disease and the lack of expertise in how it was best to control/contain it and treat it, data became a necessary tool to identify priorities and ways of action at different levels:

> I think the biggest learning from this pandemic, is that finally the health sector has understood that data analysis and data in general are indeed useful for action. (Representative, Health Observatory, Bogotá, SHB012).
>
> We read consensus, listen to suggestions amid controversies and from that we make decisions. But most importantly, I need real-time information. So we have our own information board for the clinic (how many patients with positive cases, how many suspect cases, if they are hospitalised or not, age group, health affiliation, etc.). (Representative, private health care provider, Bogotá, SHB015)

Another common strategy found across healthcare organisations was the establishment of internal technical committees. In Bogotá, private clinics, public hospitals, the Red Cross, health insurance companies and other healthcare providers have set up teams of doctors and other health experts for revising data and organisational and clinical decisions on a daily basis. The regularity of such meetings obeyed the rate of constant change and adaptation that these types of organisations went through, particularly during the first four months of the pandemic. Interestingly, besides the constitution of these formal committees, other less formal groups had established through social platforms such as WhatsApp. For instance, a key member of a national research organisation advocated this more flexible form of communication for rapid data consumption replaced the need for systematic literature reviews and reports, as the latter are not really put into practice:

> In reality, there is a rapid and daily consumption of data. Everyday there is something new. I know there is a lot of junk in Whatsapp but when you form groups there that are serious around a subject, this really has

> meant a shortcut to reach the evidence. (Representative, National research organisation, SHA018)

In summary, at the beginning of the emergency, information from international sources, particularly know-how coming from hospitals and clinics, was of importance for stakeholders' decisions. But, in general, information of local origin or applicability was prioritised in planning responses to COVID-19 at the national and local level. Although international sources of evidence were used (e.g. Germany's approach to oxygenation of patients or international professional networks that included Spain), there was recognition that such experiences needed to be tailored to the particular contextual challenges facing Colombia. Within the country, the sharing of emerging research on, and practical experiences with, responding to COVID-19 was enhanced through the ramping up of local mechanisms for collecting and sharing data, including real-time data collection, centralised synthesis and sharing of data, clinical experience surveys, and technical committees, that drew on formal and informal channels for sharing data (including WhatsApp groups used by technical committees).

Processes of Learning in Relation to Past Change Initiatives

The interview data underlined the importance of the learning processes health system stakeholders drew on to respond to COVID-19. In the context of COVID-19 in Colombia, the response has been characterised by previous experience and ad hoc actions. Experience from previous pandemics informed the response at the national planning level. Due to the geographic position and its tropical climate, Colombia is a country that has experienced and faced other epidemics at national level such as Chikungunya, Dengue, Zika and H1N1. The previous experiences have provided the possibility to build relationships and international collaborations. For instance, in the case of a national research organisation, the Centre for Disease Control (CDC), Zika provided the opportunity to build an alliance with an international scientific organisation in order to produce scientific papers, access training in pathology and latterly develop capabilities renowned in Latin America, and laboratory capacity, that were then used to respond to the challenges posed by COVID-19. A national-level interviewee commented on the relationships developed over time:

> We started with chikungunya in the first epidemic making great relationships, but I think Zika opened a door for us, a bigger golden opportunity, bigger than COVID-19, if you ask me, bigger than COVID-19 because remember that with Zika the world is turned to see the countries that had what had happened to Brazil...The institute had already had relationships with CDC for many years, in fact it had the first-field program for 26 years, 27 years, but when we made such a large agreement with CDC to investigate Zika, in fact Today the article was published in the New England Journal, today our third article on Zika came out. (Representative, National research organisation, SHA018)

At the national planning level, the use of past experiences acquired through previous epidemics has also provided knowledge to respond to the virus. Some actions taken by national authorities were based on previous experiences and were more carefully planned rather than improvised. Previous experience of managing influenza enabled health system planners to estimate financial expenses associated with the emerging demand for clinical equipment, building forecasting models and management of intensive care units. As the interviewee from the national entity claimed:

> To determine how much to buy (equipment, drugs, etc) we first based our estimates thinking about Influenza. But we also had to gather new evidence and build possible scenarios (thinking in influenza) knowing that the Ministry could not go and buy the maximum number of things because if things didn't get to that level there could be a patrimonial loss. (Representative, National health system lead, SHA017)

At the local planning level of Bogotá, planners had benefited from shared experiences of planning for a previous pandemic (H1N1), as one interviewee from a local entity planning remarked:

> Many of the staff, not to mention the majority... had already lived H1N1. So, in H1N1 there was an over-acting, then, many health secretariats in Colombia, not only here, bought the drugs for H11 and bought a lot of things, then those drugs expired, nothing happened, the morbidity and all were not the statistics that were expected worldwide. (Representative, Health planning organisation, Bogotá, SHB003)

The H1N1 experience—where the actual impact was less than that planned for—made the planners more cautious in their early responses to COVID-19. At the local planning level, stakeholders had access to established evidence and information about past events and this had a positive impact on their current learning process. The documentation of previous experiences enabled organisations to store actions taken in previous epidemics and have ready access easily to the information:

> We did a very large bibliographic review, documents, articles and well, the Ten-Year Public Health Plan is a document that the secretary made that is very, very good and we told them in effect, it is a document that can, can give us an orderly path of how to group the information so that the citizen and the academic and the scientist understand it in a good way. (Representative, Health Observatory, Bogotá, SHB012)

In addition to learning from past experience, there was evidence of ad hoc learning at different levels of the health system. COVID-19 has necessitated a new way of learning among healthcare providers, who have been exposed to situations where the decisions made had to be taken in relation to ongoing processes and existing services facing increased demand. Tracking fluctuation of positive cases by area over time, and having the flexibility to adjust the provision of health services to patients accordingly, were important to implement ongoing responses to a situation that had not been handled before and was totally unknown to those involved in health planning and delivering services:

> Some decisions are made in complete uncertainty, and it is hard to get used to that. We have to work as a team, doing the best we can't, without doing harm to patients, and being willing to adjust things all the time. (Representative, private health care provider, Bogotá, SHB004)

A process of 'ad hoc' learning recognises context variability and the pace of evidence production, as well as the novel needs and requirements posed by the virus. This has encouraged stakeholders to keep track of information emerging from health authorities and other relevant actors. This continuous learning process by healthcare providers and planners has been needed on a daily basis in order to keep updated and respond to the different challenges posed by COVID-19:

> I think that this has been, from the emergency line, one of the most relevant actions that we have had to adapt to in the face of this situation, which is new for everyone and continues to be lifelong learning, because news

> or requirements continue to appear every day or needs regarding how the pandemic is behaving in the environment. (Representative, Humanitarian NGO, SHA005)

The learning processes involve a kind of uncertainty due to the novelty of the virus and the fast pace by which evidence keeps emerging, sometimes in a contradictory way. It is an ad hoc learning process where actors at national and local level are learning as the emergency situation emerged and evolved:

> I would start by saying, this is our first pandemic. And if you mention it that way, the first thing you have to recognise is that epidemics, since we do not know, you have to have great humility but a great capacity to understand what works and what does not work. So today we say that it's the right thing to do, tomorrow we have to say, "no, it wasn't", okay? So, I think that is perhaps the aspect, for me, that is most relevant. (Representative, health insurers' association, SHA016)

In a context of crisis, the learning process has allowed different actors from the national and local entities to work in a collaborative way. This interaction has permitted the sharing of opinions that before were not accepted or taken into account. The crisis has forced acknowledgement of the barriers to coordination associated with the pre-existent conditions related to the Colombia health system. For instance, one interviewee from the local planning level described the lack of coordinated relationships historically among health services from different providers. Since COVID-19 arrived in Bogotá, the importance of working together towards a common goal was realised by local authorities, health insurance companies and healthcare providers. This interviewee suggests that the crisis was seen as an opportunity to overcome historic coordination problems instead of allowing the problems to inhibit the response to the crisis:

> The fact that it is an event that affects people's daily life is an element that has facilitated communication. It is an event that if coordination between providers, between insurers and others had not been achieved, it would have been very expensive and many lives would have been lost in the response, by having a fractional response. So, on the one hand, the most cost-efficient way is coordination. On the other hand, affecting the commercial performance, the work, the educational part, makes all the other sectors look towards the health sector and, in quotation marks,

> wait for answers to be able to continue with the development of life in those other aspects. (Representative, health planning organisation, Bogotá, SHB002)

In summary, responding to COVID-19 involved a combination of utilising past learning from other infectious diseases and engaging in more ad hoc and continuous learning. In relation to the past, established relationships with an international organisation, resources (laboratory capacity and personnel training) and documentary evidence were cited as important for initial responsive planning. However, it was acknowledged that COVID-19 also posed many unprecedented challenges for decision-making—leading to "complete uncertainty" as described by one interviewee. In response, there was an emphasis on improvised responses to COVID-19—denoted by terms to describe responsive actions such as "adapting" and "lifelong learning", as well as acceptance of uncertainty in decisions taken. There appeared to be emphasis on trial-and-error learning rather than enacting pre-defined plans, as one interviewee remarked:

> so today we say that it's the right thing to do, tomorrow we have to say, "no, it wasn't", okay? (Representative, health insurers' association, SHA016)

Discussion and Conclusion

Using the conceptual framework of MSC in relation to the "attending to history" rule, this study shows some of the learning mechanisms through which different organisations of the health system in Colombia have responded to COVID-19. Knowing and assessing previous efforts for change and building on "familiar ideas and activities" has been proposed in the theory of MSC as relevant elements to improve the success of large system change (Best et al., 2012). It is considered that if leaders of change take into account local histories, past "failures" or critical events there is increased feasibility for judicious planning of change. Through a qualitative study of the response to COVID-19 by various organisational actors, at the national level and within Colombia's capital city, Bogotá, we examined how local learning and its relationship to past events are related to change planning under conditions of pressure, uncertainty and limited resources. This study adds to the literature on major system change, large system transformation and healthcare reform that call for evidence that addresses issues of complexity and context from the Global South.

Being hit in a 'third wave' gave LATAM countries a learning advantage. Yet it was an advantage that could not translate into programmatic action. Colombia, as any other Latin American country, had to boost its local resources (in terms of health professionals, national and local information systems, technology production, laboratory capacity, scientists, managers, etc.) for implementing new forms of rapid learning. In the midst of urgent actions to counter the rapid spread of the virus and avoid the collapse of the health system, health providers, health insurance companies and health system leads at national level and in Bogotá, all had to quickly adapt to the new reality. For health providers, this meant reconfiguration of spaces, human resources and services. For health insurance companies, it meant new tasks and services. For government agencies, the intensification of their activities of planning, control and vigilance as well as more community work.

We found different examples of learning processes. Especially during the early stage of the emergency in Colombia, some of them were based on the interaction with the international community. Learning from the experiences of different clinical settings in Europe was stressed by stakeholders as a relevant source of information to prepare and adjust the infrastructure, and logistics of health services delivery for COVID-19 patients. However, even though international sources were highly relevant for some organisations, information of local origin or applicability was prioritised in planning and implementing responses to COVID-19.

Our findings also show that the response to COVID-19 involved a combination of learning from previous responses to other infectious diseases and more ad hoc and continuous learning. In particular, ad hoc learning acquires more relevance and weight under circumstances of uncertainty and emerging scientific evidence. In general, learning processes were highly mediated by a "trial-and-error" approach. Learning takes place in practice, while strongly fed by experiences of others. Learning processes, in the response to COVID-19, were continuously in the making.

Implications for MSC Theory, Research and Practice

We conducted our research when Bogotá was under lockdown. Without the possibility of conducting fieldwork, our study had to rely on interviews conducted virtually and documentary research. Our findings are thus mainly based on the narratives of stakeholders, having the limitation of not being able to explore how learning processes or coordination takes place in everyday practice. Relying on interview data, the study does not make an emphasis in discrepancies between what is said and what is done. Triangulating the interview data with observations of practices would be relevant for future research.

MSC theory mainly addresses conditions for longer-term planning of change. COVID-19 hit health systems worldwide unexpectedly. Given that our data collection took place during the first six months of the emergency in Colombia, it is not possible to determine what kind of changes will be sustained over time. This relates to a wider criticism of studies of health system change, that they tend to focus on the beginning of change, rather than ongoing processes involved in sustaining change (Langley et al., 2013). We would recommend a future evaluation study to analyse whether the changes implemented according to the processes of learning described result in MSC; such a study would benefit from the use of mixed methods, to define quantitative outcome measures for MSC and qualitative process evaluation. During our interviews, it was common for participants to state that no one was prepared to face the challenges raised by COVID-19. Thus, due to its unexpected, novel and highly risky nature, COVID-19 has demanded rapid adaptations without copious planning. MSC theory had yet to be explored in contexts of public health emergency, as well as of developing countries.

The 'simple rules' or recommendations for guiding MSC processes suggested by Best et al. (2012) have to be reconsidered in the light of current events. In particular, in relation to the "attend to history" rule, this study highlights that, as suggested by the authors, local forms of learning are of upmost importance. However, participation in international health systems and scientific networks also had an impact on how Colombia's health system responded to COVID-19. The MSC framework considers that processes of change can be multiple and operate at different levels, but more conceptual clarity is needed to address issues of scale. In the writing on MSC, while involving inter-organisational collaboration, the unit of change is often assumed to be geographically defined and territorially bound (e.g. a metropolitan area); however, the relevance of non-local knowledge flows and forms of learning need to be given greater recognition in shaping MSC processes. If the boundaries of the unit of change are expanded to acknowledge a wider variety of actors that can influence change processes within particular settings, use of the term "major" in future research should be qualified as to whether this denotes the geographical scale of a particular change or its perceived significance for patients and population health. Future research should focus on relationships between local adaptive systems (e.g. a metropolitan area) and enabling and constraining processes associated with wider professional networks, national policy and planning, and international agencies.

The attending to history rule emphasises the importance of learning in relation to past initiatives—a condition that is challenged in COVID-19 times. We did found examples of learning from the past that coexisted with ad hoc learning. Colombia's previous experience with serious outbreaks of chikungunya, Zika and dengue gave the country an important capacity for public health planning and response. These past experiences were particularly relevant to government agencies, but less so to other actors of the health system such as healthcare providers and health insurance companies. This indicates that, when speaking of MSC, it is important to address that the weight of shared past experiences on decision-making can differ according to the stakeholder. In terms of practice implications, making past experiences available to inform current actions appears important (e.g. documenting organisational knowledge related to pandemics and maintaining a network of inter-organisational ties, including diverse local organisations and international links, that can be utilised rapidly when a shock affects the health system).

As well as addressing issues of scale, MSC studies also need to address temporality issues. More than looking to the past, it seems that COVID-19 has pressed for actions in anticipation to an uncertain future. Fear of a potential collapsed health system, in particular as reflected in the occupation of ICU units, made stakeholders mobilise their resources and take unprecedented actions (closure of clinics, reconversion of public spaces into transitory healthcare facilities, expansion of physical space and staff, among others). Acknowledgement of the need for aspects of trial-and-error learning in making health system changes (i.e. "the right thing to do" may need revising from day to day, as one interviewee put it) contrasts with the mechanisms of learning assumed in MSC theory, which tends to emphasise rational and judicious planning. For example, MSC appears to rely on building a robust case for change, i.e. selection of evidence-based interventions (Ramsay et al., 2015) and thorough stakeholder engagement in health system decision-making, including patient and public involvement (McKevitt et al., 2018). An open question for health system leadership navigating change remains: how can rapid adaptation of services to meet emergent needs be encouraged while ensuring decision-making processes remain open to emerging evidence and stakeholder consultation?

To our knowledge, issues of temporality have not been addressed in the MSC literature. The relationship between systems thinking and future studies is marginal (Hodgson & Midgley, 2014). The role of the future (as represented in roadmaps, forecast plans, future scenarios, etc.) has scantly appeared in discussions of change implementation. Lukas et al. (2007), in their model for transformational change in healthcare systems, mention the role of vision and mission to set out strategies and directions for organisational change. However, COVID-19 as a still-emergent crisis has made evident the need for predictive models for decision-making in cases of scant evidence for urgent action.

As much as we have learned that learning from past events and other people's previous experiences is important for conducing significant change across organisations, the current pandemic has also made evident the relevance of predictive models for decision-making. Anticipatory governance, meaning the application of risk-evaluations, model-based predictions and scenario-building to avoid unwanted futures (i.e. health system collapse), is a common feature of government and health systems responses to COVID-19 (Lidskog et al.). Considering the MSC framework under conditions of crisis opens new research avenues. To further explore the role of the future, MSC theory can engage with developments in sociological and anthropological thinking that address issues of temporality in contexts of risk, crisis and/or uncertainty (see Appadurai, 2013; Beck, 2009; Koselleck, 2002; Roitman, 2012, 2013). It is worth analysing the effect of "future visions" in planning for the implementation of significant changes across several health organisations. If anticipatory practices allow actors to navigate uncertain terrains, how do they learn from them? Does the decision-making process differ if it is prospective rather than retrospective? What aspects of the imagined future matter more for planning systematic change and how are they used? If the quest for anticipatory leadership is accelerated in times of crisis, as exposed by COVID-19, it is necessary to study its effects for organisational action.

Funding Statement The study was funded by the Colombian Ministry of Science, Technology and Innovation, project code 1204101577001. The call was titled 'Invitation to present projects that contribute to solving current health problems related to the COVID-19 pandemic' (Invitación a presentar proyectos que contribuyan a la solución de problemáticas actuales de salud relacionadas con la pandemia de COVID-19). ST also acknowledges support from 'Fondo de Apoyo a Profesores Asistentes' (FAPA) de la Universidad de los Andes

References

Al-Dabbagh, Z. S (2020) The role of decision-maker in crisis management: A qualitative study using grounded theory (COVID-19 pandemic crisis as a model). *Journal of Public Affairs*, e2186.

Andrus, J. K., Evans-Gilbert, T., Santos, J. I., Guzman, M. G., Rosenthal, P. J., Toscano, C., Valenzuela, M. T., Siqueira, M., Etienne, C., & Breman, J. G. (2020). Perspectives on Battling COVID-19 in Countries of Latin America and the Caribbean. *The American Journal of Tropical Medicine and Hygiene, 103*(2), 593–596.

Appadurai, A. (2013). *The future as cultural fact. Essays on the global condition.* Verso.

Apuzzo, M., & Kirkpatrick, D. (2020). *COVID-19 changed How the world does science, together*. https://www.nytimes.com/2020/04/01/world/europe/coronavirus-science-research-cooperation.html. Accessed 29 August 2020.

Beck, U. (2009). *World at risk.* Polity.

Belser, P. (2020). *COVID-19 cruelly highlights inequalities and threatens to deepen them.* International Labour Organisation (ILO). http://www.ilo.org/global/about-the-ilo/newsroom/news/WCMS_740101/lang--en/index.htm. Accessed on 28 August 2020.

Best, A., Greenhalgh, T., Lewis, S., Saul, J. E., Carroll, S., & Bitz, J. (2012). Large system transformation in health care: A realist review. *The Milbank Quarterly, 90*(3), 421–456.

Burki, T. (2020). COVID-19 in Latin America. *The Lancet Infectious Diseases, 20*(5), 547–548.

Bradley, E. H., Curry, L. A., & Devers, K. J. (2007). Qualitative data analysis for health services research: Developing taxonomy, themes, and theory. *Health Services Research, 42*(4), 1758–1772.

Cárdenas, M., & Martínez, H (2020). *COVID-19 in Colombia: Impact and policy responses.* CGD Center for Global Development Note. https://www.cgdev.org/publication/COVID-19-colombia-impact-and-policy-responses?fbclid=IwAR2iZ8aJHEITBuGQEN-f95WeQQiljvQ9fj4cz3iH7uJgjM4_DJol6rVA3lc#ftn5. Accessed on 28 August 2020.

Congreso de la República. (2010). *Ley 1419 de 2010: Por la cual se establecen los lineamientos para el desarrollo de la Telesalud en Colombia*. http://www.secretariasenado.gov.co/senado/basedoc/ley_1419_2010.html. Accessed on 28 August 2020.

de la Hoz-Restrepo, F., Alvis-Zakzuk, N., de la Hoz-Gomez, J. et. al. (2020). Is Colombia an example of successful containment of the 2020 COVID-19 pandemic? A critical analysis of the epidemiological data, March to July 2020. *International Journal of Infection Diseases, 99*, 522–529.

Djellouli, N., Jones, L., Barratt, H., Ramsay, A. I., Towndrow, S., & Oliver, S. (2019). Involving the public in decision-making about large-scale changes to health services: A scoping review. *Health Policy, 123*(7), 635–645.

Escobar, M. L., Giedion, A. G., & Glassman, A. (2009). Colombia: After a decade of health system reform. In A. Glassman et al. (Eds.), *From few to many: Ten years of health insurance expansion in Colombia* (pp. 3–13). Inter-American Development Bank.

Fraser, A., Baeza, J. I., & Boaz, A. (2017). 'Holding the line': A qualitative study of the role of evidence in early phase decision-making in the reconfiguration of stroke services in London. *Health Research Policy and Systems, 15*(1), 45.

Franco-Giraldo, A. (2015). El Rol de los Profesionales de la Salud en la Atención Primaria en Salud (APS). *Revista Facultad Nacional De Salud Pública, 33*(3), 414–424.

Fulop, N. J., Ramsay, A. I., Perry, C., Boaden, R. J., McKevitt, C., Rudd, A. G., Turner, S. J., Tyrrell, P. J., Wolfe, C. D., & Morris, S. (2016). Explaining outcomes in major system change: A qualitative study of implementing centralised acute stroke services in two large metropolitan regions in England. *Implementation Science, 11*(1), 1–13.

Guillermoprieto, A. (2020). *Fear, anger, desperation: How Bogotá's residents are coping with COVID-19*. https://www.nationalgeographic.com/history/2020/05/fear-anger-desperation-how-bogota-residents-are-coping-covid-19/. Accessed 29 August 2020.

Guerrero, R., Gallego, A. I., Becerril-Montekio, V., & Vásquez, J. (2011). Sistema de Salud de Colombia. *Salud Pública De México, 53*, s144–s155.

Hodgson, A., & Midgley, G. (2014). *Bringing foresight into systems thinking: A three horizon approach*. 58th Annual Meeting of the International Society for the Systems Sciences, ISSS.

Jones, L., Fraser, A., & Stewart, E. (2019). Exploring the neglected and hidden dimensions of large-scale healthcare change. *Sociology of Health & Illness, 41*(7), 1221–1235.

Koselleck, R. (2002). Some questions regarding the conceptual history of "crisis". In *The practice of conceptual history: Timing history, spacing concepts*. Stanford University Press.

Langley, A. N. N., Smallman, C., Tsoukas, H., & Van de Ven, A. H. (2013). Process studies of change in organization and management: Unveiling temporality, activity, and flow. *Academy of Management Journal, 56*(1), 1–13.

Legido-Quigley, H., Asgari, N., Teo, Y. Y., Leung, G. M., Oshitani, H., Fukuda, K., et al. (2020). Are high-performing health systems resilient against the COVID-19 epidemic? *Lancet,* 395(10227), 848–850.

Lidskog, R., Elander, I., & Standring, A. (2020). COVID-19, the climate, and transformative change: Comparing the social anatomies of crises and their regulatory responses. *Sustainability, 12*(16), 6337.

Lukas, C., Holmes, S., Cohen, A., Restuccia, J., Cramer, I., Shwartz, M., & Charns, M. (2007). Transformational change in health care systems: An organizational model. *Health Care Management Review., 32*(4), 309–320.

McKevitt, C., Ramsay, A. I., Perry, C., Turner, S. J., Boaden, R., Wolfe, C. D., & Fulop, N. J. (2018). Patient, career and public involvement in major system change in acute stroke services: The construction of value. *Health Expectations, 21*(3), 685–692.

Ministerio de Salud y Protección Social. Estadísticas de Covertura. https://www.minsalud.gov.co/proteccionsocial/Paginas/cifras-aseguramiento-salud.aspx

OECD. (2020). *COVID-19 in Latin America and the Caribbean: An overview of governmental responses to the crises.* https://www.oecd.org/coronavirus/policy-responses/COVID-19-in-latin-america-and-the-caribbean-an-overview-of-government-responses-to-the-crisis-0a2dee41/. Accessed on 28 August 2020.

Orjuela, A., González, L., Pardo, H., & Angulo E. (2014) *La tutela y los derechos a la salud y a la seguridad social, 2014.* Defensoría del Pueblo (Colombia). https://www.defensoria.gov.co/public/pdf/LatutelaylosderechosalaSalud.pdf. Accessed 28 August 2020.

Pablos-Méndez, A., Vega, J., Aranguren, F., Tabish, H., & Raviglione, M. (2020) COVID-19 in Latin America. *British Medical Journal*, 370:m2939

Prada, C., & Chaves, S. (2019). Health system structure and transformations in Colombia between 1990 and 2013: A socio-historical study. *Critical Public Health, 29*(3), 314–324.

Ramsay, A. I., Morris, S., Hoffman, A., Hunter, R. M., Boaden, R., McKevitt, C., Perry, C., Pursani, N., Rudd, A. G., Turner, S., & Tyrrell, P. J. (2015). Effects of centralizing acute stroke services on stroke care provision in two large metropolitan areas in England. *Stroke, 46*(8), 2244–2251.

Rojas-García, A., Turner, S., Pizzo, E., Hudson, E., Thomas, J., & Raine, R. (2018). Impact and experiences of delayed discharge: A mixed-studies systematic review. *Health Expectations, 21*(1), 41–56.

República de Colombia. (2020). *Decreto 444 de 2020 Por el cual se crea el Fondo de Mitigación de Emergencias -FOME y se dictan disposiciones en materia de recursos, dentro del Estado de Emergencia Económica, Social y Ecológica*. https://dapre.presidencia.gov.co/normativa/normativa/DECRETO%20444%20DEL%2021%20DE%20MARZO%20DE%202020.pdf. Accessed 10 August 2020.

Riveros-Pérez, E., & Amado-González, L. N. (2012). Modelo de salud en Colombia: ¿Financiamiento basado en seguridad social o en impuestos? *Revista Gerencia y Políticas De Salud, 11*(23), 111–120.

Rodriguez-Morales, A. J., Gallego, V., Escalera-Antezana, J. P., Méndez, C. A., Zambrano, L. I., Franco-Paredes, C., Suárez, J. A., Rodriguez-Enciso, H. D., Balbin-Ramon, G. J., Savio-Larriera, E., Risquez, A., & Cimerman, S. (2020). COVID-19 in Latin America: The implications of the first confirmed case in Brazil. *Travel Medicine and Infectious Disease, 35,* 101613.

Rodríguez-Villamizar, L. A., Ruíz-Rodríguez, M., & Acosta-Ramírez, N. (2016). Evaluación de un modelo de atención primaria en salud en Santander, Colombia. *Revista Facultad Nacional De Salud Pública, 34*(1), 88–95.

Roitman, J. (2012). Crisis. In *Political concepts: A critical lexicon*. Tel Aviv.

Roitman, J. (2013). *Anti-crisis*. Duke University Press.

Ruiz, F., Avila-Burgos, L., & Trujillo, A. J. (2018). How does managed competition affect hospital prices in a social health insurance system? The Colombian case. *Health Policy and Planning, 33*(9), 1037–1046.

't Hart, P, Rosenthal, U, & Kouzmin, A. (1993). Crisis decision making: The centralization thesis revisited. *Administration and Society*, *25*(1), 12–45.

The Economist. (2020). Latin America's health systems brace for a battering. https://www.economist.com/the-americas/2020/04/11/latin-americas-health-systems-brace-for-a-battering. Accessed 11 April 2020.

The Lancet. (2020). COVID-19: Learning from experience. *The Lancet, 395*(10229):1011. https://doi.org/10.1016/S0140-6736(20)30686-3

Turner, S., & Niño, N. (2020). Qualitative analysis of the coordination of major system change within the Colombian health system in response to COVID-19: Study protocol (forthcoming). *Implementation Science Communications*

Turner, S., Ramsay, A., Perry, C., Boaden, R., McKevitt, C., Morris, S., Pursani, N., Rudd, A., Tyrrell, P., Wolfe, C., & Fulop, N. (2016a). Lessons for major system change: centralization of stroke services in two metropolitan areas of England. *Journal of Health Services Research & Policy, 21*(3), 156–165.

Turner, S., Goulding, L., Denis, J., et al. (2016b). Major system change: a management and organisational research perspective. In *Challenges, solutions and future directions in the evaluation of service innovations in health care and public health Health Services and Delivery Research*. NIHR Journals Library.

United Nations. (2020). *Policy brief: The impact of COVID-19 on Latin America and the Caribbean*. https://www.un.org/sites/un2.un.org/files/sg_policy_brief_COVID_lac.pdf. Accessed on 28 August 2020.

Vargas, I., Mogollón-Pérez, A. S., de Paepe, P., Ferreira da Silva, R., Unger, J. P., & Vazquez, M. L. (2016). Barriers to healthcare coordination in market based and decentralized public health systems: A qualitative study in healthcare networks of Colombia and Brazil. *Health Policy and Planning.*, *31*, 736–748.

Vargas-Zea, N., Castro, H., Rodríguez-Páez, F., Téllez, D., & Salazar-Arias, R. (2012) Colombian health system on its way to improve allocation efficiency—transition from a health sector reform to the settlement of an HTA agency. *Value in Health Regional Issues, 1*(2), 218–222.

Vindrola-Padros, C., Ramsay, A. I., Perry, C., Darley, S., Wood, V. J., Clarke, C. S., Hines, J., Levermore, C., Melnychuk, M., Moore, C. M., & Morris, S. (2020). Implementing major system change in specialist cancer surgery: The role of provider networks. *Journal of Health Services Research & Policy*. https://doi.org/10.1177/1355819620926553

Waring, J., Bishop, S., Clarke, J., Exworthy, M., Fulop, N. J., Hartley, J., & Ramsay, A. I. (2018). Healthcare leadership with political astuteness (HeLPA): A qualitative study of how service leaders understand and mediate the informal 'power and politics' of major health system change. *BMC Health Services Research, 18*(1), 918.

Werner, A. (2020). *Outlook for Latin America and the Caribbean: An intensifying pandemic*. IMFBlog. https://blogs.imf.org/2020/06/26/outlook-for-latin-america-and-the-caribbean-an-intensifying-pandemic/. Accessed 28 August 2020.

Yin, R. K. (2009). *Case study research design and methods* (4th ed.). Sage.

Yin, R. K. (2013). Validity and generalization in future case study evaluations. *Evaluation, 19*, 321–332. https://doi.org/10.1177/1356389013497081

CHAPTER 5

COVID-19 and the Flexibility of the Bureaucratic Ethos

Kirstine Zinck Pedersen and Paul du Gay

Introduction

Large bureaucratic organizations are commonly associated with a lack of the responsiveness, flexibility and innovative capability deemed necessary for an organization to change rapidly when circumstances dictate. While operating well in stable and predictable environments, bureaucracies are regularly assumed to be slow, ineffective and conservative in times of crises. While this so-called customary view (Perrow, 1972/2014) within the broader field of management and organization studies continues to claim that flexibility is a product of de-bureaucratization, the same argument is repeated in more specialized fields of crisis, emergency and risk management. For instance, crisis management has been described as an organizational paradox because, 'on the one hand, emergency response

K. Z. Pedersen (✉) · P. du Gay
Copenhagen Business School, Copenhagen, Denmark
e-mail: Kzp.ioa@cbs.dk

P. du Gay
University of London, London, UK

J. Waring et al. (eds.), *Organising Care in a Time of Covid-19*, Organizational Behaviour in Healthcare,
https://doi.org/10.1007/978-3-030-82696-3_5

requires meticulous organization and planning, but on the other hand it is spontaneous. Emergency managers have to innovate, adapt, and improvise because plans, regardless of how well done, seldom fit circumstances' (Waugh & Streib, 2006: 132). Here, a tension is identified between what is deemed 'bureaucratic values' and the necessary adaptation and resilience needed for crisis management to be well-functioning (Stark, 2014). More specifically, it is common to assume that 'rule-adherence limits individual creativity and innovation' in times of crisis and emergency (Stark, 2014, see also Weick, 1993).

With the COVID-19 crisis, however, evidence is emerging that large professional bureaucracies, such as hospitals, have been able to change their organization, retrain their staff, establish new physical facilities, and introduce new guidelines, technologies and safety procedures with an astonishing speed. The current chapter seeks to explore the grounds of bureaucratic responsiveness, both analytically and empirically. Hereby it adds to a number of empirical studies that have suggested how bureaucracy can be configured to enable flexibility and learning in organizations and teams (Adler et al., 1999; Briscoe, 2007; Bunderson & Boumgarden, 2010; Klein et al., 2006) and how formal systems can support responsiveness in volatile contexts (Bigley & Roberts, 2001).

The chapter begins by outlining and interrogating the 'customary view' of bureaucracy generally, and the professional bureaucracy more specifically, as inflexible and unresponsive. We then introduce our alternative to this position arguing that bureaucracies can indeed both innovate and exhibit flexible responses in times of crisis. Such responsiveness can be linked equally to technical and more normative/ethical characteristics of bureaucracy, not least its 'formality'. Following this, we present our case based on interviews with Danish healthcare professionals during the COVID-19 crisis. For this chapter, we focus specifically on the emergency response of a large Danish University hospital. Our analysis is based on interviews with the emergency response manager as well as the chief physicians of the three most affected departments, namely the intensive care unit, the infectious disease department and the emergency department. All four interviewees have been part of the hospital's Emergency

Response Team. The interviews are part of a larger qualitative virtual-interview study with 23 Danish healthcare professionals conducted on Teams from mid-April to the end of June 2020.[1]

The case shows that within the Danish healthcare system, rapid and flexible responses during the crisis were linked to classic bureaucratic features such as clear lines of command, explicit hierarchies, formalization, authority based on expertise and office-holding, and a focus on the duties, purposes and ethics of office (that engender a sense of 'vocation') as the driving force in making the reorganizations happen. We conclude by indicating how our analysis contributes to questioning received orthodoxies pertaining to the functioning of large professional bureaucracies, and suggest how our argument may also have implications for other formalized organized settings, in both public and private sectors.

The 'Customary View' of Bureaucracy as Inflexible and Unresponsive

In his classic Complex Organizations, the organizational sociologist Charles Perrow (2014 [1972]) famously argued that within the social sciences, a 'customary view' of bureaucracy was evident, one that had carried and indeed continues to carry considerable explanatory reach across a range of disciplinary and interdisciplinary fields. Perrow noted that within this customary view, bureaucracy was largely viewed negatively, and he pointed, in particular, to two enduring lines of criticism that led to that conclusion. The first associated bureaucracy with rule-bound inflexibility, inefficiency, and, at times of rapid environmental change, with a lack of innovative capacity and a pervasive unresponsiveness. The second represented bureaucracy as stifling the creativity, freedom, and self-realization of those in its employ. Perrow observed too, that both lines of criticism were often combined by a single author and were

[1] Most of the interviewees are employed in the Danish hospital sector ($N = 20$) where they represent both the administrative level of the hospital organization—with titles such as risk-managers, quality coordinators, emergency response managers—and the clinical level represented mainly by chief physicians at intensive, emergency and infectious diseases wards. They represent university hospitals and smaller regional hospitals in three out of five regions in Denmark. For this paper, we have chosen to focus our analysis on interviewees from one university hospital. The quotes are translated from Danish and we used synonyms to secure anonymity.

inter alia 'echoed by such diverse groups as the radical right, the radical left...and the counterculture' (2014: 6).

The first of these critiques has not only been dominant in descriptions of more traditional bureaucracies (such as state agencies) but also in accounts of what has been termed 'the professional bureaucracy', a moniker including, for instance, hospitals, universities, and private professional organizations such as law firms. The professional bureaucracy, a term largely associated with Henry Mintzberg in his classic The Structuring of Organizations (1979), is characterized by having professionals hired at the operating core supported by an administrative structure. In Mintzberg's original account, the professional bureaucracy is understood as decentralized and democratic, steered mainly by the standardization and internalization of professional skills, knowledge and practices, which are the result of the intensive training of professionals within their given areas of expertise. When the professional bureaucracy operates in a stable environment, it has considerable advantages in perfecting skills and knowledge. However, according to Mintzberg, the professional bureaucracy also exhibits various problems. It has to deal with particular problems of coordination, because professionals are primarily steered through standardization of skills rather than through hierarchy and administrative office (1979: 361). Moreover, the professional bureaucracy tends to suffer from what might be termed un-official discretion caused by professionals' loyalty toward their peers rather than to the organization or their clients (1979: 374). Lastly, Mintzberg adds to the list of potential dysfunctions the issue of innovation.

> Like the Machine Bureaucracy, the Professional Bureaucracy is an inflexible structure, well suited to producing standard outputs but ill-suited to adapting to the production of new ones. All bureaucracies are geared to stable environments: they are performance structures designed to perfect programs for contingencies that can be predicted, not problem-solving ones designed to create new programs for needs that have never before been encountered. (1979: 375)

Mintzberg explains that the problem of innovation is rooted in the fact that professionals are driven by convergent thinking and deductive reasoning, which encourages them to force new problems into old pigeonholes. However, Mintzberg argues, 'great art and innovative problem solving' requires inductive and divergent thinking and that 'flies in the face of everything the Professional Bureaucracy is designed to do' (1979: 375). As such, professional bureaucracies are inherently conservative and hesitant to change their ways. Mintzberg indicates that this problem might be particularly acute in professional bureaucracies compared to the classic machine bureaucracy. Although classic bureaucratic managers might well be slow to realize the need for change, at least they have the power to force the change down the hierarchy once the need is recognized. This is not possible in the professional bureaucracy, Mintzberg argues, where bottom-up decisions diffuse the power for making change: 'Everybody must agree on the change, not only a few managers or professional representatives. So change comes slowly and painfully, after much political intrigue and shrewd maneuvering by the professional and administrative entrepreneurs' (1979: 376). Following Mintzberg's proposition, then, we would assume the professional bureaucracy to be inherently inflexible and unresponsive in times of change, crisis and emergency.

Exploring the Relationship Between Bureaucracy, Flexibility and Responsiveness

As we indicated above, Charles Perrow (2014) argued that the customary view of bureaucracy as inflexible and resistant to change was considerably wide of the mark when it came to understanding this organizational form as classically articulated by Max Weber (1978, 1989, 1994; see also du Gay, 2000, 2009).[2] As Perrow concluded, 'the sins generally attributed to bureaucracy are either not sins at all or are consequences of the failure to bureaucratise sufficiently' (2014: 5). Specifically, when it came to matters of organizational responsiveness, Perrow argued that bureaucracy was not inherently unadaptive. He argued that the bureau had proven itself fully capable of undertaking what March (1991) described as 'exploration and exploitation' to some effect. In Charles Goodsell's (2005: 23) related terminology, bureaucracy had proven over time almost uniquely capable of both 'rule and response'.

[2] Charles Perrow started his academic career studying hospitals (1960, 1967). Here he quickly understood that as an organization the hospitals did not 'constitute a major and significant deviation from concepts of bureaucracy that steemed from the analysis of governmental bureaucracies and economic organization' (1967: 947).

While Perrow noted that the role of rule-bound bureaucratic authority and accountability relations in the reduction of particularism and featherbedding within organizations, and in the protection of individual employees from arbitrary decision-making, was relatively uncontroversial (Perrow, 2014: 23), he also indicated that those very same rules were also the source of considerable unease, not least to those for whom formalization connoted a loss of freedom, flexibility, and creativity, both organizationally and individually. In making this case, Perrow (2014: 21, 30) referred at various points to the work of Wilfred Brown, an experienced and successful executive and organizational analyst. Brown's experience of working within and simultaneously analyzing the operations of bureaucracy led him to argue that the latter was not inherently inflexible or unresponsive. In particular, Brown stressed that the very formalities—what others described as 'rigidities'—of bureaucratic hierarchy were not antithetical to flexibility but rather its precondition.

Brown (1965: 152) refers time and again to assumptions about bureaucratic formalization articulated by both practicing managers and executives and in the literatures devoted to analysing and intervening in their conduct. One such assumption, a key element of 'the customary view' as we indicated earlier, relates to the feeling that the greater the degree of 'informality' the more flexible and adaptive the organization will be. Brown, 1974: 35) states that the rallying cry here is: '"Let's keep it vague so that…creativeness can have a greater chance." But there is plenty of evidence that vague and confused organization is the great enemy of creativeness'.

> Informal, non-explicit organization is felt to be necessary because it enhances adaptability; explicit or formal organization is rejected because it is felt to make for rigidity. Both of these sentiments are the converse of my…experience. Looked at in this way it becomes clear that 'Informal Organization' creates an environment which allows, or even encourages, a subordinate to come to the conclusion that his manager is wrong or ineffective and to make his (sic) own decision concerning what tasks he should attempt and what degree of discretion he should assume in working on those tasks. Thus a deliberate policy of leaving organization unformulated is tantamount to the deliberate setting up of a situation of anarchy. I use the word 'anarchy' in its original sense, i.e., 'the want of government in a state'. (Brown, 1965: 153–154)

In Brown's (1965, 1974) analysis, bureaucratic formalization was viewed as a supple and multifaceted organizational device enabling people and tasks to be deployed at complementary levels. For Brown (ibid.), formal organizations consist of an executive system or employment hierarchy comprising the network of positions to which fulfillment of the organization's work is assigned. This system or hierarchy is made up of a number of roles of offices and consists of all members of the operating organization, a member being in such a role when s/he is carrying out their job responsibilities or tasks. Every such office carries with it specified responsibility and authority, which are taken on by the member assuming the role. Work roles themselves here consist of the totality of discretion which an organizational member is expected to exercise, and the prescribed acts s/he must discharge in carrying out the responsibilities of the role to which s/he is attached. The benefit of such formalization, Brown argues, is that everyone knows their place, and this provides the security required by the individual employee before they can become free fully to develop the discretionary (flexible, creative, responsive) component in their own role. Rather than infantilizing employees, by robbing them of liberty or agency, such security fosters their freedom to act in circumstances where ambiguity may exist (where policy or guidelines may leave alternative courses of action from among which the employee has to choose). In other words, rigidity and flexibility are not here seen as inevitably antithetical to one another. Rather, the former can be viewed as the condition of the latter. In other words, only when the structure and operating procedures are clear can authority be delegated effectively.

> If one knows, in objective terms, the task content of roles and the degree of discretion needed to complete it, then it becomes possible to provide people with quite explicit terms of reference. Once something is stable, then it comes under intellectual control; it can be talked about or thought about in explicit terms. This leads to adaptability and makes the result of change more predictable. (Brown, 1965: 153)

Thus, Brown argues that hierarchy is not essentially undynamic, that formalization is not inherently or largely antithetical to creativity and adaptability, and that the nature of the work that takes place in different employment hierarchies does need to be made explicit and precisely specified if authority is to be legitimately and effectively delegated and the 'proper type' of flexibility developed (1974: 33).

These sentiments are echoed by others' writing in very different contexts about organizational flexibility, such as Herbert Kaufman (2007/1971) and Stephen Holmes (2009). Kaufman, for instance, argues in his classic The Limits of Organizational Change, that 'flexibility' can become a talisman or 'hurrah word' detached from a realistic understanding of the attributes necessary for the securing of an organization's purpose or 'core tasks'. As he puts it,

> For one thing, organizational flexibility is not unequivocally beneficial; it, too, entails risks to survival. For another, survival means the maintenance of many established behavioural and structural patterns; organized entities are essentially lasting patterns of these kinds. If many prevailing patterns in a given organization are disrupted, the organization loses its form and character, its identity, it's very existence as an ongoing entity. (Kaufman, 2007: xi)

In so doing, the purposes which it has been instituted to pursue are thereby placed in question. This was evidenced, acutely in Wedel's (2004, 2009) studies of 'flex' organizations in Eastern Europe, and elite circles in US foreign policy making.

Similarly, Stephen Holmes (2009: 303–304), in his discussion of the relation between formality and flexibility in the so-called War on Terror, argues that rules 'do not function always and exclusively as disabling restraints, binding our hands; they can also serve as steadying guidelines, focusing our aim, and reminding us of long-term objectives and collateral dangers that might otherwise slip from view in the flurry of unfolding events'. Deploying examples derived from the conduct of hospital emergency room personnel, Holmes (2009: 302), suggests that a regimented adherence to pre-existing rules in emergency circumstances is key to flexibility in those situations, rather than its antithesis.[3]

Thus, in contrast to the assumptions animating the customary view including Mintzberg's account of the professional bureaucracy, and as we now seek to indicate with our case study of the response of Danish hospitals to COVID-19, Brown, Kaufman, and Holmes's arguments have considerable plausibility.

[3] As Holmes (2009: 302) puts it, 'Emergency-room doctors and nurses are not the only professionals who, when faced with a disorienting crisis, limit discretion and abjure gut reactions, embracing instead a strict adherence to rules and protocols that provide them with a kind of artificial "cool head"'.

Bureaucratic Responsiveness in Danish Hospitals During the Pandemic

In the following, we examine the organization of emergency responses at a large Danish university hospital in the first months of the COVID-19 pandemic. Compared to Southern Europe, the UK, and neighboring Sweden, Denmark went through the first wave of the pandemic relatively unscathed. The first incident of COVID-19 on Danish soil was identified on March 10 2020, and in the beginning of April, the first wave peaked with a maximum of 535 hospitalizations (April 1) and 153 intensive care admissions (April 2) (Danish Health Authority, 2020). Subsequently, the pandemic stabilized and at the beginning of June, less than 100 patients were hospitalized with COVID-19. Until after the peak, the hospitals prepared for the worst. Based on reports from hospitals, the health authorities estimated on March 23 that a total of 940 intensive care beds for COVID-19 patients could be prepared through massive hospital reorganizations and retraining of staff. The infection pressures were somewhat unevenly distributed among Denmark's five regions with most infected in the Capital Region, and relatively less in the remaining regions (Danish Regions, 2020). The University hospital at the heart of our study is located in one of these lesser affected regions. However, while it ended up facing a manageable amount of COVID cases, this did not affect the emergency planning and responsiveness needed in the beginning of the pandemic, where the hospital prepared for the worst scenarios while also dealing with constant new guidelines and instructions from the health authorities. As previously indicated, the following analysis is based on interviews with four members of the hospital's Emergency Response Team, including the emergency response manager (Sarah) and the chief physicians of intensive care unit (Gitte), the infectious disease department (John) and the emergency department (Peter).

The chief physician of the emergency department, Peter, provides a concrete example of the responsiveness needed in hospital organization in the early days of the COVID-19 outbreak. At one point in March, the Danish Health Authorities decided that patients with symptoms of the virus could no longer be seen by their general practitioner (GP) but had to go through the hospital route. For the University hospital, this meant that they had to be able to receive patients from approximately 800 GPs almost overnight. As Peter puts it:

> The acute-COVID clinic – which was to receive the patients that the GP sent us – we got that established within one day. Over the course of two days, we got it staffed so that we had a staff-schedule for two months. We then created space in the emergency department by moving the emergency room physically as well as the somatic emergency patients, so we increased capacity. We did that in a week.

To understand this capacity to change, we must look to the hospital's emergency response organization, and especially to how this organization was able to secure a rapid response through characteristics such as planning, formalization, division of labor and an in-built flexibility and discretion in the set-up of the response to fit the particular emergency in question.

The Emergency Response Team

In the beginning of February, more than one month before the first Danish patient had been identified, the emergency response manager, Sarah, wrote an email to hospital management and recommended a Level 1 activation of the hospital's Emergency Response Team (ERT). 'Here we are actually not activated yet but we gather the team and make sure to keep everybody informed and ready' she explains. The Emergency Response Team is a pre-constituted entity that consists of a representative from the hospital management (one of four hospital directors), the emergency response manager, the emergency response coordinator, the Press Officer, chief physicians from the emergency ward and the anesthetic ward, and the manager from the technical department. This pre-established team is then supplemented with ad-hoc members selected in relation to the particular type of crisis, which adds a flexibility to the otherwise fixed and pre-determined structure. In the weeks that followed, ad-hoc members were identified and brought in, including the chief physicians from the infectious disease ward and the intensive care unit, the operations manager from the product supply unit, the chair of the Hygiene Committee (who also represented the biochemical department), and some staff lawyers. In the beginning of March, still before the first confirmed Danish COVID-case, the team was activated at Level 3, which meant they were operative and thereby temporally took over central decision-making responsibilities from the hospital's traditional line-management structure (that is dependent on the involvement of the hospital's approx. 50 head of clinics, and various types of decision-making forums, for instance). The team met every day including at the weekends and had a fixed agenda for each meeting. Peter, the chief physician of the emergency ward, describes the relationship between the typical hospital organization and the emergency response organization like this:

> Generally, I think hospitals are a little conservative. Confident that they are doing the right thing, even if they are doing the same thing as yesterday. But emergency response management is something you activate when you have a situation that needs to be handled here and now. Here at the hospital we chose to activate the emergency team, when we could see that COVID-19 was on its way and probably would hit Denmark as well. We gathered the group very early on and started to look at the challenges and make the preparatory efforts. This meant that we declared the hospital in a state of emergency, of course at a low level, because the disease was not here yet. But the idea is that the emergency response organization is able to handle change very quickly, because we bypass the usual decision-making process: The hospital had to adjust to the requirement from the Danish Health Authority; we initially planned 150 intensive care beds, and several hundred COVID-beds; and we decided on how to adjust the emergency room in order to receive all the many infected patients. For all of this to happen, we needed an organization that was maneuverable and energetic, avoiding the super-thought phenomenon that we experience in everyday life where decision-making processes take a very long time.

Peter's depiction of hospitals as traditionally exhibiting a conservative ethos through slow and democratic decision-making processes is not far from Mintzberg's description of the professional bureaucracy. However, with the formal activation of emergency plans and the pre-constituted emergency organization, this traditional slowness is temporarily substituted with agility and responsiveness. One reason for the agility of the Emergency Response Team is the low number of people involved in the decision-making. Peter explains that with this temporary decision-making structure some people, who are normally part of the decision-chain, are not included: 'it is obvious, that when we establish an emergency response organization like this, we will step on someone's toes, because we do not have time to involve everyone'. However, the general impression from our interviewees is that the healthcare professionals accepted the new management organization and its authority to bypass some of the traditional decision-making forums and procedures because it was believed to be necessary. As Peter explains:

> In the beginning, nobody objected because everybody could see that we needed to act. And this agility and the power to act was a little intoxicating throughout the organization, right? Now we just do what is needed, because otherwise we risk being left with a dysfunctional hospital that is not properly prepared. (…) One could of course disagree with different initiatives, but people just did what they were told. If you are not capable of doing that, then you are not aware of your responsibility as an emergency hospital – and this goes especially for those of us who are in the trauma centre. We are the backbone of emergency preparedness in relation to single incidents, but certainly also when it is something big, like this.

In line with this description, the emergency response manager Sarah describes how emergency response management has certain advantages in terms of giving orders and expecting them to be followed:

> You can be somewhat militaristic. That is, you do not need to discuss things, you can just impose tasks on people and then expect them to be solved. And that goes for all levels – equally the management level and the clinical level, right? There is an extreme readiness throughout the organization, when we say emergency. And that is also the reason I say that it cannot be approached as an emergency situation for long, because then we draw the energy out of it.

Both Sarah and Peter emphasize how important it is to go back to traditional line management as soon as possible. In line with the argument of Herbert Kaufman that flexibility is not always beneficial, they are acutely aware that the organization can only be in a state of emergency for a limited period.

Emergency Response Between Rules and Flexibility

The hospital's emergency response was characterized by a very large degree of formalization in terms of the pre-constituted Emergency Response Team, the pre-defined activation levels, pre-described emergency response plans, and so on. In line with Brown's proposition that formality and rigidity are often a precondition for flexibility, the formalization of the emergency response was part of the answer as to why it was so swiftly, effectively and authoritatively activated. It established a clear line of command and delegated discretion and responsibility for decision-making to specific roles in the organization—also within top management:

> We have a very, very strong hospital management, which consists of four very equal hospital directors. The fact that you could call it an emergency also helped them, that's my guess, because then they knew who 'had it'. Namely, the one who was already part of the Emergency Response Team. So also for that reason, it was very important to define it as an emergency situation because then they knew who was responsible. (Sarah, Emergency Response Manager)

The formalization was also visible in something as mundane as the minutes written to document the meetings in the Emergency Response Team. As argued by Peter:

> It is well documented, what we have done. The minutes are there. And the administration got a very unusual recognition for this job, because it was so significant to document the decisions that were made, so we can go back to them and know what we decided.

As already indicated it is important to notice how the formalization of the emergency response also left room for flexibility, discretion and adaption to the situation at hand, for instance in the establishment of the emergency response team which consisted of, as described earlier, a permanent core plus members selected in relation to the particular emergency situation. The same type of situational adaptation is characterizing for the emergency response plans. When we ask Sarah what she had learned from the COVID-19 situation so far, she answers:

> When I look at our emergency response plans, they are actually not very well described. There are some things we choose not to describe in detail because we think it would be a disadvantage. For some types of emergencies, we need much detail, but with a pandemic it is different because it is not time-critical and unannounced to the same degree. We have to describe major accidents with a large degree of detail, because everything can happen within the first one or two hours. But with an emergency that

> comes rolling, and where we have time to prepare, here it is probably much better that we take as our starting point the exact incident, so we can make a proper plan. Otherwise, we have to make an entire organization unlearn what they think they are supposed to do. Then we later have to say: "We will not do it like we have trained this time, because this pandemic is very different from the last one". So, there might well be something about the organization of our emergency response that needs to be described more clearly, but I am quite pleased that we did not have a detailed plan for where to establish the isolation-areas, for instance. Nobody would even have had the imagination to make plans for as many patients as we calculated with in the beginning. With this flexibility, we could make a plan that provided us with a good solution for the particular situation.

Once again, then, we see that formalization in the organizational set-up does not rule out flexibility and discretion in the design of the emergency response. As Brown and Holmes have indicated, bureaucratic rules and formalization are not antithetical to adaptability but rather its presupposition. One reason for this is that formalization does not necessarily entail standardization, a one-size-fits-all attitude or that every task is explicitly and precisely specified (Brown, 1974: 33). Rather, bureaucratic rules and office-holding might define the bounds within which discretion and flexibility can be exercised—or included in planning or design—in order to secure situated and case-based responses when needed (Du Gay & Pedersen, 2020; Pedersen, 2018).

Division of Labor and the Authority of Expertise and Office

Another reason for the agility and responsiveness of the hospital had to do with the way responsibility was delegated through the hierarchical authority of expertise and office—what Brown termed the formalized 'executive system'. Peter describes the efficiency of the Emergency Response Team, as well as its authority in the organization, as being intimately connected to the composition of the group:

> It is a small group with the strongest professional insight and one which knows the hospital in such a way that they can see where the opportunities lie to create, for example, more isolation areas, separate entrances to the emergency room, and convert operating rooms into intensive care rooms. All the knowledge needed to move in the right direction must be present in the group. These people have to be part of the group and take on part of

the responsibility, so that when you look at the Emergency Response Team, the rest of the hospital will think, "well, the people who have the most experience and knowledge are members, and they choose this solution, then it must be the right solution".

The authority of the Emergency Response Team, it seems, was granted equally because of expertise and the nature of the office occupied by those in charge. As Gitte—the hospital's relatively newly appointed chief physician of the intensive care unit—indicates when we ask her to highlight lessons learned from the COVID-19 experience:

Gitte: 'Then I would say that there is something…well you create an emergency team. You gather them because each has a specific role or function. I'm there because I'm the chief physician of the intensive care unit. The others are there because they are chief physicians. We are gathered, not because of who we are as individuals but because of our jobs and, then, we can actually solve the task (…) It might not have been in my job description that I should prepare for a major emergency, but when you are met with trust from your base then it actually works out to be surprisingly efficient. (…)

Interviewer: Your base?

Gitte: Although I'm new here at the ward I'm met with trust from the personnel, but also from the wider hospital organization that is, the hospital management and other wards and their management. You are confident that the people who occupy these positions, can solve this task, also if they are new in the job'

Interviewer: Where does this trust come from do you think?

Gitte: Well I do not think that it is coincidental that some are chief physicians and some are not. We are used to being presented with certain issues and pretty quickly consider for or against (...) So there is something about the position but also something in the hierarchical system. That if the chief physician of the infectious disease department or clinical microbiology department says it, then we can count on it. That's how the usual hierarchy works here. It also goes for me: 'even though she is new this Gitte, she probably has it under control'.

Although, then, the traditional line-management structure of bureaucratic decision-making within the hospital is temporarily put on hold during the emergency organization, the authority of decision-making is still based on the role or office, and their associated status, occupied by those within the bureaucratic hierarchy characteristic of the hospital's normal organization. This is also evident in the fact that certain parts of the decision-making chain are working as usual, as Gitte describes in relation to her plan for the massive reorganization and expansion of the intensive care unit in order to make space for the possible intake of COVID-patients.

Gitte: 'We made the plan and got it approved by the hospital management. We just needed them to say ok. (…) We said: "We suggest that we organize it like this, in these steps and"…and they then said "okay".

Interviewer: You are laughing – why?

Gitte: Because when I say it now, it sounds a bit funny how it just worked out like that. You asked earlier whether any of our already established systems worked. Well, there have been some structures and paths for making decisions. We have department management and hospital management, and this very clear command route was followed in relation to planning our emergency response. What has changed is not so much the command routes but the speed and the will to execute.'

As is evident here, the responsiveness of the organization was to a large degree based on an existing bureaucratic executive system, with an established division of labor and responsibility to people and groups in the organization, that then acted with a fairly large degree of discretion in relation to handling the crisis. In this way, as Brown indicated (1974: 33), hierarchy is not inherently undynamic. Rather, hierarchy can effectively and legitimately delegate authority, responsibility and decision-making capacity to organizational roles that exhibit the expertise and competences needed for creative problem-solving. This was also evident in an organizational initiative introduced by the Emergency Response Team in the early weeks of the COVID-19 crisis, namely what they called Pandora Groups: a selection of experts appointed to work on a particular problem with a set deadlines for coming up with a workable plan. Groups were established for organizing the patient flow in the emergency department, the nursing resources, protective equipment, and so on. Peter explains:

> The advantage of a Pandora Group is that someone with a particular type of expertise are given a task to solve. They then involve whoever they need to solve it and then they come back with a plan. When they return with a plan, it is the one you go with and communicate out. And then you dissolve the group.

Likewise, questions of expertise, training and experience were dominant in decisions about the reorganization of the hospital and not least the retraining of personnel who were to take on new roles. Here, decisions were made on the basis of experience with similar types of tasks, skills and patient groups. For instance, the personnel trained to work with infectious diseases had obvious advantages. As the head physician of the infectious diseases ward, John, explains:

> There are two important things to be mentioned. It is partly the technical training in handling protective equipment and dressing and undressing and stuff like that. And then there is the more mental part of it: 'I'm not afraid to be here'. That means a lot. Therefore, they can adjust relatively quickly to this group of patients.

Another important competence is routine in emergency response, as stressed by Holmes (2009). As Gitte explains when describing the retraining of her personnel at the intensive care unit:

> The personnel group I work with, the intensive care nurses and physicians, they are used to acuteness. They are used to act. 'Well okay then, we will do this. We have to solve it'. They are, routinely actually, used to take care of acute situations. I think that makes it much easier.

While all of our interviewees agree with some amount of pride that the emergency response of the hospital was efficient, well-functioning and incredibly swift, they also identify different kinds of problems. Interestingly, these are especially problems related to unclear lines of command and frames for operating. As Sarah explains, such problems have been particularly evident in the shift from the emergency response organization and back to traditional line management.

> Well a main problem was connected to our existing hospital management's ability to inform us about the framework within which we could act. It was not always optimal. So I was fencing a bit in the wild and said, well, if you do not tell me what the framework is, then it's not easy to be operational, right? (...) but at the end of week twelve [March 16-22], I held a meeting with our hospital director and said that we should either stay in the emergency response organization or go back to normal line-organization, because right now we stand with one foot in each place, and that is not working. Either we are operational or not. Then we decided that we should return to normal line-organization as soon as possible.

Thus, not unlike Perrow's statement that the 'sin' of bureaucracy is a consequence of the failure to bureaucratize sufficiently, and Brown's argument that 'informality' is not the best friend of adaptability, it seems that problems of responsiveness can here be linked to a failure of formalizing and bureaucratizing sufficiently in the transition between one management system to another.

Discussion and Concluding Remarks

As we have had cause to note, a customary and enduring criticism of bureaucracy as a rule-infused hierarchical form of organization concerns its presumed inability to be adaptive to changes in its environment and thus to be inherently inefficient, unresponsive, inflexible, and uncreative in times of emergency. In addition to being described as inflexible, the professional bureaucracy specifically has been represented as containing a problem of coordination and of discretion that add to the idea of an organizational form that is not able to act effectively in response to crisis. In this chapter, we have challenged this common critique of bureaucracy by arguing that as an organizational form, bureaucracy is both capable of rule and response and that formality can be, and often is, a precondition for flexibility and responsiveness. Empirically, we have discussed a Danish University hospital's emergency response during COVID-19 to support and develop our proposition. During the early days of the pandemic, the hospital organization showed a remarkable ability to act swiftly and effectively when needed. This agility was directly linked to the emergency response of the hospital—a highly formalized and largely planned exercise, based on clear hierarchies and decision-making structures. But also an exercise that allowed for flexible and situation-based decision-making not least through the bureaucratic division of labor and hierarchical delegation of responsibility based on role-based expertise and office-holding within an established executive system. This response suggests that the arguments concerning the relationship between formality and flexibility we developed from the work of Brown, Kaufman, and Holmes's do indeed have some clear plausibility and can contribute to studies of organizing care in a COVID-19 context.

Without wishing to over-extend the explanatory power or reach of our analysis, it is nonetheless worth stating, by way of concluding our chapter, that the ongoing and widespread repudiation of bureaucracy as a formal organizing device, can have profound real-world effects, both in occluding the remarkable successes bureaucracies have and continue to achieve in any number of organized contexts, and in disappearing it as an organizational option to be deployed to confront 'wicked' public governance challenges, for instance. As Hadas (2020) has argued, echoing our analysis, while 'it's easy to mock faceless, rule-bound bureaucracies', this criticism is deeply unfair, 'particularly from those who enjoy modern comforts. As the coronavirus spreads around the world, millions of people are belatedly learning the virtues' of bureaucratic capacity, for the evidence emerging from cross-national comparisons suggest that those states with well-functioning bureaucracies are considerably more adept at dealing with COVID-19 than those without such capacities. As Hadas puts it, crises such as pandemics

> put terrible strains on medical systems and disrupt normal economic activity. Only government bureaucracies have the power and competence to respond. The Herculean labour of administrative agents cannot succeed without firm political leadership. Yet the politics are not supportive. Strong, popular and bureaucratically savy leaders are in short supply. U.S. President Donald Trump and British Prime Minister Boris Johnson seem to prefer Weber's charismatic leadership, and owe much of their electoral success to anti-bureaucratic rhetoric. (XX)

This echoes points made by Lodge and Wagrich (2014) and Zacka (2017) in their discussions of the essential role of public bureaucracies in confronting governance challenges in the EU and the United States, respectively. As Zacka, argued, shortly after the election of Donald

Trump to the Presidency of the United States in 2016, public bureaucracy began to enjoy a reversal of fortune. Almost overnight, its image was transformed from being seen as a thorn in the side of government to something akin to its saving grace. In the space of a few days following Trump's inauguration, the media was full of accounts detailing how bureaucracy and bureaucrats could serve as a bulwark against populism (Zacka, 2017: 4). The very attributes of governmental bureaucracy that had earned it condemnation from across the political spectrum—its alleged inertia, red-tape mentality, and lack of responsiveness to political control—suddenly became virtues. To these current tropes about the indispensability of well-functioning public bureaucracies to the constitution and preservation of civil security and peace, and to the individual and collective liberties that derive from this (Byrkjeflot & du Gay, 2012; du Gay, 2000), we add in this chapter an appreciation of the bureaucratic ethos in supporting swift and effective emergency responses in large formal organizations, such as hospitals. As our case study shows, in major emergencies, there is not necessarily a tension between rule-bound and office-based organizational conduct and the resilience and adaptation needed in order for crisis management to be creative, swift and well-functioning. Rather, bureaucracy can function as the precondition for the delivery of safe and appropriate care even during emergencies such as the COVID-19 crisis.

References

Adler, P. S., Goldoftas, B., & Levine, D. I. (1999). Flexibility versus efficiency? A case study of model changeovers in the Toyota production system. *Organization Science, 10*(1), 43–68.

Bigley, G. A., & Roberts, K. H. (2001). The incident command system: High-reliability organizing for complex and volatile task environments. *Academy of Management Journal, 44*(6), 1281–1299.

Byrkjeflot, H., & du Gay, P. (2012). Bureaucracy: An idea whose time has come (again)? *Research in the Sociology of Organizations, 35*, 85–109.

Briscoe, F. (2007). From iron cage to iron shield? How bureaucracy enables temporal flexibility for professional service workers. *Organization Science, 18*(2), 297–314.

Brown, W. (1965). *Exploration in management*. Penguin.

Brown, W. (1974). *Organization*. Penguin.

Bunderson, J. S., & Boumgarden, P. (2010). Structure and learning in self-managed teams: Why "bureaucratic" teams can be better learners. *Organization Science, 21*(3), 609–624.

Danish Health Authority. (2020, June 9). COVID-19 i Danmark: Status 15. *Epidemiuge*. Sundhedsstyrelsen.

Danish Regions. (2020, August 14). Regionernes erfaringer med omstilling af kapacitet. *Notat*. Danske Regioner

Du Gay, P. (2000). *In praise of bureaucracy*. Sage.

Du Gay, P. (2009). Max Weber and the ethics of office. In P. Adler (Ed.), *Oxford handbook of sociology and organizational studies: Classical foundations* (pp. 146–173). Oxford University Press.

Du Gay, P., & Pedersen, K. Z. (2020) Discretion and bureaucracy. In T. Evans & P. Hupe (Eds.), *Discretion and the quest for controlled freedom* (pp. 221–236). Palgrave Macmillan.

Goodsell, C. T. (2005). The bureau as unit of governance. In P. du Gay (Ed.), *The values of bureaucracy*. Oxford University Press.

Hadas, E. (2020). *Good bureaucracy is a ultimate virus slayer*. Reuters Breakingviews. Accessed at https://www.reuters.com/article/us-health-corononavirus-breakingviews-idUSKBN20R25R

Holmes, S. (2009). In case of emergency: Misunderstanding tradeoffs in the war on terror. *California Law Review, 92*(2), 301–356.

Kaufman. (2007/1971). *The limits of organizational change* (3rd ed.). Routledge

Klein, K. J., Ziegert, J. C., Knight, A. P., & Xiao, Y. (2006). Dynamic delegation: Shared, hierarchical, and deindividualized leadership in extreme action teams. *Administrative Science Quarterly, 51*(4), 590–621.

Lodge, M., & Wagrich. M. (2014, April 23). *Bureaucracy may be the solution not the problem, for issues of European Governance*. blogs.lse.ac.uk. Accessed at https://blogs.lse.ac.uk/europpblog/2014/04/23/bureaucracy-may-be-the-solution-rather-than-the-problem-to-issues-of-european-governance/

March, J. M. (1991). Exploration and exploitation in organizational learning. *Organization Science, 2*(1), 71–87.

Mintzberg, H. (1979). *The structuring of organizations: A synthesis of the research*. Prentice Hall.

Pedersen, K. Z. (2018). *Organizing patient safety: Failsafe fantasies and pragmatic practices*. Series: Health, Technology and Society. Palgrave Macmillan.

Perrow, C. (1960). *Authority, goals and prestige in a general hospital* (PhD thesis). University of California.

Perrow, C. (1967). Hospitals: Technology, structure and goals. In J. G. March (Ed.), *Handbook of organization*. Rand McNally.

Perrow, C. (2014/1972). *Complex organizations: A critical essay* (3rd ed.). Echo Point Books.

Stark, A. (2014). Bureaucratic values and resilience: An exploration of crisis management adaptation. *Public Administration, 92*(3), 692–706.

Stinchcombe, A. (2001). *When formality works: Authority and abstraction in law and organizations*. University of Chicago Press.

Waugh, W. L., Jr., & Streib, G. (2006). Collaboration and leadership for effective emergency management. *Public Administration Review, 66*(Special Issue), 131–140.

Weber, M. (1978). *Economy and society: Vols I and II*. University of California Press.

Weber, M. (1989). Science as a vocation. In P. Lassman & I. Velody (Eds.), *Max Weber's AQ4 science as a vocation*. Unwin Hyman.

Weber, M. (1994). *Weber: Political writings* (P. Lassman & R. Speirs, Eds.). Cambridge University Press.

Weick, K. E. (1993). The collapse of sensemaking in organizations: The Mann Gulch disaster. *Administrative Science Quarterly, 38*, 628–652.

Zacka, B. (2017). *When the state meets the street: Public service and moral agency*. The Belknap Press of Harvard University Press.

CHAPTER 6

Dancing with a Virus: Finding New Rhythms of Organizing and Caring in Dutch Hospitals

Iris Wallenburg, Bert de Graaff, Jenske Bal, Martijn Felder, and Roland Bal

Introduction

When COVID-19 hit the Netherlands early March 2020, it was first tried to stop the outbreak at the border of 'the Great Rivers', separating the southern regions (Limburg and North Brabant) from the rest of the country. Against the backdrop of the fast and worldwide expansion of the virus outbreak, this, however, proved a hopeless endeavor—although the upper north experienced a much lower number of infections as it benefitted from stringent government measures that were taken to 'flatten the curve' in order to protect the healthcare system from an overflow of severely ill patients (Bal et al., 2020; Wallenburg, Jeurissen, et al., 2020). In the course of March, general hospital care was more or less dispelled by COVID care and hospitals turned into crisis-organizations: non-emergency care was postponed, nursing wards turned into COVID

I. Wallenburg (✉) · B. de Graaff · J. Bal · M. Felder · R. Bal
Erasmus School of Health Policy and Management, Erasmus University Rotterdam, Rotterdam, The Netherlands
e-mail: wallenburg@eshpm.eur.nl

J. Waring et al. (eds.), *Organising Care in a Time of Covid-19*, Organizational Behaviour in Healthcare,
https://doi.org/10.1007/978-3-030-82696-3_6

wards, and general practitioners (GPs) and nursing homes sought to keep hospital referrals at a minimum to soften the pressure on hospitals. Hospitals moreover faced a shrinking stock of personal protection equipment (PPE) and medical technical equipment (especially ventilators) (de Graaff et al., 2020). In the last weekend of March, hospitals in the south started to overflow nevertheless, sending out alarming requests to take over patients. A national and army-led coordination center was established to coordinate the redistribution of infected patients and equipment and to prepare for a possible worsening of the situation; one in which even more patients would need intensive care treatment. In the following weeks, the curve, however, flattened. Experts warned for a lack of non-COVID care, stating that lives were lost due to lack of regular care provision (i.e., cardiovascular treatment, diabetes care, cancer treatment). They stated that hospitals should prepare for dual care provision ('COVID and non-COVID care'), which would perhaps fluctuate over time following the yet unknown rhythm of the virus outbreak and development of clinical knowledge.

In this chapter, we study how hospitals in the Netherlands engaged in organizing and delivering care during the first months of the COVID-19 outbreak. We build on an extensive (and ongoing) ethnographic study in one university hospital that plays a key role in the Dutch COVID crisis.[1] As embedded researchers, we have been able to study the crisis 'from within'. In addition, we conducted semi-structured interviews with nurses in four other hospital setting to gain a better understanding of daily hospital practices. We use the metaphor of 'the dance' to show and reflect on how healthcare organizations (including healthcare professionals, managers, patients) have engaged with the virus and its emerging consequences, thereby reconfiguring vested hospital routines, socio-spatial interactions, and rhythms of organizing and providing care.

The analogy of the dance is appealing as it comprehends elements of rhythm, space, relationality, movement, and time; aspects that were all assembled in the organizational response to the virus outbreak. Dance as a metaphor and methodology has gained ground in the organization- and management literature in the past two decades (Chandler, 2011, e.g. Biehl, 2019; Hujala et al., 2016). It draws attention to the embodied

[1] We have also closely followed one of the safety regions in which this hospital is located. While our analysis is also informed by this data, we did not use it explicitly for this paper.

and relational practices of collaborative action, 'connecting spaces and contexts and each other, "leading" and 'following' and making sense of the spaces in-between' (Biehl, 2019: 20). In this paper, we use the analogy of the dance to envision how hospital organizations have sought to *move with* the virus in a fluid and open-ended manner, as a kind of modern choreography in which actions are emerging and improvised, responding to how other people and 'things' (not the least the virus itself) behave (Biehl, 2019). We use the dance analogy specifically to affectively describe how hospitals have engaged in finding situated solutions to emerging and often uncertain organizational and practical issues through improvising and creating new strategies and routines, and how rhythms and (inter)actions changed as the crisis unfolded.

Dancing Organizations

We adopt the definition of dance coined by Ortmann and Sydow (2018: 903). They apply dancing as a metaphor for '*moving with ease and facility, partly playing by, partly deviating from, the old rules and creating new ones as well.*' In doing so, Ortmann and Sydow use the notion of dance to envision the creativity of organizations working within self- and externally imposed constraints. Dancing, they argue, is about '*taking steps, turning around, moving (parts of) the body, improvising and relating to others following conventions and rhythm*' (p. 909). In organization science, the analogy of the dance is used to understand the dynamic, fleeting, and invisible structures of interaction in organizations and how they are negotiated and transformed (Biehl, 2017). It enables to foreground aspects of movement, appearance, and emotion, often in relation to the unknown. The metaphor of the dance draws attention to the rhythms, complex movements, and affective interactions in space and time. Dance also includes the material environment and how actors move through and alter space (Merriman, 2010). In doing so, it transcends the often-used metaphor of organizational improvisation (e.g., Weick, 1998) that focuses on the coordination of 'normal' and temporarily disrupted organizational procedures and rhythms, connecting 'clock time' (as a linear process) with 'event time'; an often sudden and temporal disruption of the normal order (e.g., Crossan et al., 2005; Orlikowski & Yates, 2002). This is particularly relevant in case of a virus that is unstable, invisible, and enduring. In a recent publication, and referring to the Ebola outbreak (a more often used comparison to COVID-19) Shrum et al. (2020)

depict the Ebola virus as a 'fire object' that generates fear because of its invisibility and possible presence, transforming spaces and humans (as well as 'stuff'—e.g., in the Netherlands some hospitals have forbidden postcards as these may carry the virus) in indeterminate dangers. The importance of moving through space, and the architectural features of (transforming) space into an (un)healthy place, has also been explained in the medical sociological literature. Recently, Brown et al. (2020) have shown how patients suffering from cystic fibrosis (CF) move through a hospital building to avoid physical contact with other CF patients (who carry other resistant bacteria) and how the building is (re)arranged to enable physical distancing to prevent (life threatening) cross infection. The authors reveal the politics of windows and air to show how dangers are accommodated in everyday hospital practice. In the case of COVID-19, we will demonstrate in this paper, the architecture of the hospital is part of the dance as well, as hospitals seek to facilitate a smooth transfer of patients from one department or hospital to another to optimize capacity and regulate work pressure among the medical and nursing staff, while also attempting to protect patients (and themselves) from contamination with the new and hardly known virus. Rather than a clearly scripted choreography of moving and acting, the uncertainties and different rhythms of care involved—e.g., due to the lack of knowledge about (the spread of) the virus and related diseases as well as adequate treatment; the nature and risk of cross infection; and financial uncertainties—require experimentation and improvisation at different organizational layers.

Building on running research projects and close contact in the field, we were able to quickly set up an empirical study when the crisis unfolded.[2] The ethnographic research in the university hospital started on March 5, 2020, just after the hospital had identified their first COVID patient and right before the first Dutch COVID fatality was reported. We engaged in non-participatory observation of policy-meetings on the level of the hospital boards, the staff, and the regional level (210 hours). We furthermore conducted 29 interviews with key actors and analyzed numerous

[2] Our research in the university hospital started directly after having received permission of the Board of Directors on March 4, 2020. Informed consent for observing meetings was derived always explicitly through the Board. Consent for interviews was obtained in writing from all respondents, and with some of our data being difficult to anonymize, quotes were approved by respondents before publication. Our research has been approved by our institutional ethical review board (reference IRB2020-08 Bal WMO, 25/03/20 and IRB 20-13 Felder, 08/05/2020).

internal documents (protocols, guidelines, notes of meetings). In the summer, when the crisis had slowed down, we organized three meetings in which we reflected on preliminary findings with key informants. Next to this specific hospital case, we approached nurse managers and nurses in four other hospitals in the Netherlands. Six of them were willing to keep a diary of their experiences working with COVID patients. Seven other nurses did not keep a diary but were willing to be interviewed. All of them were interviewed ($N = 17$ as some respondents were interviewed various times). We asked them about their role and the impact of the crisis on care provision and how hospitals organized and accounted for the care delivered.

The fieldwork in the university hospital and the diaries and interviews with nurses provided us with an elaborate dataset which we analyzed iteratively by moving back-and-forth between the data itself and the literature (i.e., organization studies and dance theory) (Timmermans & Tavory, 2012). Based on this analysis, we aim to provide a layered and in-depth account of how hospital organizations improvised and established new organizational rhythms of organizing and providing care in uncertain times.

The Hospital/Acute Care Setting in the Netherlands

The Dutch healthcare system is usually defined as a social insurance system. It has a strong corporatist tradition in which the state highly depends on private healthcare providers and professional associations for the provision of care. In 2006, a system of regulated competition has been introduced to enhance competition among insurers as well as healthcare providers in order to enhance efficiency and quality of care (Bal & Zuiderent-Jerak, 2011; Helderman et al., 2005). However, the Dutch healthcare system is a layered system (van de Bovenkamp et al., 2014), in which 'the healthcare market' operates next to, and intermingles with, other institutional arrangements. This became highly visible in governing the COVID-19 outbreak (Wallenburg, Helderman, et al., 2021).

A setting important to this study is acute care provision that is organized at the regional level, and which more or less exists next to the model of regulated competition (although, as we will demonstrate in this paper, they also intermingle). Acute care provision (i.e., ambulance services, emergency departments, ICUs) is organized in 11 regions, directed by

Regional Acute Care Coordination units (in Dutch: Regionaal Overleg Acute Zorg, or ROAZ). Acute care regions cover both primary and hospital care and play an important coordinating role across healthcare providers that remain autonomous nevertheless. In the COVID crisis, the ROAZ has played a central role in coordinating care in the region, as well as in organizing collaboration with other regions through the National Network of Acute Care Regions.

Next to the ROAZ, which is focused on healthcare, Safety Regions are institutionalized in (geographic) infrastructures to foster public safety. In the Netherlands, 25 Safety Regions exist. They are usually presided by the mayor of the biggest town in the region. Based on the Public Health Act, a Safety Region can call on different 'crisis levels' corresponding with different levels of incidence in the region. In doing so, a Safety Region can centralize decision-making power when incidence levels are rising. During the COVID-19 crisis, all Safety Regions were (and, at the time of writing, still are) in level four, which means that decision-making is largely centralized on a regional level. National coordination between the Safety Regions occurs through the Safety Council.

At the national level much decision-making has also been centralized, with the Prime Minister's cabinet being in the lead, together with the Minister of Health and the Minister of Justice & Safety. A national Management Outbreak Team (OMT), led by the director of the infection prevention unit of the National Institute of Public Health and largely consisting of medical experts, advises the Prime Minister. Responding to the Dutch public debate (e.g., RVS, 2020) and to reports that have been published during the summer on a decline in public acceptance of stringent measures, the cabinet has endeavored to broaden the scope of the experts included in their advisory committees, like social scientists. However, when infection rates went up again after the summer, resulting in a second wave and with a probable third wave ahead, policy focus has again increasingly narrowed on curbing the spread of the virus again (Wallenburg, Helderman, et al., 2021).

Findings: Dancing with a Virus

We present our findings following the unfolding dance in the (early) spring and summer of 2020. In the first instance, hospitals were at risk of becoming overwhelmed with severely ill and (perhaps) highly infectious patients suffering from yet unknown diseases. In this first but rather short phase (3–4 weeks, of which central actors said 'it felt like months') of immediate crisis, our participants 'learned how to dance'. This first phase was followed by a second phase in which a new choreography of organizing and caring emerged in which personnel, spaces, and materials were rearranged through both national and local infrastructures to make optimal use of the available capacity while attempting to mitigate the virus outbreak. We view this process as a 'dance-marathon', as our participants were making long hours, holding on to one-another, building new organizational structures. In this second phase, the ROAZ and the national government took in a more central role in governing hospital care. In the third phase, with the virus slowly under tentative control in the Netherlands, hospitals sought to engage with physical distancing, restarting non-COVID care and preparing for an expected second wave. Whereas the initial moments of the crisis seemed a focused affair, here we find participants' 'dancing to a cacophony' as different voices and rhythms started to intermingle.

Learning to Dance

> We were kind of preparing that week, but we were mostly looking at what was happening over there (...) It was still far away. But that weekend my Italian colleague phoned me, saying that we should start preparing now, that it was much worse than we thought. Until then, we had still been thinking, chatting and planning what to do... (Physician ICU)

The dance started quite unexpectantly. Although physicians had informed themselves about China and (later on) Italy, the virus still seemed far away and something that might fly over. Hospital facility staff members in the university hospital had, however, already noticed a sudden and worrisome decline in the supply of PPEs and medicines from China as well as from southern European countries. The phone call from an Italian colleague the physician above refers to, which took place in the first week of March, made him realize that immediate action should be taken to prepare for an inflow of patients at the intensive care departments. This inflow indeed happened one week later in the south, where people had been celebrating Carnival two weeks before (a tradition in the Netherlands that is mainly restricted to the catholic south). Southern hospitals could not manage this sudden influx of patients, urgently requesting other hospitals to take over some of their patients. When hospitals responded hesitatingly, some patients were put in ambulances and sent out to hospitals in the north:

> I was phoned by an ambulance nurse, saying that they had been circling on the Amsterdam motorway for quite some time, and that they would bring in the patient within 10 minutes. (Hospital manager)

The suggestion to put a severely ill patient in an ambulance without clear destination had been quite unlikely (and perhaps even considered a crime) just a few weeks before, but became real in this first phase of the crisis. It exemplifies the panic that (at least some) hospitals experienced during these first weeks in which they could hardly accommodate the inflow of patients. It made other hospitals realize that they had to act immediately. Some of our respondents recalled how hospital care was rearranged overnight; establishing special COVID wards to take in new patients. A manager recalled how they had first planned to use the isolation rooms for (possible) infected patients, but soon realized that these few rooms would never be enough. They subsequently cleared two nursing departments; cancelling operations and sending patients home or transferring them to other departments. The ward's architecture was furthermore adjusted in order to strictly separate positively tested and possibly positive patients:

> Patients who had tested positive we laid in the back, other patients [who might be infected and awaited test results] were in the front with 1.5 m distance between them and separated with curtains. Both parts (of the nursing ward) were separated by a plastic curtain with a zipper. When a patient appeared positive, (s)he was sent through the plastic curtain to the other side. (Nurse)

Improvisation was key in these first days, involving many uncertainties about treatment and safety. Protocols and guidelines were frequently (i.e., several times a day) 'written and rewritten' (Callon, 2002) to keep up with the latest insights while simultaneously dealing with the increasing problem of lacking test capacity and a quickly diminishing stock of PPEs, especially protective aprons and mouth masks. The threatening lack of protection caused great worries among hospital directors and staff:

> It [the troubles] only became more, more and more… at some point we discussed that we only had face masks for two more days. That was it! Each time I left the [local] OMT, I thought: 'What the f*ck is happening?!'

> Then we decided that we could put two patients in the same room, so we rewrote the protocol. (...) and then finally there was a decrease in the number of new patients. This gave us some air. But I kept on thinking; who [of us] will get sick? We had some infectious disease specialists who were really ill... It all was so very close. (Hospital director 2)

The shortage of PPEs stood central in this first phase in which all actors had to learn to dance with a hardly known virus, threatening the health of patients, nurses, and physicians, as well as the continuity of care. Hospital directors struggled with the severe shortage of PPEs, seeking to use them as efficient as possible. In some hospitals, whole wards were declared 'dirty' so that practitioners could move from one patient to the other without having to change (and hence throw away) disposable cloths; in other hospitals, like the one mentioned in the quote above, single rooms were refurnished to accommodate two patients. In yet others, corridors were declared 'clean', meaning that nurses and physicians had to use more PPEs but also had space where they could pull off protective equipment and have some time 'in between' to relax a bit. Many nurses complained about headaches, and there was a lot of emotion involved as patients passed away suddenly and often in loneliness—visitors were strictly limited due to the danger of cross infection as well as to save PPEs for the staff.

It was heavily discussed who exactly needed to wear PPEs and with what level of protection. At first, healthcare professionals but also cleaners had worn high-level surgical masks offering optimal protection. However, when these masks became scarce, it was decided to 'scale off' and offer a different kind of face mask or to no longer use one at all in specific circumstances (for instance when no patient was around)—causing a lot of fear and frustration among practitioners. In one hospital, nurses resisted a new protocol stating that, following new insights, disposable hats were no longer needed. They insisted on wearing the hats as they felt they deserved optimal protection as they had already put themselves and their loved ones at risk. Being a fire object (Shrum et al., 2020), it was felt that the virus and maybe 'death' could catch them or their loved ones without noticing. Some nurses confessed how they had slept separately from their spouses these first weeks and did no longer hug their children. However, at the same time respondents underscored the solidarity they had experienced, and that it has also been 'a very special time period'. Nurses recalled how hierarchical relationships seemed to disappear, as physicians and nurses had to figure out together how patients responded to treatment, and how and when clinical situations deteriorated and an immediate transfer to the ICU was needed. They furthermore received all kinds of public support—e.g., citizens hang up banners in front of the hospitals thanking 'their heroes', and local shop owners brought in food and presents.

In sum, the music had started abruptly—leaving actors not yet knowing how to dance. Learning to dance involved lots of improvisation (e.g., can PPE be disinfected, and will they then still work?), the redesigning of nursing wards to separate patients and save scarce resources, and clinical reasoning to figure out how to treat patients and protect hospital personnel. This learning involved both situated probing and tinkering (i.e., how to deal with the virus in this hospital?) and collective learning—as almost the whole medical world was involved in uncovering the threatening mystery of the disease. The rhythm of the first wave was quick and unpredictable, rendering it hard to anticipate on a next move. This resulted in collective action at the ward level, the hospital management level, and in the contact with other hospitals (e.g., training films how to pull on protective gear safely were quickly shared among neighboring hospitals) and national agencies.

Dance Marathon—Hanging in There

Respondents all referred to the first weeks as incredibly difficult and tiresome (some worked 24/7, almost literally). Hospital directors and managers struggled with the pressure that was put on the nursing staff[3]:

> The chair is closing the meeting. Yet one of the infectious disease specialists wants to add something. 'We need to organize psychological assistance. A social worker had visited a nursing ward and four of them had started crying immediately'. One of the managers agrees; they are trying to organize things, like serving croquettes.[4] Others underline the heaviness of what's going on. (field notes university hospital)

Hospital directors worried about their healthcare professionals who were put under a lot of pressure, struggling to find some way of offering relief

[3] Interestingly, it's only about the pressure that is put on nurses and not medical doctors, also in the media.

[4] A quite popular snack in the Netherlands.

(like serving snacks, as is suggested in the above). Nurses who had not been trained for ICU care assisted ICU nurses, and medium care nurses and nurses from the operation theater received a speed course in ICU treatment. As a consequence, regular surgeries were canceled, also because ventilators and other technical equipment were needed for the COVID patients. This shift in care provision did not only have clinical and practical consequences, but also impacted on a hospital's financial position as it was unclear if and how COVID care, and the loss of normal care production, would be reimbursed. Hospitals struggled to keep regular care-delivery going. A solution was to divide COVID patients among the hospitals. However, hospitals that treated COVID patients were afraid that regular patients could be lost to other hospitals in the region—underscoring the ongoing competition between hospitals:

> Already at the very first meeting we have been thinking about the post-COVID crisis; we can't turn into a COVID-hospital. We must keep working on our patient portfolio. If we now shift care to [name hospitals], we lose it. (...) We have some hospitals in this region that like to offer more specialized care. We have negotiated about this; who does diabetic care, or transplants. Others [non-university hospitals] won't do the heart transplants, but there still is a grey area they might step in. If they take it now, we won't get it back after the crisis. (Staff member university hospital)

At this point in time (late March, early April), the pressure on hospitals and especially ICU care was reaching a peak. Physician associations as well as politicians in parliament feared a 'Code Black' in which choices had to be made who could go to the ICU (and have a chance to survive) and to whom access would be denied. At the same time, the problems in nursing homes heavily increased. Many residents were infected and died,[5] often through nurses that had to work without PPE, nursing homes did not have enough at stock, and the PPEs that were imported were sent to the hospitals, which was increasingly criticized in the media. To get a grip on the distribution of patients as well as PPEs and technical equipment, and to soften the pressure on some of the hospitals, a national coordination

[5] In this paper we focus on hospitals, which perhaps is a bit painful as we now may make the same choice as policymakers did during this phase of the crisis; not paying enough attention to the severe and rather undefined problems in nursing homes. It would have been interesting to include the nursing homes as the nursing home-hospital discussion is a dance in itself, particularly regarding the use and distribution of PPEs.

center for patient distribution (*Landelijk Coördinatiecentrum Patiënten Spreiding*, or LCPS) was established. The Dutch army was involved in establishing the LCPS, which was located in one of the university hospitals. It aimed to establish a national patient logistic center exceeding local interests:

> It had to be done in a such a short notice. We first had to solve the acute problem in Brabant, as they were overwhelmed with patients. We searched for other spots [in other ICU departments, also across the border in Germany], and asked hospitals to reveal their capacity. That way, we knew where to send the patients. The army and local consultants were involved, and we had it going in just a couple of days. It all happened under a lot of pressure. We started during day time and in the evening, and within a week it was running 24/7. (Hospital director 1)

Staff members of the LCPS requested the numbers of ICU patients of each hospital (COVID and non-COVID) on a daily basis. Based on these numbers, patients were redistributed. Physicians, however, complained that these figures did not meet the real number of patients, and that national bed-coordination was moreover unwanted as they also wanted to keep some space for local citizens that were sent in by their GPs. They admitted to 'save' some spots to have room for patients already admitted to the hospital who might clinically deteriorate, or patients that would be brought to the emergency department late at night.

In short, the eclectic dance of the first weeks turned into a tiring dance marathon in which multiple dances had to be performed at the same time—each with its own rhythm, dancers, and music. Nurses and physicians worked long shifts to care for the increasing number of patients, and gradually became more familiar with the rhythm in which disease symptoms developed. The protocols and guidelines that had been quickly drawn up and endlessly revised in the first phase now guided patient treatment as well as the distribution of patients among hospitals. The dance also involved precarious movement, attempting to mitigate the ongoing crisis by offering help while at the same time protecting the hospital's competitive and financial position as well as care for local citizens; hence seeking to synchronize acute, elective, and future care.

Dancing to a Cacophony

> You can see it in the time line, how the curve was flattening. The week after, you could feel the urgency fading away. Maybe as quick as it had appeared, peacefulness returned. On Monday we thought 'let's see what will happen', and on Wednesday we said 'it's really flattening'. Immediately, the tone was changing. (staff member 2, university hospital)

In the second half of April, the number of admitted COVID patients started to decrease; 'the curve was flattening'—which, until then, had been the main policy concern: mitigating the pressure on the healthcare system (instead of fighting the virus) (Wallenburg, Jeurissen, et al., 2020). As the staff member in the quote above points out, the decreasing number of patients evoked a change of rhythm. Some experienced this as a loss as they had enjoyed the solidarity. Others argued that the high-speed organization was doomed to fail in the long run: '*You can do all this driven by emotion; it provides the energy to keep going. But you can never hang on to it, that would be utopian, I'd say. I don't even think it'll be healthy*' (staff member 3, university hospital).

The tone and rhythm of the music changed. Actors no longer served one main goal, and in the discussions many old and new interests popped up, sometimes as a result of decisions that had been taken in the heat of the moment. A striking example is the opening of a hospital unit in a big events hall that the Safety Region had turned into a shelter for infected patients. The events hall opened just after the peak was reached and hence was no longer necessary. However, after all the preparations and investments the Safety Region had made, the directors of the university hospital felt they had no other option. It was decided to engage in the municipality's initiative, although the events hall remained empty and the consensus was that it would deliver sub-optimal care if a patient was to be admitted. Events like these happened in other regions as well and led to many discussions about responsibility (also financially).

At the same time, a new dance unfolded between regional hospitals about starting up (profitable) non-COVID care while also preparing for the expected second wave of the virus outbreak. Preparations especially concerned scaling up ICU care. The government generously invested in expanding the number of ICU beds, which made it attractive to establish a few more beds:

> The director (and chair of the meeting) stresses the regional agreements that are already in place: the university hospital will scale up with 92 ICU-beds. Yet, other hospitals now want to have 'a few beds more' as well. It is said that scaling up with 2-5 beds per hospital won't make the difference, and that it embarks on plans to employ more nurses. Yet all hospitals seem to want to have their share. The numbers are discussed but are confusing to the participants. One of them points at Hospital X, one of the smaller hospitals in town. 'Increasing the number of ICU-beds will enable them to upgrade their ICU-level' [which would be a significant change in the task division in the acute region]. (field notes university hospital)

A cacophony of voices emerged in this third phase of the crisis, in which 'back to normal' was no option. Hospitals, like the rest of Dutch society, had to deal with national measures like 1.5-metre physical distancing (hampering their goal of increasing regular care provision to treat patients that had more or less been excluded in the months before) and prepared for a new phase in which COVID and non-COVID care had to exist next to each other. Here, 'quick wins' could be made. This is exemplified in the quote above in which the ICU of a small hospital could 'level up' and, through that, employ another ICU physician to enable 24/7 ICU services and, as a result, conduct more complex surgical procedures that require high-level ICU care—also revealing the politics of the COVID hospital crisis.

Whereas especially during the peak of the crisis, work routines as well as expert opinion had been authoritative and more or less unified, flattening the curve seemed to be inversely related to the number and diversity of opinions coming to the fore. Both in the media and in the regional coordination structures, more and more voices were heard, and also explicitly called for (RVS, 2020; Wallenburg, Helderman, et al., 2021). Within the hospitals, different disciplines tried to start up non-COVID care and were calling for attention and resources. Within the Safety Regions, more emphasis was placed on long-term, primary and social care. Here, next to the ROAZ-structure, non-acute care coordination teams were erected. The media, in addition, started staging experts arguing for more and for less stringent measures. Last but not least, in the House of Parliament, the COVID crisis increasingly became politicized, with the opposition calling the leading government parties to account for measures taken. In the cacophony of voices, hospitals still had to function—now serving both COVID and increasingly more non-COVID patients—and learn how to deal with this mixture of (dance) styles and rhythms.

Discussion

Few were expecting to have to learn how to dance with a new virus, yet the COVID-19 pandemic thoroughly changed the rhythms of Dutch healthcare delivery—as well as life in general. Despite early warnings, the surge of COVID-19 patients, particularly in the south, almost overwhelmed the Dutch healthcare system, as it had done in other countries. Such fate, for now, has fortunately been abated, among others by the effort of the board(s) of directors, nurses, and other healthcare professionals to make healthcare work in pandemic times; yet with great cost, particularly among vulnerable groups (Wallenburg et al., 2020). In this paper, we have aimed to offer an in-depth account 'from within' healthcare practice on how hospital organizations have improvised and established new organizational rhythms of organizing and providing care in uncertain times. To do so, we have used the analogy of the dance, offering a perspective on how actors felt about, worked with and through disrupted and new spatial-temporal orders of organizing and caring.

In a beautiful essay in *The New York Review of Books*, Clair Wills (2020) describes dancing as reading and being read, as dance partners constantly must relate to each other in order to not only move together but also engage in an affective interaction to produce a performance. In this paper, we have envisioned the dance in three phases. In the first phase, we found our participants and respondents learning how to dance—uncertainty about the virus and about the availability of PPE triggered an immediate crisis which, next to negative affect, also engendered feelings of camaraderie and trust. Rhythm was sped-up, fast-forward and improvisation at all levels was key. In the second phase, the speed of the crisis slowed down to a 'dance-marathon'; long hours, fatigue, and new organizational structures emerged to deal with the virus and its diseases. The third phase occurred when the 'first wave' of COVID-19 patients in the Netherlands had fallen to such a level upon and government-imposed measures were loosened. Hospitals worked hard to implement social distancing, and to prepare for a next wave of COVID patients. Different and conflicting rhythms, such as that of COVID and non-COVID care, started to intermingle, engendering new or re-living old goals like leveling up an ICU ward.

The analogy of the dance is powerful and we find it particularly productive to provide an affective story of how hospitals operated at different levels and in various ways to accommodate a new group of patients while finding new ways of organizing and caring in a highly political and uncertain context. It enables to account for the tensions between the loose acts of improvisation, such as the quick clearing of whole nursing departments, and the emergence of coordination efforts such as the LCPS. The first phase we identified necessitated healthcare organizations to improvise and act quickly—there was little room for hesitation nor reflection requiring high levels of trust. In the second phase, the rhythm stabilized and became enduring. Nurses sometimes sighed that providing intensive care to COVID-19 patients proved in fact to be 'rather boring' because of the numerous repetitions. The dance marathon is tiresome. The cacophony that ensued when the first wave subsided mixed-up the now newly established orders. New (e.g., long-term COVID patients) and old (competition between hospitals) voices problematized how our participants had learned to dance with the virus, offering among others the reflection that was missing previously, but also necessitating the actors to learn to dance with an increasing amount of participants, albeit according to different and sometimes conflicting rhythms.

Dancing as a metaphor focuses attention on the relationality, reflexivity (e.g., 'reading and being read'), materiality as well as the rhythm with which actors move through organizational life. It makes us researchers aware of the changes in organizational choreographies and creates space for providing an affective narrative of these changes. In our case, changes in choreographies include the different waves of the virus but also the interactions between the different 'levels' of the healthcare and political system in which the dance is embedded and needs to respond to. Learning to dance to the different rhythms and choreographies then also becomes the challenge that actors within such a layered system must respond to.

The dance of healthcare organizations with COVID-19 has not finished yet, but its sudden emergence has offered us researchers of the organization of healthcare a historic opportunity to do empirical research. Thus far, little in-depth empirical work such as we provide in this paper is available, but the need to reflect concretely on what happened—emphasized by the great willingness of our informants and respondents to share their experiences—and the need to offer concrete, lived, reflections on the effects and consequences of this pandemic is great. In this paper, we focused on the organization of healthcare, but the consequences of decision-making structures and practices, the mediatization of the pandemic, the organization of healthcare systems, and the role of expertise are similarly urgent matters to which research should attend (Bal et al., 2020). Learning to dance to the different rhythms that will emerge in subsequent phases of the pandemic will remain imperative.

References

Bal, R., de Graaff, B., van de Bovenkamp, H., & Wallenburg, I. (2020). Practicing Corona: Towards a research agenda of health policies. *Health Policy, 124*, 671–673.

Bal, R., & Zuiderent-Jerak, T. (2011). The practice of markets in Dutch healthcare: Are we drinking from the same glass? *Health Economics Policy and Law, 6*(1), 139–145.

Biehl, B. (2017). *Dance and organisation: Integrating dance theory and methods into the study of management*. Routledge.

Biehl, B. (2019). Dance in new areas: Integrating dance methods into business and management for personnel and leadership development. *Research and Dance in Physical Education, 3*(1), 17–30.

Brown, N., Buse, C., Lewis, A., Martin, D., & Nettelton, S. (2020). Air care: An 'areography' of breath, buildings and bugs in the cystic fibrisis clinic. *Sociology of Health & Illness, 42*(5), 972–986.

Callon, M. (2002). Writing and (re)writing devices as tools for management complexity. In J. Law & A. Mol (Eds.), *Complexities: Social studies of knowledge practices* (pp. 191–217). Duke University Press.

Chandler, J. (2011). Work as dance. *Organization, 19*(6), 865–878.

Crossan, M., Pina e Cunha, M., Vera, D., & J. Cunha. (2005). Time and organizational improvisation. *The Academy of Management Review, 30*(1), 129–145.

de Graaff, B., Bal, J., & Bal, R. (2020). *Layering risk work amidst an emerging crisis; an ethnographic study on the governance of the COVID-19 pandemic in a university hospital in the Netherlands*. Health.

Helderman, J. K., Schut, F., van der Grinten, T. E. D., & van de Ven, W. P. M. M. (2005). Martket-oriented health care reforms and policy learning in the Netherlands. *Journal of Health Policy, Politics and Law, 30*(1–2), 189–210.

Hujala, A., Laulainen, S., Kinni, R. L., Kokkonen, K., & Puttonen, K. (2016). Dancing with the bosses: Creative movement as a method. *Organizational Aesthetics, 5*(1), 11–36.

Merriman, P. (2010). Architecture/dance: Choreographing and inhabiting spaces with Anna and Lawrence Halprin. *Cultural Geographies, 17*(4), 427–449.

Orlikowski, W. J., & Yates, J. (2002). It's about time: Temporal structuring in organizations. *Organization Science, 13*(6), 684–700.

Ortmann, G., & Sydow, J. (2018). Dancing in chains: Creative practices in/of organizations. *Organization Studies, 39*(7), 899–921.

RVS. (2020). *(Samen)leven is meer dan overleven – Breder kijken en kiezen in tijden van corona* Raad voor Volksgezondheid en Samenleving (The Council of Public Health & Society) (Den Haag).

Shrum, W., Aggrey, J., Campos, A., Pamplona da Costa, J., Joseph, L., Kreimer, P., Kroeger, R., Medina, L. R., Miller, P., Palackal, A., Pandal de la Peza, A., & Traore, A. (2020). Who's afraid of Ebola? Epidemic fires and locative fears in the Information Age. *Social Studies of Science*. https://doi.org/10.1177/0306312720927781

Timmermans, S., & Tavory, I. (2012). Theory Construction in Qualitative Research: From Grounded Theory to Abductive Analysis. *Sociological Theory, 30*(3), 167–186. https://doi.org/10.1177/0735275112457914.

van de Bovenkamp, H. M., de Mul, M., Quartz, J. G. U., Weggelaar-Jansen, A. M. J. M. W., & Bal, R. (2014). Institutional layering in governing healthcare quality. *Public Administration, 92*(1), 208–233.

Wallenburg, I., Helderman, J. K., Jeurissen, P., & Bal, R. (2021). Unmasking a healthcare system: The Dutch policy response to the Covid-19 crisis. *Health Economics, Policy and Law*. https://doi.org/10.1017/S1744133121000128.

Wallenburg, I., Jeurissen, P., Helderman, J. K., & Bal, R. (2020). *The Netherlands response to the coronavirus pandemic*. Cambridge Core blog (blog), Cambridge University Press. https://www.cambridge.org/core/blog/2020/04/06/the-netherlands-response-to-the-coronavirus-pandemic/

Weick, K. E. (1998). Introductory essay: Improvisation as a mindset for organizational analysis. *Organization Science, 9*(5), 543–555.

Wills, C. (2020). Stepping out. *The New York Review of Books*. https://www.nybooks.com/articles/2020/08/20/stepping-out/

CHAPTER 7

Professional Engagement in Management: Learnings from the COVID-19 Crisis in France

Olivier Saulpic and Philippe Zarlowski

Introduction

The engagement of healthcare professionals in managerial decision-making has been considered for some time as critical to the transformation of, and improvement of the performance of, healthcare organizations (Baker & Denis, 2011). During the first phase of the COVID-19 crisis in France, healthcare professionals have precisely been placed at the center of the governance in public hospitals, to facilitate the management of patients and the delivery of care in this situation of crisis. Administrative teams, in turn, have been placed in a supporting role of medical practitioners. Thanks to this mode of governance, exclusively focused on the medical priorities of the pandemic, operational processes have been reorganized quickly across medical services and departments, with a timely

O. Saulpic (✉) · P. Zarlowski
ESCP Business School, Paris, France
e-mail: saulpic@escp.eu

J. Waring et al. (eds.), *Organising Care in a Time of Covid-19*, Organizational Behaviour in Healthcare,
https://doi.org/10.1007/978-3-030-82696-3_7

reallocation of resources and scaling up of capacities, especially of intensive care units for patients in need of respiratory assistance. Overall, a variety of stakeholders have underlined the resilience of the public hospital system to the crisis (Dumez & Minvielle, 2020). Even though the system has been put under an unprecedented level of pressure for a long period of time, very few cases, if any, of patients not receiving the care they needed, have been reported.

Our objective in this chapter consists in describing and analyzing the internal governance of hospitals during the crisis, with the view to draw propositions on hospital governance when hospitals are not placed in the context of a crisis. To that end, we have conducted interviews with a sample of doctors and administrative managers. We have also analyzed the reports and syntheses produced for, and in the wake of, a general consultation of healthcare practitioners representatives organized in June and July, 2020 by the French government to assess and "rebuild" the hospital and healthcare systems in France.[1] With this chapter, we intend to contribute to the literature on physicians' engagement in the governance and management of healthcare organizations by focusing on the practical organizational arrangements that are likely to support and sustain this engagement.

In section "Theoretical Background: Some Elements", we present elements for the theoretical background of our study. We then detail our methodology (section "Context and Methods") and analyses (section "Findings"). We discuss these propositions drawn from our analyses in section "Discussion" before concluding.

Theoretical Background: Some Elements

The interest in academia and policy making for the study of the engagement of healthcare professionals in managerial decisions is relatively recent and follows a period in which the managerialization of healthcare organizations has been construed in policies in several Western countries as the main answer for the successful transformation of these professional bureaucracies and the improvement of their performance.

[1] This consultation has been called *Ségur de la santé* (literally, "Ségur of health" as the French Ministry of health is located avenue de Ségur in Paris).

Since Mintzberg's (1979) seminal contributions to organizational theory, hospitals in Western countries have been analyzed as typical examples of professional bureaucracies: highly skilled, powerful healthcare professionals form the operating core of the organization while managers undertake the administrative work and support clinicians in their practices. In spite of their effectiveness as mode of organizing, professional bureaucracies have been depicted, as organizations in which decision-making is slow, and organizational change is difficult to implement as it has to be consensual (Baker & Denis, 2011; Mintzberg, 1979). In the managerialist view, the implementation of structural changes in hospitals, whereby new medical responsibility centers are created and managed by a newly created, or extended, category of medical managers would be instrumental to the achievement of higher performance goals for the quality, effectiveness, and efficiency of care (Kirpatrick et al., 2005, Llewellyn, 2001).

While the debate between advocates of a return to modes of governance typical of professional bureaucracies and managerialists remains open, echoing approaches and viewing organizations and professionalism as two opposing modes of coordination, students of healthcare organizations have proposed that the opposition is outdated and that healthcare organizations should be studied in terms of "organized professionalism" (Noordegraaf, 2011). Healthcare organizations are faced with social, cultural, and technological changes that make it necessary to engage professionals in the management of the organization. "Economic and corporate" changes, in turn, would explain the evolution in control modes and the decline in professionals' engagement. In addition to these institutional or contextual changes, the analytical opposition drawn between professionalism and organization would be excessive as "organizational tasks – planning, scheduling, allocating resources, management development, and the like – are not necessarily at odds with professional work" (Noordegraaf, 2011), and professionals have always been involved in organization and coordination work (Postma et al., 2015). Nordegraaf identifies three social factors that affect the position of professionals in the management of their organizations: changing work preferences, calls for multi-professionalism, new risks. These factors explain the development of management-minded professionals and connective organizational forms.

This literature is inviting contributions on the engagement of professionals that would not be in conflict with the managerial organization, but it leaves open the question of the modalities of this engagement. Professional engagement, in both practice and research, is often approached as being played out in the positions held by professionals: either by professionals taking on leadership positions (Rotar et al., 2016) or by creating hybrid positions in which professionals have responsibility for both medical and economic outcomes (Kurunmäki, 2004; Llewellyn, 2001). As we will see, this is exemplified in the context of public hospitals studied in this chapter.

The limitations of this approach have been underlined, notably as it "would have a limited impact if not coupled with a more active strategy to get doctors involved in improvement efforts" (Baker & Denis, 2011). It can therefore only be one element of a strategy to foster engagement, which must also include the definition of "clear improvement goals at the strategic and operational levels of the organization" and "a more collective view of organizational leadership where leadership development occurs at all levels of a system in a concerted manner". To our knowledge, the modalities by which this distributed leadership can be organized, and "what form a reinvigorated professionalism should take (…) is unclear" (Martin et al., 2015). More precisely, what practical organizational arrangements and managerial choices are more likely to sustain and enhance organized professionalism and collective leadership in hospitals—e.g., what modes and forms of communication and decision-making processes, what formal or material arrangements in which these processes are incorporated and which enable them could be associated with organized professionalism in hospitals? With this study, we aim to contribute to this line of research.

Context and Methods

The Context of Public Hospitals in France

We describe hereafter the institutional elements of the French healthcare and hospital systems that, in our view, are important to provide the contextual information for our analyses.

The hospital system comprises a variety of actors: public hospitals, not-for-profit private hospitals, and for-profit private hospitals but it is centrally regulated by public healthcare authorities. Since 2008, hospitals in France are mainly financed through a DRG system, called T2A (*Tarification à l'activité*, Activity-Based Pricing). Nation-wide prices are determined on a yearly basis by healthcare authorities. The T2A pricing system has been designed as a way to promote efficiency within the hospital system and to regulate the offer of care (Or, 2014; Or & Renaud, 2009).

Our study concentrates on public and not-for-profit private hospitals as they had to cope with the demand for care related to the pandemic, as planned in the policies designed to face sanitary crises. Public hospitals, as well as many not-for-profit private hospitals, share a same internal governance structure. Hospitals are run by an executive committee chaired by chief executive officer (CEO). With few exceptions, CEOs are not and have not been healthcare practitioners. They are administrative managers who have been specifically trained and recruited to serve as hospital directors in the public sector. The medical profession is represented by a different body, the medical committee of the entity (CME, *Commission médicale d'établissement*), chaired by a president elected by their peers. The president of CME also is the vice-president of the hospital executive committee. Since 2006, and the implementation of a new policy for the internal governance of public hospitals (*Nouvelle gouvernance hospitalière*), medical services are grouped into medical divisions that are placed under the responsibility of a medical doctor, who reports to the hospital CEO (and not to the president of CME). Heads of medical divisions are accountable for the performance of their division, in particular its economic results, as the hospital as a whole has to achieve profitability targets—at the very least, public hospitals in France are expected to balance their costs with their revenues and to generate operating cash-flows to contribute to financing of the maintenance and renewal of their fixed assets. The internal governance of public hospitals therefore presents some of the characteristics of managerialist principles that have infused healthcare and public sector organizations in many Western countries.

The combined and contemporary implementations of T2A and *Nouvelle gouvernance* have created the conditions for a shift in the power structure of hospitals, from medical practitioners to professional managers, with, in practice, a prominence of activity, cost, and efficiency indicators in the internal performance management and reporting systems of hospitals.

Hospital's CEOs themselves report to a regional health authority (ARS, *Agence régionale de santé*) that deconcentrates the action of the French Ministry of Health at the regional level. ARSs cover territories with a population of between 200,000 and 12,000,000 people (the latter for the ARS covering the territory of and around Paris) and are responsible for organizing the entire medical and health system in this territory.

In each region, ARS have been coordinating and organizing the supply of care and the scaling up of resources and capacities amongst hospitals during the crisis.

The actual structuring of the hospital system in France is therefore the result of relatively recently implemented reforms. In particular, these reforms involved a shift to DRG-type funding and the related focus on activity-based and efficiency indicators, the reinforced territorialization of aspects of the healthcare system with the creation of ARS, the empowerment of directors, and the creation of hybrid roles for physicians through the creation of both medical divisions and the position of medical managers of these divisions. The reforms are infused by some of the core principles of the managerialist approach in the organization of hospitals and demonstrate a willingness to break with the organizational and institutional arrangements typical of professional bureaucracies.

The Organization of Responsibilities During the Crisis

Coordination on the territory was ensured by regional health agencies (ARS). ARSs made decisions to stop certain programmed activities and less-urgent cares, played a role in forecasting needs and managing availability/capacity (opening beds, managing transfers). A crisis cell with representatives of both ARS and hospitals was convened every day as well. It was including representatives of the hospitals, in particular the medical doctors in charge of the crisis units in their hospitals. It was at this regional level that decisions were made on activity closures or patient transfers to other regions. This cell also disseminated information on capacity, bed occupancy, and the evolution of the epidemic.[2]

In all hospitals, the crisis procedure called "white plan" (*plan blanc*) has been implemented. In particular, this procedure provides for the management of the hospital by a dedicated crisis unit or cell headed jointly by a crisis medical director and a crisis director. This crisis cell is made up of medical and paramedical practitioners (the latter being, however, less numerous) and managers. During the crisis, meetings were organized every day. It was the responsibility of the crisis units to make decisions on the opening of COVID-19 and resuscitation beds. They also had to solve operational problems (procurement of medical equipment

[2] For complementary elements on the (re-)organization of the healthcare system during the COVID-19 crisis in France, see, for instance, Barro et al. (2020).

and protective gear; staffing, sizing and recruitment of caregivers; etc.). During the crisis, the activity-based funding system (T2A) was suspended and the constraints on financial resources were lifted.

For some of the hospitals we have studied, there were two levels of governance: that of the hospital and that of the hospital group it was part of, with a crisis cell at each level.

Data

Our work is based on interviews with medical professionals and hospital managers, on documents produced during the consultation initiated by the Ministry of Health to make proposals for the reform of the French healthcare system after the acute period of the first wave of the pandemic ("*Ségur de la santé*"). It is also informed by our knowledge of the French healthcare and hospital system and previous work on the management of public hospitals.

More precisely, we conducted 8 interviews in 4 Parisian hospitals (including 2 in AP-HP, the largest group of hospitals in Paris and in France) with 3 directors (all crisis unit coordinators: a cross-functional project director responsible for on-site crisis units, a general manager of a hospital group and a medical affairs director of a hospital group) and 5 doctors (head of the pneumology department, member of a crisis unit in an establishment; president of CME, head of the surgery department, medical manager of the GH crisis unit; head of the resuscitation and anesthesia department, member of the hospital's crisis unit; head of the resuscitation department, member of the hospital's crisis unit; head of the mobile emergency resuscitation unit, head of the hospital's crisis unit). Our questions focused on changes in activities during the crisis; on governance and decision-making; on our interviewees' analysis of the results of the crisis management in their hospitals, on what made the observed changes possible and what could be sustained; and on their views on the post-crisis period.

As far as the "*Ségur de la santé*" is concerned, the consultation was held for 5 weeks by the French government from May 25, 2020, following a commitment made by the President of the French Republic on March 25, 2020. Its mission was to define measures to reform the hospital and the healthcare system, taking into account the experience gathered from the crisis. Four "pillars" or areas of work were identified for this consultation: careers; compensation and staff training; investment plan and funding reform; governance reform and simplification; territorialization of the healthcare system. The consultation has drawn contributions from representatives of stakeholders in the healthcare system. It included the organization of a digital consultation of healthcare and medico-social professionals and the analysis of the feedback on the crisis gathered on a regional basis. The consultation resulted in agreements on careers, professions and compensations signed by the Prime Minister, the Minister of Solidarity and Health and union representatives. During the consultative process, medical societies and institutions representing various stakeholders in the healthcare system have contributed reports and proposals, and a report and several documents have been published by the organizing committee of the consultation as it had been commissioned to make recommendations to the Minister of Health.

Findings

We focus our analysis on four recurring elements in our interviewees' discourses on how the hospital operated during the crisis and the ways by which the crisis was managed: goal alignment, transparency and collegiality in decision-making, cooperation.

Goal Alignment

In a context of strong pressure on capacities and uncertainty about the extent of the epidemic, our interviews highlight an alignment of all the players on a single objective of operational efficiency dictated by the crisis: to ensure the admission of COVID-19 patients and the quality of care for these patients. The management of scarce resources has led to very deep and rapid reorganization of activities and roles. For example, in one hospital, almost all services have been transformed to treat COVID-19 patients. In all hospitals, resuscitation capacities have been very significantly increased (sometimes multiplied by 3). Caregivers who did have any practice is this medical field have been trained to reinforce the resuscitation teams. Surgeons have taken on guards as nursing assistants. Etc.

Collegiality in Decision-Making and Transparency

Despite their workload, frontline medical doctors were highly engaged in the functioning of the crisis units. Even though it could be expected that the roles of the latter would be central in these units, given the primacy of operational efficiency goals during the crisis, all of our interlocutors emphasized the collegiality of the decision-making processes and the consensual nature of the decisions taken. For example, although many decisions were debated, one director has indicated that in his perception, "decisions were self-imposed".

> Why we were happy ? We didn't know who the crisis director was. Decisions were made together. (medical doctor)
>
> It was an idyllic moment in terms of the organization of care. Eventually, we sat around a table to discuss. We built something together. (medical doctor)

Our interviewees also stressed that during the crisis, there has been a high level of transparency in the information flow in their hospital and that it has been important for the smooth running of operations.

> Normally we can say we don't know what's going on, but in this case everyone had all the information so decisions were easy to make. (manager)

In all hospitals, a report prepared by the heads of the crisis cell was distributed very quickly and widely, even though in some cases, medical directors of the crisis cell have had, in their perception, to overcome the initial reluctance of the management.

> Everything was transparent with minutes sent daily to all staff. I was doing it because it's not in [the hospital CEO's] culture to be transparent. From the first committee on, I told [the CEO] we need minutes. We did it and sent it out. (medical doctor)

Transparency in the information was perceived as reciprocal between the administrative and medical spheres. The role of the regional health authority (ARS) in communicating on the available capacities and the observed and anticipated evolution of the epidemic was also emphasized.

Cooperation

A high degree of cooperation has been established between medical and administrative staff on the one hand, and among medical and paramedical practitioners on the other.

All our interlocutors highlighted seamless operating processes, in sharp contrast, according to the medical doctors interviewed, with the habitual functioning of hospitals in which administrative hurdles tend to hamper their activities (in procurement, staff sizing, management of beds, etc.). Even though in one hospital, according to the head of the crisis cell interviewed, the administrative staff looked overwhelmed as detailed procedures were not readily available, in general, in medical practitioners' discourses, the administrative staff was praised for their facilitating role in implementing decisions (e.g., to create partitions in wards, to organize the procurement of scarce medical equipment, to develop and deploy a specific COVID-19 application on the intranet of the hospital)

> It was magical. Usually, if you need supplies and equipment, it takes ages to get them. There we snapped our fingers, and the problem was solved in 24 hours. (medical doctor)
>
> The role of the administration has been to help us. To make sure that we could develop what we had to do. Put up plastics [walls] to separate the emergencies in two. (medical doctor)

A strong cooperation was also quickly established between medical specialties, overcoming the operational or organizational tensions that were not unusual before the crisis.

> Tensions between emergency, medicine and ICU disappeared very quickly. It was a good surprise. There was a very high fluidity of operations. It's been a great help in crisis management, a very good surprise. There were no point of resistance in the patient's journey. The medical community was close-knit. (manager)

Several interviewees praised the form of solidarity that existed among the staff in their hospital: between doctors whatever their specialties; with the paramedical staff; with the administrative staff; etc. This solidarity has resulted in the removal of barriers related to the profession and function.

> We worked well together. There was an extraordinary solidarity [...], the impression that everyone was working hand in hand. (medical doctor)

For example, given their aptitude for this type of gesture, surgeons have done a job as assistant nurses to help turn patients over in their beds. This solidarity led some doctors to hope that the hospital would return to a collective existence that, in their perception, had been undermined by recent reforms.

Our interviewees also deemed unanimously that operations were very effective.

> And we assumed our role as a public service: every time the [Regional health authority] asked us to increase capacity, we did it. (manager)
>
> The bet we took was to stop the wave in Paris; we ran at our maximum capacity for two weeks. It was quite hard, but we succeeded. (medical doctor)
>
> We are not going to congratulate ourselves, but it went well. (medical doctor)
>
> Yes, it has been effective. If it hadn't worked like that there would have been more death. We were very scared but we never felt overwhelmed. (medical doctor)

Deep and swift reorganizations made it possible to deal with a particularly acute crisis in and around Paris, without having to compromise the quality of medical practices when taking care of COVID-19 patients. Still, concerns have been raised for the quality of non-COVID-19 care as most planned cares were postponed to the post-crisis period, to allocate the maximum medical capacity that could be available to the treatment of COVID-19 patients.

Discussion

Professionals' Engagement in the Management of Hospitals

Conducive Changes

Our analyses are aligned with results put forward in research on professional engagement and also allow us to draw propositions on the practical modalities by which the engagement of medical practitioners in management can be sustained and promoted.

The COVID-19 crisis created a context calling for professional engagement and the development of their organizing capacities, as already outlined in the literature.

Firstly, our study tends to confirm the ability of professionals, under specific circumstances, to become effectively engaged in hospital management, notably, without their engagement resulting in a problem of slow and difficult decision-making (Baker & Denis, 2011; Dickinson et al., 2015; Noordegraaf, 2011). Indeed, during the outbreak, in many respects, medical doctors had the lead in decision-making processes yet consensual decisions were settled quickly between both medical doctors and managers, e.g., to restructure the medical services, reorganize the flow of patients, and reallocate resources.

This engagement do not resemble the vision of either professional bureaucracy or pure managerialization. In that, it is in line with the literature that recognizes forms of organized professionalism. Indeed, decision-making processes described in our study are collective, multidisciplinary, and consensus-based. This mode of engagement is therefore more aptly depicted by that of multi-professional work (Noordegraaf, 2011) and differs from the ideal type of professional bureaucracy in which *individual* professionals are primarily focused on assessing the cares needed for their patients. Many decisions involved all the specialities in the hospital (transforming services bed into COVID-19 beds, prioritizing activities, etc.). Medical doctors were confronted with new cases and new risks, two changing circumstances (new cases calling for multi-professionalism and new risks) which have been identified as drivers for the development of professionals' organizing capacities (Noordegraaf, 2011).

We can also note that in the context of the crisis, actors could align themselves on a clear objective (here, of operational effectiveness), which has been analyzed as a factor likely to promote their engagement (Baker & Denis, 2011). However, the high level of clinical resources that were made available to medical doctors during the first phase of the crisis, together with their consensual allocation to the COVID-19 public health priority, may have facilitated this alignment.

Our study allows us to formulate assumptions about how other traits of the organizational arrangements during the crisis may have contributed to the engagement of professionals.

As was pointed out by one of our interviewees, meetings had very operational scopes and purposes: They were aimed at exposing and resolving problems. It could be argued that a very operational purpose is more likely to support the engagement of professionals. In addition to this, a doctor was leading the meetings, in his/her capacity as the crisis medical director for the hospital. It should be noted that the function of crisis medical director is usually intended for extreme but transient situations (e.g., a terrorist attack, a natural disaster). In this case, medical directors had to lead daily crisis meetings over a long period of time (almost three months).

Our interviewees have mentioned to us how smooth the decision-making processes have been during the crises. For some of them, the decisions to be made "had not much to do with management". Others went even so far as to say that "decisions were self-imposed" even though in reality, decisions were made when views were originally very different (an example of debated decision was whether family members and relatives should be allowed to visit COVID-19 patients). It follows that professionals would more easily engage in collective decision-making processes when the matters that need to be discussed have a direct impact on their work practices. This relates to the conceptualization of organized professionalism where professionals find in organizational assets all sorts of resources to improve their practice or the effectiveness of their interventions.

Most of our interviewees have mentioned to us that in practice, crisis meetings were co-facilitated by the site administrative manager and the crisis medical director. Still, they seemed to be sensitive that doctors were formally leading these meetings. Meetings were organized every day, and involved a large number of participants. Convening meetings with a larger number of participants were not deemed to be a problem (with the exception of one hospital, in which actors preferred not to have too many participants in the crisis meetings). On the contrary, in the words of one of our interviewees, participating in the meeting was the best way to make sure that all relevant information was shared by, and communicated to, everyone. This underscores the ability of professionals to facilitate meetings involving large numbers of participants and to address topics that fall within both the organizational and professional spheres.

They willingly agreed to participate in these daily meetings despite their heavy workload. This may echo a work practice that is habitual to them, when they participate in medical staff meetings in their units or departments. Finally, the minutes of these meetings were made available very quickly and widely disseminated in the hospital. In several instances, the medical heads of the crisis cell were more instrumental in the diffusion of the minutes than their managerial counterparts, which may indicate differences in actors' sensitivities to transparency.

Regarding the engagement of professionals in management, our analyses are in line with the literature emphasizing that the engagement of physicians is not, or no longer, a mere question of professional culture. We propose that the practical modalities of the participation of these professionals in management (for instance, the definition of objectives, the purpose of meetings, who facilitates the meetings who participates in them, etc.) are important features of the context of action that could promote or, on the contrary, hamper professionals' engagement. This differs from, and is complimentary to, conclusions in literature on organized professionalism which emphasize the role played by the setting of standards, more precisely new work standards for building positions in professional labor markets, new delivery standards, and new standards to assess quality and safety effects (Nordegraaf, 2011). Our propositions also support and complement the attention directed in existing research to the managerial context of professionals' engagement, for instance, when physicians would take up new managerial roles in their hospitals or would develop their individual leadership skills (Baker & Denis, 2011; Dickinson et al., 2015).

A Specific Context?

The crisis situation analyzed was in several respects very specific. There were no constraints on the use of financial resources during the time of the crisis: The DRG funding system had been put on hold and at the national level, the government clearly took the political position that the priority was to face the COVID-19 crisis, whatever the economic costs or longer-term social and medical consequences. Medical and paramedical personnel was not scarce: Non-COVID-19, non-emergency activities were closed down in frontline hospitals and frontline medical services of hospitals in and around Paris benefitted from the voluntary work of private sector or recently retired practitioners, or from practitioners working in other hospitals in France, in regions much less impacted by the crisis, and who came to reinforce the Parisians teams. In addition to that, the objectives were clear and were not conflictual.

The question therefore arises as to what extent these factors explain the successful engagement of professionals during the crisis. Addressing it would go beyond the scope of the present study and the empirical base on which it relies. However, we propose that several levers of professional's' engagement could be transferable to studies in different contexts.

First, our analyses tend to indicate that the engagement of professionals in management could be fostered by practical forms of organizing that are not traditionally viewed as recommended management practices: for instance, meeting agendas dictated by operational priorities, a high number of participants in meetings, the possibility for all participants to intervene in these meetings, the transparency of exchanges and conclusions, etc.

With regard to the clarity and acceptance of the objectives, the situation analyzed is very specific since the whole healthcare system was oriented toward the cure of COVID-19 cases, and the financial constraints tightening the situation of many hospitals in France were lifted. In habitual times, objectives are multiple, actors have different views and interests, pursue a variety of objectives, and compete for resources that are scarce. However, the work conducted in the specifically dedicated cell to manage the crisis sometimes entailed the genuine discussions on objectives between participating actors (for instance, there have been competing views among doctors on the scale and intensity of the crisis and level of adaptation in the healthcare organizations that it would require). Professionals were involved and participating in the decision-making process. Therefore, involving professionals in the upstream phase of the identification of objectives could promote their engagement in the management processes of their organization. We return to this point in the next section.

Finally, the clarity of purpose of the management meetings organized may also play a role in sustaining professionals' engagement. Not all meetings are problem-solving oriented as in the case of the crisis. However, meetings pursuing a variety of ambiguous, sometimes inexplicit purposes may not facilitate professionals participation in, and appropriation of, these formal instances that are meant to structure managerial work in their organizations and make it visible (see also Saulpic & Zarlowski, 2020).

Internal Governance and Opportunities of Collaboration

The main proposals of the general consultation "*Ségur de la santé*" were focused on the internal governance of hospitals, and on the policy choices at the health care system level—namely, in terms of funding—directly impacting hospitals' internal governance and management processes and practices. The proposals were as follows: (1) Medicalizing the governance of the hospital and restoring the role and power of the medical commission of the hospital, (2) Refocusing management processes in medical departments, at the lower level, and at the level of the hospital general management, at the top, in a contrast with the previous reforms that had created the divisional structure (this structure becomes optional, while its adoption used to be compulsory), (3) Supporting local experimentation, (4) Simplifying and automating reporting processes and, (5) Changing the funding system away from the "all DRG" system, i.e., funding based almost exclusively on activity.

Several of these proposals could be interpreted as a political response to the crisis, in an attempt to recognize the results and efforts of the medical profession during the first wave of the outbreak. Indeed, the operational efficiency during the crisis was attributed, by the professionals interviewed as well as in the political conclusions of "*Ségur de la santé*", to medical practitioner's' decision-making power in the crisis management units. The crisis indeed created the conditions for a shift of power in hospitals as doctors were no longer supposed to report to the CEOs and general management teams of their hospitals. Given practitioners' achievements in their management of the crisis, the general mindset both in public discourses and in the comments of the interviewed practitioners stipulated that changes in the internal governance of hospital were necessary to improve their operational effectiveness. The aim would be to medicalize the governance of hospitals, refocus the internal structure on medical departments as healthcare production entities, and deemphasize the two flagship systems in which pre-crisis governance was embodied: medical divisions and French DRGs ("*T2A*").[3] The relative power of professionals and managers was already a central point in the 2006 and 2009 reforms, but with an opposite diagnosis leading to the strengthening of the power of managers.

Both diagnoses seem to revolve around the centrality of the opposition between two social groups in hospitals: professionals and managers, with the assumption that one must have power over the other. However, the crisis has demonstrated that under particular conditions of governance and with specific decision processes and structures, power games and differences between cultures and frameworks do not prevent hospital

[3] See section "The Context of Public Hospitals in France".

actors from working together and making decisions that are accepted by all. Therefore, it would be worthwhile to further investigate how the practical arrangements in which and by which these two social groups can cooperate and coordinate in practice impact decision-making processes and, more specifically, whether specific arrangements are more likely to overcome the opposition driven by the different logics and identities that are theirs.

During the crisis, the hospital's operations were radically simplified, and budgetary issues were temporarily overshadowed by operational capacity issues. The alignment on the sole medical objectives dictated by the COVID-19 crisis has also erased the specialized logics that govern the various medical disciplines (medicine, surgery, emergency, resuscitation)—in particular, almost all surgical departments have been closed down to free up capacities in post-surgery resuscitation wards. Therefore, while concluding that the crisis would have demonstrated the effectiveness of a medicalized mode of governance of hospital could seem premature, our study calls for further research on how the place devoted to medical practitioners in the internal governance of hospitals impacts management processes in the hospital at large, and their organizational performance.

Further research could also question the ways by which the practical and operational complexity of processes are addressed in the internal organizational arrangements of hospitals. The reforms conducted in 2000s in France, which led to the empowerment of managers, put the emphasis on incentives for hospitals and medical divisions heads, in relation with a focus on financial objectives (called "medico-economic" performance objectives in France: turnover, expenditures, operating income) and the most apparent associated performance levers (volume of activity, length of stay, occupation rates). The underlying assumption was that operational challenges were concentrated, and could be properly addressed, in each medical division, neglecting the key problems of coordination between divisions (the management of inpatients when they are discharged from the emergency units, the coordination between medical and technical divisions, such as imaging or biology) or between the hospital and the "outside world" (e.g., that of general practitioners, or follow-up care and rehabilitation facilities). The analysis of the functioning of hospitals during the crisis indicates that major operational questions may not be addressed within each responsibility center, which calls for the study and experimentation of new forms of governance likely to foster organizational capacities of both professionals and managers.

In addition to this, while there is a general agreement that multidimensional objectives constitute one of the key specificities of healthcare systems, questions of governance tend to be analyzed without taking it into account. In French, public hospitals, management control systems are strongly focused on financial or budgetary reporting and rely in that on an overly simplified representation of the hospital (Saulpic & Zarlowski, 2020). During the crisis, missions have been reduced to a single dimension, but for reasons that were shared by all the actors involved the management of the crisis in hospitals and this clarity in objectives may have played a role to sustain the effective engagement of professionals (Baker & Denis, 2011). How the multidimensionality of objectives could be accounted for in habitual times remains an open question and should not be overlooked by concerns centered on the balance of power between stakeholders in the internal governance structures. As a consequence, to further our understanding of professionals' engagement, studies could analyze the processes by which priorities are set in a context of multidimensional performance objectives, the positions and possible contributions of a variety of stakeholders in this process, and the features, such as transparency, that could impact its results.

Conclusion

In this chapter, we describe and analyze the internal governance of hospitals during the crisis, to draw more general propositions on the professionals' engagement in the management and governance of hospitals.

To that end, we have conducted interviews with a sample of medical doctors and administrative managers and analyzed the documentation published for, and in the wake of, a consultation convened in June and July 2020 by the French government, to change the governance of the French healthcare system.

Our analyses are consistent with studies that conceptualize hospitals in terms of organized professionalism (Noordegraaf, 2011) and that analyze new forms collective and distributed leadership in these organizations (Baker & Denis, 2011). We suggest possible developments to this literature by focusing on the practical organizational arrangements by which professionals' engagement happens. Our analyses also suggest possible pathways to inform the study of the internal governance structures in hospitals, notably by analyzing the processes by which priorities are set in a context of multidimensional performance objectives and more broadly, the ways by which the multidimensionality of objectives can be addressed in multi-professional settings. Attention could also be granted to the purposes and forms of management meetings, the place of operational issues in these meetings, or the expectations attached to transparency and participation in decision-making.

Our analyses confirm that the forms and intensity of professionals' engagement in the management of hospitals are related to the overall multidimensional performance of these organizations and invites to pay attention to the micro-organizational processes by which this engagement is performed and sustained, beyond the internal governance choices that define responsibility and power structures.

References

Baker, G. R., & Denis, J.-L. (2011, September). Medical leadership in health care systems: From professional authority to organizational leadership. *Public Money & Management*, 1–8.

Barro, K. A., Malone, A., Mokede, A., & Chevance, C. (2020). Management of the COVID-19 epidemic by public health establishments–Analysis by the Fédération Hospitalière de France. *Journal of Visceral Surgery, 157*(3)(Suppl. 1), S19–S23.

Dickinson, H., Bismark, M., Phelps, G., & Loh, E. (2015). Future of medical engagement. *Australian Health Review, 40*(4), 443–446.

Dumez, H., & Minvielle, É. (2020). *Comment le système hospitalier français a-t-il géré la crise COVID-19? Une contribution des sciences de gestion*. Rapport de recherche, Palaiseau, École polytechnique, I3G-CRG.

Kirkpatrick, I., Ackroyd, S., & Walker, R. (2005). *The new managerialism and public service professions*. Palgrave Macmillan.

Kurunmäki, L. (2004). A hybrid profession—The acquisition of management accounting expertise by medical professionals. *Accounting, Organizations and Society, 29*(3–4), 327–347.

Llewellyn, S. (2001). 'Two-way windows': Clinicians as medical managers. *Organization Studies, 22*(4), 593–623.

Martin, G. P., Armstrong, N., Aveling, E.-L., Herbert, G., & Dixon-Woods, M. (2015). Professionalism redundant, reshaped, or reinvigorated? Realizing the 'third logic' in contemporary healthcare. *Journal of Health and Social Behavior, 56*(3), 378–397.

Mintzberg, H. (1979). *The Structuring of Organizations*. Prentice-Hall, Englewood Cliffs.

Noordegraaf, M. (2011). Risky business: How professionals and professional fields (must) deal with organizational issues. *Organization Studies, 32*(10), 1349–1371.

Or, Z. (2014). Implementation of DRG payment in France: Issues and recent developments. *Health Policy, 117*(2), 146–150.

Or, Z., & Renaud, T. (2009). Principes et enjeux de la tarification à l'activité à l'hôpital (T2A). Enseignements de la théorie économique et des expériences étrangères. Document de travail Irdes n° 23. 2009/03.

Postma, J., Oldenhof, L., & Putters K. (2015). Organized professionalism in healthcare: Articulation work by neighbourhood nurses. *Journal of Professions and Organization, 2,* 61–77.

Rotar, A. M., Botje, D., Klazinga, N. S., Lombarts, K. M., Groene, O., Sunol, R., & Plochg, T. (2016). The involvement of medical doctors in hospital governance and implications for quality management: a quick scan in 19 and an in depth study in 7 OECD countries. *BMC Health Services Research, 16*(Suppl. 2), 99–109.

Saulpic, O., & Zarlowski P. (2020). *Le rôle des outils de gestion pour améliorer l'efficacité du dialogue de gestion au sein des hôpitaux.* Rapport de recherche, Fédération Hospitalière de France.

CHAPTER 8

Theorizing Reorganizations of Care: Boundary Work and the Professions During Ontario's COVID-19 Response

Paula Rowland, Mathieu Albert, and Simon Kitto

Introduction

Healthcare workers often took center stage in the early unfolding drama of the COVID-19 pandemic. Heralded as "heroes" but also marginalized as potentially infectious "pariahs" (Lefkowitz, 2020), these workers embodied debates about the duties of professionals, the responsibilities of employers, and reasonable expectations of publics (Cox, 2020). As the urgency and uncertainty of the COVID-19 pandemic prompted radical transformations in the organization and delivery of health and care services, these debates became ever more salient. In Canada, the first set of transformations oriented toward increasing the critical care capacity of health systems, reallocating and redeploying healthcare workers and

P. Rowland (✉) · M. Albert
University of Toronto, Toronto, ON, Canada
e-mail: paula.rowland@utoronto.ca

S. Kitto
University of Ottawa, Ottawa, ON, Canada

J. Waring et al. (eds.), *Organising Care in a Time of Covid-19*, Organizational Behaviour in Healthcare,
https://doi.org/10.1007/978-3-030-82696-3_8

resources in anticipation of surges of critically ill patients. Later, as the fragilities of long-term and community care systems became increasingly apparent, a second wave of reorganization shifted services and resources once again.

Through these dynamics of redeployment, relationships between patients, professions, the state, and health service organizations were all brought into stark relief. These relationships and their inherent tensions have long occupied sociologists studying professions (Anteby et al., 2016; Muzio et al., 2019). However, the high stakes, high profile, and enormously complex reorganizations in response to COVID-19 prompts a thoughtful re-appraisal of the conceptual tools available to study these dynamics. As the crisis abates, these relationships are likely to become an area of focused attention. Attending to these dynamics incites engagement with current theories while also pointing our attention toward how our conceptualizations of professions and professional work may be meaningfully expanded.

In this chapter, we explore how healthcare workers were reorganized in response to the COVID-19 pandemic. We accomplish this through an analysis of publicly available texts, chronicling how healthcare workers were redeployed in Ontario Canada and the associated cascades of activity required to enact those redeployments. Our phenomenon of interest is how various actors connected knowledge domains, scopes of practice and emerging structures of professional work in order to meet the demands of COVID-19. The unit of analysis became the interface between employers, professions, and the state as played out through governmental orders and organizational policies. With our data collection limited to texts available in the public domain, we sought out documents from key stakeholders such as employing organizations, professional associations, regulatory bodies, and various levels of provincial government. To contain the scope of this study, we limited our interest to those professions most implicated in the first wave of the COVID-19 response (e.g., physicians, nurses, respiratory therapists, physiotherapists) and later added occupational groups implicated as health human resources began to shift to long-term care centers (e.g., personal support workers, Canadian Armed Forces). Collection of documents was an iterative process, leading us to key pieces of legislation, newly enrolled stakeholders, and public debates playing out in social media. In doing so, we trace the historical, political, and cultural dynamics that have made current strategies of redeployment possible within our particular context.

Our aim is twofold. First, we contribute to real-time theorization of the effects of these redeployments. Second, we reflect back on our current theoretical tools and the capacity to grapple with complexity inherent in the relationships between professions, the state, members of the public, and health services organizations. In this way, we join a growing body of scholarship that calls for more attention to relationships between the sociology of the professions and the social organization of work (Adams et al., 2020; Eyal, 2013).

Systems of Professions: Understanding Cascades of Redeployment

For the purposes of our study, we required analytical purchase on a quickly evolving situation that entangled various groups of actors. These groups include multiple professions and occupations, health service organizations, governments, publics, patients, educational institutions, professional associations, and unions. Further, these entanglements were being played out in three arenas: workplaces, media, and legislation. Finally, while the response required by the pandemic is largely unprecedented in the lifetimes of these various actors, the responses mobilized are underpinned by the cultural and political tools available at this particular moment. Responses may be unprecedented, but they are not ahistorical.

To inform our analysis, we used Andrew Abbott's concepts from the *Systems of Professions* (Abbott, 1988), later elaborated through concepts of boundaries and boundary work (Abbott, 1995a, 1995b) and linked ecologies (Abbott, 2005). Situated within the power or conflict tradition within the sociology of the professions, Abbott's work was influential for shifting the focus away from individual professions and onto wider ecologies of professions engaged in competing projects. In Abbott's system of the professions, the proper unit of analysis is a profession's jurisdiction, defined as the link between the profession and its work. Professions made jurisdictional claims, based on their professional logics. In these claims, knowledge is the "currency of competition" (p. 102). As Abbott noted, many occupations fight for turf but only the professions with a claim to abstract knowledge were able to capture new jurisdictions and define those jurisdictions as their proper work. Thus, in this theorization, the history of professions became a history of turf wars, with jurisdictions in constant flux (Abbott, 1995a). Further, the professions were enrolled in an interdependent system, such that a change in one jurisdiction would launch a chain of effects with implications for other professions. This, according to Abbott (1988), was the proper focus of a study of the professions: how jurisdictional maps are made, contested, and sustained. Once established, the internal social structure of professions is maintained through relationships between professional groups, various forms of internal control (e.g., schools, exams, competency frameworks), and the places where the professionals work. For Abbott, the proper sites for exploring the edges of those jurisdictions are in the arenas where claims were being made and contested, namely in worksites, in public discourse, and in legislation.

Abbott later elaborated his theorizing, acknowledging that his conceptualization of systems of professions was "in short, a theory of boundaries" (Abbott, 1995a: 552). Following this line of thinking, Abbott moved toward a more intently processual view, arguing that social entities (such as professions and the objects of professional work) are actively constructed by agents as they pull together various boundaries into coherent units (Abbott, 1995b). In this conceptual reorientation, "boundaries come first, then entities" (p. 860). The concept of ecology was used as a metaphor, drawing attention to the complexities of networked interactions that characterize these entities. Abbott also further expanded his core ideas to include "linked ecologies". The concept of linked ecologies adds another layer of contingency, taking into account "the simultaneous existence of numerous adjacent ecologies, all of whose actors seek alliances, resources, and support across ecological boundaries" (Abbott, 2005: 247).

The analytical threads opened up by Abbott's theorizing allows us conceptual purchase on the cascades of movement between professions and occupations as part of the COVID-19 response. Further, the notion that jurisdictional claims are made—and contested—in the three arenas of worksites, public discourse and legislation provide a ready empirical site for us to explore. This focus allowed us to consider boundary work within and between professions, but also between professions and members of the public.

Expanding the Bounds of "Boundary Work"

In Abbott's framing, boundary work was always competitive (Lamont & Molnár, 2002). Furthermore, abstract professional knowledge served as the currency of that competition (Abbott, 1988). While we could certainly trace displays of competitive boundary work in our dataset, this interpretation of boundary work was insufficient to capture the complexity of what was going on. Here, we turn to a recent interpretive and integrative review of boundary work scholarship by Langley et al. (2019). These authors articulate three conceptually distinct but interrelated forms of boundary work: *competitive*, *collaborative*, and *configurational*.

Competitive boundary work refers to processes of constructing, defending, or maintaining boundaries in order to confer some kind of advantage. Langley et al. (2019) describe this as work *for* boundaries. This form of boundary work is defined as competitive, as the self-oriented process construes boundaries in order to secure some kind of legitimacy, status, or resource for those that engage in it. Gieryn's (1983) work is conceptually foundational here, as he described processes of demarcation that served to separate science from non-science. Bourdieu's theorizations on reproductions of power, social position and status in sites of class struggle (Bourdieu, 1980, 1993, 1996) are also exemplary of competitive boundary work. Indeed, this kind of boundary work must anticipate struggle and contest, as inclusion within the boundary cannot be conceptualized without also anticipating some kind of "other" outside of the boundary. This "other" may well push back on this exclusion (Langley et al., 2019).

Langley et al. (2019) describe collaborative boundary work as occurring when agents draw on, negotiate, blur or realign boundaries in interaction with others in order to collaborate, coordinate, or otherwise get work done. Where competitive boundary work is described as work *for* boundaries, collaborative boundary work is characterized as the work *at* boundaries (Langley et al., 2019). Rather than considering boundaries as obstacles to be overcome, this form of work considers boundaries as junctures that may enable rather than inhibit collaboration. Theories that inform this understanding of boundaries include Strauss' negotiated order perspective (Strauss, et al., 1985; Strauss, Schatzman, et al., 1963) as well as work from Latour and others that describe active assemblages of actor-networks (Latour, 2007). A particularly insightful contribution from the analysis of this kind of boundary work is the notion that it is possible to have cooperation across boundaries without consensus among stakeholders, a feat mediated through boundary objects (Star, 2010).

Configurational boundary work refers to specific instances where agents from outside existing boundaries work to design, organize, or rearrange the set of boundaries influencing other's behaviors for the express purpose of producing particular kinds of collective action (Langley et al., 2019). Where competitive boundary work is characterized as work *for* boundaries and collaborative boundary work is work *at* boundaries, configurational boundary work is work *through* boundaries (ibid.). Here, outside forces actively use boundaries to bring certain activities within a common space while working to keep others apart. It is this manipulation of boundaries that creates the conditions for collective work. In this framing, boundaries are not just something simply a source of legitimacy and self-protection (as in competitive boundary work) nor a juncture to be aligned (as in collaborative boundary work), but a tool to be deployed to bring together people, objects, and powers into new configurations (ibid). From Langley et al.'s (2019) literature review, this is a less frequent form of boundary work. They cite foundational concepts from social movements theory and institutional entrepreneurship to explain how outside actors have been successful in framing the need for collective work and consequently generating creative and relational spaces.

In summary, Langley et al. (2019) revive the concept of boundary work. Through their analysis, they elaborate the concept in a way that draws attention to ongoing processual work. Rather than attending to boundaries with the sole intent of mapping jurisdictions, they argue for a dynamic inquiry that links together agency, power dynamics, materiality, and temporality. It is a movement from thinking of the analysis of boundaries as an exercise of cartography, to thinking of the analysis of boundary work as tracing processes and their effects. In our analysis of the redeployment process, we were sensitized to these conceptualizations of boundary work. Rather than focusing exclusively on competitive boundary work, we attended to how boundaries were constructed, the agents involved in constructing (and shifting) those boundaries, and the possible implications of that boundary work. The dynamism of the unfolding COVID-19 pandemic provided a rare opportunity to trace boundary work during a compressed moment in time.

Background Information and Description

To put our analysis into context, we first begin with public health and demographic data. Ontario has a population of approximately 15 million. As of July 29, 2020, Ontario Public Health reported 38,986 confirmed cases of COVID-19, with 13,153 of those confirmed cases reported in individuals over the age of 60. As of that date, 4,656 individuals have been hospitalized with 997 of those hospitalized individuals requiring care in an intensive care unit (ICU). The first reported provincial death from COVID-19 was on March 11, 2020, the same day the World Health Organization declared the pandemic. As of July 29, 2020, there have been 2,769 reported deaths in the province of Ontario.

In Ontario, there were two phases of reorganization in response to COVID-19. The first phase was in preparation for a feared surge of critically ill patients, potentially overwhelming available critical care resources. This phase involved a rapid cascade of resource redeployment, oriented toward bolstering critical care capacity within each of the provinces. As the surge of critically ill patients did not materialize in the Canadian context, national attention shifted toward the long-term care sector, recognizing these settings as particularly vulnerable. This second phase of redeployment involved an unprecedented amount of organizational permeability as resources were shifted from the newly bolstered acute care settings into long-term care (LTC) settings struggling with virus outbreaks, staffing stability, and scarcity of supplies. With each phase of redeployment, cascades of educational and training needs were mobilized as redeployed staff were required to quickly learn new skills in order to function within their newly configured worksites.

Along with the redeployment of healthcare workers and resources, two other groups emerged as key players in the reorganization dynamics. These groups are interesting and important for the ways they were excluded and included in the reconfigured worksites. The first group to note is for their exclusion. On March 13, 2020, citing the guidance of the Chief Medical Officer of Health, the government of Ontario and the Ontario Ministry of Health and Long-Term Care advised LTC facilities and hospitals to exclude all visitors to health care facilities. Only "essential visitors" were to be allowed access and only under certain limited circumstances. As COVID-19 cases began to decline, patients and residents were allowed limited and physically distant outdoor visits. However, this gradual resumption of family visitors and caregivers did not begin until June 11, 2020. Further, there was no distinction in the Ministry's language between "visitors" and "caregivers", with both groups subjected to the same requirements for limited interactions within hospitals and LTC facilities. While studies of the professions do not typically include family members in their conceptual framing, we attend to these exclusionary dynamics in our analysis. Recent policy trajectories have emphasized the important roles of patients and families in the care team. Using language of "experts" and arguing for a dismantling of the power differential between health care providers and health care recipients, there has been a strong push for patients and their caregivers to be considered as part of the health care team (Martin & Finn, 2011). The decision to exclude caregivers from healthcare spaces and places stands in direct contrast to that policy trajectory and warrants exploration.

The second group to note is based on their inclusion. The provincial emergency declaration also allowed the province to request assistance from the Canadian Armed Forces (CAF) as a means to address the pandemic. On April 15, 2020, the CAF mobilized Operation LASER, providing medical and support personnel to assist with day to day operations, support infection control procedures, and provide general care support in seven LTC facilities in Ontario. The CAF continued to provide care within these settings until July 2020. We primarily attend to these dynamics of inclusion as they stand in contrast to dynamics of exclusion. In attempting to understand how these decisions were made (and justified), we tap into arguments about expertise, accountability, and risk that shape boundary work.

Configurational Boundary Work: Government Powers and Employer's Roles

As anticipated, displays of boundary work were prominent through the texts analyzed. However, the primary empirical story was not about competitive or exclusive boundary work, as we might have expected if we only followed Abbott's earlier work on jurisdictions. For the purpose of our analysis, we focus on the prominent displays of configurational boundary work. Here, outside forces actively use boundaries to bring certain activities within a common space while working to keep others apart (Langley et al., 2019). What is on display in our analysis is the powerful role of the provincial government and the Ministry of Health and Long-Term Care in reconfiguring worksites and the cascades of activity mobilized in response to those reconfigurations.

On March 17, 2020, the government of Ontario declared a state of emergency in response to COVID-19. As a result of the state of emergency, the Ontario government mobilized a series of emergency orders. These included orders relevant to the general public, but also a series of orders related to extraordinary work deployment measures within and across health service organizations. These series of governmental orders had several immediate effects. The first set of orders gave hospitals the power to redeploy their employees to areas of high need within their own networks. A second set of orders allowed hospitals to redeploy their staff into LTCs and retirement homes (RHs). Here, it is useful to make note of the organization of health care services in Ontario. While hospitals are publicly funded, they are independent organizations with their own Boards of Directors and governing structures. Further, many unions operate within hospitals, with some larger hospitals negotiating labor practices with upwards of 25 unions at a time. In contrast, LTCs and RHs may be publicly or privately funded. Regardless of their funding source, LTCs and RHs are also independent organizations, separate from hospitals and with their own dynamics of labor relations. To have staff crossing boundaries between hospitals and other health service organizations is an exceptional and unprecedented amount of workforce mobility.

In one sense, this scenario displays the power of the provincial government to quickly reconfigure worksites. Professional and organizational boundaries were temporarily suspended as healthcare work was organized around shifting tasks, first in acute care settings and later in long-term care. Arguably, this was an exceptional circumstance and may not foreshadow any future relationships between the state and the professions. However, sociology of professions analysis brings attention to the historical maneuvers that have made such powers possible. We found explanatory propositions in sociological examinations of the regulation of health professionals in Ontario, particularly studies of the 1991 Regulated Health Professional Act (RHPA) (Adams & Saks, 2018; Coburn, 1993; Coburn et al., 1997; William et al., 1995). The RHPA is characterized as an attempt to loosen boundaries among the health occupations. Rather than articulating exclusive domains of practice for the health professions, the RHPA provides a shortlist of protected acts that a health care professional may provide with subsequent delineations about which professions may perform which acts. The effect of this legislation is to shift the focus away from the exclusive territory of groups to the risks and responsibilities associated with certain tasks. Thus, the ability to quickly mobilize configurational boundary work in order to be responsive to changing demands was not a new innovation, but one that had been the express trajectory of legislation for almost 30 years (Bourgeault & Mulvale, 2006). This has been latent but accruing power achieved through steady incursion of the government into not just the context of Ontario health care services, but also the content (Coburn, 1988, 2006; Coburn et al., 1997).

As much as the reconfiguration of worksites was enabled through the actions of the provincial government, the actual work of redistribution was delegated to the health service organizations. In these acts of redeployment, the emergency orders from the government gave employers the power to use "their reasonable opinion" to fill any staff position with a person who "has the adequate skills, training, and knowledge to perform the duties required of that position" (Ontario Regulation 95/20). Along with these powers, employers were "authorized" to provide "appropriate training or education as needed to staff and volunteers to achieve the purposes of the redeployment plan" (Ontario Regulation 77/20). In this unusual situation, professional regulatory bodies acknowledged that health care professionals may be asked by their employers to work outside of their traditional scope of practice. The professional regulatory Colleges acknowledged this delegated power of employers and primarily advised registrants to use their best professional judgment when making decisions about specific assigned tasks. Some regulatory Colleges also chose to emphasize their registrants' duty to care, citing the limited scenarios where a professional may refuse a care assignment or discontinue services. The effect is that powers that had been historically distributed across the internal social structures of professions became temporarily consolidated under the jurisdiction of employers, now able to make decisions about scopes of practice, continuing education needs, and competency of their professional employees. While this was an unusual circumstance, the speed at which this consolidation of power was accomplished is telling. Historically, sociologists have identified four key actors in the development of the professions: practitioners, the recipients of professional services, states and universities. The way power was reconfigured in response to this pandemic strongly suggests that future theorizing on the professions must also consider a fifth potentially powerful actor: employing organizations (Evetts, 2016).

Exclusive Boundaries: Intersections of Governance and Knowledge

We have described much of the configurational work of the government as working to bring previously separated workers together, oriented toward a common aim. However, configurational boundary work also serves to exclude actors. In this section, we describe a particular exclusion, analytically relevant for the implications of how professional work and professional knowledge are organized. The exclusion of family members from health care spaces stands in direct contrast to earlier rhetorical displays from the government that have emphasized patient and family centered care, describing family members as valued partners in care (Rowland et al., 2016). This exclusion was justified by concerns to ensure "a safe and secure environment for residents" and was given legitimacy through reference to the Chief Medical Officer of Health's advice to the Ministry (MOHLTC Newsroom, March 16, 2020). Health professionals took to social media, describing the extents to which they were working to try to ameliorate the social isolation created for seniors living in LTC due to these exclusions. Family members also took to social media, describing the continued exclusion as "heartbreaking", "infuriating", and "unsafe". Thus, this decision to exclude family caregivers from healthcare spaces was contentious. However, it was presented as a necessary evil (Molinsky & Margolis, 2005) in an exceptional circumstance.

It might seem unusual to focus on the exclusion of caregivers from healthcare workspaces as part of this analysis. By virtue of their employment relationships, caregivers may already be considered outside of the phenomenon of interest. However, we draw attention to this exclusion as it reflects an interruption of a recent policy trajectory in Canada. For more than 15 years, Ontario has been pursuing an agenda related to patient centered care. This agenda takes shape through engagement strategies, "using patient and caregiver experiences to improve care" (Health Quality Ontario, 2015). In this policy trajectory, much is said about the expertise of patients and caregivers. The argument is that the expertise that is gained through experience as a patient or a caregiver warrants a place for patients and caregivers at decision-making tables at all levels of healthcare organizations and healthcare governance (Kerr et al., 2007; Sanderson & Angouri, 2013). Further, patients and their caregivers are repositioned as "members of the care team", rather than objects of professional service. This notion of patient and caregiver expertise has received considerable attention in sociological literature (Epstein, 1995; Voronka, 2016), including some of the tensions introduced when using these claims of patient or caregiver expertise to reconfigure multi-professional healthcare teams (Martin & Finn, 2011). Thus, the scholarly conversation on the inclusion of patients and caregivers in healthcare spaces has emphasized boundary work. However, those boundaries have largely been considered as constructions (and contests) of knowledge, legitimacy, and expertise (Rowland et al., 2018).

In the context of the pandemic, these claims of expertise were rendered fragile, if not irrelevant. What emerged instead was a focus on risk, as family caregivers were constructed as (additional) bodies of risk. Uncertainty about mechanism of virus spread, wide-spread concerns about adequate supplies of personal protective equipment, and organizations mobilizing around systems of infection control and surveillance all converged around decisions to limit risk as much as possible. Whereas traditional lines of inquiry about boundary work in the professions would draw attention to dynamics of exclusion based on jurisdictional claims to expertise, this scenario draws attention to dynamics of risk (and accountability) as they play out in boundary work. This example is particularly striking as is it reflects an abrupt shift in an emerging policy trajectory that had positioned patients and family caregivers as "valuable members of the care team".

This exclusion was rendered particularly contentious when placed in contrast to newly arrived stakeholders who *were* allowed access to health care spaces: the Canadian Armed Forces (CAF). Members of the CAF provided many of the care tasks that had been previously been accomplished by family visitors: providing meals, feeding residents, assisting with personal hygiene, and offering reassurance (Operation LASER, accessed July 23, 2020). The appeal being made by excluded family members took on new urgency when the CAF documented alarmingly poor levels of care in LTC facilities. Framed as an obligatory response to report on the conditions of a mission, the Operation LASER report released in May 2020 detailed conditions of resident neglect, poor infection control practices, expired medication, inadequate staff training, poor communication, and inappropriate staff behavior (Operation LASER, May 20, 2020). This report aggravated an existing sense of public mistrust in the ability of these centers to provide adequate care in the absence of continued vigilance and presence from committed family members (Rowland & Kuper, 2017). This aggravation played out in social media, as members of the public and health care professionals further demanded the exclusion of family members in LTC be lifted. As the visiting restrictions were slowly eased, the Ministry primarily credited the staff of LTC facilities, saying "thanks to the hard work of our frontline workers and the collective effort of everyone in stopping the spread, we can now allow families to reunite with their loved ones safely and in person with strict public health measures" (MOHLTC Newsroom, June 11, 2020). Staff were hardworking. Family members were "allowed" re-entry into healthcare spaces. The institutional boundaries are stark.

The persistence of this boundary troubles the notion that knowledge is the primary justification of the boundary between professionals and "lay" members of the public. Given that LTC facilities opened their doors to new stakeholders during the pandemic, the persistence of this exclusion of family visitors cannot be explained by knowledge and training alone. If members of the Armed Forces, volunteers, and new hires could be rapidly trained to provide safe personal care to residents during the pandemic, arguably family members could have been as well. Following this line of reasoning, the exclusionary boundary cannot be explained by appeals to professional knowledge or skill. Instead, likely explanatory mechanisms for the persistence of this boundary may have been about the preservation of resources (e.g., limited supplies of personal protective equipment being reserved for health care providers, limited time of health care providers to supervise infection control practices of visiting family members) and the limited ability of employers to *govern* the infection control procedures of family members. Despite the moral valence of describing family members and caregivers as members of the care team, these relationships were rendered fragile in the face of institutional accountabilities and assessments of risk.

Again, the powerful role of the employer in governing the work of health care professionals and employees emerges as a more salient social factor than knowledge alone. Arguably, long-time family caregivers could make a credible claim to specialized knowledge about their family members' care needs. That health service organizations continue to exclude family members as caregivers suggests that these boundaries are maintained based on assessments of risk, of accountability and governance, not knowledge. This offers another layer by which to understand the boundaries between professions and "lay" members of the public, one that considers organizational powers and accountabilities. This analysis also troubles the assumed role of knowledge and expertise in maintaining boundaries, instead shifting attention to twinned concepts of accountability and governance. Thus, a fruitful way forward in understanding that professions would include grappling with changing fields of knowledge and expertise, but also shifts in concepts of professional responsibility and accountability (Fenwick, 2016). This analytical attention provides a necessary and continued complement to more recent theorizations of professions that focus on concepts of expertise (Eyal, 2013) while also attending to concepts of responsibility and governance.

Discussion

Our aims in this study were twofold. First, we aspired to explore these dynamics of redeployment in order to better understand their potential effects, both short term and potentially far-reaching. Second, we reflect back on our current conceptual tools, exploring their potential fit for purpose during these exceptional times. While these times are exceptional, it is their extremity that makes both long-standing and newly emerging dynamics particularly visible. Through this visibility, we may consider our existing tools and see how well they approach current dynamics while also considering historical foundations. To those aims, we turn to our discussion to two main themes: (1) theoretically exploring potential effects of reorganization and their implications for relationships between publics, professions, and the state and (2) reflecting back on our conceptual tools and how they might be meaningfully expanded.

Potential Effects of Reorganization: Existing Policy Trajectories

Through our analysis, we attempted to connect current efforts to reorganize health care and health care professionals to existing policy trajectories. On one hand, we see a continuation of an existing policy trajectory. In this case, we see how the Ministry of Health and Long-Term Care was able to take an active role in the reconfiguration of professional work as a result of more than 30 years of steady incursion into not just the organization of health care, but also the content. Not only was this a continuation of an existing policy trajectory, it may have been an escalation, as responses to the unfolding crisis consolidated a great deal of power under the jurisdiction of employing organizations. On the other hand, we saw an interruption of a nascent policy trajectory. In this case, we saw a relatively shorter history of policies related to shared power with patient and family caregivers abruptly halted in response to concerns of risk, governance, and accountability. The associated consequences of this latter move played out in social media, primarily framed as moral dilemmas and interruptions of compassionate care. However, the consequences of this abrupt shift in the policy trajectory may be more far-reaching, as they potentially solidify boundaries between (paid) health care workers and (unpaid) caregivers.

Attending to the history of policy trajectories is an important thread of analysis. In understanding these historical dynamics we may develop a more nuanced understanding of the present (Adams et al., 2020). In this case, is it not new to consider professions as embedded in complex webs of relationships with other professionals, state actors, patients, publics, and employers. What we are drawing attention to are the shifts in power and accountability revealed in these evolving relationships. Further, by placing the current dynamics of reorganization in the context of existing policy trajectories, we are able to see both continuities and disruptions. In doing so, we are more capable of exploring intended and unintended consequences of these decisions. This kind of reflection will be necessary for any future attempts to unravel unintended consequences of decisions made during the crisis.

Expanding Empirical and Conceptual Range: Focusing on the Role of Employing Organizations

Throughout our analysis, employing organizations steadily emerged as central players in the unfolding dynamics. This focus on employing organizations is in contrast to earlier work in the sociology of professions that have described systems of professional production but ascribed employing organizations a rather marginal role in those dynamics (Evetts, 2016). Where employing organizations have been considered, they are often positioned in opposition to the interests of professions. This has resulted in a binary in the scholarly literature on the professions. On one side of the binary, researchers have oriented toward advocating for a "return to the professions" as a way to protect occupational spaces and rescue professional work. On the opposite side of the binary, researchers have argued to move "beyond professions" in ways that restrict professional autonomy and discipline professional work toward organizational interests (Noordegraaf, 2011).

Newman (2013) argues that the way out of this conceptual binary is to shift the focus away from the various actors involved in systems of professions and instead attend to the relationships between them. Describing relationships between professions, governments, publics, and employing organizations as tangled in "knowledge-power knots", Newman maps out different formations of power and their implications for public service professionals.

As publics place new expectations, governments make new demands, employing organizations tighten controls, and professions potentially become more fractured, the relational dynamics of professions begin to shift. In this analysis, we saw these knowledge-power knots shift toward government-organizational relationships. However, we also saw the necessity of large-scale organizational efforts to allow professionals to do their work. This was not a binary between professions and employing organizations, but a dynamic shift in the ordering of long-established relationships in response to a large-scale crisis. What remains to be seen is whether those shifts will persist beyond this immediate crisis.

Perhaps provocatively, Waring (in Adams et al., 2020) argues that traditional sociology of the professions has long been shaped by the combined dominance of neo-Weberian and neo-institutional theories. In the process, the field may be losing conceptual purchase on important shifting relationships that would be better appreciated using ecological or relational perspectives. Adams and Waring (in Adams et al., 2020) both argue that these webs of relationships have long characterized the professions. What is potentially changing is the power within these relationships, the associated accountabilities and norms, as well as the institutional arrangements that allow people to accomplish their various tasks. By bringing the unit of analysis to these relationships, the focus shifts away from the professions and their interests and moves toward questions of how autonomy, expertise and authority are realized in wider systems of work (Waring in Adams et al., 2020). Thus, we are in agreement with this call to focus on the relationships between actors in systems of professions and we further argue that employing organizations are a key actor in this complex web. This is both an empirical expansion and a conceptual shift in the sociology of the professions.

Conclusions

Following a traditional read of Abbott's system of the professions, we may have expected to find conditions of competition between the professions, an elevated role for profession-specific abstract knowledge, and a relatively distant role for the state in shaping the work of the professions. Instead, we found the conditions being set for professions to mobilize around shared tasks and a directly intervening state mobilizing its power through the health service provider organizations where health professionals work. The longer-term consequences of all of this boundary work remain to be seen. However, we propose our conceptual framing requires elaboration in order to grasp the social and political complexity of all of this activity and to ask meaningful future questions.

One empirical consequence of this line of thought is to look more carefully and directly at the role of employing organizations in the sociology of the professions. Another consequence is a focus on the continued utility of the concept of boundary work. Elaborating this concept beyond competitive boundary work to be inclusive of configurational boundary work provides a powerful analytical lens to explore emerging processes of organizing (Langley et al., 2019). We also argue there is both an opportunity and a need to attend to shifting constructions of professional responsibility and how those constructions of responsibility participate in the boundary work of professions. This was particularly apparent in the analysis of the exclusion of caregivers from healthcare spaces, where assessments of risk, responsibility and governance were far more salient than arguments for expertise.

We have approached this analysis as a snapshot in some very exceptional times. At this moment, we draw attention to reconfigured relationships between professions, the state, employing organization, publics, patients and their family members. Whether these reconfigurations will persist beyond this crisis remains to be seen. However, taking stock at this moment reveals how these shifts have been made possible, how they are manifestations of dynamics already set in place, and what these shifts potentially imply for future reordered relationships. Rather than attempting to predict the longer-term organization and governance of care in post-COVID era, our analysis points toward questions we might ask as the current flux begins to settle into something more durable. Will this tight coupling between the government and employing organizations persist and to what potential effect across the health professions? Now that professional tasks have been redistributed across the healthcare workforce, will these tasks ever be returned to their original jurisdictional space? How will aspirations of increased appreciation for patient, family and caregivers' knowledge continue to interact with institutional logics of risk and accountability? What might be gained and what might be lost in all of this configurational work? We argue that these kinds of questions are consequential.

The response being mobilized in the social sciences communities is not garnering the same kind of public attention as the medical sciences. However, the insights being generated in the social sciences will be essential in shaping the next phase of our collective futures. Exploring the role of healthcare professionals in the COVID-19 response is just one small thread of inquiry in a much broader project. Pulling these threads together is important for the future of the professions, but also participates in the futures of the kinds of societies we want to create.

References

Abbott, A. (1988). *The system of professions: An essay on the division of expert labor*. University of Chicago Press.

Abbott, A. (1995a). Boundaries of social work or social work of boundaries?: The social service review lecture. *Social Service Review, 69*(4), 545–562.

Abbott, A. (1995b). Things of boundaries. *Social Research, 62*(4), 857–882.

Abbott, A. (2005). Linked ecologies: States and universities as environments for professions. *Sociological Theory, 23*(3), 245–274.

Adams, T. L., Kirkpatrick, I., Tolbert, P. S., & Waring, J. (2020). From protective to connective professionalism: Quo Vadis professional exclusivity? *Journal of Professions and Organization*. https://doi.org/10.1093/jpo/joaa014

Adams, T. L., & Saks, M. (2018). Neo-weberianism and changing state-profession relations: The case of Canadian health care. *Sociologia, Problemas e Práticas, 88*(88), 61–77.

Anteby, M., Chan, C. K., & DiBenigno, J. (2016). Three lenses on occupations and professions in organizations: Becoming, doing, and relating. *The Academy of Management Annals, 10*(1), 183–244. https://doi.org/10.1080/19416520.2016.1120962

Bourdieu, P. (1980). *The logic of practice*. Stanford University Press.

Bourdieu, P. (1993). *Sociology in question*. Sage.

Bourdieu, P. (1996). Understanding. *Theory, Culture & Society, 13*(2), 17–37.

Bourgeault, I. L., & Mulvale, G. (2006). Collaborative health care teams in Canada and the USA: Confronting the structural embeddedness of medical dominance. *Health Sociology Review: Medical Dominance Revisited, 15*(5), 481–495.

Coburn, D. (1988). Canadian medicine: Dominance or proletarianization? *The Milbank Quarterly, 66*(2), 92–116.

Coburn, D. (1993). State authority, medical dominance, and trends in the regulation of the health professions: The Ontario case. *Social Science & Medicine, 37*(7), 841–850.

Coburn, D. (2006). Medical dominance then and now: Critical reflections. *Health Sociology Review, 15*(5), 432–443.

Coburn, D., Rappolt, S., & Bourgeault, I. (1997). Decline vs retention of medical power through restratification: An examination of the Ontario case. *Sociology of Health & Illness, 19*(1), 1–22.

Cox, C. L. (2020). 'Healthcare heroes': Problems with media focus on heroism from healthcare workers during the COVID-19 pandemic. *Journal of Medical Ethics, 46*(8), 510–513. https://doi.org/10.1136/medethics-2020-106398

Epstein, S. (1995). The construction of lay expertise: AIDS activism and the forging of credibility in the reform of clinical trials. *Science, Technology & Human Values, 20*(4), 408–437. https://doi.org/10.1177/016224399502000402

Evetts, J. (2016). Trust and professionalism: Challenges and occupational changes. *Current Sociology, 54*(4), 515–531. https://doi.org/10.1177/0011392106065083

Eyal, G. (2013). For a sociology of expertise: The social origins of the autism epidemic. *American Journal of Sociology, 118*(4), 863–907.

Fenwick, T. (2016). *Professional responsibility and professionalism: A sociomaterial examination*. Routeledge.

Gieryn, T. F. (1983). Boundary-work and the demarcation of science from non-science: Strains and interests in professional ideologies of scientists. *American Sociological Review, 48*(6), 781–795. https://doi.org/10.2307/2095325

Kerr, A., Cunningham-Burley, S., & Tutton, R. (2007). Shifting subject positions: Experts and lay people in public dialogue. *Social Studies of Science, 37*(3), 385–411. https://doi.org/10.1177/0306312706068492

Lamont, M., & Molnár, V. (2002). The study of boundaries in the social sciences. *Annual Review of Sociology, 28*(1), 167–195.

Langley, A., Lindberg, K., Mørk, B. E., Nicolini, D., Raviola, E., & Walter, L. (2019). Boundary work among groups, occupations, and organizations: From cartography to process. *Academy of Management Annals, 13*(2), 704–736.

Latour, B. (2007). *Reassembling the social: An introduction to actor-network-theory*. Oxford University Press.

Lefkowitz, A. (2020, May 11). Fourteen days on the COVID ward. *Toronto Life*. Retrieved from https://torontolife.com/city/fourteen-days-on-the-covid-ward-at-sunnybrook-a-memoir/

Martin, G. P., & Finn, R. (2011). Patients as team members: Opportunities, challenges and paradoxes of including patients in multi-professional healthcare teams. *Sociology of Health & Illness, 33*(7), 1050–1065. https://doi.org/10.1111/j.1467-9566.2011.01356.x

Molinsky, A., & Margolis, J. (2005). Necessary evils and interpersonal sensitivity in organizations. *Academy of Management Review, 30*(2), 245–268.

Muzio, D., Aulakh, S., & Kirkpatrick, I. (2019). *Professional occupations and organizations*. Cambridge University Press.

Newman, J. (2013). Professionals, power, and the reform of public services. In M. Noordegraaf & B. Steijn (Eds.), *Professionals under pressure: The reconfiguration of professional work in changing public services* (pp. 41–54). Amsterdam University Press.

Noordegraaf, M. (2011). Risky business: How professionals and professional fields (must) deal with organizational issues. *Organization Studies, 32*(10), 1349–1371. https://doi.org/10.1177/0170840611416748

Rowland, P., & Kuper, A. (2017). Beyond vulnerability: How the dual role of patient-health care provider can inform health professions education. *Advances in Health Sciences Education, 23*(1), 115–131. https://doi.org/10.1007/s10459-017-9777-y

Rowland, P., McMillan, S., Martimianakis, M. A., & Hodges, B. D. (2018). Learning from patients: Constructions of knowledge and legitimacy in hospital-based quality improvement programmes. *Studies in Continuing Education, 40*(3), 337–350. https://doi.org/10.1080/0158037x.2018.1465402

Rowland, P., McMillan, S. E., McGillicuddy, P., & Richards, J. (2016). What is "the" patient perspective in patient engagement programs? Implicit logics and parallels to feminist theory. *Health: An Interdisciplinary Journal for the Social Study of Health, Illness and Medicine, 21*(1), 76–92.

Sanderson, T., & Angouri, J. (2013). 'I'm an expert in me and I know what I can cope with': Patient expertise in rheumatoid arthritis. *Communication & Medicine, 10*(3), 249–261.

Star, S. L. (2010). This is not a boundary object: Reflections on the origin of a concept. *Science, Technology, & Human Values, 35*(5), 601–617. https://doi.org/10.1177/0162243910377624

Strauss, A., Fagerhaugh, S., Suczek, B., & Wiener, C. (1985). *The social organization of medical work*. The University of Chicago Press.

Strauss, A., Schatzman, L., Ehrlich, D., Bucher, R., & Sabshin, M. (1963). The hospital and its negotiated order. In E. Friedson (Ed.), *The hospital in modern society* (pp. 169–XXX). Free Press.

Voronka, J. (2016). The politics of 'people with lived experience' experiential authority and the risks of strategic essentialism. *Philosophy, Psychiatry, & Psychology, 23*(3), 189–201. Retrieved from https://muse.jhu.edu/article/648226

William, A. P., Eugene, V., May, L. C., Christel, A. W., & Barbara, M. F. (1995). Medicine and the Canadian state: From the politics of conflict to the politics of accommodation? *Journal of Health and Social Behavior, 36*(4), 303–321.

CHAPTER 9

The Impact of COVID-19 on Primary Care Practitioners: Transformation, Upheaval and Uncertainty

Emily Burn, Louise Locock, Rebecca Fisher, and Judith Smith

Introduction: A System in Flux

The COVID-19 pandemic led to a wholesale re-ordering in 2020 of primary care service delivery in both the UK and other countries. Virtually overnight, general practices radically re-structured care provision, and consultations moved from face-to-face to telephone calls or online interactions wherever possible (Clarke et al., 2020; Thornton, 2020). Service changes which had been the source of protracted debate, and which would ordinarily have taken years to implement, quickly became normal

E. Burn (✉) · J. Smith
University of Birmingham, Birmingham, UK
e-mail: e.burn@bham.ac.uk

L. Locock
University of Aberdeen, Aberdeen, Scotland, UK

R. Fisher
The Health Foundation, London, UK

J. Waring et al. (eds.), *Organising Care in a Time of Covid-19*, Organizational Behaviour in Healthcare,
https://doi.org/10.1007/978-3-030-82696-3_9

practice (Brant et al., 2016; Lay, 2020; Marshall et al., 2020). At the same time, other challenges and changes included the development of 'hot hubs' for COVID-19-related primary care across cities or districts, and the addition of new staff and roles into what became large extended general practice teams (including formerly retired staff, part-time staff working full-time and extra hours, clinical academics, and volunteers).

While primary care was braced for a large wave of COVID-19-related workload, as the pandemic evolved in the UK, concern emerged that patients who needed to seek help for non-COVID-19 conditions were not doing so, and a backlog of ill-health was building rapidly in the community (NHS England and Improvement, 2020a; Spencer & Oung, 2020). Primary care staff then faced a new series of challenges as the government issued guidelines in the summer of 2020 for a gradual return to restoring practices to their full range of services, also recommending that some new ways of working—including offering a greater proportion of phone or online consultations—should continue to be part of the offer (NHS England and Improvement, 2020b).

We view this as an example of 'punctuated equilibrium' in both national policy and local practice. Punctuated equilibrium is a metaphor borrowed originally from evolutionary biology, where it described long periods of evolutionary stability 'punctuated' by sudden rapid change in the fossil record, before the re-establishment of a new stability. In social theory, Baumgartner and Jones (1993/2010) borrowed the term to explain shifts in American policymaking. They argued that 'the course of public policy in the United States is not gradual and incremental, but rather is disjointed and episodic. Long periods of stability are interrupted by bursts of frenetic policy activity' (2010: xvii). While the causes of such bursts of change might sometimes be because of electoral shifts, more often than not they are observed to result from the confluence of multiple factors in specific policy arenas, where 'the stars can align' (p. xxv) for a change to break through. Health policy is frequently subject to reform. COVID-19, however, created a very different context compared to the usual fluidity of health policy. COVID-19 initiated a violent rupture where all-encompassing changes had to be made to local practice at extraordinary speed. These circumstances were exceptional in modern times and created a great sense of initial uncertainty.

This chapter presents the initial findings of a study, started in early spring 2020, that has captured the narratives of primary care practitioners during a time of pandemic. General practitioners, practice nurses, and practice managers were invited to participate in the study to ensure a range of experiences were documented. The research team periodically sent questions for participants to consider, these being designed to reflect topical discussion points as the response to the pandemic progressed. Participants were able to contribute as frequently as they wished and could also choose how they shared their experiences. Some participants decided to record voice notes on their phone which were then sent securely to the research team, whereas others contributed written notes or via a telephone or online interview with a member of the research team. Narratives are still being collected from 16 participants and thematically analysed (Braun et al., 2018) at the time of writing, reflecting the ongoing pandemic.

COVID-19 represents a fascinating intersection between the biological and social theory versions of punctuated equilibrium. A powerful virus emerged in a landscape where the advent of digital technologies was already, gradually, reshaping health care and its forms of communication and consultation, and accelerated this process at previously unimaginable speed. Whereas before much of the discussion about 'modernising primary care service delivery' was couched in terms of—for example—organisational facilitators and barriers to change, resistance to new ways of working, incremental adoption, and professional identities, a tiny invisible organism caused a sudden and major acceleration of this change. This has resulted both in enforced, unplanned service transformation and the emergence of 'policy windows' (Kingdon, 2002) which have given policy actors an opportunity to pursue intended change. Tuohy (1999) uses the term 'accidental logics' to describe how external events can create unanticipated windows to implement change within health systems.

Professionals in Transition

Such upheaval has profound consequences not just for organisational systems but also for individual people. It is undoubtedly the case that changes arising from COVID-19 have been disconcerting, stressful and emotional for general practice team members. As one GP colleague observed to us, 'I've been a GP for 25 years, and overnight I felt I didn't know how to do my job any more' (personal communication). In his work on role transitions, Ashforth (2000) examined how people move between role identities—sometimes just as day-to-day transitions (e.g. transitioning between work and home life personas) but sometimes as a result of changes within their work environment. He considers the use of Lewin's (1951) model of change (unfreeze-change-refreeze) to articulate how a previously stable state becomes fluid and disrupted before resettling into equilibrium, although both Lewin and Ashforth note that there may be repeated fluctuation and blurring between change and stability along the way. The predicted waves of COVID-19 infections until the discovery of a vaccine, and associated impact on health services, makes this repetition and cycles of change very likely.[1]

Ashforth argues that 'one may need a mechanism—a *transition bridge*—to preserve a sense of personal continuity as one moves between roles [....] even if the transition is welcomed as a means of furthering personal development' (p. 12). Transition bridges may include identity narratives, transitional roles, grieving and mementos, which help maintain attachment to the past while performing in a new role. However, 'a particularly disruptive transition [...], typically a high magnitude, socially undesirable, and involuntary transition, may simply overwhelm the efficacy of bridging mechanisms precisely when they are most needed' (p. 12), leading to potential heightened 'role shock' or the discontinuity generated through a 'discrepancy between expectations and experiences' (p. 159).

Ashforth argues that when workplace roles are in flux, a series of 'psychological motives' come into play. Team members have to work to create and maintain: a sense of workplace identity; meaning; control; and belonging. The better each individual is able to resolve these motives at a personal level, the better they will be able to deal with disruption to their role and organisational upheaval. Reflecting on the COVID-19 pandemic, Wiedner et al. (2020) explore how crises can lead to 'improvised innovation'—innovation borne of 'dealing with unforeseen events without the benefit of preparation' (p. 1). Wiedner et al. note how the shared experience of responding to the pressures of a crisis can facilitate a positive 'collective identity'. Despite the potential for the COVID-19 pandemic to fragment primary care teams, there is also potential for healthcare workers to feel a strengthening of team identity and shared purpose, and greater affinity with the wider health system which can challenge silo working and encourage greater support for change.

[1] Note a vaccine had yet to be developed at the time of the fieldwork reported here.

At a more experiential level, Bury's (1982) concept of biographical disruption offers an additional lens through which to understand individual transitions. This concept was originally derived from studying the diagnosis of chronic illness and how this disrupts one's sense of self, one's anticipated trajectory in life and one's ability to maintain relationships and activities. People who experience biographical disruption, Bury suggests, will work hard to mobilise material and social resources to restore or repair their biography, and find a new way of being. While they may normalise their new situation, further changes in health status may require repeated adaptations and repair work.

In the case of primary care workers, the source of the disruption is not usually personal illness but rather the dramatic effects of a virus and associated pandemic on society, which has transformed primary care staff's working lives, and left them scrambling to regroup in a situation of ongoing radical uncertainty.

In this chapter, we first outline the changes that took place in primary care during 2020 and continue to take place at the time of writing. We then present findings from a small longitudinal study of the experiences of individual primary care staff, including GPs, practice nurses and practice managers. These narratives were collected from April 2020 onwards and were therefore able to capture in real time the evolving lockdown of UK society and health service re-opening situation. In this analysis, we focus particularly on what the virus enabled, enforced and prevented, and how this has affected the lives, work and professional identities of individual primary care staff.

Findings

A reduction in GP consultations since the start of the pandemic has been widely reported and has led to concerns about the care of non-COVID-19 patients, people with long-term health conditions, and the potential for delayed diagnoses. In April 2020—the first full month of UK 'lockdown'—there were 8.7 million GP consultations, compared with 12.4 million in the same month in 2019. The proportion of consultations taking place by telephone jumped significantly, as the number of face-to-face consultations fell (NHS Digital, 2020). Health Foundation analysis of data from the clinical practice research datalink (CPRD) shows that over the period from March to June 2020, there was a fall in the number of referrals, medical tests, new prescriptions and immunisations in general

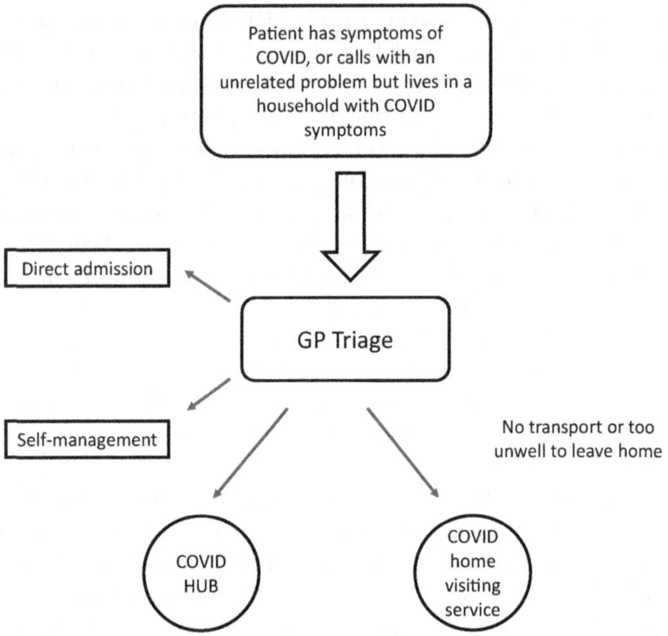

Fig. 9.1 Triage process in COVID-19 hubs

practice. As time and the pandemic have progressed, the number of GP appointments carried out in England has risen again.

Describing Change

The participants in this study all highlighted the vast array of changes that were made to general practice during the first half of 2020. These changes included: the advancement of digital consultations, primary care practitioners working remotely, restructuring and adapting the physical layout of practices to maintain social distancing, and the increased use of personal protective equipment. Below, Dr. Rebecca Fisher, a practising GP, describes the establishment of COVID-19 hubs in Oxford, along with other aspects of change to general practice as the pandemic progressed and attempts were made to restore non-COVID-19 primary care services.

Creating a COVID-19 Primary Care Service

Since 2014, GP practices in Oxford have collaborated through OxFed, a not-for-profit healthcare organisation owned by Oxford's NHS GP practices. Prior to the COVID-19 pandemic OxFed ran several services, shared by practices across the city. This included a 7-day access service (allowing practices to meet their extended hours commitments), and a home visiting service. In early March, as COVID-19 loomed large, OxFed rapidly re-configured services to provide COVID hubs and a COVID home visiting service.

What happened?

Almost overnight OxFed worked with a variety of local stakeholders, including GP practices and the clinical commissioning group to develop an entirely new service. This aimed to provide excellent primary medical care for patients with COVID-19, and people with COVID-19 symptoms in the household, and to do so in a separate location from GP surgeries in the city. This allowed practices to keep their sites as safe as possible for staff and for patients without COVID-19 symptom. Three sites were found and were turned into 'COVID-19 hubs'. These were staffed by a mix of GPs who usually work for the (temporarily paused) 7-day access service, and GPs who agreed to work for the service as additional hours. Patients were triaged into the service via their own GP practice as shown in Fig. 9.1.

Triaging GPs at city surgeries booked patients into COVID-19 clinics, whereupon clinic administrative staff phoned the patient, ascertained that they had their own transport (important for infection control), and offered a specific appointment time and location. COVID-19 hub sites were set up to maximise infection control, with minimal contact time between patients and GPs. Most history was ascertained by telephone with the patient in their car, and patients were examined face-to-face only where necessary. Staff observed social distancing within hub sites to try and minimise spread of infection, with GPs working in separate rooms where possible, and an infection control lead at each site. GPs working at COVID-19 hubs had full read and write access into the patient's usual medical notes, and so informational continuity of care was preserved.

OxFed additionally re-purposed their home visiting service, to become a COVID-19 home visiting service—seeing patients with probable COVID-19 who either did not have their own transport to enable safe attendance at a hub, or who were housebound. Initially this meant the temporary suspension of the usual home visiting service, and individual practices resumed responsibility for all non-COVID-19-related home visits to their patients. In April 2020, the Oxford COVID-19 hubs saw 354 patients in clinic, and 190 patients via the COVID-19 home visiting service, and 342 patients were seen in clinic and 206 on home visits in May.

As demand for COVID-19 services dropped in May 2020, the three COVID-19 hub sites were condensed to a single site. OxFed have divided their home visiting service into 'green' (non-COVID-19) and 'red' (possible COVID-19 symptoms) patients, releasing some capacity back to routine general practice. This enables general practice in the city to continue to operate a 'hot' and 'cold' site system, where patients' with possible COVID-19 are seen outside of their usual GP surgeries.

Throughout this period GP surgeries in Oxford continued to 'see' patients, but with a 'telephone first' approach. Patients requesting appointments would have an initial telephone or e-consultation with a clinician, through which their concern would either be addressed, or a face-to-face appointment arranged at their practice if required.

Sudden and Unsettling Change

Narratives were collected throughout the pandemic, as such they captured the reorganisation of practices, along with primary care practitioners' response to the pandemic at both a professional and personal level. Recurrent themes throughout the initial narratives were the great speed at which changes were made to primary care, and the profound consequences for professional identity.

Frequently, participants discussed feeling lost as they had little choice but to get used to a new approach to consulting. Remote consultations often denied primary care professionals access to some of their much-honed skills to detect subtle signs and clues—for example, someone's gait when entering the consultation room—that could inform their investigations. As a result of the fast-changing character of the pandemic, participants highlighted that initially there was not a key, overarching guideline or policy that could inform practices' response. Some participants noted that guidance and plans were shared by clinical commissioning groups (CCGs) and health boards, with practices at times working with others within the primary care network to create their own plans. At the initial stages of the pandemic, these plans frequently changed according to the shifting situation. As demonstrated by the participant below, there was frequent acknowledgement of an early overload of information in some areas, but limited guidance on others. Participants reported that the pace of change did decrease as the pandemic progressed but that there was a continual need to plan for the future organisation of care (e.g. the delivery of the flu vaccination programme, and eventual roll-out of a COVID-19 vaccine).

> I think the volume of stuff to read to keep up, certainly in the first phase, felt pretty overwhelming. There was this kind of, on some levels, complete silence in that there was no national guidance for what to do, on numerous levels, so both how we should structure our services, but also what we should do about specific treatment decisions. [Participant 1]

While practices developed their own response in respect of how to organise patient services in a time of societal lockdown, some participants discussed how the subsequent release of local or national NHS guidance meant that such plans had to be revised on multiple occasions, leading to further uncertainty, as identified here:

> Initially it felt very much like we were trying to build something and make changes on shifting sands. Every day there was new guidance coming out, there were new rules coming out, there were new definitions coming out, and we had to rethink our plans all the time. [Participant 7]

> There's lots of information coming out, it was very information overload. You'd read one thing one day and it all changed the next...Do you follow your local guidelines? Do you follow your national guidelines? Medically, legally where do you stand? It was very difficult. [Participant 12]

This sense of uncertainty was also expressed when discussing the move from face-to-face to remote consulting in primary care. One participant framed the role of GPs as being similar to a detective [participant 1], working with patients to take a medical history and make inferences from their observations. Working remotely was suggested to reduce the number of senses that primary care practitioners could call upon within their diagnostic role. Participants frequently reported that the effects of the pandemic meant they could no longer rely on their experience, succinctly articulated by one GP [participant 5] as '*we're all beginners together*' and also expressed in the quotation below:

> But I think the main difficulty has been in the way that we think and work. We've had to completely change our normal thought processes, whether it be simple things like getting investigations, radiology or referrals done, or even whether we assess people face-to-face, has all had to have been viewed through the lens of the coronavirus. And this is proving really hard, because you can't fall back on the heuristics built up over years of experience, because they're all now wrong. We're having to relearn them, have to do a lot of type two thinking and it's effortful. So although demand has been lower, the effort involved in work has been high and it's really quite stressful, and exhausting working in this environment. [Participant 7]

> So it was very difficult to know whether we were giving people the right advice or not and I found it really unsettling and very anxiety provoking really as to whether I was telling people, you know, 'actually no you don't need to be shielding' and then leaving them vulnerable, that was my worry, that I was mis-, you know, advising them incorrectly, that was not a comfortable place to be. [Participant 12]

> We're very much sort of controlling – we are the best, we are the perfectionists, and then all of a sudden to be put in a place of deep uncertainty and doubt, is quite – has a quite sort of existential sort of moments of what is the point of me? Why did I think I could do this? And that kind of really questioning what your core reason for being in general practice, or not just in general practice, but I think particularly general practice, because so much of what we do is relationship based medicine. So much of what we do is around establishing those relationships with trust. And I don't know, all of a sudden everything changed, and we had to get our heads around everybody being safe and us being safe. And I think we lost something in that moment initially. [Participant 10]

The changes involved were thus unsettling in several ways—not just in terms of disrupting routines and ways of practising, and facing a new, baffling condition, but also in terms of emotion and a fundamentally disrupted sense of self, as the above quotation reveals. GPs described feeling they had lost their professional bearings, cast adrift without their normal navigational aids.

While participants highlighted the confusion and difficulties of the initial phase of the pandemic, some also welcomed a new sense of liberation to pursue innovation. It was also noted that pre-pandemic attempts to pursue change in general practice service delivery had at times been frustrated due to professional resistance or other factors. While some participants felt that progress had already been beginning to be made within some of these areas (e.g., phone triage of GP appointments, online consultations), the pandemic had '*added an impetus that wasn't there previously*' [participant 7].

Related to this point about impetus and energy for change, participants often mentioned that there had been an initial welcome reduction in what was identified to be excessive monitoring by NHS England and Improvement and the local clinical commissioning group, and greater autonomy for practices and primary care networks to get on and make local decisions during the height of the pandemic. Reduced oversight facilitated the 'improvised innovation' (Wiedner et al., 2020) required by the COVID-19 pandemic. One participant discussed this in terms of their practice embedding the '*freedom to fail*' [participant 1] when trying out new ways of working, with another reflecting that the pandemic had '*created an environment where basically nothing was sacred anymore*' [participant 11], a sentiment captured in the following quotation:

> I think one thing I'd like to say actually is that what was really freeing was a bit of the not having problems with the bureaucracy. So normally if you'd wanted to make these changes, you'd have probably had to go through many layers of decision making and approval processes, but actually we just did it, now. Ideally, there are some things that do need approval and whatever, but actually shaking off some of the shackles of regulation, because that's actually been one of the things that has bogged practitioners down. [Participant 12]

The speed at which the COVID-19 pandemic hit meant that primary care practitioners had little choice other than to devise responses to ensure that those patients experiencing both COVID-19 and non-COVID-19 symptoms received appropriate care. Services were redesigned rapidly in exceptional circumstances and it was clear from the study participants that there was an element of testing out new ways of doing things, adapting them so that they worked best, and trying to ensure that they met the requirements of evolving guidance. However, six months into the pandemic, there are signs of some return to centralised and sometimes contradictory oversight as seen in NHS England and Improvement's (2020c) letter advising that practices must prioritise face-to-face appointments. Although practices never stopped offering face-to-face appointments, this appears to conflict with a letter issued in July 2020 exhorting practices to ensure that online and phone appointments continue to be provided in future. Throughout the first six months of the pandemic, primary care practitioners operated within a complex and ever-shifting environment which generated much uncertainty within primary care. The character of this uncertainty, and the effects on primary care practitioners are explored in the following section.

The Effects of Uncertainty

The future evolution of the pandemic is impossible to predict and the resulting uncertainty is complex and multifaceted. As noted by Rutter et al. (2020) it is not possible to eradicate uncertainty within a pandemic and the focus should be on how to manage and respond to this uncertainty. Study participants' narratives reflect two distinct forms of uncertainty: (1) clinical uncertainty and (2) the effects of rapid service change on the primary care profession and the effects on their own role and team relationships.

Clinical Uncertainty

Turning first to clinical uncertainty, participants frequently identified concerns about unmet patient need and potential high levels of future demand. The decrease in consultations at the start of the pandemic (outlined above) was noted by participants, who shared concerns that unmet need for health care was building up within communities, worrying that primary care lacked capacity to respond to a potential surge in demand:

> I'm really worried about unmet need. I think lots of us are, after that initial kind of burst of activity, general practice, in terms of patient demand, at least has been kind of eerily quiet and I'm worried about what's going on there. Because yeah, OK, some may be that people aren't getting, aren't coming to see us with mild self-resolving things that perhaps wouldn't have needed to be seen. But actually I really just don't believe that that accounts for the level of the drop off that we've seen, and I think there is an awful lot that we're not seeing and we should be seeing and I'm really worried about that. I'm also worried that we're generating a massive backlog that we won't necessarily have capacity to deal with. [Participant 1]

Participants also highlighted the challenges of having to respond to a new disease when very little was known about the progression of a COVID-19 infection. As a result, participants frequently experienced clinical uncertainty and the potential for such uncertainty to threaten their professional identity.

Some participants highlighted that patients often expected GPs to offer reassurance and provide answers; however, the novelty of COVID-19 meant that GPs felt they could not always meet this expectation. One participant made particular reference to the lack of knowledge on 'long COVID' (a condition where COVID-19 symptoms persist over many weeks or months) and being unable to advise patients on the likely duration and development of their symptoms:

> The doctors don't know and that, that I think it's really hard for the patients because they've come to us, expecting us at least if we don't have a kind of 'I know that you will be better in X amount of time', we can say that 'Well, other patients I've met with this condition, this is how it usually goes' but I don't know, all I can say at the moment is 'I know there are lots of other people in your situation, but I don't know what happens next'. We haven't had a next yet. [Participant 16]

In normal times, GPs may consider themselves to be defined by their professional ability to deal with uncertainty—to manage whatever comes in through the door. These new conditions of more radical uncertainty represent a fundamental challenge to GP and wider primary care team identity. COVID-19 also impacted relationships between primary and secondary care, with GPs unable to make anything except urgent referrals (for example, possible cancer) to hospitals from April to June 2020. Some participants discussed the initial closing of many areas of non-COVID-19 care and the inability to make onward referrals, meaning that '*other stuff that's not COVID [is] just kind of sitting on our doorstep*' [participant 16], representing a further degree of clinical uncertainty and anxiety for GPs, as well as having to respond to a sense of frustration from patients.

> So we've got more people kind of perhaps slightly upset that they can't get the care that they feel they should receive, I think probably the majority of that is the expectation of when things will come back in secondary care. So a classic example is people waiting for hip and knee ops, you know, people who are in pain, and you've been waiting and in pain for a while and then to be told 'You got to wait longer' and I think it's one of those, in fact,

> it's quite disempowering because we know that there's nothing I can do to change that. Except potentially tinker with some meds or, you know, there's not much I can do and so I think that kind of natural frustration, I think, you know, I think we see it probably in the population in general, I think. [Participant 11]

What was particularly striking in this respect was the sense of disempowerment felt by GPs, and feeling unable to do their normal job, with this leading to a profound sense of uncertainty and concern.

The Effects of Rapid Service Change on the Primary Care Profession

Uncertainty was also reported in respect of rapid service reorganisation having an impact on the primary care profession. For example, some participants raised concerns that the prioritisation of remote consultations might be exacerbating health inequalities as not all patients had access to the technology and private space required for a virtual consultation to take place. Safeguarding of their patients was also a concern acknowledged by a number of participants, unable to be sure who else might be present during a phone or online consultation, and it proving difficult or impossible for a patient to report concerns. These changes could be viewed as challenging the responsibility participants felt towards their patients and as a potential threat to their ability to fulfil their professional role. This example highlights the lack of control primary care practitioners felt about these difficulties:

> I am worried about the things that I was worried about before – the big things, like child protection, intimate partner violence, consultations with people for whom English isn't a first language. I am worried about our kind of known unknowns in that, the stuff that is hard to, in some ways, be able to do anything about. If people aren't phoning into the practice, because they don't feel that they can communicate with us adequately, how do we know to what extent that's a problem? [Participant 1]

As the pandemic progressed, participants raised in their narrative reports the challenges of deciding who needed to be seen face-to-face, as opposed to a virtual or phone consultation. This concern about ensuring an appropriate pattern of primary care services took place as patients began to come forward again, particularly those with a more complex mix of conditions, as illustrated here:

> I mean, certainly the mix of cases that we're getting now on the telephone consultations are getting more difficult to manage just on the phone. I don't think it's just that my tolerance for the risk and the uncertainty has changed – I think people are ringing us with other things now that they've been hanging onto for a while. And some things you really can only resolve by seeing them face-to-face. [Participant 12]

> So it's been it's been very odd and it's, I think to start with, there's a kind of relatively easy bit where you, you are doing emergency triage you're taking calls from patients who are deciding, are you really ill. Do I have to see you to save your life now or prevent something drastic? And that's a relatively easy question to answer, but as it drags on over several months, that's not, that's not good enough really, you actually have to address all the other needs that there are and it becomes much more difficult to make that decision of who you see and who you don't need to see. [Participant 16]

Frequently, participants praised the efforts of the wider practice team in working together to implement vast changes to service delivery. In particular, a renewed emphasis on checking in on colleagues' wellbeing and a collective sense that everyone was 'in it together' was often noted. Wiedner et al. (2020) highlight this shared experience can facilitate social bonding and, as captured in the following quotation, developing knowledge about COVID-19 precipitated increased discussion between colleagues:

> One of the things as well is that as a team, actually one of the things I've benefited from, is more discussion around cases. So general practice can sometimes be quite isolating and you can feel, particularly when you've got a busy surgery, everybody else is busy too, you've just got to make these decisions. And sometimes you ruminate on them and worry about whether you've made the right ones. There isn't really time set aside in the day for you to discuss cases and talk about things, you're conscious everybody else is busy. But one of the things is that we've been better as a team I think in sharing our discomfort and saying 'Well what would you do?' [Participant 12]

The Sustainability of Changes Made to Primary Care

Turning to the uncertainty felt about the effects of the pandemic on the future organisation of primary care, narratives highlighted the value placed on positive relationships with patients. In the initial phase of the pandemic, some participants questioned whether remote consulting would challenge their consultation skills and their ability to develop rapport with patients. However, other participants highlighted that some patients would prefer remote consultation as appointments were potentially less time consuming and easier to schedule around work commitments. Both responses demonstrate how participants called upon the professional identity of a primary care practitioner—changes to practice were framed via their effect on the quality of relationships with patients. Some participants reflected that they felt the increased use of remote consulting was here to stay and that '*we won't probably go back to general practice as it was before*' [participant 14].

> I think it will suit a lot of people, I mean, just, you know, I've always been interested in health inequalities and there are lots of barriers to accessing healthcare for a group of people that I think that this sort of technology would be really helpful for. So the kind of people I'm talking about are the people in really low paid jobs who will get the sack if they take a day off, or who certainly won't get paid if they take a day off. And, you know, let's just say you're a labourer working on the roads for example, then you don't get paid if you take a day off and you might be working remotely, you might be staying in a caravan to do your job, you can't get away to see your GP. [Participant 2]

As the pandemic progressed, a small number of participants did note that remote consulting, while based at home, could feel a little isolating, with some saying how much they appreciated the times when they did see patients face-to-face. Some participants raised concerns about how remote consultation affected their own perception of being a primary care practitioner, highlighting concerns that the future of primary care would be '*much more of a transactional role and almost call centre medicine*' [participant 12].

> I think the only other thing I have to say about sort of remote first, when you are working from home, you do start to feel disenfranchised very quickly. So I had to do a week of sort of what I was waiting for swab results for my daughter and although you are sort of on the list, you don't really feel part of a team, you just feel like you're kind of going back to that. 'I'm just processing, I'm just getting through work', and I'm not having that shared interaction with my colleagues, I'm not going

> to coffee with them and those sorts of things. So it's difficult, because I think naturally there is a question mark over what can we do more of from home now, which I think we can at a push, but I don't think that should be what we're aiming for. We should be working in a virtual model, but actually, where we're in the same room together because I think that, you know, you're working in a hub, you're working as a core group working together. [Participant 11]

Participants' narrative accounts repeatedly highlighted the personal challenges presented by the initial stages of the pandemic. Participants referenced the difficulty of being able to switch off from work and the challenges presented by living in lockdown which frequently obstructed the deployment of their usual coping methods. Participants frequently discussed the high level of exhaustion they were experiencing which was often linked to the difficulty of maintaining morale, both at an individual level and also within practices. Those participants with school-age children also discussed the strain of managing childcare and the difficulties of balancing the demands of work and home life and the additional demands this could place on their partners. Our participants' narratives demonstrated that the challenges of responding to COVID-19 extended from the workplace into their home life.

Discussion

The outbreak of the COVID-19 pandemic occurred rapidly and unexpectedly, throwing the usual procedures and routines of primary care up in the air, this disruption occurring within a wider societal and global context in which few areas of life were untouched by the sudden and yet sustained effects of COVID-19. Change in primary care took place at an organisational, team and personal level, impacting on the professional and home lives of all those working in general practice. In this way, the equilibrium of daily life and professional identity was truly punctuated and external influences created the conditions whereby, in Baumgartner and Jones' terms, there were 'bursts of frenetic policy activity' (2010: xvii). In parallel, individuals experienced disruption to both their professional identity and their personal sense of biography and life plans, with the extent of this becoming more evident as pandemic restrictions tightened (Bury, 1982).

This blending of policy and organisational change, with disruption and uncertainty at a personal and professional level, is interwoven in the narrative accounts given by the primary care practitioners in our study. It is important to note that alongside different degrees of uncertainty, anxiety and isolation, our research participants also reported a sense of liberation at times, being free to innovate in how primary care services are organised and delivered, seemingly released from what they previously considered the burden or constraint of regulation, performance monitoring, or policy control. While inspection and regulation have as their intent the preservation and improvement of standards of quality and safety of care (Furnival et al., 2018), it has been noted in other studies of healthcare organisations that such scrutiny can be experienced by local managers and professionals as 'regulatory throttle' (Chambers et al., 2018, p. 179).

The collected narratives of a group of primary care practitioners, recounting their individual story of the first six months of the COVID-19 pandemic reveal a complex set of paradoxes. Sudden change to the organisation of care delivery, yet such developments becoming sustained, and policy makers seeking increasingly to make them permanent. For clinicians, a strong sense of uncertainty about the treatment and course of COVID-19, alongside rising concern about all the non-COVID-19 patients who were not presenting for care, seemingly a ticking time bomb of morbidity and need. The service changes themselves appeared to be experienced in a paradoxical manner—sometimes energising, refreshing and different, and at others exhausting, worrying, and unsatisfactory in their apparent inability to meet the many and nuanced needs of the full population of patients. Furthermore, the effects of the pandemic are increasingly experienced as longer term, and likely to come in cycles of more or less virulence, societal restrictions, and attempts to 'control' infections and outbreaks. Hence, general practice remains in a state of flux and uncertainty, the accounts of our study participants revealing their desire for a period of stabilisation, or equilibrium, and also a recognition that the long-term effects of the pandemic on primary care, and indeed its practitioners, are as yet unknown.

Primary care is accustomed to the management of uncertainty, for it is concerned with the diagnosis, management and treatment of undifferentiated illness and symptoms, being available to people as their first point of contact with the health system, and having a concern for wider population and public health (Starfield, 1998). Our collected narratives of primary care practitioners demonstrate however the extent to which the COVID-19 pandemic has increased the level of uncertainty within general practice, and in complex and overlapping ways. From being unable to refer patients during the initial stages of the pandemic, having the 'heuristics' of consultation disrupted by the increased use of remote consultation, and concerns over virus transmission to themselves and others, primary care practitioners have had to respond to a high level of uncertainty within their practice, and in its impact on both their professional and personal life.

The uncertainty arising from COVID-19 marked a challenge to participants' ontological security, defined by Giddens (1991) as an individual's sense of continuity and certainty on which they ground their perceptions of who they are—their self-identity. Narratives from primary care practitioners reflected the discontinuities within participants' sense of their professional identity. Monrouxe (2010) notes that professional identities 'are not fixed cognitive schemas; rather, identities are what we do. Identities are asserted and claimed through continual interactions' (p. 44). Arguably the fragmentation and physical dispersal of practice teams caused by COVID-19 interrupted this identity work—this process of mutual shaping and enactment of professional identity—just at the moment when GPs as a profession were most in need of ways to anchor to a new situation. Gordon et al. (2020) describe the transition from trainee to trained in medical education as a 'dynamic liminal phase, in which the sense of 'who I am' gives way to a sense of 'who I'm becoming' (p. 1007). In some senses, primary care experienced COVID-19 as a reverse of this process, disrupting their collective professional biography as skilled managers of uncertainty and holistic face-to-face practitioners, leaving them uncertain how to practice and back to being 'beginners together' as one participant put it. For many, the identity work needed to regain a sense of who they were or who they are becoming is still work in progress. In Lewin's terms what has unfrozen remains fluid and may take some time to refreeze.

There are instances within the narrative accounts where Ashforth's concept of a 'transition bridge' (the mechanisms by which people process the disruption or role shock they experience) can be identified. For example, participants frequently highlighted their pride in the way the practice team had worked together to facilitate necessary changes during the pandemic response—fostering collective identity work despite the physical separation, in line with Wiedner et al. (2020). Furthermore, some of them highlighted the potential positive long-term changes to primary care that might result from the response to COVID-19, such as greater ease of access to consultations through phone and online methods. And yet others reported on how the new ways of working had enabled a more measured and sometimes calmer experience of the working day, including the option to work from home. These forms of transition bridges facilitate individuals in making sense of the profoundly challenging situation in which they find themselves, as they foreground the perceived benefits that might arise from working through the COVID-19 pandemic.

As identified by Waring and Bishop (2011), clinicians who transitioned from the NHS to working within an independent sector treatment centre often interpreted the change in a way that maintained their biographical narratives. Some identified that the move offered the opportunity to shape services, with a renewed focus on efficiency allowing a higher number of patients to access treatment. Others viewed the changes as an opportunity to defend the threatened ethos of the NHS. Those who did not appear to reposition their identities were 'characterised by their enduring sense of isolation, anxiety and loss' (p. 673). Often, within our study, participants responded to the ontological insecurity surfaced by COVID-19 through the reconstruction and reassertion of their self-identity as a primary care practitioner. Participants address the ontological dilemmas of self-doubt and questions surrounding the future of primary care through the construction of transition bridges. The transition bridges invoked are rooted in the participants' sense of what it is to work in primary care—they emphasise the relationship between practitioner and patient, along with the quality of care. This sense-making (Weick, 1995) is not however guaranteed to withstand the continued cycles of uncertainty and paradoxes of living and working with COVID-19 in the long term.

The context in which primary care practitioners operate has changed in a sudden and disruptive manner, and some participants openly questioned whether changes might occur to professional identities within primary care, questioning how they personally might be able to adapt and fit in with a future form of primary care that was as yet unknown. Some questioned whether there might be a shift away from an emphasis on relational medicine which they saw as foundational to their identity. Other participants used their professional identity as a primary care practitioner as an anchor amidst the uncertainty. As we write at what we think is the beginning of a second surge of the COVID-19 pandemic, transformation, upheaval and uncertainty remain the watchwords. This chapter is a tribute to the diligence and willingness of a group of primary care professionals who have taken the time to reflect, record their experiences, and do so in the hope of making sense of global change experienced in their personal and professional lives, when almost everything is uncertain. As T. S. Eliot (1944) wrote 'And what you do not know is the only thing you know'.

References

Ashforth, B. (2000). *Role transitions in organizational life: An identity-based perspective*. Routledge.

Baumgartner, F., & Jones, B. (2010). *Agendas and instability in American politics*. The University of Chicago Press (First published 1993).

Brant, H., Atherton, H., Ziebland, S., McKinstry, B., Campbell, J. L., & Salisbury, C. (2016). Using alternatives to face-to-face consultations: A survey of prevalence and attitudes in general practice. *British Journal of General Practice, 66*(648), 460–466. https://doi.org/10.3399/bjgp16X685597

Braun, V., Clarke, V., Hayfield, N., & Terry, G. (2018). Thematic analysis. In P. Liamputtong (Ed.), *Handbook of research methods in health social sciences*. Springer.

Bury, M. (1982). Chronic illness as biographical disruption. *Sociology of Health and Illness, 4*(2), 167–182.

Chambers, N., Thorlby, R., Boyd, A., Smith, J., Proudlove, N., Kendrick, H., & Mannion, R. (2018). *Responses to Francis: Changes in board leadership and governance in acute hospitals in England since 2013* (The Full Report). Available at: https://www.research.manchester.ac.uk/portal/files/66318094/responses_to_francis_report.pdf. Accessed 14 September 2020.

Clarke, G., Pariza, P., & Wolters, A. (2020). *How might COVID-19 have affected people's ability to see their GP.* Health Foundation. Available at: https://www.health.org.uk/news-and-comment/charts-and-infographics/how-might-covid-19-have-affected-peoples-ability-to-see-GP. Accessed 01 September 2020.

Eliot, T. S. (1944). *Four quartets*. Faber.

Furnival, J., Boaden, R., & Walshe, K. (2018). Assessing improvement capability in healthcare organisations: A qualitative study of healthcare regulatory agencies in the UK. *International Journal for Quality in Health Care, 30*(9), 715–723. https://doi.org/10.1093/intqhc/mzy085

Giddens, A. (1991). *Modernity and self-identity*. Polity.

Gordon, L., Rees, C. E., & Jindal-Snape, D. (2020). Doctors' identity transitions: Choosing to occupy a state of 'betwixt and between'. *Medical Education, 54*(11), 1006–1018. https://doi.org/10.1111/medu.14219

Kingdon, J. (2002). *Agendas, alternatives, and public policies* (2nd ed.). Pearson (First published 1984).

Lay, K. (2020, April 4). How pandemic is set to future-proof the NHS. *The Times*. Available at: https://www.thetimes.co.uk/article/how-pandemic-is-set-to-future-proof-the-nhs-ms63678r8. Accessed 01 September 2020.

Lewin, K. (1951). *Field theory in social science: Selected theoretical papers* (D. Cartwright, Ed.). Harper and Brothers.

Marshall, M., Howe, A., Howsam, G., Mulholland, M., & Leach, J. (2020). COVID-19: A danger and an opportunity for the future of general practice. *British Journal of General Practice, 70*(695), 270–271. https://doi.org/10.3399/bjgp20X709937

Monrouxe, L. V. (2010). Identity, identification and medical education: Why should we care? *Medical Education, 44*(1), 40–49. https://doi.org/10.1111/j.1365-2923.2009.03440.x

NHS Digital. (2020). *Appointments in general practice*. Available at: https://digital.nhs.uk/data-and-information/publications/statistical/appointments-in-general-practice. Available at: Accessed 01 September 2020.

NHS England and Improvement. (2020a). *Help us help you: NHS urges public to get care when they need it*. Available at: https://www.england.nhs.uk/2020/04/help-us-help-you-nhs-urges-public-to-get-care-when-they-need-it/. Accessed 01 September 2020,

NHS England and Improvement. (2020b). *Third phase of NHS response to COVID-19*. Available at: https://www.england.nhs.uk/coronavirus/publication/third-phase-response/. Accessed 01 September 2020.

NHS England and Improvement. (2020c). *Updates and guidance for general practice. Access to GP practices*. Available at: https://www.england.nhs.uk/coronavirus/wp-content/uploads/sites/52/2020/09/C0765-access-gp-practices-letter-14-september-2020.pdf. Accessed 14 September 2020.

Rutter, H., Wolpert, M., & Greenhalgh, T. (2020). Managing uncertainty in the covid-19 era. *BMJ, 370*, m3349. https://doi.org/10.1136/bmj.m3349

Spencer, J., & Oung, C. (2020). *How has lockdown affected general practice and where do we go from here?* Nuffield Trust Comment. Available at: https://www.nuffieldtrust.org.uk/news-item/how-has-lockdown-affected-general-practice-and-where-do-we-go-from-here. Accessed 01 September 2020.

Starfield, B. (1998). *Primary care: Balancing health needs, services, and technology*. Oxford University Press.

Thornton, J. (2020). Covid-19: How coronavirus will change the face of general practice forever. *BMJ, 368*. https://doi.org/10.1136/bmj.m1279

Tuohy, C. H. (1999). *Accidental logics: The dynamics of change in the health care arena in the United States, Britain, and Canada*. Oxford University Press.

Waring, J., & Bishop, S. (2011). Healthcare identities at the crossroads of service modernisation: The transfer of NHS clinicians to the independent sector? *Sociology of Health & Illness, 33*(5), 661–676. https://doi.org/10.1111/j.1467-9566.2010.01311.x

Weick, K. E. (1995). *Sensemaking in organizations*. Sage.

Wiedner, R., Croft, C., & McGivern, G., (2020). Improvisation during a crisis: Hidden innovation in healthcare systems. *BMJ Leader*. (Published Online First: 10 June 2020). https://doi.org/10.1136/leader-2020-000259

CHAPTER 10

Professionalism in a Pandemic: Shifting Perceptions of Nursing Through Social Media

Charlotte Croft and Trishna Chauhan

Introduction

Nurses are the largest professional group in global health systems, and a key resource in the ongoing drive for high quality care, cost improvements and service innovation. Yet, traditionally, nurses have struggled to successfully leverage a significantly influential role in the organization of care beyond their professional jurisdiction. However, the COVID-19 pandemic has brought the important, yet previously undervalued, role of nurses to the forefront of public consciousness. In particular, nurses around the world are taking to social media to emphasize the importance of the profession to the pandemic response, and to promote the reality of their highly skilled modern roles to an unusually engaged public. In this chapter, we examine how nurses' expressions of their professional identity and professional work have changed over the course of the pandemic, and explore how this change has created the potential for the emergence

C. Croft (✉) · T. Chauhan
Warwick Business School, University of Warwick, Coventry, UK
e-mail: Charlotte.croft@wbs.ac.uk

J. Waring et al. (eds.), *Organising Care in a Time of Covid-19*, Organizational Behaviour in Healthcare,
https://doi.org/10.1007/978-3-030-82696-3_10

of new models of professionalism, influencing the organizing processes of health systems as nurses leverage new-found political influence.

The findings we present in this chapter build on the work of a research project ongoing at the outset of the global pandemic, analysing over 600 social media blogs by nurses to understand how they communicate their profession to others. As COVID-19 progressed, we noted changes in the way nurses attempted to explain the complexities of their many and varied clinical skills, increased the frequency of posting pictures of themselves in uniform, and agentically positioned themselves as a key resource in the pandemic response. We subsequently engaged in additional data collection of over 600 nurses' social media blogs and posts in "real time", to gain insight into a professional group's use of social media before, during, and potentially after, a time of crisis. To aid the data collection process, a series of hashtags were used as search terms (e.g. #NHSNurse; #NHSPayRise #ICUNurse). We then engaged in snowball sampling as we further engaged with content which was re-tweeted, re-posted, or linked to a blog on a different social media site.

Social media platforms give opportunities for individuals to communicate their opinions, views and desired identity (Stieglitz et al., 2018) in relation to other users and to an imagined audience (Cassinger & Thelander, 2020). However, there are some limitations to this approach. We acknowledge that social media platforms are not utilized by everyone, and may only cover specific audiences of a certain demographic such as age.[1] Our search was limited by a reliance on the use of hashtags. Unless hashtags are actively used some posts may not be widely viewed and their visibility and impact subsequently reduced. Finally, social media accounts may be private, meaning individuals may actively engage in debates but their responses cannot be seen by others without permission.

We acknowledge these limitations in terms of the intersubjective nature of social media use. However, the use of social media data also gives valuable real-time insight into the opportunity for a profession to create their own online community, and influence others outside of that professional community, through the use of hashtags and trends. Where certain posts gain traction (i.e. through the most number of interactions), they are often highlighted as the "top" post and can gain immense visibility within

[1] As of September 2020 in the UK, the highest percentage of Instagram users fell into the age bracket of 25–34 years old (Statista, 2020).

a broader argument (likes, retweets, shares)—a benefit for sharing interests quickly in "real-time" (comparative to print news articles or academic papers). Social media posts which gain visibility outside of the professional community on the Internet may also be reported by traditional media outlets, further enhancing the ability of the profession to communicate their desired message to a more general audience (Parmelee & Bichard, 2011).

Through comparative analysis of over 1361 articles of social media content, we identified three intertwined areas in which nurses' communication changed: challenging stereotypes about the profession; highlighting the physical and emotional demands of their work; and leveraging increased political influence. We continued to track social media "conversations" over time, with a focus on how shifting narratives of professional identity, work and political influence have the potential to influence broader processes of organizing.

We propose the COVID-19 pandemic has the potential to influence models of professionalism, as groups which have not traditionally been at the forefront of public consciousness, with regard to the organizing of health care, now take centre stage on social media. We suggest the pandemic acts as a communal space through which professional groups are able to shift public perceptions about their identity, work and potential role in organizing processes, leveraging increased political influence over more powerful actors. We explore the potential implications of shifting models of professionalism on organizing care, and set out a research agenda to further enhance understandings of how under-represented professional groups may communicate, perpetuate or change perceptions of their profession through agentic use of social media platforms.

Organizing Professionalism and Nursing

The benefits of engaging health professionals in processes of organizing have long been established in both management research and international policy (Ham & Zollinger-Read, 2012; Shortell et al., 2014). Professional actors working across managerial and professional boundaries theoretically have the ability to exert influence over organizational decision making, while at the same time enjoying continued influence among professional colleagues (Coburn et al., 1997; Currie et al., 2012; Martin et al., 2015; McDonald et al., 2009). However, the increased involvement of professionals in organizing processes has raised interesting questions about the resultant influence of that involvement on models of professionalism, the means by which workers are organized beyond explicit managerial or bureaucratic control (Evetts, 2013). Traditional models of professionalism, often termed "occupational professionalism", rely on internal forms of professional control, governed by collegial authority and shared meaning (Freidson, 1994). However, as professional groups become more engaged with organizing processes, models of professionalism change in response to the interaction of hierarchical, market and community influences (Adler et al., 2008).

The involvement of professionals in organizing processes is viewed by some as a process of co-option, to encourage proliferation of managerial priorities among a professional group. This represents a form of "controlled professionalism", whereby professionals are controlled by top-down processes encouraging them to behave in organizationally desirable ways (Evetts, 2013; Faulconbridge & Muzio, 2008). Conversely, to resist managerial encroachment on their autonomy and jurisdiction, professionals may become competent in management practices, co-opting managerial expertise into professional practice through a process of reverse colonization (Waring & Currie, 2009). Noordegraaf (2015) suggests this merging of professional and managerial principles are now common in modern-day organizations. Termed "organizing professionalism", modern professionals embed managerial processes within professional work, to establish connections across multiple domains to jointly tackle complex issues of organizing. Going beyond a model of controlled professionalism in which professionals become involved in organizational decisions to buffer the profession from managerial intrusion, Noordegraaf (2015) argues that, for modern professionals, "organizing is part of the job".

Problematically, extant understandings of the interplay between models of professionalism and processes of organizing draw conclusions from the experiences of more dominant professional groups. In health care, this is reflected in a plethora of research considering how models of professionalism develop among doctors taking on increasing roles in organizing processes, where they are assumed to occupy an established, powerful role and voice within a dominant coalition with general managers, controlling health services (McDonald et al., 2009; Noordegraaf, 2007; Veronesi et al., 2013). While we acknowledge there is variation within the medical profession about the nature of their role in organizing (McGivern et al., 2015), there is limited consideration of how models of professionalism in other professional groups shape, and are shaped by, involvement in organizing processes.

One professional group where involvement in processes of organizing is distinct from the medical profession is nursing. Globally, the last twenty years has highlighted the potential role of nurses in leading organizational innovation and service improvement, driving calls for more engagement of nurses in organizing health systems (Allen, 2014; Kan & Parry, 2004; Neubert et al., 2016). Problematically, nurses engaging in organizing processes commonly suffer emotional distress as they struggle to align expectations associated with stereotypes of their professional identity with a model of organizing professionalism (Croft et al., 2015). Despite the increasing technical skills and academic education required by modern nurses, prior to COVID-19, nursing was often perceived as a "girl's job" with nurses positioned as angels, sex objects, or hardened matrons (Apesoa-Varano, 2007; Goodrick & Reay, 2010). Compounding these challenges, the role of nurses is further undermined by the "invisibility" of their work, and their exclusion from organizing processes by political leaders who often devalue the non-medical, caring work central to nursing practice (Allen, 2014; Bishop & Waring, 2019).

In short, nursing has historically aligned more with models of occupational or controlled professionalism than organizing professionalism, complicating, and at times undermining, the widespread involvement of nurses in organizing processes (Blomgren, 2003; Croft et al., 2014, 2015). However, as we outline below, the COVID-19 pandemic unexpectedly created an opportunity for nurses to challenge outdated professional stereotypes, promote the skilled reality of their day to day work and increase their political influence to emphasize the importance of their potential role in organizing health services, facilitated through agentic use of social media.

The proliferation of social media platforms has seen an increased interest in the way traditional models and understandings of professionalism manifest through social media (O'Connor et al., 2020). While some have voiced concerns about the potentially negative influence of the misuse of social media on societal perceptions of nursing (Wang et al., 2019), others view agentic use of social media as an opportunity to redress stereotypical perceptions of the nursing profession, which do not reflect the experiences of modern nurses (Castro & Andrews, 2018; Hoeve et al., 2014; Kelly et al., 2012). Social media content also gives researchers insight into how nurses from across the profession deal with, respond to, and perpetuate ideas about nursing held within wider society (Castro & Andrews, 2018).

In sum, social media platforms offer a vehicle through which to challenge and reconstruct assumptions about nurses' professional identity and work, increasing the potential for alignment with models of organizing professionalism. Additionally, social media campaigns hold the potential for nurses to leverage increased political influence outside of their profession. For example, Blomberg (2016) previously illustrated how Swedish nurses harnessed social media platforms to engage in political debates and increase public awareness around nurses' professional identity, working conditions, and limited role within organizing processes. However, prior to COVID-19 the extent to which nurses' social media activities were successful in leveraging influence over organizing processes remained unclear, largely due to the ongoing "invisibility" of nursing work (Allen, 2014). In contrast, as we outline below, the pandemic brought nurses to the forefront of public consciousness, and social media became a powerful tool through which they were able to challenge and reconstruct stereotypical assumptions about the profession and their work, and leverage increased political influence.

Findings

Challenging Stereotypes

Before the COVID-19 pandemic nurses on social media often referred to the need to address widely held, but incorrect, societal perceptions of nursing held by the public. Such misconceptions "*come from the media, from both TV and the movies. How nursing is portrayed in those settings embeds itself to people's minds and influences their perception of nursing. The point I'm making is that for many, this becomes nursing, this stereotypical view or misrepresentation becomes linked in the public minds, it forms part of their expectations when seeing a nurse. To be frank it damages us as individuals and also greatly harms our profession*" (644920). There was a sense of frustration that nurses were often perceived in terms of stereotypes, such as "the sexy nurse": "*Some of you may recall the sexualised view of nursing given in the Carry On movies; some may even remember the main nurse from M.A.S.H, 'Hot lips'... Representations like these lead the public to perceive nursing as almost a 'fantasy' profession, one in which the staff seem to become objects of male desire rather than professional care providers*" (644920).

The influence of stereotypical perceptions undermined the extent to which the important role of nurses was recognized by those outside of the profession: "*I believe nurses should be recognised to their fullest extent, for at the minute, nurses are undervalued and underappreciated*" (599781). Public perceptions based on nursing stereotypes were seen as undermining the ability of nurses to construct and communicate a professional identity to others outside health services which aligned with the reality of their skilled role: "*so sick of nurses being undermined by the angel trope. We aren't inherently good - no-one is. We are professionals, doing our job; our complex, multifaceted, dynamic & disgustingly underpaid job. Don't present us with invisible halos & pointless badges, just pay us accordingly*" (21866).

The COVID-19 pandemic created an opportunity for nurses to challenge these stereotypes and communicate to an audience outside of the profession that "*nurses do more than wipe arses and make tea*" (16958); "*Pre pandemic I am not sure that positive public perception in its entirety was well married to the profession. COVID has absolutely enhanced public perception. It's needed. Hoping it has positive impacts on lobbying post pandemic!*" (19646). Nurses turned to social media to enhance the public perception of nursing by communicating their pivotal role in managing the crisis, and raising awareness of the highly skilled nature of their work: "*I think the handmaiden image exists - my grandparents have a very narrow view of what I do. But #COVID19 has shone a light on the skill, scienceand understanding behind nursing, as well as the humanity #NurseBloggers2020*" (14779); "*#COVID has put the world's spotlight on the very best of our skills & professionalism*" (13386). Their identity as skilled professionals, rather than handmaidens or sex objects, was further strengthened when UK Prime Minister Boris Johnson was admitted to Intensive Care due to COVID-19, following which he extolled the professionalism and skill of the nurses caring for him.

However, while the pandemic gave nurses the opportunity to combat some of the stereotypes undermining their profession, it also gave rise to a new stereotype. Internationally, conceptualisations of nurses outside of the profession were communicated in both social and print media as the "heroes" of the pandemic. This perceived heroism was supported by pictures of nurses with marks on their faces due to the heavy protective equipment they were required to wear. Problematically, the "hero" stereotype was almost as constraining as the "sexy nurse" stereotype, as it normalized the horrific working conditions nurses found themselves in due to inadequate provision of PPE (personal protective equipment such as masks, visors, hazmat suits, aprons etc.), low pay, and increasing number of COVID-19 deaths among healthcare professionals: "*calling us 'heroes' takes the onus off of the governmentfor treating NHS HCPs (healthcare professionals) like excrement for the past 10 years. It means they can get away with providing us with inadequate PPE, stripping our resources and paying us less than we deserve. THAT'S why I can't stand the word...They KNEW this war was coming and they sent us into battle armed with pea shooters*" (13537).

In a departure from the enduring stereotypes characterizing nursing pre-pandemic, nurses were quick to turn to social media to actively reject the hero stereotype. Although proud to step up to the frontline and help in the pandemic, nurses were strongly against being called heroes: "*we're not heroes, we're human. We too have a breaking point*" (20817). This was also publicly re-affirmed by Chief Nurse Officer for England Ruth May: "*I've seen a few (misconceptions) about us being heroes, about us being there with our hat", Ms May said. "No, we're not heroes – we are expert professionalswho are doing our jobs and providing skilled, compassionate care, and nurses and midwives across England should be very proud of themselves right now*" (57284).

Initially, social media was used as a platform through which nurses could challenge societal stereotypes. Problematically, these stereotypes were replaced with the "hero" stereotype. However, due to their increased exposure on social media nurses were able to reject this narrative and communicate their professional identity in their own terms. In particular, they did so by emphasizing the reality of the emotional and physical demands of their work.

Communicating the Emotional and Physical Demands of Nursing Work

Prior to the pandemic nurses frequently referred to the lack of recognition for how "*physically, mentally and emotionally demanding*" (585057) their work was: "*I do not believe nurses or nursing students are offered enough mental health or emotional support in what is a very demanding, all-consuming profession. Nurses are expected to be able to deal with anything that is thrown at them*" (599569). Supporting their attempts to challenge stereotypical perceptions of their professional identity, nurses used their increased exposure on social media to demonstrate the emotional and physical aspects of their work.

First, nurses highlighted the emotional toll of altruism which is central to the profession: "*we signed up to help people in possible the lowest moments of their life and that's what we will continue to do*" (13230). For example, they used social media to talk about leaving their families and staying in hotels to protect them from exposure to the virus: "*It was a super hard decision to leave my beloved family but they knew as soon as I got the call to go to Nightingale*[2] *that I wouldn't turn it down*" (34633); "*I have made the heartbreaking decision to leave my children safe with their grandparents for the foreseeable. It's so I can continue to educate our NHS heroes and join them on the units in the fight. If I can do this. YOU CAN STAY HOME*" (18890).

In addition, they talked about the emotional labour of their role in caring for extremely unwell patients: "*I've looked after the sickest patients that I've ever come across, nursed them on ventilators on their fronts as it's the only way that we could get enough oxygen in for them to breathe. I've held the hands of terrified patients who have watched every other patient around them die and are worried that they are next*" (39499); "*as much as I try and show that I care I'm limited by how much I can do to keep them and me safe. I cannot begin to imagine how frightening this is to people. I'm frightened*" (41013).

Nurses openly used social media to discuss the emotional toll they had to manage due to their own fears about working on the frontline, and to highlight the impact this was having on many people within the profession: "*I know I'm not alone (particularly in my profession) in suffering with anxiety at the minute. I have always been a confident and outgoing person but COVID has really knocked me and I am more anxious than ever*" (41159); "*everyone is COVID +ve and poorly. And I mean really, really poorly. You move - roll them, they desaturate, you suction them, they*

[2] In the UK several 'Nightingale' hospitals were built to cope with surge demand from the COVID-19 pandemic. They were commonly established in large conference or exhibition centres and had capacity for 4000 patients. Many frontline staff volunteered to be re-deployed to the Nightingale hospitals during the pandemic. It is interesting that these field hospitals were named after Florence Nightingale, one of the enduring stereotypes of the profession.

desaturate. All you do is touch them and they literally desaturate... it's impossible to deal with" (36323).

Nurses also used social media to emphasize the physically demanding nature of the work. In particular, they used PPE as a sociomaterial resource in two ways. First, as an image through which they could directly challenge perceptions of nursing work. Nurses often posted photographs of themselves donned in PPE and gave detailed descriptions of working in such conditions: "*My ears are red and swollen, my face indented and I've never been more dehydrated in my life*" (20334). They discussed the physically uncomfortable reality of having to perform nursing work in such conditions "*It has been really tiring and hot and sweaty wearing this PPEon 12.5 hour shifts. It's hard to communicate too as you can't hear each other speak clearly and the patientsstruggle to hear you too*" (37825); "*As an ICU nurse at one point, I had not eaten, drank or passed urine for more than 6 hours*" (19579). Alongside this, nurses talked about their concerns for patients they were attempting to care for, giving insight into the harrowing experience of being hospitalized with COVID-19, beyond the associated medical illness: "*surrounded by 'space aliens' wearing PPE, cut off from your family! Can't see our faces. Cannot feel our touch thru 3 gloves. Voices muffled by PPE*" (13222).

Second, nurses used PPE, or more specifically the lack of it, as a sociomaterial resource to illustrate how nurses are often undervalued in the organizing of health services. Poor logistical planning on the part of the UK government led to significant shortages of PPE for frontline workers as the pandemic progressed, and became a prominent theme on social media "*We're making massive sacrifices. We don't have PPE*" (62709); "*I didn't sign up to have little PPE, exposing myself to a deadly virus*" (18908). However, the government did not take responsibility for the lack of PPE and refused to apologize to nurses for it "*Hancock (Secretary of State for Health and Social Care) didn't only refuse to acknowledge that there had been failures. Instead, he went on to disgustingly talk about how complicated the 'logistics' of delivering PPEare*" (57289).

In response to what was seen by many as a dismissive attitude from the government, nurses took to social media to highlight the lack of PPE and the way the nursing profession felt undervalued as a result "*I was really upset to see the health secretary not apologising to the poor nurses and health-care workers who have lost their lives because of a lack of PPE, something that should just not be the case. A builder wouldn't go to work without a toolbox or a hairdresser wouldn't go to work without scissors, so why on earth are nurses 'expected' to not wear PPE when they are riskingtheir lives, breaks my heart to see the lives lost*" (36070). They posted pictures of themselves in improvised PPE and campaigned for better provision: "*Three nurses who wore bin bags on their shifts due to a shortage in personal protective equipment (PPE)have reportedly tested positive for coronavirus. Just weeks ago, the nurses had shared a photo of themselves with clinical waste bags on their heads and feet as they issued a plea for proper masks, gowns and gloves*" (59450).

Communicating the emotional and physical demands of their work further strengthened their attempts to reconstruct stereotypical perceptions of nursing outside of the profession and highlighted the reality of their role. In particular, by using PPE (or a lack of it) as a sociomaterial resource, nurses were able to communicate two key messages about the profession: the physically demanding nature of their work which required them to put their own comfort aside for the sake of their patients; and a continual undermining by political leaders who were seen as dismissive of nurses' concerns. This dismissive attitude drove nurses to social media to campaign for better working conditions, leveraging changing societal perceptions of the profession to enhance their political influence.

Increasing Political Influence

Prior to the pandemic nurses often felt they had little ability to politically influence broader processes of organizing beyond the profession: "*I wonder why sometimes in nursing we are conditioned to ask first and prove ourselves before being allowed to try? Is it because we don't want to appear to be too pushy, a throwback to our female dominated professionacting collectively in the culturally manner associated with women? Or similarly, are we too afraid to step out of line in case we fail?*" (599485). As a result, nurses often found themselves excluded from political discussions about organizing health care, "*Some nurses have often felt as though their voice cannot make a difference*" (599569) or found their role in organizing processes undermined: "*There was no recognition or acknowledgment of my dedication, my professionalismor of my continuous 43 years services as a committed nurse*" (661570).

During the first wave of the pandemic, an increased public awareness about the importance of nursing, and the skilled nature of their work (particularly in critical care), gave nurses the opportunity to use social media to leverage increased political influence. COVID-19 generated public awareness of the centrality of nurses in providing health care and nurses reinforced this by using social media to share images of themselves in PPE, and narratives around their role on the frontline of the pandemic response. Combined with their strengthened professional identity, nurses used their social media platforms to position themselves as leaders of the health service alongside doctors, managers and politicians; "*Nurses are the same people who don't take our own kids to hospitalunless we see a bone poking through So when we tell you this is real you might want to listen #Covid19 #StayAtHome #Stay2mApart #WashYourHands U can spread the virus even if you don't have symptoms*" (15469). Aligning themselves with messages from UK central government about the need for non-key workers to socially isolate, nurses would often accompany their pictures on social media with hashtags such as #StayAtHomeSaveLives #StayAtHome #StopTheSpread.

Soon after the first wave of COVID-19 began to subside in the UK, the government announced a public sector pay rise which excluded nurses. The news provoked uproar from the profession who turned to social media to highlight the injustice of this decision given their central role in the pandemic response: "*Pay rise for everyone in the public sector! Wait-…WHAT? Not for nurses? This governmentis really, openly, laughingly shitting on us, right? I'm only going to say one thing, trying not to disrespect the rest of the public sector. Even though I could. Easily. But anyway, without nurses, ALL patientswould've died. And I don't mean now, I mean always. We are the constant presence at the bedside. Hospitalscannot survive without nurses. Never. But especially during this pandemic, we have been the absolute main reason for patients surviving. Yes, NURSES. We deserve more. What a joke*" (34565).

Nurses' increased political influence was leveraged through social media to promote a campaign for more equitable pay for nurses, creating a social media "trend" through the use of hashtags. #NHSPay15 and #NHSWorkersSayNO subsequently gained significant traction with an audience outside of the profession on social media platforms: "*And we are off! When our patientsare under attack, what do we do?? Stand up, fight back! #NHSPay15 #NHSWorkersSayNO @NurseSayNO*" (19342) and "*Proud to be part of the NHS protest yesterday. #NHSPay15 #NHSWorkersSayNO #nhsfairpay #NHSheroes #proudtobeastudentnurse @SUSTNU @HumanandHealth*" (19444).

In addition to trending hashtags, nurses used the "Clap for Carers"[3] campaign to highlight the hypocrisy of refusing them a pay rise: "*Now, gonna go see if my mortgage supplier will accept a round of applause as payment this month...*" (34551); "*It's ok though, I've got 10 weeks of Thursday night clapping stashed in the bank #payrise #NHS #nhspayrise #nursespay*" (19124); "*As if a clap is enough to recognise the dedication, hard work, loss and ongoing struggles we STILL face day to day*" (38489). They talked about how the transience of the appreciation for their work, and the constraining political influences over their role in organizing health care was enough to make them want to leave the profession: "*A proud NHS nurse was reduced to tears as she told James O'Brien how the government'smishandling of the coronavirus crisis has made her want to quit. It scares me to live in this country. I used to adore being part of the UK. I made sure I worked in the NHS and I would never work anywhere else. But after all this, I've questioned even being a nurse*" (65699). The continued refusal by UK politicians to consider a pay rise for nurses was seen as hypocritical by nurses who took to social media to post a widely shared image relating to "backstabbing" (Fig. 10.1): "*The hypocrisy of them all standing clapping on their doorsteps, whilst undermining the value of our work is deafening*" (79110).

While nurses were ultimately unsuccessful in persuading the UK government to provide better pay and working conditions, they were able to leverage political influence on another matter. In the English NHS, final year student nurses were asked to qualify early and take on paid roles to assist with staffing pressures. After they had started working Health Education England stated they no longer had funding to honour this payment, and that student nurses would not be paid for the work they undertook during the crisis as "student nurses are not deemed to be providing a service". The nursing community took to social media using the hashtag #IamProvidingAService, documenting the importance of their work and the value they offered alongside registered nurses: "*I am a student nurse, I smile, I listen, I observe the smallest changes, I advocate for my patients, I make your voice heard, I comfort, reassure, and do my best everyday. We are here everyday for you until your very last day always by your side. #IAmProvidingAService*" (11363). Registered

[3] The 'Clap for Carers' campaign was initiated in the UK during the first wave of the pandemic. Every Thursday at 8 pm people would stand outside their door and clap or cheer to show their appreciation for those working in the NHS.

Fig. 10.1 The widely shared "backstabbing" image (Copyright: https://www.instagram.com/p/B-18ciyqcrQ/)

Nurses also supported the message, highlighting "*Without students there are no nurses. Without nurses there is no NHS. #IAmProvidingAService*" (16991); "*#IAmProvidingAService qualified ITU (intensive care unit) RN (Registered Nurse). Without our student nurses helping when we had wards full of incredibly sick COVID patients, we would of never been able to provide the level of care the patients deserve, as well as complete all of our paperwork and jobs to make it safe*" (13423). A public outcry followed, forcing the UK government to reverse their decision and honour the payment contracts.

The COVID-19 pandemic gave nurses an opportunity to use social media to increase their political influence within the health system. They were successful in positioning themselves as leaders of the health service with regard to public health messaging and were able to reverse a government position on the non-payment of student nurses by campaigning on social media. While they were not successful in securing a pay rise, they used social media to raise awareness with a wider audience about the hypocrisy of this decision, drawing on the "Clap for Carers" campaign to highlight the injustice, and further strengthening reconstructed public perceptions about the skilled and highly valuable nature of nurses as a profession.

Discussion and Conclusions

The COVID-19 pandemic created an opportunity for nurses to communicate the reality of their skilled role to an unusually engaged general public. While the use of social media for professional advocacy is not a new phenomenon (Blomberg, 2016; Castro & Andrews, 2018; O'Connor et al., 2020), nurses have hitherto not experienced much success in elevating the perceived value of the profession within society. However, during the pandemic nurses used social media in three key ways: challenging professional stereotypes; communicating the emotional and physical demands of their role; and increasing their political influence.

Professionals wearing personal protective equipment (PPE) has become one of the most enduring images of the COVID-19 crisis. As a sociomaterial resource, nurses were able to use images of themselves in PPE alongside communications of the more skilled, technical aspects of their work. In doing so they were able to challenge the stereotypical imagery of Florence Nightingale which perpetuates unrealistic assumptions about nursing (Apesoa-Varano, 2007; Goodrick & Reay, 2010) and align perceptions of the work they do with a modern professional identity. Further to this, amplifying the importance of their role to the pandemic response began to redress the challenge of the invisibility of nursing work (Allen, 2014; Bishop & Waring, 2019). Photographs of nurses in PPE created a tangible image in the public consciousness of nursing work beyond misconceptions of their role as making beds or acting as doctor's handmaidens (Fealy, 2004), elevating the perceived value of nursing work and the centrality of the profession in organizing health services.

An elevated awareness of the important role of nurses had a subsequent influence on the ability of nurses to leverage political influence. We highlighted how they used their social media presence to initially align with government policies (#stayhome) and manage the immediate response to the virus, before later challenging policies which undermined the profession (#Iamprovidingaservice). These hashtags can be seen as "action" tags

(Lovejoy & Saxton, 2012) through which professionals attempt to get others to "do something" in response to their campaigning. The public support for nurses emanating from their increased visibility as central to the pandemic meant that, during the first wave, nurses briefly enjoyed enhanced political influence and increased social appreciation for their work as skilled professionals.

However, the amplified political voice of nursing quickly became muffled by more powerful groups, most notably politicians. Following the first wave of the pandemic, after the initial crisis had passed, the UK government returned to systematic undermining of the profession—rejecting pleas for pay increases and suggesting that student nurses did not perform valuable work. While nurses had managed to move away from "angel" stereotypes by posting their pictures in PPE, a "hero" stereotype soon replaced it. By positioning nurses as "altruistic heroes", influential political actors were once again able to undermine nurses' professional role in organizing health care, perpetuating the challenges previously experienced by nurses in taking on those roles (Allen, 2014; Bishop & Waring, 2019; Croft et al., 2015).

The constraining influence of more powerful groups rendered nurses' political voice and influence transient, limited to the emergency context of the first wave. However, a societal change in perceptions about nursing's professional identity and work seems to have had a more permanent impact (at least for the moment). Confidence in the skills of nursing, and public appreciation, seem to remain high—reflected in a 15% increase in applications to study nursing at University in the UK in September 2020 (Lintern, 2020). Further to this, and perhaps more importantly, the profession itself seems to have found a common voice through social media platforms, creating a shared space for a more cohesive professional community. As a result, they may have more potential for influencing political decisions in the future.

What does this mean for our understandings of shifting models of professionalism? As previously highlighted, nursing has traditionally been more aligned with occupational or controlled professionalism, which ultimately undermines their involvement in organizing processes (Blomgren, 2003; Croft et al., 2014; Evetts, 2013). A key limitation in moving towards a model of organizing professionalism (Noordegraaf, 2015) has long been identified as the misalignment between the work associated with nurses and the work associated with organizing, generating internal and external tensions (Croft et al., 2014; Currie et al., 2010; Hogg,

2001; Jung et al., 2009). However, shifting constructions of professional identity emerging from nurses' social media use during the COVID-19 pandemic can give insight into how these tensions may be changing. Increased public awareness of the complexity of their professional role and centrality to health provision, coupled with an increased, albeit bounded, political voice and influence, has set the stage for the nursing profession to move towards a model of organizing professionalism.

More work is needed to continue to observe the emergence of this new model of professionalism, framed by a volatile and ever-changing backdrop of a global health crisis. Research should continue to track how nurses construct and reconstruct their professional identity and work over time as the COVID-19 pandemic continues, and consider how this changes again when the crisis is over. Similarly, the extent of nurses' political influence should be of ongoing interest to researchers interested in changing models of professionalism. Our work has focused on nurses, who were focal actors in the health service response to the pandemic, but other professional groups are now emerging as key actors in other sectors, for example teachers. Future research should consider how different professional groups move in and out of the public consciousness and interrogate how social media acts as a vehicle through which they can change public perceptions about their profession and leverage increased political influence.

In conclusion, we acknowledge the difficult circumstances faced by health professionals around the world in responding to COVID-19 and do not seek to promote the contribution of nurses to that response above the role of others, such as Doctors, Healthcare Assistants or Allied Health Professionals. However, the unique and extreme circumstances of the pandemic have created an unprecedented opportunity for a professional group whose work is largely invisible, and broadly undervalued in society, to more accurately communicate their profession. While talk of "heroes" has the potential to normalize the marginalization or devaluing of nursing work by political groups, it has at least allowed nurses to move away from an enduring idea that they are passive "angels". Social media allowed nurses to reiterate the message that "*No, we're not heroes – we are expert professionalswho are doing our jobs and providing skilled, compassionate care*", moving them into a more opportune position from which to step forward into more central involvement in organizing processes. It is our view that the pandemic has acted as a catalyst for the nursing profession to evolve into a new model of organizing professionalism and begin to challenge enduring assumptions which have, for so long, inhibited nurses from unleashing their full potential within healthcare organizing.

Acknowledgements This project was funded by a research grant from NHS Horizons.

References

Adler, P. S., Kwon, S.-W., & Heckscher, C. (2008). Perspective—Professional work: The emergence of collaborative community. *Organization Science, 19*(2), 359–376.

Allen, D. (2014). Re-conceptualising holism in the contemporary nursing mandate: From individual to organisational relationships. *Social Science & Medicine, 119*, 131–138.

Apesoa-Varano, E. C. (2007). Educated caring: The emergence of professional identity among nurses. *Qualitative Sociology, 30*, 249–274.

Bishop, S., & Waring, J. (2019). From boundary object to boundary subject; the role of the patient in coordination across complex systems of care during hospital discharge. *Social Science & Medicine (1982), 235*, 112370.

Blomberg, H. (2016). Nurses' blogs as part of a political process—Professional identity as a rhetorical resource for negotiating responsibility and blame. *Discourse, Context & Media, 13*, 82–88.

Blomgren, M. (2003). Ordering a profession: Swedish nurses encounter new public management reforms. *Financial Accountability & Management, 19*(1), 45–71.

Cassinger, C., & Thelander, Å. (2020). Voicing the organization on Instagram: Towards a performative understanding of employee voice. *Public Relations Inquiry, 9*(2), 195–212.

Castro, A., & Andrews, G. (2018). Nursing lives in the blogosphere: A thematic analysis of anonymous online nursing narratives. *Journal of Advanced Nursing, 74*(2), 329–338.

Coburn, D., Rappolt, S., & Bourgeault, I. (1997). Decline vs. retention of medical power through restratification: An examination of the Ontario case. *Sociology of Health & Illness, 19*(1), 1–22.

Croft, C., Currie, G., & Lockett, A. (2014). Broken 'two-way windows'? An exploration of professional hybrids. *Public Administration, 93*(2), 380–394.

Croft, C., Currie, G., & Lockett, A. (2015). The impact of emotionally important social identities on the construction of a managerial leader identity: A challenge for nurses in the English National Health Service. *Organization Studies, 36*(1), 113–131.

Currie, G., Finn, R., & Martin, G. (2010). Role transition and the interaction of relational and social identity: New nursing roles in the English NHS. *Organization Studies, 31*(7), 941–961.

Currie, G., Lockett, A., Finn, R., Martin, G., & Waring, J. (2012). Institutional work to maintain professional power: Recreating the model of medical professionalism. *Organization Studies, 33*(7), 937–962.

Evetts, J. (2013). Professionalism: Value and ideology. *Current Sociology, 61*(5–6), 778–796.

Faulconbridge, J., & Muzio, D. (2008). Organizational professionalism in globalizing law firms. *Work, Employment and Society, 22*(1), 7–25.

Fealy, G. (2004). 'The good nurse': Visions and values in images of the nurse. *Journal of Advanced Nursing, 46*(6), 649–656.

Freidson, E. (1994). *Professionalism reborn: Theory, prophecy, and policy*. University of Chicago Press.

Goodrick, E., & Reay, T. (2010). Florence Nightingale endures: Legitimizing a new professional role identity. *Journal of Management Studies, 47*(1), 55–84.

Ham, C., & Zollinger-Read, P. (2012). What are the lessons from the USA for clinical commissioning groups in the English National Health Service? *The Lancet, 379*(9811), 189–191.

Hoeve, Y. t., Jansen, G., & Roodbol, P. (2014). The nursing profession: Public image, self-concept and professional identity. A discussion paper. *Journal of Advanced Nursing, 70*(2), 295–309.

Hogg, M. A. (2001). Social identification, group prototypicality, and emergent leadership. In M. A. Hogg & L. D. Terry (Eds.), *Social identity processes in organizational contexts* (pp. 197–212). Psychology Press.

Jung, D., Yammarino, F. J., & Lee, J. K. (2009). Moderating role of subordinates' attitudes on transformational leadership and effectiveness: A multi-cultural and multi-level perspective. *The Leadership Quarterly, 20*(4), 586–603.

Kan, M. M., & Parry, K. W. (2004). Identifying paradox: A grounded theory of leadership in overcoming resistance to change. *The Leadership Quarterly, 15*(4), 467–491.

Kelly, J., Fealy, G. M., & Watson, R. (2012). The image of you: Constructing nursing identities in YouTube. *Journal of Advanced Nursing, 68*(8), 1804–1813.

Lintern, S. (2020, July 9). Student nursing applications surge 15 per cent in a year. *The Independent*. https://www.independent.co.uk/news/health/student-nursing-applications-ucas-coronavirus-nhs-a9608556.html

Lovejoy, K., & Saxton, G. D. (2012). Information, community, and action: How nonprofit organizations use social media. *Journal of Computer-Mediated Communication, 17*(3), 337–353.

Martin, G. P., McKee, L., & Dixon-Woods, M. (2015). Beyond metrics? Utilizing 'soft intelligence' for healthcare quality and safety. *Social Science & Medicine, 142*, 19–26.

McDonald, R., Checkland, K., Harrison, S., & Coleman, A. (2009). Rethinking collegiality: Restratification in English general medical practice 2004–2008. *Social Science & Medicine, 68*(7), 1199–1205.

McGivern, G., Currie, G., Ferlie, E., Fitzgerald, L., & Waring, J. (2015). Hybrid Manager-Professionals' identity work: The maintenance and hybridization of medical professionalism in managerial contexts. *Public Administration*. https://doi.org/10.1111/padm.12119

Neubert, M. J., Hunter, E. M., & Tolentino, R. C. (2016). A servant leader and their stakeholders: When does organizational structure enhance a leader's influence? *The Leadership Quarterly, 27*(6), 896–910.

Noordegraaf, M. (2007). From "pure" to "hybrid" professionalism: Present-day professionalism in ambiguous public domains. *Administration & Society, 39*(6), 761–785.

Noordegraaf, M. (2015). Hybrid professionalism and beyond: (New) Forms of public professionalism in changing organizational and societal contexts. *Journal of Professions and Organization*. https://doi.org/10.1093/jpo/jov002

O'Connor, S., Chu, C. H., Thilo, F., Lee, J. J., Mather, C., & Topaz, M. (2020). Professionalism in a digital and mobile world: A way forward for nursing. *Journal of Advanced Nursing, 76*(1), 4–6.

Parmelee, J. H., & Bichard, S. L. (2011). *Politics and the Twitter revolution: How tweets influence the relationship between political leaders and the public*: Lexington Books.

Shortell, S. M., Addicott, R., Walsh, N., & Ham, C. (2014). *Accountable care organisations in the United States and England: Testing, evaluating and learning what works*. The King's Fund.

Statista. (2020, November 9). UK: Instagram users by age 2020. Statista. https://www.statista.com/statistics/1018012/instagram-users-united-kingdom/

Stieglitz, S., Bunker, D., Mirbabaie, M., & Ehnis, C. (2018). Sense-making in social media during extreme events. *Journal of Contingencies and Crisis Management, 26*(1), 4–15.

Veronesi, G., Kirkpatrick, I., & Vallascas, F. (2013). Clinicians on the board: What difference does it make? *Social Science & Medicine, 77*, 147–155.

Wang, Z., Wang, S., Zhang, Y., & Jiang, X. (2019). Social media usage and online professionalism among registered nurses: A cross-sectional survey. *International Journal of Nursing Studies, 98*, 19–26.

Waring, J., & Currie, G. (2009). Managing expert knowledge: Organizational challenges and managerial futures for the UK medical profession. *Organization Studies, 30*(7), 755–778.

CHAPTER 11

Population Health Management in the NHS: What Can We Learn from COVID-19?

Kath Checkland, Jonathan Hammond, and Sharon Spooner

Introduction

Population health management is an increasingly popular concept in many health systems. Lauded by the World Health Organisation (WHO) (2020), it is intimately tied to the growth of 'big data' and the ideal of moving 'health and well-being from reactive care models to active community- based models' (World Health Organisation, 2020: 1). In England, the NHS Long Term Plan (NHS England, 2019) sets out the agenda for NHS services in England for the next decade. Population health management forms an important strand of the Plan, briefly defined as: *[the use of] predictive prevention (linked to new opportunities for tailored screening, case finding and early diagnosis) to better support people to stay healthy and avoid illness complications* (NHS England, 2019: 12). Later in the document, it is explained that such an approach involves the active identification of people at risk using digital tools and large data

K. Checkland (✉) · J. Hammond · S. Spooner
Division of Population Health, Health Services Research and Primary Care, University of Manchester, Manchester, UK
e-mail: Katherine.H.Checkland@manchester.ac.uk

J. Waring et al. (eds.), *Organising Care in a Time of Covid-19*, Organizational Behaviour in Healthcare,
https://doi.org/10.1007/978-3-030-82696-3_11

sets, and the provision of care of some kind to prevent future health problems. In keeping with the WHO agenda, population health management is characterized as being 'proactive' in contrast to previous 'reactive' care. The evidence underpinning the introduction of such an approach is not described.

The COVID-19 crisis provides us with an opportunity to interrogate the population health management approach in more depth, and to consider critically what it might offer, what the problems might be and what this means for the post-COVID-19 organization of the NHS and of health systems more generally. Early in the COVID-19 pandemic, it was announced that, in the UK, a cohort of 'clinically extremely vulnerable' patients would be identified using digital tools and singled out for special care to prevent them contracting the virus. This process was called 'shielding' (https://www.gov.uk/government/publications/guidance-on-shielding-and-protecting-extremely-vulnerable-persons-from-COVID-19), and it was described as '*a measure to protect people who are clinically extremely vulnerable by minimising all interaction between those who are extremely vulnerable and others*'. This represents an example of population health management: a cohort of people at risk were actively identified using digital tools, and preventative care (e.g. requirement to self-isolate, provision of social support and welfare parcels) was provided to prevent future health problems.

In this paper, the 'shielding' scheme is explored as an example of the population health management approach and critiqued using three theoretical lenses. Firstly, it is considered as an example of *categorisation* (Bowker & Star, 2000). Who is in, who is out and the basis of those decisions are considered, and the implications addressed, including the uncertainties surrounding the classification schema and the political factors at work. Secondly, it is considered as an example of the *construction of risk* (Johnson & Covello, 2012). Within the policy discourse around shielding, reducing the death rate from COVID-19 is presented as a simple matter of identifying risk-bearing individuals. But risk is socially and culturally constructed (Adams, 2001), and biomedical risk is only one type of risk which might be considered (Adam, 2011). Moreover, the construction of the category of 'high risk' is neither transparent nor straightforward. Finally, the paper explores population health management as a *framing device* which highlights particular causes of disease and distress and obscures others (Jones & Exworthy, 2015).

The experience of GPs in the UK in operationalising the shielding policy is explored through these lenses to bring to the surface the inherent contradictions and unexamined assumptions which underpin the rhetoric associated with the population health management approach. We do this in the tradition of autoethnography (Ellis et al., 2011), in which the experiences of two authors (KC and SS) as GPs are used to contextualize and illuminate the operation of the shielding policy as it unfolded in real-time. Autoethnography is a family of methods in which researchers use their own experiences as their research material:

> We all engage in [...] identity work, this presentation of self to others and to oneself. At its most basic, autoethnography may be understood as the practice of doing this identity work self-consciously, or deliberately, in order to understand or represent some worldly phenomenon that exceeds the self; it is 'a form of self-narrative that places the self within a social context' (Reed-Danahay 1997b,9). (Butz & Besio, 2009: 1660)

In keeping with the ethnographic tradition of problematizing the familiar (Rodriguez et al., 2017), both KC and SS found themselves engaging with the day to day realities of the practical implementation of a shielding policy that they found troubling. Whilst the mechanics of the process—using searches to identify groups of patients and providing them with care—is both deeply familiar and recognized as a standard part of current primary care practice, its application in this case proved difficult in ways which went beyond the material difficulties of any programme introduced at speed. In conversation together and in reflective writing, these difficulties were reflexively analysed and considered from a number of theoretical perspectives, eventually generating this account.

Our discussion considers the intersection between population health management and public health approaches, with a focus on the role of advocacy and community action (Hall et al., 2018). The implications for the post-COVID-19 organization of health and care systems are discussed. What follows is divided into five sections. An initial section describes the rise of population health management as a concept, and its current place in the English NHS. The COVID-19 'shielding' scheme is described, and this is then examined through the lenses described above. A final discussion section considers the implications for public health and health system organization.

Population Health Management: Panacea or Chimera?

The origins of the concept of population health management are not entirely clear, but some authors highlight the role of the Canadian Institute for Advanced Research (CIAR) (Labonte et al., 2005; Raphael & Bryant, 2002) in the 1990s. According to Raphael and Bryant (2002), the approach was first set out in a paper in Social Science and Medicine (Evans & Stoddart, 1990), in which it was argued:

> The health of individuals and populations is affected by their health care, but also by other factors as well. Expansion of the healthcare system uses up resources which would otherwise be available to address those other factors. (Evans & Stoddart, 1990: 1360)

Building upon the classic WHO definition of health as 'complete physical, mental and social wellbeing', and highlighting the importance of social determinants of health, the approach appears, at first sight, to be a progressive one, which locates health as the product of the interaction between an individual, their personal circumstances, and the environment and social context within which they live. However, it has been criticized, not least by the health promotion and critical public health communities, who argue that this approach fails to consider how measured disparities in health arise, or facilitate political action to remove them (Labonte et al., 2005; Raphael & Bryant, 2002). Notwithstanding these critical voices, the CIAR approach has been attractive across international health systems.

Developed by quantitative epidemiologists, with a focus on using rigorous data analysis to demonstrate how health expectations differ between sectors of the population, the CIAR approach has found resonance in a world increasingly driven by big data. One of the first communities to adopt the approach was that of Health Management Organisations (HMOs) and Accountable Care Organisations (ACOs) in the USA. Developed to try to halt the rapid rise in health costs in the US privately funded health system, HMOs and subsequently ACOs represent healthcare providers which take responsibility for a defined population (Barnes et al., 2014; Goodrick & Reay, 2016; Havighurst, 1970; Luft, 1978; Shortell et al., 2010). Perhaps one of the best known examples is the Kaiser Permanente organiszation. Originating in California, Kaiser Permanente provides comprehensive health care for its enrollees, using data analytics and integrated teams to try to maximize outcomes at the lowest cost (Chen et al., 2009). ACOs, a more recent development, also use a data-driven approach, with proponents arguing:

> Overall, the goals of an ACO are to empower people to take charge of their health and engage in shared decision making with providers; eliminate waste and unnecessary spending while also meeting patients' preferences for care; increase preventive care and other strategies that could help keep people well; and increase overall satisfaction with care. (DeVore & Champion, 2011: 41)

Population health management in this context is described as going:

> ...far beyond an electronic health record and requires IT resources and tools to collect data on individual health status; stratify and target populations based on their risk and need for care; engage people in their health using patient health records or online portals; connect to a health information exchange to ensure portability of records; and direct physicians toward appropriate, evidence-based care protocols. (DeVore & Champion, 2011: 44)

This description illustrates one of the key tenets of the population health management approach: the risk stratification of populations in order to target interventions and support. Linked to the concept of 'case management' (Boaden et al., 2006), risk stratification involves using algorithms with large data sets to identify what are often called 'segments' of populations most at risk of particular problems (Cerezo & Lopez, 2018).

Population health management in this latest guise of algorithmic analysis of large data sets to target interventions has been enthusiastically embraced in the English NHS. The NHS England website explains:

> A new approach – called Population Health Management (PHM) – is helping us understand our current, and predict our future, health and care needs so we can take action in tailoring better care and support with individuals, design more joined up and sustainable health and care services, and make better use of public resources. It is how we use historical and current data to understand what factors are driving poor outcomes in different population groups. It is how we then design new proactive models of care which will improve health and wellbeing today as well as in 20 years' time. This could be by stopping people becoming unwell in the first place, or, where this isn't possible, improving the way the system works together to

> support them. (https://www.england.nhs.uk/integratedcare/building-blocks/phm/)

As this quote illustrates, population health management has become intimately linked with ideals of prevention, with 'proactive' care again lauded as an important 'new' approach. A prevention Green Paper (UK government discussion paper) published in 2019 (Parliamentary Under Secretary of State for Public Health and Primary Care, 2019) takes this further, suggesting that large data sets offer the possibility of 'personalised' and 'predictive' prevention. Explicitly referencing the CIAR population health model, the Green Paper locates potential health problems in individuals, but argues that big data approaches can identify relevant groups of these individuals so that preventative efforts can be appropriately targeted.

Alongside these utopian dreams of 'predictive' prevention, recent structural reorganization of the NHS in England is also built upon an ideal of population health management. Integrated Care Systems (Lorne et al., 2019) are voluntary non-statutory collaborations between large scale healthcare commissioners and providers across geographical footprints covering between 1 and 3 million people. Primary Care Networks are also voluntary collaborations between general practices, offered contractual incentives to work together to provide additional services across populations of between 30 and 50,000 people (Morciano et al., 2020). Both Primary Care Networks and Integrated Care Systems are explicitly enjoined to take a population health management approach, analysing their respective populations and providing appropriately targeted care (NHS England, 2019).

Thus, in 2020, there seems to be a global movement towards population health management as an underlying organizing principle for health systems, with utopian ideals. Han et al., (2020) exemplify this approach, with their title referencing 'precision population health management'. Such use of persuasive rhetoric is widespread in the field, with far-reaching claims made and frequent juxtapositions of pairs of concepts such as 'proactive' and 'reactive', in which one is clearly situated as being obviously preferable to the other. However, evidence to back up these rhetorical claims is limited (Taylor-Robinson & Kee, 2018). In the rest of this paper, we explore an example of the population health management approach which emerged in England during the COVID-19 pandemic in 2020. We consider the operation of this programme and use it to explore some of the unspoken and potentially problematic ontological and epistemological assumptions underlying population health management as an approach to improving the health of the public.

UK 'Shielding' Policy

The so-called shielding policy emerged in the early stages of the COVID-19 pandemic in the UK. As the 'lockdown' started, GPs were notified that a cohort of 'extremely vulnerable' patients would be identified who would be asked to adhere to a stricter version of lockdown, refraining from leaving their homes, and avoiding all social contact (NHS England, 2020). It was argued that in order to reduce mortality from the virus and protect NHS capacity, such patients needed to be 'shielded' from the virus by special measures, with arrangements put in place to support them with primary care support, food deliveries, social support, etc. Those who fell into this category would be centrally identified and informed using large-scale databases (NHS Digital, 2020). As eventually established, the programme had all the hallmarks of the population health management approach: identification of characteristics driving risk or vulnerability to a particular health problem; identification of an at-risk population based on these characteristics using electronic records; and the provision of targeted measures to these individuals to prevent ill health.

The programme did not run particularly smoothly. An initial cohort of individuals was identified using national hospital records, and a first tranche of what came to be known as 'shielding letters' were sent out. These letters explained to individuals that their health conditions meant that they were at higher risk of complications should they contract COVID-19, and that they should remain at home, avoiding all social contact. The criteria by which risk status was ascribed to individuals were publicized, including, for example, those with compromised immune systems, those with severe asthma and those having chemotherapy for cancer. A letter was then sent to GPs by their professional bodies, the Royal College of General Practitioners and the British Medical Association, explaining that, in addition to this centrally identified 'at risk' group, GPs should start running searches on their own systems to identify high-risk individuals, who should be notified to the central authorities in order to log them on the central list of those eligible for support (British Medical Association et al., 2020). An email address was provided for this purpose (NHS Digital, 2020). This letter arrived at the end of the last week in March. As the GP responsible for the programme in her practice, KC spends some time with her practice secretary constructing searches and devising communications to be sent to the people identified. An initial tranche of letters were sent. By the beginning of the following week, these instructions had been withdrawn, with GPs now told to stop identifying people as they would be provided with automated search facilities by their electronic record suppliers. In the meantime, our own and other practices who had begun to identify and inform their list of patients were left unsure what to do, with some commentators suggesting that this process had over-identified vulnerable people (Serle, 2020a). The administrative and secretarial staff working in our practices were at the front line of this confusing process, trying to get to grips with changing guidance and dealing with queries from confused patients. Over the next few weeks, shifting guidance and electronic record search algorithms were provided to practices, whilst at the same time, criteria were adjusted and additional national searches were run which triggered a further round of national letters (Bostock, 2020; Serle, 2020b). As GP computer system suppliers caught up with the guidance, new automated searches were provided, and practices sent letters to those that they felt satisfied with the criteria, simultaneously entering a code on the record which would be picked up at national level (Brennan, 2020). Local Authorities were given access to lists of identified patients generated by this national coding process, who were provided with food deliveries. In a slightly bizarre twist, supermarkets which were struggling to keep up with demand for online delivery slots stated that they would give priority to those 'on the shielding list' (Nott, 2020), triggering multiple requests from patients and their families to their GPs asking to be 'put on the list'.

Through the month of April, GPs were required to check their 'extremely vulnerable' lists, and in performing this time-consuming task, KC and SS discovered, in common with many of their colleagues, that some people had been erroneously identified by the national process, whilst others had been left off the list for no obvious reason. Phone calls to both groups of patients could be fraught, with some angry that they were on the list whilst others were angry that they were not. Even as clinicians who were simultaneously engaging in reflexive critique of the shielding process, we found that removing someone from the list felt risky, despite good reasons for doing so, in that it wasn't clear if we would be vulnerable to criticism should the patient concerned subsequently develop a severe illness. At the same time, voluntary and professional groups such as Asthma UK and the British Rheumatology Society (BRS) started to issue their own guidelines as to what constituted 'high risk' which, at times, were at odds with official definitions (Merrifield, 2020). For example, the DHSC risk algorithm identified those receiving the drug methotrexate as extremely vulnerable, whilst guidance from the BRS suggested that two or more immunosuppressant drugs were required to put patients in this category. Finally, employment issues featured highly in the process, with those ordered to 'shield' asking for sick notes to cover them when they failed to attend work, even though this was officially discouraged. Those living with 'shielding' patients were concerned as to whether to not they should go to work (official guidance was that they should) and some people with chronic conditions who did not meet shielding criteria asked to be 'put on the list' in order to support them in conversations with their employers as to whether or not they could work from home. Dealing with these issues was time-consuming and emotionally draining, and it threw into sharp relief the complexities of categorization and assigning risk status to individuals which we were beginning to discuss in our reflexive conversations. Whilst some of the issues we have highlighted which arose during this fraught period were due to the speed at which the programme was put in place, others were not. Indeed, the time element acted to draw attention to issues which are inherent in all programmes of population health management. Thus, for example, deciding who was or was not 'on the list', and the criteria used to establish this are common to all programmes built on identification of risk, whilst the contestation of risk-bearing status by both those identified as high risk and those who were not highlights variation in attitudes to risk within the population with which accounts of population health management programmes often fail to engage. In the next sections, we explore these issues in more depth.

Critique 1: The Problem of Classification

Bowker and Star (2000) define classification as 'a spatial, temporal or spatiotemporal segmentation of the world' (p. 10). They suggest that an ideal classification system meets the following criteria: classificatory principles are consistent and unique; categories are mutually exclusive; and the system is complete—i.e. it can cover all eligible units which exist. In our example, the classificatory system contained three categories: extremely vulnerable, identified individually and associated with special treatment; vulnerable, not individually identified; and everyone else. Only the extremely vulnerable category received any additional support, and it is this group upon which we will focus, as they are the group whose health was 'managed'.

The classificatory principles by which individuals were identified as extremely vulnerable were somewhat obscure. Whilst a clear list of conditions deemed to render individuals vulnerable was issued (https://digital.nhs.uk/coronavirus/shielded-patient-list#publication), the underlying principles upon which the selection of conditions to include was made were not discussed publicly. Thus, for example, whilst severe asthma was deemed to render an individual extremely vulnerable, severe heart failure, which also leads to chronic lung problems and breathlessness, was not. In the absence of a clear justification for this, we can only speculate, but it is possible that this apparent anomaly rests upon an unacknowledged feature of the idea of risk classification which underpins population health management: the need for identified 'high risk' populations to be of a manageable size. If a programme aims to provide supportive or preventative care to a population identified as at high risk, then the number of people identified must be one to which the required services can be provided. In this case, identified patients were to be provided with food parcels and contact from a central support hub. If the high-risk population was too large, then such services could not be provided. It thus seems likely that the features used to identify risk did not reflect an objective category; rather, they represented a negotiation in which potential risk factors were chosen which would identify a vulnerable cohort of a suitable size. Include too many factors, and available support would be too thinly spread as to be useful, whilst too narrow a definition would fail in the declared goal of reducing mortality and easing pressure on the NHS. Perhaps more contentiously, considerations of ability to benefit may also figure in the development of such classification systems. Thus, for example, it is possible that identified 'high risk' populations might actually be those with relevant characteristics who are deemed most likely or most able to benefit and so provide the greatest return on investment.

Thus, classifications such as this appear neutral and objective, whilst in fact, embodying negotiations which may include political or economic factors and which may or may not be transparent. In the case of the shielding list, the underlying principles determining categorization were not publicly discussed, and we can therefore only speculate as to what drove the decisions made. This lack of transparency drove many of the difficult conversations which GPs had with their patients, as those with poor health who did not fall into the official shielding category strove to understand why they were at less risk than friends with a different combination of diseases. This illustrates an important truth about population risk categorization applied to individuals: whilst it is possible to look at populations and determine which groups are most likely to suffer from particular problems, at individual level, risk categorization will always be approximate and contingent. The operation of the shielding list, and its association with material benefits such as priority supermarket deliveries, highlighted this issue, with an approximate designation of risk status translated into a concrete categorization of in or out—an all or nothing status of being protected or not.

Further issues arose out of the dichotomous assignment of people as either in or out of the shielded group. Support and lobby groups working on behalf of patients with particular diseases argued publicly for 'their' disease to be included in the high-risk category. Those excluded from the list felt less valued, and commentators argued that the exclusion of some diseases/disabilities from the risk algorithm represented a lack of priority given to their patients (Ryan, 2020). Even the ending of the scheme generated some controversy, with some arguing that the ending of food deliveries, etc. represented an abandonment of those most at risk (Busby, 2020).

The problems highlighted here are clearly exaggerated by the unique issues arising out of a global pandemic. The identification of high-risk groups and the provision of preventative health care associated with the usual operation of population health management approaches do not usually generate so much angry commentary or individual angst. Indeed, individuals are often unaware that they have been designated as 'high risk' against some or other criteria. However, the underlying issues driving the problems we have highlighted are always present. The criteria used to identify high-risk population 'segments' are never wholly objective and will always arise out of negotiations which take account of economic, political, or social issues, and the categorization of individuals as in or out of the high-risk group will always be approximate. In the next section, we will consider the concept of risk in more detail.

Critique 2: The Problem of Constructing Risk

In contrast to the common understanding of risk in early modern societies where it was considered to have positive as well as negative dimensions, in modern societies, the term has come to refer to the possibility of a negative event or outcome and is associated with danger, hazard, or threat (Lupton, 1999). It is '...the product of the probability and consequences (magnitude and severity) of an adverse event' (Bradbury, 1989: 382): a techno-scientific interpretation founded on knowledge from various scientific domains of practice including economics, statistics, and engineering. Indeed, it is through developments of scientific expertise and technology that awareness of risks is increased, coupled to an expectation of the ability to exercise control to mitigate them.

Adam (2011) shows how HIV prevention attempts to focus particularly on the discovery and development of biomedical technologies. This is part of an '...epistemological frame characteristic of biomedical individualism...' (Adam, 2011: 8) where social dimensions of the epidemic, and social tools for helping to address it, lack prominence in prevention discourse and interventions. We can see the same dominance of biomedical individualism in the COVID-19 shielding policy. This is articulated in the extract from the shielding letter sent to those designated extremely vulnerable in Box 11.1.

Box 11.1: Exert from the shielding advice for the extremely clinically vulnerable letter sent to patients from NHS organisations in March 2020 (bold text reflects original).

The NHS has identified you, or the named person you care for, as someone at risk of severe illness if you catch Coronavirus (also known as COVID-19). This is because you have an underlying disease or health condition that means if you catch the virus, you are more likely to be admitted to hospital than others.

The safest course of action is for you to stay at home at all times and avoid all face-to-face contact for at least 12 weeks from today, except from carers and healthcare workers who you must see as part of your medical care. This will protect you by stopping you from coming into contact with the virus.

The broader risk calculus involved in the shielding policy was the probability of an individual catching the virus (i.e. the extent to which a person is exposed to others, and the estimated prevalence of COVID-19 in the population at that time) combined with the potential consequences (i.e. the magnitude and severity) of infection in terms of both costs to an individual's health and the healthcare resources expended in treating what is assessed likely to be a severe illness. The risk is, therefore, to both the individual in terms of detrimental consequences to their health as well as risks to the broader population dependent on a functioning healthcare system, which threatened to be overwhelmed with the sheer volume of patients requiring intensive care during the first wave of infection.

Beck's (1992) 'risk society' is one in which scientific and industrial development creates the conditions for both the creation of significant, globalized risks, and the expectation that these can be controlled through the application of expertise. For Beck, the defining risks of late modernity are more evenly distributed across populations than had previously been the case, and it is harder for the wealthy to pay to personally circumvent them. As such, individualized risk positions tend to supersede social class and other characteristics (Nygren & Olofsson, 2020). Curran (2016) argues instead that contemporary risks tend towards intensification of class differences, and this warrants particular consideration in relation to COVID-19.

In the early stages of the pandemic, the virus was referred to by some as 'the great leveller' because of its ability to infect and affect anyone, including the UK Prime Minister. Since then, however, it has become clear that the risks of COVID-19 are not distributed at all equally, with certain groups in society disproportionately affected in association with age, occupation, deprivation, and ethnic background, for example. Medical classifications previously ascribed to the bodies of individuals may be the most practical and objective basis on which to ascribe risk to citizens when faced with the threat of a new virus, but it also fails to address socio-political dimensions of the pandemic. As we have discussed, the initial risk-identification algorithm was focused solely upon biological risk associated with particular treatments or diseases. As the pandemic progressed, and it became clear that socio-economic, ethnic, and occupational factors were driving both risk of infection and risk of severe illness, the algorithm was not adjusted, leaving many vulnerable people unprotected (Bowleg, 2020). The wealthy may not simply be able to pay to avoid infection but they do benefit from a system where 'essential workers', many with multiple structural risk factors, continue to expose themselves to the risk of infection in order to continue to provide goods and services for society at large.

A further issue relating to risk is a lack of attention in shielding policy to the risks associated with shielding for those doing so. The consequences of contracting a virus are relatively immediate and measurable. However, the consequences of staying at home and not seeing other people (including friends and family) face-to-face for extended periods of time are more psychological and social in nature as well as variable, contingent, diffuse, and unpredictable. Those with good access to technology, for example, may have been relatively protected, as they were able to keep in contact with family and friends via video calls. Those with low digital literacy or no access to technology were thus differentially exposed to the psycho-social risks of shielding.

Shielding policy thus constructed risk around the single dimension of biological vulnerability based on the presence or absence of particular diseases, with socio-economic or ethic-origin driven risks not considered. The population health management approach as set out by NHS England and espoused by US health care providers similarly largely focuses upon individual biological characteristics which are captured by large databases. Such databases are constructed for a variety of purposes, often focused on patient management, and they will thus only capture characteristics which have been pre-specified as relevant. Socio-economic status and ethnic origin are rarely the focus of such databases, and may be poorly captured (Jorm, 2015), and new or previously unconsidered risk-driving characteristics will not feature. Moreover, the 'interventions' offered are individual in focus, framing 'risk' as something to be addressed by individual action (better nutrition, more exercise, etc.) rather than by attention to the structural factors driving that risk. Just as the shielding policy addressed risk by asking individuals to behave in certain ways, population health management programmes tend to focus upon actions to 'engage people in their health' (DeVore & Champion, 2011: 44) rather than interventions to change the societal factors driving individual risks.

Discussion

The COVID-19 shielding programme in the UK represents an example of the Population Health Management approach lauded in current UK and international health policy. Whilst some of the problems that we have identified arise out of the unique context of a global pandemic, we argue that this context has simply acted to bring into sharp relief problems which are inherent in this approach. Much of the commentary on the shielding programme has focused upon the specifics of the risk algorithm, with advocates arguing that their particular client group should have been included. However, we have demonstrated that the issue with this population health management approach is more fundamental, which no tweaking of the algorithm or adjustment of the parameters will solve. We have highlighted how the categorization of 'high' or 'low' risk offers a spurious precision, which, whilst defensible at a population level, unravels when applied to individuals. Moreover, we have shown how the factors underlying such categorizations are not necessarily transparent and may conceal negotiations based around undeclared considerations such as the volume of care to be provided or perceptions of ability to benefit. We have also interrogated the concept of risk, arguing that population health management built around large healthcare databases tends to foreground biological risk at the expense of other risks which may arise out of structural inequalities in society. Individually focused ('precision') interventions will thus fail to grapple with the underlying features of society which drive differential health outcomes.

What we have called the 'categorisation problem' and the 'risk construction problem' both illustrate the importance of problem *framing* in driving or focusing action to improve health. As Jones and Exworthy, (2015) demonstrated in their study of hospital planning, how a problem is framed has a powerful impact upon how it is perceived, including the potential for a particular framing to bracket out important aspects of any given situation whilst at the same time constraining potential responses. Shielding from COVID-19 in the UK was framed as a biomedical issue, with individuals assigned to risk categories based upon their biological characteristics. As with population health management more generally, this framing had an important impact on what was done to ameliorate risk, with a neoliberal focus on responsibilizing individuals (Liebenberg et al., 2013) to take action to improve or protect their health rather than upon societal-level action.

This in turn raises questions about the relationship between population health management and public health. In England, since 2012, responsibility for public health has rested with Local Government. The rationale for the shift of responsibility from the NHS was the opportunity offered for Local Authorities to take a more holistic approach to health, considering housing, transport, and employment issues alongside medical care and health system actions (Marks et al., 2015). Population health management approaches, by contrast, are being driven by the NHS, with NHS

England a prominent advocate (NHS England, 2019). This raises important questions about the role and identity of public health practitioners, and the potential for co-ordination between NHS-driven individually focused PHM and LA-driven community-based action. Public health practitioners themselves identify advocacy and campaigning on behalf of vulnerable populations as important roles (Hall et al., 2018; Tillmann et al., 2014). Our examination of the COVID-19 shielding policy has highlighted the potential disconnect between this social activism approach and the more biomedical approach embodied in population health management. At present, it seems as if these two approaches are talking past one another, framing the problem differently and therefore identifying different avenues for intervention. We have demonstrated the problems associated with PHM, not least the fact that it has limited potential to engage seriously with the underlying structural issues driving risks within the population. As Raphael and Bryant argue with respect to the CIAR approach which underpins current PHM:

> CIAR offers no theory of society (Coburn and Poland, 1997). Lack of a theory of society leads to a neglect of how the current state of health determinants come to be and the potent forces that either support or oppose the status quo. Population health has a troubling blind spot (as does health promotion at times) to work in the political economy area that sheds lights on the forces that drive health determinants. (Raphael & Bryant, 2002: 192)

PHM is currently being embedded ever more deeply in the developing health system in England as well as in other countries, and it is unlikely that this can be reversed. Indeed, it is probably undesirable, as undoubtedly the ability to use accumulated data to understand health inequalities is important. However, our analysis would suggest that PHM alone is problematic, and that it needs to be married with a traditional public health advocacy and campaigning approach, refusing to accept at face value identified disparities, but digging beneath to expose and interrogate the structural factors at work. In the context of COVID-19, this would mean protecting those vulnerable due to their biological characteristics, but also looking seriously at employment conditions, poverty, and racial injustice to tackle the underlying problems which have caused the shocking inequalities in the impact of the pandemic.

References

Adam, B. D. (2011). Epistemic fault lines in biomedical and social approaches to HIV prevention. *Journal of the International AIDS Society, 14*(Suppl. 2), S2.

Adams, T. (2001). The social construction of risk by community psychiatric nurses and family carers for people with dementia. *Health, Risk & Society, 3*(3), 307–319.

Barnes, A. J., Unruh, L., Chukmaitov, A., & van Ginneken, E. (2014). Accountable care organizations in the USA: Types, developments and challenges. *Health Policy, 118*(1), 1–7.

Beck, P. U. (1992). *Risk society: Towards a new modernity*. Sage.

Boaden, R., Dusheiko, M., Gravelle, H., Parker, S., Pickard, S., Roland, M., Sargent, P., & Sheaff, R. (2006). *Evercare evaluation: Final report*. NPCRDC, University of Manchester.

Bostock, N. (2020, April 24). U-turn as splenectomy patients added to COVID-19 shielding list. *GP Online*.

Bowker, G. C., & Star, S. L. (2000). *Sorting things out: Classification and its consequences*. MIT press.

Bowleg, L. (2020). We're not all in this together: On COVID-19, intersectionality, and structural inequality. *American Journal of Public Health, 110*(7), 917–917.

Bradbury, J. A. (1989). The policy implications of differing concepts of risk. *Science, Technology, & Human Values, 14*(4), 380–399.

Brennan, S. (2020). Covid vulnerable patient list balloons by 500,000. *Health Services Journal*. https://www.hsj.co.uk/primary-care/covid-vulnerable-patient-list-balloons-by-500000/7027503.article

British Medical Association, Royal College of General Practitioners and NHS England. (2020, March 23). *Vulnerable patients—The role of general practice during COVID 19*. https://www.pulsetoday.co.uk/wp-content/uploads/c_files/uploads/b/w/l/Shielded-letter---23-March.pdf

Busby, M. (2020). 'Perverse' to tell vulnerable to stop shielding from coronavirus, says Age UK. *The Guardian*.

Butz, D., & Besio, K. (2009). Autoethnography. *Geography Compass, 3*(5), 1660–1674.

Cerezo, J. C., & Lopez, C. A. (2018). *Population stratification: A fundamental instrument used for population health management in Spain*. World Health Organisation.

Chen, C., Garrido, T., Chock, D., Okawa, G., & Liang, L. (2009). The Kaiser Permanente Electronic Health Record: Transforming and streamlining modalities of care. *Health Affairs, 28*(2), 323–333.

Curran, D. (2016). *Risk, power, and inequality in the 21st century*. Palgrave Macmillan.

DeVore, S., & Champion, R. W. (2011). Driving population health through accountable care organizations. *Health Affairs, 30*(1), 41–50.

Ellis, C., Adams, T. E., & Bochner, A. P. (2011). Autoethnography: An overview. *Historical Social Research/Historische Sozialforschung, 36*(4) (138), 273–290.

Evans, R. G., & Stoddart, G. L. (1990). Producing health, consuming health care. *Social Science & Medicine, 31*(12), 1347–1363.

Goodrick, E., & Reay, T. (2016). An institutional perspective on accountable care organizations. *Medical Care Research and Review, 73*(6), 685–693.

Hall, A., Hammond, J., Bramwell, D., Coleman, A., Warwick-Giles, L., & Checkland, K. (2018). Beyond the parish pump: What next for public health? *BMC Public Health, 18*(1), 856.

Han, A., Isaacson, A., & Muennig, P. (2020). The promise of big data for precision population health management in the US. *Public Health, 185*, 110–116.

Havighurst, C. C. (1970). Health maintenance organizations and the market for health services. *Law and Contemporary Problems, 35*(4), 716–795.

Johnson, B. B., & Covello, V. T. (2012). *The social and cultural construction of risk: Essays on risk selection and perception*. Springer Science & Business Media.

Jones, L., & Exworthy, M. (2015). Framing in policy processes: A case study from hospital planning in the National Health Service in England. *Social Science & Medicine, 124*, 196–204.

Jorm, L. (2015). Routinely collected data as a strategic resource for research: Priorities for methods and workforce. *Public Health Research & Practice, 25*(4), e2541540.

Labonte, R., Polanyi, M., Muhajarine, N., McIntosh, T., & Williams, A. (2005). Beyond the divides: Towards critical population health research. *Critical Public Health, 15*(1), 5–17.

Liebenberg, L., Ungar, M., & Ikeda, J. (2013). Neo-liberalism and responsibilisation in the discourse of social service workers. *British Journal of Social Work, 45*, 1006–1021.

Lorne, C., Allen, P., Checkland, K., Osipovic, D., Sanderson, M., Hammond, J., & Peckham, S. (2019). *Integrated care systems: What can current reforms learn from past research on regional co-ordination of health and care in England?* (pp. 1–84).

Luft, H. S. (1978). How do health-maintenance organizations achieve their savings? Rhetoric and evidence. *New England Journal of Medicine, 298*(24), 1336–1343.

Lupton, D. (1999). *Risk*. Psychology Press.

Marks, L., Hunter, D. J., Scalabrini, S., Gray, J., McCafferty, S., Payne, N., Peckham, S., Salway, S., & Thokala, P. (2015). The return of public health to local government in England: Changing the parameters of the public health prioritization debate? *Public Health, 129*(9), 1194–1203.

Merrifield, N. (2020). Asthma UK admits its earlier shielding guidance 'caused confusion'. *Pulse Today*.

Morciano, M., Checkland, K., Hammond, J., Lau, Y. S., & Sutton, M. (2020). Variability in size and characteristics of England's Primary Care Networks: observational study. *British Journal of General Practice, 70*(701), e899–e905.

NHS Digital. (2020). *Shielded patient list*. https://digital.nhs.uk/coronavirus/shielded-patient-list

NHS England. (2019). *The NHS long term plan*. NHS England.

NHS England. (2020). *At risk patients coronavirus*. https://www.england.nhs.uk/coronavirus/publication/guidance-and-updates-for-gps-at-risk-patients/

Nott, G. (2020, April 17). How to get an online supermarket delivery slot if you are shielding by George Nott. *The Groceer*. https://www.thegrocer.co.uk/online/how-to-get-an-online-supermarket-delivery-slot-if-you-are-shielding/604081.article

Nygren, K. G., & Olofsson, A. (2020). Managing the Covid-19 pandemic through individual responsibility: The consequences of a world risk society and enhanced ethopolitics. *Journal of Risk Research, 23*, 1031–1035.

Parliamentary Under Secretary of State for Public Health and Primary Care. (2019). *Advancing our health: Prevention in the 2020s—Consultation document* (Department of Health and Social Care, Ed.). https://www.gov.uk/government/consultations/advancing-our-health-prevention-in-the-2020s/advancing-our-health-prevention-in-the-2020s-consultation-document

Raphael, D., & Bryant, T. (2002). The limitations of population health as a model for a new public health. *Health Promotion International, 17*(2), 189–199.

Rodriguez, E., Shofer, S., Harter, M., & Clark, N. (2017). First guiding process: Problematizing what you know for new-self insight. In S. Hughes & J. Pennington (Eds.), *Autoethnography: Process, product, and possibility for critical social research*. Sage.

Ryan, F. (2020). Disabled people left off coronavirus vulnerable list go without food. *The Observer*.

Serle, J. (2020a). 100,000 people incorrectly told they needed to self-isolate because of coronavirus. *Health Services Journal*. https://www.hsj.co.uk/coronavirus/100000-people-incorrectly-told-they-needed-to-self-isolate-because-of-coronavirus/7027575.article

Serle, J. (2020b). GPs given new deadline to identify 'at risk' patients. *Health Services Journal*. https://www.hsj.co.uk/coronavirus/gps-given-new-deadline-to-identify-at-risk-patients/7027390.article

Shortell, S. M., Gillies, R., & Wu, F. (2010). United States innovations in health care delivery. *Public Health Reviews, 32*(1), 190–212.

Taylor-Robinson, D., & Kee, F. (2018). Precision public health—The Emperor's new clothes. *International Journal of Epidemiology, 48*(1), 1–6.

Tillmann, T., Baker, P., Crocker-Buque, T., Rana, S., & Bouquet, B. (2014). Shortage of public health independence and advocacy in the UK. *The Lancet, 383*(9913), 213.

World Health Organisation. (2020). *Draft global strategy on digital health 2020–2024*. WHO.

CHAPTER 12

The Temporal Dimensions of Health Technology Adoption During the Covid-19 Pandemic: Revisiting Roger's Diffusionist Innovation Theory

Jean Ledger and Minal Bakhai

Introduction

The Covid-19 global pandemic has created an atypical innovation adoption context resulting in radical shifts in health service delivery. These include the widespread uptake of telemedicine and remote consultations in primary and secondary care and greater use of digital health tools by patients. Practical problems requiring urgent solution during Covid-19 displaced common implementation barriers to service innovation in health

J. Ledger (✉)
Department of Applied Health Research, University College London, London, UK
e-mail: j.ledger@ucl.ac.uk

M. Bakhai
Digital First Primary Care, NHS England and NHS Improvement, London, UK

J. Waring et al. (eds.), *Organising Care in a Time of Covid-19*, Organizational Behaviour in Healthcare,
https://doi.org/10.1007/978-3-030-82696-3_12

care, such as lengthy procurement and administrative processes, professional resistance and cultural barriers, and risk aversion (The King's Fund, 2021).

Traditional diffusionist innovation theory focuses on variable adoption timescales. In Rogers' seminal work (Rogers, 2003), a socially based model of diffusion conceptualises innovations as taking variable time to spread due to a number of inter-relating factors, with innovations largely spreading through communication channels and peer networks (Greenhalgh et al., 2004: 589). When new ideas or innovations are taken up quickly, this is due to the specific attributes of the innovation, coupled with communication of knowledge about its benefits. The actions of dedicated opinion leaders and innovation champions are critical to persuading others to adopt, especially persons who are reluctant to change.

In this chapter, I revisit Roger's highly cited and widely recognised conceptualisation of innovation spread, arguing that it is worthy of re-examination in the light of the Covid-19 pandemic and given the fast-paced implementation and widespread uptake of digital health innovations across international health systems from March 2020. In particular, innovation adoption timescales were compressed across health systems on account of the pandemic necessitating the overhaul of dominant service delivery models which have been conventionally designed around the face-to-face clinical encounter. In both primary and secondary care, such as in the UK's National Health Service (NHS), managers and health professionals rapidly implemented digital tools during the pandemic to deliver care safely to patients through remote clinical assessments and consultations (NHS England and NHS Improvement, 2020a, b).

In the English primary care system, which is the focus on this chapter, different types of digital innovations underwent an accelerated uptake during 2020: online consultations (i.e. enquiries submitted by patients online); video consultations; group video consultations; and online/digital remote triage. In practice, each of these approaches is mediated by different digital suppliers which in turn shapes the end user experience and system functionality.[1] These digital innovations were already available to healthcare providers in the NHS in England; however, many had not deployed them (NHS England and Improvement, March 2020c; The Health Foundation, 2020; The King's Fund, 2021). In

[1] Providers include AccuRX, e-Consult, DoctorLink, AskMyGP, Bablyon—each offering slightly different services.

parallel, in the secondary care sector, technology was leveraged at pace with virtual clinics being established in service areas such as orthopaedics and outpatient services, with one specialist NHS hospital reporting a shift to 87% remote consultations within a six-week period (Gilbert et al., 2020). Rapid change was brought about due to the necessity of physical distancing and protecting the most vulnerable members of society and health workers from exposure to the virus, drastically altering the health care landscape in the process—in the UK and internationally. Critically, within a short period of time, health care consultations transformed from bounded interactions associated with physical place (e.g. hospital outpatients departments, local surgeries) to a service mediated by digital platforms and undertaken within and outside of health care settings, such as in people's homes.

This chapter draws on review of grey literature (e.g. commentaries, news and think tank reports), national NHS and clinical guidance, and published peer-reviewed research about primary care. To explore innovation adoption dynamics theoretically, the chapter is structured as follows: I begin by revisiting Rogers' diffusionist theory, taking into consideration a number of criticisms and exploring how time is presented in his work to explain different rates of innovation adoption within a social system. I then apply Rogers' theory to help understand the changes witnessed in the English primary care sector (as a social system) during Covid-19, given that much of the focus on telehealth and telemedicine has been traditionally focused on secondary care and has not occurred in the context of a global crisis.

Roger's Diffusion of Innovation Theory During the Covid-19 Global Pandemic: The Temporal Dimensions of Innovation Adoption

In Rogers' classic text, *Diffusion of Innovations*, time is a central aspect of the diffusion process (Lundblad, 2003; Rogers, 2003). Rogers emphasised that the temporal dimension of innovation diffusion had previously been overlooked in research and sensitised readers to time as a variable influencing innovation adoption in three distinctive ways:

1. During the 'innovation-decision process': this is the time between an individual and group first knowing about an innovation and adopting or rejecting it.
2. The time taken for an individual or group to adopt an innovation within a social system compared to others, as influenced by their relative 'innovativeness': this refers to the five well-known adopter categories: *innovators; early adopters; early majority; late majority; laggards.*
3. The rate of adoption and time taken to scale up an innovation: this is a quantitative measure of how many people/groups/organisations adopt the innovation during a specific period of time (the 'S' adoption curve).

These distinctive, time-sensitive activities are influenced by individuals and groups within social systems and their choices and behaviours. It is worth exploring in more detail these different temporal aspects and how they can be applied to studying innovation adoption in health care settings, before moving on to apply them to the Covid-19 context.

Temporal Variable 1: The 'Innovation-Decision Process'

According to Rogers, it is in the first preliminary stage, the 'innovation-decision process', when knowledge is first acquired about an innovation and a person persuaded to form a more or less favourable disposition towards it. This process has both a subjective and social element to it. Individuals seek out new knowledge to provide greater certainty about whether or not to implement an innovation and at this point are receptive to new information about how an innovation might alleviate a particular problem or challenge. In this early stage, the individual is chiefly concerned with the question: *will information [about the innovation] be beneficial to me in my particular situation?* (Rogers, 2003: 21).

According to Rogers, the innovation-decision process is comprised of five stages that typically 'occur in a time ordered sequence' (p. 21) as follows:

1. Knowledge
2. Persuasion
3. Decision

4. Implementation
5. Confirmation.

Consideration of others' opinions (persuasion) eventually leads to a choice about whether or not to implement an innovation (decision). Once implemented, individuals gather additional information to confirm (or reaffirm) the appropriateness of their initial decision choice and observe the effects of the innovation. Importantly, this process is time-sensitive and shaped by the attributes of the innovation: its *relative advantage; compatibility; complexity; trialability; and observability* (Rogers, 2003: 222).

Access to information about the innovation is, importantly, a socially mediated process wherein an individual—or adopting unit/organisation—leverages 'interpersonal communication networks' to access information (ibid.: 21). Indeed, for Rogers, it is key individuals within a social system that primarily influence a person's evaluative judgement about the acceptability of an innovation or new idea (ibid.: 223). Interpersonal peer networks are critical for persuading more cautious adopters about the potential advantages of an innovation, whilst 'mass media channels' are better for raising general awareness (ibid.: 18). Today's phenomenon of widely accessible information as is found in the health sector and on social media is a less accurate predictor of innovation adoption timescales because, for Rogers, it is the interpersonal communication channels and 'face-to-face exchange between two or more individuals' that are most persuasive in the innovation-decision process (p. 18).

Temporal Variable 2: The Relative 'Innovativeness' of Adopters

Now to one of the most widely cited aspects of Rodger's theory of innovation diffusion: the distinctive 'adopter categories' which describe the time taken for an individual or group to adopt an innovation or new idea relative to others. The archetypes used by Rogers are *innovators; early adopters; early majority; late majority; laggards.*

'Innovators' and 'early' adopters are amongst the first to adopt an innovation, even if they are cautious since uncertainty about the innovation and its effectiveness is typically higher in the early stages (Rogers: 204). The case of tetracycline adoption by the medical community, as studied by Coleman et al. (1966), is cited by Rogers as an example of doctors having initial exposure to limited scientific evidence about a drug's efficacy—pushed by drug companies—resulting in reliance on 'near peers' for additional information about real-world use cases. As Rogers interprets the study, 'innovators had to conduct their own personal experimentation with the new idea in order to assure themselves that it was indeed advantageous under their conditions' (ibid.).

Later adopters, the so-called 'late majority' or 'laggards', reap the benefits of these early risk-takers and experimenters. That is why late adopters 'profit' from preceding developments and adopt rapidly when decision uncertainty is lower. Rogers is clear that slow adopters are more sceptical in orientation and require a greater degree of persuasion through their networks, resulting in longer decision timescales. The personal characteristics of adopters are reduced to broad generalisations: earlier adopters and innovators are noted for their higher education and social status, and greater exposure to social media channels and external sources of information, than laggards; they are more 'cosmopolite' (ibid.: 298). By contrast, the late majority and laggards are sceptical and traditional (ibid.: 298).

Interestingly, recent research on antibiotic prescribing by GPs in primary care (Walker et al., 2019) underscores the heterogenous behaviours and variable timescales to implement change within modern health care systems. Through statistical analysis, researchers were able to detect changes in antibiotic prescribing for over 8000 GP surgeries in England following the introduction of new national guidelines. This included a recommendation for the use of nitrofurantoin instead of trimethoprim for uncomplicated urinary tract infections (UTI) (the authors also looked at prescribing a generic version of a branded contraceptive pill). The results of the research suggested that later adopters of national recommendations—the 'late majority' or 'laggards' to apply Rogers' categorisation—did change rapidly, albeit far later. The authors hypothesised that this could be due to a sudden sense of urgency amongst later adopters, and, at later time points, adopters merely need to catch up.

The point here is to emphasise the heterogenous time variations found within health systems such as primary care when it comes to innovation adoption and evidence-based practice, even in circumstances where national guidance is widely disseminated to professional groups at the same time. The researchers in the case above, for example, concluded that improved communication systems to share information and automated audit feedback to health care professionals might see more GP practices fall in line with the early adopters. But the research was less clear about the organisational characteristics of practices that do adopt early, and how local factors might lead some practices to be slower in taking up national recommendations than others, despite obvious cost benefits.

Temporal Variable 3: The Overall Rate of Adoption Within a Social System

The discussion above foregrounds the complexity behind understanding why there are differential rates of adoption of innovations within social systems. Overall, there are five main variables that Rogers views as influencing the rate of adoption of an innovation:

1. Perceived attributes of the innovation—relative advantage; compatibility; complexity; trialability; observability.
2. Type of Innovation-Decision—optional; collective; authority.
3. Communication Channels (e.g. mass media or interpersonal).
4. Nature of the Social System.
5. Extent of Change Agents' Promotion Efforts.

The variation in the rate of adoption is explainable by the features of the innovation and interactions between the factors listed above. When considering the rate of adoption, the attributes of the innovation are paramount in terms of how it will 'fit' with the norms of the adopting social system and help solve practical problems. Yet hugely important are the opinion leaders who, according to Rogers, determine the rate of adoption by being directly connected to mass media and having extensive interpersonal networks that allow them to communicate knowledge about the innovation—somewhat like today's marketing 'influencers'. To understand the diffusion, therefore, you have to understand these underlying networks and change agents (ibid.: 331).

Criticisms and Observations

Before applying Rogers' theory to health care during Covid-19, it is necessary to address some valid criticisms of his framework.

McMaster and Wastell (2005) have rightly challenged the underlying positivist foundations and assumptions of 'diffusionist' thinking, in particular, amongst writers on technological innovations that have used Rogers' work in an uncritical manner that promulgates the idea that the failure to implement an innovation is essentially negative—an act of resistance or passivity (pp. 385–386). They write:

> On the one hand, we have courageous innovators, and at the other pole, we have "laggards"; bumpkins with no aspirations, resources or initiative of their own. (p. 387)

This cautions researchers against naively linking an innovation 'laggard' with negative attributes or characteristics. Rogers' himself warned researchers to not fall prey to 'pro-innovation bias' which 'leads diffusion researchers to ignore the study of ignorance about innovations, to underemphasise the rejection or discontinuance of innovations, to overlook re-invention… and fail to study antidiffusion programs designed to prevent the spread of "bad innovations"' (Rogers, 2003: 107). After all, the 'failure' to adopt an innovation could be justified because it is unsafe, inequitable or lacking in evidence on effectiveness; in health care, this would be a valid justification for slow adoption, non-adoption or abandonment. Likewise, analysis of the diffusion of management practices by organisations has shown that following the majority is not necessarily associated with superior performance. Organisations can be strongly influenced by 'fads and fashions' and new management trends by persuasive broadcasters—business schools, gurus, management consultants and media (Abrahamson, 1991; Piazza & Abrahamson, 2020).

For McMaster and Wastell, Rogers nevertheless divides the world into a binary of non-adopters and adopters. They link this to a history of Eurocentric ideology and colonialist assumptions about insiders and outsiders; the world divided into those who innovate and those who imitate (p. 393). Such criticisms sensitise the research to the risks of pro-innovation bias and unreflexively suggesting that technological developments and innovations are inherently superior and will yield benefits. The rise of Responsible Research and Innovation (RRI) frameworks and policies, for example, encourages more nuanced and fine-grained analysis of the socioeconomic, environmental, organisational and legal risks of innovations and new technologies within social systems, recommending inclusive stakeholder engagement to understand different values and beliefs across social groups (Pacifico Silva et al., 2018). On the flip-side, Rogers' categorisation of adopters could be used to explain why some groups gain benefits from early adoption and others do not (e.g. because of social capital), an issue that needs to be understood given inequalities in the use of health technologies and innovations that reflect wider divisions in society (Timmermans & Kaufman, 2020).

Another criticism is that there is 'no single adoption decision' when it comes to implementing an innovation in a complex system such as health care (Fitzgerald et al., 2002: 1432). Diffusionist theory generally foregrounds the individual—the farmer or doctor, for example—who makes an independent choice about whether to change their practice via an '*optional innovation-decision*'. This person is envisaged as having a high degree of autonomy, yet in practice, decisions usually involve overlapping networks of professionals and organisations that intersect and influence each other in unpredictable ways. It is rare that a single individual becomes the ultimate arbiter of a decision to implement an innovation or idea. Indeed, whether or not to adopt an innovation or technology can lead to conflict and disagreements, highlighting professional jurisdictions that may hamper the innovation adoption process (Ferlie et al., 2005).

It is due to these complex social and cultural dynamics that faster access to information is not on its own sufficient to change daily practice. Diffusionist theory is often criticised for overlooking the role of different contexts and organisational characteristics in the innovation process and for emphasising a rather simplistic model of decision-making based around influential individuals and their peers (Fitzgerald et al., 2002; Greenhalgh et al., 2004; Lundblad, 2003). For example, there is now greater understanding that health care organisations and local systems differ in their capabilities to search out and apply new knowledge and evidence to solve problems, as suggested by the theory of Absorptive Capacity (Harvey et al., 2015). Health care organisations operate from different baselines in terms of their internal resources for exploiting and acting upon new information and data, and this will influence innovation-adoption decision processes and timelines. Indeed, there is a sizeable amount of social scientific evidence from empirical studies that demonstrate that mobilising knowledge—such as clinical evidence or information about service innovations—is effortful and time-consuming in multi-layered, profession-based organisations (Ferlie et al., 2018; Swan et al., 2016). This applies even if there is professional consensus at a national level about optimal treatments that reduce the potential for patient harm (Born et al., 2019).

A final criticism is the way in which collective decisions are downplayed in Rogers' theory. For Rogers, '*authority innovation-decisions*' made by a few on the behalf of others (such as when a law or mandated policy is decreed) expedites innovation adoption, whereas '*collective innovation-decisions*' are slower. However, this framework overlooks the many provisional, emergent and collective decisions found during the implementation of an innovation in a social system, and necessary for its success. As Pope et al. (2013) observed in their study of the implementation of computer decision support systems in urgent care settings, 'collective purposive action' was enacted through health care teamwork. In health care as well as other settings, teamwork cannot be overlooked vis-à-vis influential change agents and innovators. One can argue that a *lack* of collective decision-making in health systems can slow down implementation efforts and doom top-down innovation projects to failure. Staff need to be on board with change. The reality is therefore less either/or than Rogers suggests and a lot more multifaceted. In health care, senior leadership and management advocacy for innovations and knowledge mobilisation have consistently been identified as an important enabler of successful service innovation and change (Bullock et al., 2016; Greenhalgh et al., 2008, 2018; Nolte, 2018). At the same time, trusted professional relationships and grassroot networks can support collective decision-making across boundaries. For example, during a study of the early establishment of Academic Health Sciences Networks in England in the period 2014–2016 (Ferlie et al., 2017), a combination of influential 'knowledge leaders' and more dispersed professional contacts was central for establishing policy-mandated networks to expedite the uptake and spread of innovations into the NHS. There was a dynamic interplay, then, between authority and collective innovation-decisions.

Taking into account these observations, it is suggested that Rogers' original theory minimises how effortful, collective and non-linear innovation processes are at the organisational level, especially when it comes to implementation. Secondly, in health care, a decision process about adopting a particularly novel, complex or risky innovation may need to be lengthy because knowledge about efficacy, costs and safety takes time to acquire—being a 'laggard' could be a perfectly rational choice. Thirdly, collective decision processes are often needed to improve the chances of an innovation being successful and implemented at scale. Finally, it is widely acknowledged in health care that evidence alone is 'not, of itself, sufficient to ensure diffusion', a finding that has held remarkably consistent despite the rise of evidence-based medicine (Dixon-Woods et al., 2011; Fitzgerald et al., 2002). In health systems, an innovation requires professional and patient support to truly spread (both supply and demand), and senior management and policy backing. At the local level, a convincing 'business case' and 'value proposition' is often needed by health care providers (Nolte, 2018).

Remote Care Delivery in Primary Care During Covid-19: Compressing the Adoption Curve

In this section, I address how innovation adoption timescales were impacted by the outbreak of the Covid-19 pandemic and the rapid rate of digital transformation seen in primary care in England from March 2020 onwards.

With the Covid-19 pandemic came the rapid shift to remote health care delivery across primary and secondary care providers in health systems internationally. Arguably, in a short period of six months, the NHS implemented more digital transformation, both technically and culturally across thousands of providers, than ever before. The health system introduced changes to customary service models to mitigate the risk of viral transmission amongst the population, especially for vulnerable and shielding groups and health care workers. Therefore, whilst face-to-face consultations remained if there was clinical need, digital care pathways became more heavily relied upon. Interestingly, the shift to implementing digital products had already encouraged through NHS frameworks and policy (NHS, 2019), yet these changes had not been delivered across general practice at scale. To understand this impact on innovation adoption timescales, it is helpful to understand trends by looking at available evidence and data on primary care consultations before Covid-19.

Evidence on Remote Consultations and Care Delivery in Primary Care

Looking at the primary care sector in England, available information on consultation type indicates a seismic shift to remote delivery and a faster rate of adoption of digital technologies during the pandemic (Hutchings, 2020). To provide a comparison, the findings of a trend report tracking general practice in England between 1995 and 2009 shows that there had been very limited change to the traditional appointment model in primary care over time which centred on in-person visits to medical premises, a small proportion of telephone consultations and home visits:

> In 1995, 86% of GP consultations were conducted in surgery premises, 3% were on the telephone, 9% were home visits and 2% were conducted at other locations. By 2008, 82% of GP consultations were conducted in surgery premises, 12% were on the telephone, 4% were home visits and 3% were conducted at other locations. (Hippisley-Cox & Vinogradova, 2009)

A survey of practices in England and Scotland undertaken 2015 found that the majority of general practices had limited or no plans to introduce remote consultations, such as video and a 'reluctance among GPs to implement alternatives to face-to-face consultations' (Brant et al., 2016). More recent estimates were that 80% of appointments were delivered face to face in general practice before Covid-19 (Hutchings, 2020) indicating a slow pace of innovation despite new tools for remote consultations entering the market place. The widespread adoption of telemedicine/telehealth has generally been slow, despite discussions of 'teleconsulting' being in the ascendence since the mid-1990s (Wootton, 1996; Lennon et al., 2017). Telemedicine has frequently focused on secondary and specialist care settings (e.g. outpatients) or interfaces that link primary care doctors and patients with secondary care experts, but less on primary care remote consultations (Al Dossary et al., 2017; Roland et al., 2006). And whilst a 2016 report by the Nuffield Trust signalled the potential for digital transformation in the sector, barriers were noted, such as limited IT infrastructure and professional resistance to change:

> patient access will be improved, supported by remote consultations, mobile working, sign-posting to other services and alternatives to GPs within the primary care team. (Castle-Clarke et al., 2016)

On the patient side, there has been limited change in behaviour over time in primary care when it comes to digital access. The GP Patient Survey for 2020, which surveys around 740,000 patients and was conducted before the Covid-19 pandemic, found that 10% of patient said their last appointment was remote, of which 9.8% were conducted via phone and 0.2% online/video (Ipsos Mori, 2020). Younger groups were more likely to have made use of online appointments, and older groups telephone appointments (ibid.). Previous surveys have also found that only 16% of patients were ordering repeat prescriptions online (GPPS, 2019; NHS England, July 2019).

Whilst insights from the GP Patient Survey during the pandemic will not be available until 2022, there is emerging evidence that a large number of patients shifted to greater use of online tools during pandemic. Before the national lockdown in England, there was a sharp increase (of 97%) in the number of repeat prescription requests made via the NHS App—from 50,341 in February to 98,984 in March 2020 (NHS Digital, April 2020a; NHS Digital, July 2020b). This was part of a broader shift in prescribing practices in primary care. By July 2020, NHS Digital data confirmed that 86% of prescriptions dispensed in primary care in England were via the electronic prescribing system (EPS) which enables prescriptions to go to a pharmacy of the patient's choice. This was a marked increase from 2019 when the figure was 68%.

In terms of understanding changes within general practice and the primary care workforce, the evidence base has started to grow in recent years and has largely drawn on surveys, pilots, feasibility and qualitative studies. Table 12.1 summarises a number of observations about different digital solutions in primary care incorporating UK and international evidence and recent evaluations and research. It is noticeable that research into remote consultations has previously found that traditional face-to-face consultations can still be preferred by patients and staff, despite overall high levels of satisfaction with alternative modalities such as video (Atherton et al., 2018; Thiyagarajan et al., 2020). Yet travel and time savings can prove popular with patients.

By contrast, far less is known about user experiences and satisfaction with digital triage and online consultations (submitted via online forms, some of which are automated templates). There is also limited quantitative data on the uptake and impact of different remote consultation modalities nationally which makes accurate trend analysis especially difficult. This is partly on account of the previously low levels of uptake of online consultations within general practice, coupled with variations in coding and data capture within local systems. There are also few Randomised Controlled Trials or quasi-experimental studies to compare outcomes across different consultation types (video, telephone, online) in primary care in the UK. Generalisability about online/e-consultations and remote triage is therefore problematic given this pre-pandemic context of

Table 12.1 Remote digital services in primary care: observations

Digital solution—primary care	*Study methods*	*Digital supplier/solution(s) mentioned (if any)*	*Observations*	*Source(s)*
Telephone/online/remote digital triage	Systematic review (mixed designs); primary research	Bablyon; WebGP (e-Consult)	Weak evidence base for online and digital symptom checkers—mostly observational studies Gap in evidence about patient safety and experience/satisfaction with online triage Issues with diagnostic accuracy AI-based tools more risk-averse than health professionals Need to consider how remote triage (whether by telephone or other modality) influences workflows—amongst clinical and non-clinical staff. Mixed evidence on increased workloads vs efficiency gains	Chambers et al. (2019) Rushton et al. (2019) Salisbury et al. (2020) Murphy et al. (2021)

Digital solution—primary care	*Study methods*	*Digital supplier/solution(s) mentioned (if any)*	*Observations*	*Source(s)*
Video consultations (VC)	Qualitative and scoping reviews; evaluation; guidelines	Attend anywhere	May be used more by younger patients and those more confident with web-based communication Positive user experiences and patient satisfaction reported (e.g. convenience, time saving, no travel) Not appropriate for all cases (e.g. sensitive issues, bad news) Technical issues reported (e.g. bandwidth, visual quality) Face-to-face consultations still perceived as 'gold standard' Patients may raise fewer issues in VCs, yet more reassuring for some patients compared to a phone call (e.g. visual cues, rapport) VC adoption requires a sociotechnical approach to implementation, with attention to IT/tech infrastructure	Donaghy et al. (2019) Thiyagarajan et al. (2020) Hammersley et al. (2019) Greenhalgh et al. (2020) Wherton and Greenhalgh (2020) Wherton et al. (2020)

(continued)

Table 12.1 (continued)

Digital solution—primary care	*Study methods*	*Digital supplier/solution(s) mentioned (if any)*	*Observations*	*Source(s)*
Online or 'e' consultations (e.g. email and secure text messaging, online forms) (OC)	Systematic review; primary studies	webGP askmyGP	Evidence that modality may be favoured by young people, the employed and women, not poorer or older age groups Convenience for non-urgent medical concerns Patients may expect more timely responses Workforce can welcome efficiencies associated with email consultations Lack of knowledge about impacts on health outcome Can complement in-person care	Mold et al. (2019, 2021) Atherton et al. (2018) Carter et al. (2018) Eccles et al. (2019)

low adoption, limited patient feedback, and a lack of comparative analyses of different approaches and their costs (Mold et al., 2019, 2021; Rushton et al., 2019). This has made it hard to draw conclusions about the most appropriate implementation and service models during Covid-19. Another point is that the evidence underpinning some systematic reviews in this area is dated (e.g. from the 1990s to early 2000s), and technological capabilities have moved on significantly in the last decade (e.g. artificial intelligence). Overall, then, there is a lack of knowledge concerning the acceptability and impacts of alternative online and video systems to end users and explanations of how their different features shape the patient encounter with health care providers.

The COVID-19 Context and Emerging Evidence

Fortunately, a number of studies and evaluations have come on board or been commissioned shortly before or during Covid-19 (Dias & Clarke, 2020; Murphy et al., 2021), and various systematic reviews have been undertaken in recent years. These help to set the context for the change that has taken place rapidly at the level of general practice during Covid-19, even if longer-term effects are not possible to quantify at this stage.

We also know that from Spring 2020 onwards, primary care in England drastically shifted to the greater use of a variety of digital tools and services, including online messaging/chat functions, digital triage, video consultations, which was accompanied by more widespread use of e-prescribing and the NHS App by patients. Many of these tools were available prior Covid-19, but they had not been taken up at scale: the rate of adoption had been slow.

Antecedent events and authority decisions helped expedite the rate of adoption in primary care. The remote 'total triage' model was encouraged by NHS England and NHS Improvement during the pandemic, aimed at minimising the exposure of patients and health care workers to the risks of Covid-19. It required clinical and non-clinical staff to determine the best response to patient needs—either a remote consultation (delivered by video, telephone or online), an online reply or in-person appointment (NHS, April 2020). The decision to adopt a remote triage model was a national decision, implemented with recommendations (Bakhai et al., 2020; NHS England and NHS Improvement, 2020a), yet inevitably slightly different forms of triaging patients have arisen at the practice level due to different online providers and approaches being used. A national rapid procurement framework for online and video suppliers for the NHS was also instigated (NHS, June 2020), helping to ensure remote consultations were possible across all of general practice.

A survey conducted by the RCGP of 829 GPs across the UK during Covid-19 (RCGP, July 2020) demonstrated a clear reliance on telephone appointments for the delivery remote care several months into the pandemic. The survey found that:

- Between 9 and 22 July 2020, on average, 61% of GP appointments were conducted by telephone and a further 16% spent doing telephone triage. 11% were conducted face to face, 6% by SMS or email, 4% online via video and 3% were home and care home visits.
- Although only 4% of consultations were reported being delivered by video, the survey found that 88% of respondents said their surgery was equipped to deliver video or e-consultations (up from 5% before the pandemic).
- When asked about the efficiency of delivering consultations remotely, 70% of respondents said telephone consultations increase efficiency, and 67% said video or e-consultations do so.
- 76% of respondents said that GP-led telephone triage increases efficiency, 66% said non-GP triage and 65% said online triage increased efficiency, respectively.

The same publication by the RCGP also reported findings from the Research and Surveillance Centre (RSC) on more than 500 GP practices in England. Data indicated that at the peak of the pandemic in 2020, around 71% of GP consultations were being conducted remotely and 25% face to face. By contract, in the same period of 2019, the opposite was the case: around 70% appointments were conducted face to face and 25% remotely (RCGP, July 2020). As social distancing restrictions lifted over the summer of 2020 in the UK, face-to-face consultations gradually did increase. But in terms of digital capabilities, by early 2021, 99% of GP practices were reported to have installed a remote consultation platform, evidencing the continuance of an accelerated innovation adoption rate (Health IT News, January 2021). Two million online consultation requests were also being reported for general practice every month (ibid.).

Yet as previously mentioned, consultations in health care systems are likely to have been recorded inconsistently during the pandemic as new technologies were implemented rapidly, and given the sudden changes to services, workflows and professional practices. Researchers are therefore right to wonder if the recording of appointment type has been accurate throughout a period of seismic transformation; for example, video consultations may not always have been captured and could be under-reported. This makes it challenging to infer changes in volume and consultation modality with absolute confidence. In primary care, the recording of appointments was also influenced by implementation of the total triage model, with both GPs and non-clinical staff supporting the remote triage of patient enquiries (whether submitted by phone or online). Nevertheless, it is clear from what data there is, that when compared to former years, primary care has seen a significant increase in remote care delivery and implemented new digital capabilities at scale, and in a very short period of time.

Discussion

In view of the emerging research and data presented above, the compression of innovation timelines during the Covid-19 pandemic becomes apparent. A pertinent question is whether the pandemic lessened the role and agency of 'early adopters' and 'innovation champions' and relied more on authority innovation decisions to accelerate change, or whether the innovation picture is more complex than Rogers' theory suggests. Another important consideration is the extent to which antecedent health policy decisions focused on digital health transformation enabled more rapid adoption within the pandemic context.

Firstly, to return to the 'innovation-decision process'. The most obvious point is that the pandemic resulted in face-to-face appointments being a riskier option for reasons of public health and safety. In-person consultations were a priority for patients requiring an assessment due to clinical need or unable to access GPs via remote means. However, the over-riding public health, legislative and policy context was clear at the macro-level and the most persuasive decision factor in the face of decision uncertainty or resistance to remote consultations using digital tools, compared to normal times. Rather than taking months or years for individual GP practices or groups of practices to reach an innovation-decision, national guidelines necessitated a new model of service delivery within weeks. This suggests there was less reliance on optional innovation decisions and autonomy, as explained in Rogers' framework, and that authority decisions had particular impact.

Secondly, antecedent factors in the health policy context set the groundwork for the expedited rate of adoption of remote consultations during the pandemic and the shift to delivering remote triage in primary care. Firstly, the General Practice Forward View (NHS England 2016) had set the policy direction for funding online consultations in GP practices with support from Clinical Commissioning Groups. The NHS Long Term Plan had then signalled the policy objective that 'every patient will have the right to online 'digital' GP consultations' within five years' (NHS 2019: 6). There was also a policy ambition to have online resources and the NHS app playing a far bigger role in patient self-management and the redirection of demand away from general practice and A&E services, especially in cases of minor ailments which can be treated within community settings, such as pharmacy. A more digitalised service model was also hypothesised as a method of supporting more flexible working in the GP workforce which faces severe shortages, particularly for GPs wishing to work part-time. Lastly, the latest iteration of the GP Contract committed practices to ensuring that patients would have the right to online consultations by April 2020 and video consultation by April 2021. Hence, it is important to recognise that in the months and years prior to the pandemic, there had been a policy drive towards implementing digital services in primary care, accompanied with reforms to contractual arrangements which were intended to encourage the widespread implementation of online consultations and new digital capabilities at the local level, supported by national frameworks and funding (NHS, June 2019).

Given the above, for time variable one (the innovation-adoption decision), the available evidence suggests that rate of innovation adoption was expedited by authority decisions at the national level during the pandemic and bolstered by an already favourable health policy context that had primed GPs to the direction of change. For Rogers, the shortening of 'the innovation-decision period is one of the main methods of speeding the diffusion of an innovation' (ibid.: 213).

In terms of time variable two (relative innovativeness/adopter categories), whilst data is emerging as to the extent to which general practice has truly relied on online and video consultations tools[2] over the past year, the vast majority of practices did move into the 'early majority' category and now have an online consultation and video system installed, meaning they have developed new organisational capabilities to triage and care for patients remotely. What is *less* clear is the extent to which a 'late majority' of adopters or 'laggards' have persisted even during the pandemic. Some practices may have—for different reasons—not engaged with remote care delivery and used online systems as easily as others. Further evaluation and research are needed to establish the extent of variation in implementation, and new knowledge will hopefully come to light about the different approaches taken by general practices, their experiences and workflow processes.

Time variable three (the rate of adoption) was clearly expedited with remote consultations delivered at scale across primary care within a narrow window of time: March–July 2020, and with further adoption continuing into 2021. This expedited the meeting of national NHS policy objectives set prior to the pandemic (e.g. in the Long Term Plan). Interestingly, the reliance on telephone technology to support remote consultations, such as following remote digital triage, is notable. Telephone is a familiar, low-tech technology. Following Rogers' theory, delivering remote consultations in general practice using existing telephone infrastructure has the relative advantage of being familiar to patients and staff compared to online and video consultations. With telephone, there is low innovation complexity and compatibility with existing social norms. Telephone consultations also have the advantage of not requiring new training on software, although patients may prefer video consultations in some instances. Either way, the vast majority of general practices in England can now offer patients more innovative forms of appointment type. How best to use these modalities across different patient cohorts should become clearer throughout the 2021–2022, as more accurate data is captured, and as research studies that started during the pandemic report their findings. The significant point is that in the face of decision uncertainty at the beginning of the pandemic, especially concerning the relative advantages of different digital providers in an emergency context, health professionals nevertheless employed new systems which is particularly noteworthy given

[2] Part of the difficulties occur in coding and data accuracy. General practices made code video calls as telephone calls. Furthermore, digital suppliers for online and video solutions vary in how they collect data.

that there are over 6,000 general practices in England each needing to offer solutions to thousands of registered patients.

Lastly, Rogers' observations about the importance of the social aspects of the innovation-decision process remain salient and are likely to have impacted on adoption time scales. Anecdotal reports of greater collaboration at the local and CCG level suggest collective decision-making and information sharing about remote consultations were happening across organisations in primary care. This warrants further understanding, especially given that Rogers' theory can be used in a way that places greater emphasis on the autonomy and agency of early adopters and innovators.

Conclusion

In this chapter, the different temporal features of Rogers' theory of innovation diffusion have been discussed in detail in the context of the Covid-19 pandemic. It has been argued that the innovation-decision process in health care systems drastically accelerated, such as in primary care. This sector shifted to remote care appointments and triage of patients within a period of less than six months in the UK after years of limited uptake of digital health care platforms. From a diffusion of innovation perspective, whilst the technology being used is not new (telemedicine has been around since mid-1990s, in a more basic form), the rapid implementation of remote consultation at scale in primary care has huge implications for service delivery, professional practice, patients and the workforce.

Going forwards, detailed knowledge to understand which digital solutions work optimally for staff and patients in terms of their usability and accessibility, and given different levels of digital literacy across the population, will be helpful. Policy makers will also require more knowledge about how to mitigate digital exclusion and when it is least appropriate to use remote consultation models in patient care, and when conversely they yield greatest health care and cost benefits.

At the present time, whilst some uncertainty remains, there are opportunities for peer-learning across primary care (and primary and secondary care) about the effective implementation of remote consultations. Whilst opportunities for in-person training have been curtailed due to the restrictions brought about by Covid-19, webinars and remote working have continued and can support knowledge transfer.

Covid-19 led the NHS to adopt a variety of digital solutions and to integrate these into routine care. However, a 'one-size-fits-all model' is unlikely to be sustainable given variable patient needs and diverse population demographics around the country.

We are likely to see shifts and variations in patient demand for these technologies over time and they must be delivered in ways that mitigate against inequalities (e.g. by online consultation platforms being accessible in different languages). Capitalising on the lessons and insights encountered during the Covid-19 pandemic will be invaluable for informing future service delivery and progressing the evidence on telemedicine and digital pathways across different health contexts.

As such, 'blended' and differentiated models combining remote and in-person care will undoubtedly feature more in future, in the NHS and beyond. The digital health solutions that are the least complex to use and confer the greatest observable benefits to health professionals and patients—as demonstrated during Covid-19—may well be the ones that are sustained over longer term, especially if they fit within existing business models. Compromises will need to be found, ideally supported by collective forms of decision-making based on the insights emerging about remote consultations. However, whilst the time to adopt digital solutions was accelerated during the pandemic, identifying the most sustainable and workable solutions for the majority is likely to take health care systems more time.

To conclude, in this chapter, I have applied Rogers' diffusion of innovation theory to explore the case of digital health adoption in the NHS, analysing how remote consultations experienced an expedited rate of use during the Covid-19 pandemic in primary care. I suggest this is because, in such a context, the combination of technological utility, a favourable policy context, available resources and urgent public health needs, created an ideal tipping point for digital tools to be adopted to address real-world problems at multiple levels: system, organisational and individual. This has resulted in faster innovation-adoption decision-making compared to normal times—shifting much of the health care workforce into the category of the 'early majority', to use Rogers schematic. Of particular interest to health researchers is the observation that the different temporal dimensions of Rogers' diffusion theory have shifted and been compressed during the pandemic, with decision-making and adoption rates expedited overall. For this reason, it is arguable that the role of individual innovators or influencers, which are strongly emphasised in Rogers' original theory, became less central during the early stages of the Covid-19 pandemic compared to the influence of collective and authority-based decision-making at regional and national levels, requiring greater inter-organisational and professional cooperation, plus dedicated investment to support staff with the implementation of digital solutions at the meso- and micro-levels.

Acknowledgements with special thanks to Dr Minal Bakhai, Professor Ewan Ferlie and the editors of this book for their helpful comments and guidance with earlier drafts. The views expressed in this publication are those of the lead author and not those of NHS England and NHS Improvement.

References

Abrahamson, E. (1991). Managerial fads and fashions: The diffusion and rejection of innovations. *Academy of Management Review, 16*(3), 586–612.

Al Dossary, S., Martin-Khan, M. G., Bradford, N. K., & Smith, A. C. (2017). A systematic review of the methodologies used to evaluate telemedicine service initiatives in hospital facilities. *International Journal of Medical Informatics, 97*, 171–194.

Atherton, H., et al. (2018). Alternatives to the face-to-face consultation in general practice: Focused ethnographic case study. *British Journal of General Practice, 68*(669), e293–e300.

Baird, B., & Maguire, D. (2021). *Understanding factors that enabled digital service change in general practice during the Covid-19 pandemic*. The King's Fund.

Bakhai, M., et al. (2020). *Using online consultations in primary care NHS England: Implementation toolkit for practices*. https://www.england.nhs.uk/wp-content/uploads/2020/01/online-consultations-implementation-toolkit-v1.1-updated.pdf

Born, K., Kool, T., & Levinson, W. (2019, November). Reducing overuse in healthcare: Advancing choosing wisely. *The BMJ, 367*, 1–4.

Brant, H., et al. (2016). Using alternatives to face-to-face consultations: A survey of prevalence and attitudes in general practice. *British Journal of General Practice, 66*(648), e460–e466.

Bullock, A., et al. (2016). 'Getting the most out of knowledge and innovation transfer agents in health care: A qualitative study', Full Report. *Health Services and Delivery Research, 4*(33), 1–156.

Carter, M., et al. (2018). Feasibility, acceptability and effectiveness of an online alternative to face-to-face consultation in general practice: A mixed-methods study of webGP in six Devon practices. *BMJ Open, 8*(2). https://doi.org/10.1136/bmjopen-2017-018688

Castle-Clarke, S., Kumpunen, S., Machaqueiro, S., Curry, N., & Imison, C. (2016). *Digital requirements for new primary care models: A briefing for clinicians and managers*. Nuffield Trust.

Chambers, D., et al. (2019). Digital and online symptom checkers and health assessment/triage services for urgent health problems: Systematic review. *British Medical Journal Open, 9*(8), 1–13.

Coleman, J. S., Katz, E., & Menzel, H. (1966). *Medical innovation: A diffusion study*. Bobbs-Merrill.

Dias, A., & Clarke, G. (2020). *How are total triage and remote consultation affecting prescribing patterns?* The Health Foundation. https://www.health.org.uk/news-and-comment/charts-and-infographics/how-are-total-triage-and-remote-consultation-affecting-presc

Dixon-Woods, M., et al. (2011). Problems and promises of innovation: Why healthcare needs to rethink its love/hate relationship with the new. *BMJ Quality and Safety, 20*(Suppl. 1), 47–51.

Donaghy, E., Atherton, H., Hammersley, V., McNeilly, H., Bikker, A., Robbins, L., Campbell, J., & McKinstry, B. (2019). Acceptability, benefits, and challenges of video consulting: A qualitative study in primary care. *British Journal of General Practice, 69*(686), e586–e594.

Eccles, A., et al. (2019). Patient use of an online triage platform: A mixed-methods retrospective exploration in UK primary care. *British Journal of General Practice, 69*(682), E336–E344.

Ferlie, E., et al. (2005). The nonspread of innovations: The mediating role of professionals. *Academy of Management Journal, 48*(1), 117–134.

Ferlie, E., Dopson, S., Bennett, C., Fischer, M. D., Ledger, J., & McGivern, G. (2018). *The politics of management knowledge in times of austerity*. Oxford University Press.

Ferlie, E., Nicolini, D., Ledger, J., D'Andreta, D., Kravcenko, D., & de Pury, J. (2017). NHS top managers, knowledge exchange and leadership: The early development of Academic Health Science Networks a mixed-methods study. *Health Service Delivery and Research, 5*(17). https://www.journalslibrary.nihr.ac.uk/hsdr

Fitzgerald, L., et al. (2002). Interlocking interactions, the diffusion of innovations in health care. *Human Relations, 55*(12), 1429–1449.

Gilbert, A. W., et al. (2020). Rapid implementation of virtual clinics due to COVID-19: Report and early evaluation of a quality improvement initiative. *BMJ Open Quality, 9*(2), 1–8.

GP Patient Survey (GPPS). https://gp-patient.co.uk

Greenhalgh, T., et al. (2004). Diffusion of innovations in service organizations: Systematic review and recommendations. *The Milbank Quarterly, 82*(4), 581–629.

Greenhalgh, T., et al. (2018). Real-world implementation of video outpatient consultations at macro, meso, and micro levels: Mixed-method study. *Journal of Medical Internet Research, 20*(4), e50.

Greenhalgh, T., Stramer. K., Bratan, T., Byrne, E., Mohammad, Y., & Russell. J et al. (2008). Introduction of shared electronic records: multi-site case study using diffusion of innovation theory. *BMJ, 337*, a1786. https://doi.org/10.1136/bmj.a1786. https://www.bmj.com/content/337/bmj.a1786.long

Greenhalgh, T., et al. (2020). Video consultations for covid-19. *The BMJ, 368*(March), 1–2.

Hammersley, V., et al. (2019). Comparing the content and quality of video, telephone, and face-to-face consultations: A non-randomised, quasi-experimental, exploratory study in UK primary care. *British Journal of General Practice, 69*(686), E595–E604.

Harvey, G., Jas, P., & Walshe, K. (2015). Analysing organisational context: Case studies on the contribution of absorptive capacity theory to understanding inter-organisational variation in performance improvement. *BMJ Quality and Safety, 24*(1), 48–55.

Hippisley-Cox, J., & Vinogradova, Y. (2009). *Trends in consultation rates in General Practice 1995/1996 to 2008/2009: Analysis of the QResearch® database*. Final Report to the NHS Information Centre and Department of Health. https://files.digital.nhs.uk/publicationimport/pub01xxx/pub01077/tren-cons-rate-gene-prac-95-09-95-08-rep.pdf

Hutchings. (2020). Briefing: The impact of Covid-19 on the use of digital technology in the NHS. *The Nuffield Trust*. Available at: https://www.nuffieldtrust.org.uk/files/2020-08/the-impact-of-covid-19-on-the-use-of-digital-technology-in-the-nhs-web-2.pdf

Ipsos Mori. (2020). *GP patient Survey: National report*. Available at: https://gp-patient.co.uk

Lennon, M., Bouamrane, M., Devlin, A., O'Connor, S., O'Donnell, C., Chetty, U., Agbakoba, R., Bikker, A., Grieve, E., Finch, T., Watson, N., Wyke, S., & Mair, F. (2017). Readiness for delivering digital health at scale: Lessons from a longitudinal qualitative evaluation of a national digital health innovation program in the United Kingdom. *Journal of Medical Internet Research, 19*(2), e42. https://www.jmir.org/2017/2/e42. https://doi.org/10.2196/jmir.6900

Lundblad, J. (2003). A review and critique of Rogers' diffusion of innovation theory as it applies to organizations. *Organization Development Journal, 21*(4), 50.

McMaster, T., & Wastell, D. (2005). Diffusion—Or delusion? Challenging an IS research tradition. *Information Technology and People, 18*(4), 383–404.

Mold, F., Hendy, J., Lai, Y., & de Lusignan, S. (2019). Electronic Consultation in Primary Care Between Providers and Patients: Systematic Review. *JMIR Medical Informatics, 7*(4), 13042.

Mold, F., Cooke, D., Ip, A., Roy, P., Denton, S., & Armes, J. (2021). COVID-19 and beyond: virtual consultations in primary carereflecting on the evidence base for implementation and ensuring reach: commentary article. *BMJ Health Care Informatics, 28*(1), e100256. https://doi.org/10.1136/bmjhci-2020-100256

Murphy, M., et al. (2021, March). Implementation of remote consulting in UK primary care following the COVID-19 pandemic: A mixed-methods longitudinal study. *British Journal of General Practice*. https://doi.org/10.3399/BJGP.2020.0948

NHS Digital. (2020a, April 2). '*Surge in the number of people using NHS tech during Coronavirus outbreak*.' Available at: https://digital.nhs.uk/news-and-events/latest-news/increase-in-nhs-tech-usage

NHS Digital. (2020b, July 7). '*Increase in use of electronic prescriptions during Coronavirus*.' Available at: https://digital.nhs.uk/news-and-events/latest-news/increase-in-use-of-electronic-prescriptions-during-coronavirus

NHS England. (2016). *General Practice Forward View (GPFV)*. Available at: https://www.england.nhs.uk/publication/general-practice-forward-view-gpfv/

NHS England. (2019, July 11). *News: GP Patient Survey 2019*. https://www.england.nhs.uk/statistics/2019/07/11/gp-patient-survey-2019/

NHS England and NHS Improvement. (2020a). Advice on how to establish a remote "total triage" model in general practice using online consultations. *Covid-19 Ad Hoc Guidelines, 2*, 17. https://www.england.nhs.uk/coronavirus/wp-content/uploads/sites/52/2020/03/remote-total-triage-model-in-general-practice-27-march-2020.pdf

NHS England and NHS Improvement. (2020b, November). *Clinical guide for the management of remote consultations and remote working in secondary care during the coronavirus pandemic*. https://www.england.nhs.uk/

NHS England and NHS Improvement. (2020c, March). *Procurement of pre-approved suppliers of online and video consultation systems for GP practices to support COVID-19*.

Nolte, E. (2018). *World Health Organization (WHO)/European Observatory on health systems and policies. How do we ensure that innovation in health service delivery and organization is implemented, sustained and spread?* (pp. 1–28). World Health Organization (WHO). https://apps.who.int/iris/bitstream/handle/10665/331980/Policy-brief-3-1997-8073-2018-eng.pdf?sequence=5&isAllowed=y

Pacifico Silva, H., et al. (2018). Introducing responsible innovation in health: A policy-oriented framework. *Health Research Policy and Systems, 16*(1), 90. https://doi.org/10.1186/s12961-018-0362-5

Piazza, A., & Abrahamson, E. (2020). Fads and fashions in management practices: Taking stock and looking forward. *International Journal of Management Reviews, 22*(3), 264–286.

Pope, C., et al. (2013). Using computer decision support systems in NHS emergency and urgent care : Ethnographic study using normalisation process theory. *BMC Health Services Research, 13*, 1–13.

Rogers, E. M. (2003). *Diffusion of Innovations* (5th ed.). Free Press.

Roland, M., McDonald, R., & Sibbald, B. (2006). *Outpatient services and primary care: A scoping review of research into strategies for improving outpatient effectiveness and efficiency*. NIHR Trials and Studies Coordinating Centre.

Rushton, S., et al. (2019). *Effectiveness of remote triage: A systematic review*. Department of Veterans Affairs (US). https://pubmed.ncbi.nlm.nih.gov/31971698/

Salisbury, C., Murphy, M., & Duncan, P. (2020). The impact of digital-first consultations on workload in general practice: Modeling study. *Journal of Medical Internet Research, 22*(6), e18203.

Swan, J., Newell, S., & Nicolini, D. (Eds.). (2016). *Mobilizing knowledge in healthcare: Challenges for management and organization*. Oxford University Press.

The Health Foundation. (2020). *How might COVID-19 have affected people's ability to see their GP? COVID-19 chart series*. https://www.health.org.uk/news-and-comment/charts-and-infographics/how-might-covid-19-have-affected-peoples-ability-to-see-GP

Thiyagarajan, A., et al. (2020). Exploring patients' and clinicians' experiences of video consultations in primary care: A systematic scoping review. *BJGP Open, 4*(1), 1–8. https://doi.org/10.3399/bjgpopen20X101020

Timmermans, S., & Kaufman, R. (2020). Technologies and health inequities. *Annual Review of Sociology, 46*, 583–602.

Walker, A. J., Pretis, F., Powell-Smith, A., & Goldacre, B. (2019). Variation in responsiveness to warranted behaviour change among NHS clinicians: novel implementation of change detection methods in longitudinal prescribing data. *BMJ, 367*, l5205. https://doi.org/10.1136/bmj.l5205

Wherton, J., & Greenhalgh, T. (2020). *Evaluation of the attend anywhere/near me video consulting service in Scotland, 2019–20: Summary report* (pp. 1–10). http://www.gov.scot/publications/evaluation-attend-anywhere-near-video-consulting-service-scotland-2019-20-main-report/

Wherton, J., et al. (2020). Guidance on the introduction and use of video consultations during COVID-19: Important lessons from qualitative research. *BMJ Leader, 4*(3), 120–123.

Wootton, R. (1996). Telemedicine: A cautious welcome. *BMJ, 313*(7069), 1375–1377. https://doi.org/10.1136/bmj.313.7069.1375

CHAPTER 13

The Politics of Life and Death in the Time of COVID-19

Joanne Travaglia and Hamish Robertson

Introduction

Early on in the COVID-19 crisis, it became clear that health systems were not prepared to cope with the anticipated demand for acute services (Argulian, 2020). Faced with the need to ration care, guidelines were issued by national bodies, and clinicians encouraged patients to exercise their right of control over their lives, and possible death. Yet unlike in previous crises, for example, Hurricane Katrina in the USA (Fink, 2013), disquiet and challenges to these directions began to emerge early on (Todd, 2020). Examined through the lens of Mbembe's framework of necropolitics, which analyses the state's right to decide who may live and who must die, these decisions and guidelines can be seen in a very different light (Mbembe, 2019). In this chapter, we utilise and extend Mbembe's concept to examine not only persistent inequalities and inequities in morbidity and mortality, but also their variation during states

J. Travaglia (✉) · H. Robertson
Centre for Health Services Management, University of Technology Sydney, Syndey, NSW, Australia
e-mail: Joanne.travaglia@uts.edu.au

J. Waring et al. (eds.), *Organising Care in a Time of Covid-19*, Organizational Behaviour in Healthcare,
https://doi.org/10.1007/978-3-030-82696-3_13

of crisis and the consequences for those people structured as not simply vulnerable but, ultimately, as surplus to requirements.

Crises, such as disasters and pandemics, increase the need for systems and services to make rapid decisions most often under conditions of uncertainty and complexity (Rijke et al., 2012). One result of the process of rapid decision-making is that societal, systems and service assumptions (including those based on racial bias or ableism) and fissures in delivery systems often come to the fore. As Hilgartner (2007: 154) argues about disasters in general '*Disasters and accidents create profoundly disturbing collective experiences that challenge the managerial vision of orderly systems*'.

All humans are vulnerable by virtue of our existence. But not all vulnerabilities pose the same risk, risk which is often magnified by the precarity of people and groups before, during and after crises or disasters. McEntire (2004: 24), in his tenets of vulnerability, notes that '*Vulnerability occurs at the intersection of the physical and social environments*'. Cutter et al. (2003: 243) go further, arguing that '*Social vulnerability is partially the product of social inequalities—those social factors that influence or shape the susceptibility of various groups to harm and that also govern their ability to respond*'.

Yet, as Columbo has identified, the two governmentalities that emerged with COVID-19 '… *monopolized the public and political debate are biomedical and economic. The former brought the defense of biological life (zoé) as the ultimate element of truth and legitimacy of the government's action. The latter, based the "true" justification upon a careful cost–benefit calculation and the protection of the interests of homo oeconomicus. The debate lacked a "social" perspective capable of placing dignity and human rights as a compass for intervention*' (Colombo, 2021: 1). Waring and Bishop (2020) made a similar argument in relation to the transition of care as experienced particularly by older and more vulnerable people. They found that the process of complex care transitions acts to reduce vulnerable patients to their bare life (zoe), which in turns makes the provision of unsafe and undignified care acceptable.

A lack of a social perspective during COVID-19, we will argue, has increased the risk for vulnerable individuals and groups. Governance structures, set up through formal regulatory or administrative channels to manage 'predict and control' functions (Rijke et al., 2012: 73) have difficulties in keeping up both with the rapid changes in demand for, and the actions of, individuals and services during times of crisis (Tierney, 2012). The events that took place at the time of Hurricane Katrina in the USA, including the involuntary euthanising of patients, are a case in point (Lugosi, 2007; Shea, 2010).

As COVID-19 spread across the globe, reports emerged about the implications of health systems attempts at prioritising care. In most cases prioritisation favoured young, well and non-disabled bodies, leaving elderly people and people with disabilities at greater risk of being denied treatment (Lund & Ayers, 2020). The rationale was that such 'non-damaged' people had a better chance of surviving. Underpinning this argument was the belief that the fairest way to allocate limited health resources was to allocate them to people where they would not be 'wasted' (Archard & Caplan, 2020). This argument is seductive, not least of all because it reads as rational, impartial and objective and presumes a form of utilitarian logic.

This approach belies the fact that it makes vulnerable individuals and groups even more vulnerable, reinforcing the inequities associated with the social determinants of health (Marmot & Allen, 2014). Feminist bioethicists and others have argued that capitalist systems have a deep antipathy towards dependent people (Dodds, 2007; Lanoix, 2007; Müller, 2019), relegating their responsibility wherever possible to their families, and more specifically to the women in their families. The neoliberal governance model includes a reduction of even this form of socially engaged care to one of commodified and poorly paid 'professional' care. As Bergeron (2016: 190) note, referencing Elson and Cagatay (2000), 'Governments cut support for childcare and healthcare, assuming these services will be picked up by women in households'. As so few healthcare systems are resourced to the level of actual population health need, they are rife with implicit and explicit narratives about the need to ration resources (Hunter, 2018). We know that access to healthcare is inequitable even without a pandemic because healthcare systems reflect our social structures and their associated inequalities (Gulliford et al., 2002). The consequences of a pandemic scenario for people whose lives are already precarious are especially serious.

Deep-seated inequities are frequently exacerbated during emergency situations as in the case of COVID-19 (van Dorn et al., 2020). But what seems to set the response to COVID-19 apart was that not only did pre-existing conditions increase already medically vulnerable peoples (like the elderly) risk of harm, so too did the decision-making of health bodies, governments and clinicians. In Britain, the National Institute for Health and Care Excellence's first release of COVID-19 critical care guidelines (later revised) disadvantaged patients with learning disabilities and autism (National Institute for Health and Care Excellence, 2020) including criteria which were said to '... *discriminate unjustly against a broad class of people with disability*' (as well as people over the age of 60 or 65) (Scully, 2020: n.p.). Across the UK there were reports of care homes placing do not attempt resuscitation (DNAR) orders on the files of elderly patients without proper consultation with or consent from the patients themselves (Booth, 2020).

While there may be no definitive answer to the question of who *should* survive, when it comes to choosing who *will* survive and who is likely to die, we need to consider how health systems and societies both historically, and currently, value and protect different patients. In this paper, we will explore the risks to the vulnerable during times of crises, and the response to these risks during COVID-19. We do this by focusing on the necropolitical dimensions of healthcare systems both in 'business as usual' and in crisis situations.

Necropolitics, Zemiology and Forms of Harm Analysis

The idea that harms occur in societies and social systems is not new. Various critical analyses from the social sciences and elsewhere have identified this for centuries. The German pathologist Virchow noted that medicine was a social science because it dealt with the problems generated at the intersection of natural and social worlds. COVID-19 is therefore not an unanticipated event in the epidemiological sense (quite the contrary to the scientific community) and nor are its social consequences for those who follow and analyse the consequences for any society's vulnerable groups and individuals. Broadly speaking, even disaster theory has produced useful tools for analysis in this space but here we focus firstly on Mbembe's necropolitical concept and, secondly on that of zemiology, a thesis arising from criminology. The reason for this is that we can observe the relationship between the nature of the state and its reliance on various forms of violence in association with the production of a variety of socially manufactured harms.

There is a tendency in the event of crisis events for official forgetting and a devaluing of public memory—unless it serves the purposes of the state. Hence World War I events continue to be celebrated in the present day while the 1918–1919 Influenza epidemic that ultimately claimed more lives than the war, is largely forgotten as a focus of and for public memory (see Outka, 2019). Thus, even the reliability of individual and collective memory as a foundation of identity is, and in our assessment remains, highly suspect. While historians may provide more nuanced analyses of past events and their current positioning, in this kind of context what is memorialised in public memory, symbols and ceremonies is more a contested performative space than an accurate record of what happened and how the state responded. And this broader construction sets the scene for much of Mbembe's ongoing project around the construct of necropolitics.

The Cameroonian philosopher and theorist has been developing his analytical frameworks and research agenda for almost 30 years. Much of his focus has been on the African experience as seen through French language, philosophy and social theory, including the role that race and racism play in both colonial and contemporary liberal democratic projects (Mbembe, 2001). His development of a specific 'take' on these issues was expressed in the term 'necropolitics', which has gained increasing interest internationally as a tool for analysing local versions of these problems and their representation within specific political and cultural environments (e.g. Davies, 2018; Valencia & Zhuravleva, 2019).

Mbembe's focus has been especially interested in the role of the state in creating the conditions for dying and death, and the role that object-making plays in this sense of disposability. In a related context, our interpretation is that colonial logics were not restricted to the colonies and thus many historically situated and contemporary social phenomena and practices within those liberal democratic states can be usefully analysed from a necropolitical perspective. This includes health systems and their position in the contemporary liberal democratic states. In this particular context, the advent of COVID-19 as a particular version of broader known problems, infectious disease and the pandemic, is clearly of timely relevance and interest. This is not only because the human cost has been very high in some specific countries where the framing of those most affected has come with some very particular discourses about vulnerable groups and their intrinsic 'value' in the social project itself.

Increasingly, in this open-ended work, Mbembe invokes the value of *caring* in delimiting the role that constructing the 'Other' plays in such practices. The need for a relational analytic and process of engagement is not new, feminist theory has posed this issue for some time now, but to break the cycle of objectification and naturalised harms that, it seems, almost inevitably result, we need to look at how our societies manufacture such practices. Medicine, for example, lauds the Socratic paradox that '*that no man does wrong willingly*' (Bambrough, 1960: 290) and yet this is clearly not the case. In addition, it elides the individual and their intent with systemic actions and their consequences. Many social policy systems and their actors in contemporary liberal democratic states continue to produce harmful outcomes while lauding their virtuous intentions. Harms are minimised, and forgotten, and responses largely ritualised in acceptable acts of performativity—such as the inquiry mechanism in the UK and associated jurisdictions.

Here we believe that the idea of harms and harming come into play as a technique for exploring just how such systems continue to reproduce themselves in ways that carry a substantial cost in terms of human suffering. It seems reasonable to suggest that if object-making and the objectification of others places them firmly within a necropolitical landscape, one in which suffering generally ensues, then the mechanisms by which this plays out warrant further inquiry. To do this, albeit briefly, in the following section we examine the additional conceptual framework of zemiology, that is the study of social harm in the belief this helps broaden and contextualise Mbembe's analysis of sovereignty and the relationship between state power and the multitude of harms that societies can generate within themselves.

From Zemiology to Necropolitics

The concept of zemiology, or the study of social harms, emerged from criminology and was a significant attempt to go beyond existing critiques by criminology of the concept of 'crime' and how 'criminals' are both generated and treated in contemporary neoliberal societies (Hillyard & Tombs, 2017). A key point here was that 'crime' has no substantive ontological basis and those actions designated as crimes can vary enormously depending on when, where and by whom they are perpetrated. Hulsman (1986) explored this issue throughout much of his career based on his own experiences under German occupation. He identified crime as the product of criminal policy and not its object. Here the idea of 'harms' came into play because many things were, he noted, able to be categorised as criminal but also many harmful activities did not attract the designation of crimes.

Hillyard (2004) expanded the concept of zemiology not only on the basis of critical criminology but by including the politics and policies of the neoliberal state in the UK, and the tranche of harms this produced and/or entrenched. Some have suggested this approach was not entirely new in that critical criminology was well-established and various contemporary approaches suggest opportunities for reconciliation between the two perspectives (e.g. Kotzé, 2018). However, certainly for the purposes of this chapter, what we see as relatively novel is that this emphasis on harms from a criminological and legal perspective had, and continues to have, so much potential utility outside of that particular discipline. Indeed, we could even suggest that inquiring into 'harms' represents a bridge from criminology not only to other critically focused social sciences but also to many applied disciplines, policy domains and systemic responses. Since we are not criminologists, it is the perceived utility of the social harms approach for patient safety and healthcare critique more generally on which we focus here.

Pemberton (2016) is closely affiliated with this discussion of harms within criminology and expanded the scope of his work to consider that it is societies which produce a wide variety of harms. In a 2012 interview he pointed to the human cost of air pollution in the UK, which was responsible for some 20,000 deaths per annum, even then, from causes that were and are perfectly well-understood but not classified as crimes. He compared this to the 600 murders a year in the UK, classified as crimes, which received enormous public attention and expenditure within and without the criminal justice system. One set of deaths, the numerically much large one, received little public attention while the other is a focus for laws, public policy and sets of institutional processes ranging from those seen in courts through to prisons. He further pointed to the distinct narratives that surround one category of deaths, from air pollution, to another category, murder and the moralising positions seen in public discourse seen about murder but not preventable deaths from air pollution (Vernall, 2012). In other words, the emphasis on harms was an attempt to break the process of silos of perfectly acceptable and unacceptable deaths into a larger focus on harms produced in and then by society itself.

If we can contemplate the idea of societies that harm, then obviously we can consider the notion of systems, sub-systems and domains of practice within societies that produce harms even though their intended outcomes, as stated, may be positive. Thus, town planning makes claims to beneficial urban redesign but frequently does so at the expense of groups stigmatised by class and race, for example, and at its most extreme through the use of hostile design which has the explicit aim of '... *pushing particular behaviour – and, ultimately, particular people – out of public areas*' (Rosenberger, 2020: 883). Thus, harms up to and including death—and stigmatisation in death—can be generated both directly and indirectly by the contemporary state.

And if a profession such as town planning, with nominally benign intent, can generate or reinforce social inequalities at scale, then the same can be true of other domains of social policy and practice including health and aged care. The issue for us here is that the consequences of professions across multiple social policy and practice domains can be interpreted through a narrow aperture lens of health or through a broader one, in which consequences such as impairment, disability and even death are not by products but intrinsic to their collective necropolitics. Thus, the concept of systems and practitioners generating harms through individual and systemic practices can be also be scaled to a zemiological and, ultimately, necropolitical narrative. Here we propose intersectional forms of analysis can enrich our understanding of how such harms are generated but also how and why they continue to occur over time. Especially so when they occur to the same or very similar groups of people marked less by biological or physiological factors but more by their social categorisation and positioning.

With a sociological lens, then, the production of social harms at a conceptual level—both directly and indirectly—can be seen to be mirrored in healthcare systems which frequently attribute social value to those harmed, including those who are disabled or die (e.g. illicit drug users). Healthcare treatments may be a path to cure for some but, as we have seen during the present pandemic, the attribution of more or less value to some lives can have significant consequences for those who are weak or vulnerable within any society and its systems. The necropolitical sense of who lives and who must die is therefore a background constant in such systems but made more overt during periods of crisis. In addition, the discourses employed to rationalise such harms (e.g. 'limited resources' or the perceived 'clinical benefit' arguments) are a form of necropolitics in action. The rational for assisting some people live while permitting others to die is a microcosm of state power in that the assumed right to undertake such decisions ultimately comes back to the authority of the state to prohibit or support such actions. Aged care, which is increasingly healthcare at one remove form acute care, continues to illustrate this necropolitical dimensions in detail and at scale.

At the time of writing, there are two Royal Commissions under way in Australia, one into aged care (Royal Commission into Aged Care Quality and Safety, 2020) and one into disability (Royal Commission into Violence Abuse Neglect and Exploitation of People with Disability, 2020). Both are producing evidence for a wide variety of historical and current harms to groups of people mostly categorisable by, and through, their dependence on institutional forms of care and their vulnerability within those systems (Hide & Bourke, 2018). These vulnerabilities include individuals with intellectual and cognitive impairments such that their capacity to even protest their care is severely restricted in many instances (Mileski et al., 2019; White et al., 2003). As with Pemberton's harms critique, these are often individualised into discrete events rather than seen in the full scope of their often ongoing, systemic failures. Healthcare systems consistently produce a landscape of harms of varying degrees of kind and severity. Indeed, the whole field of patient safety can be seen as a response to, study of and attempt to intervene systemically in the harms that healthcare and the health professions (and others including managers and technicians) produce, or allow to be produced, within healthcare settings and institutions.

Necropolitics

Necropolitics, as conceptualised by Mbembe (2003: 11), addresses the State's '… *ultimate expression of sovereignty* [which he argues] *resides, to a large degree, in the powerand the capacity to dictate who may live and who must die*'. Mbemebe's concern is with a particular conceptualisation of sovereignty which is characterised as being 'My concern is those figures of sovereignty whose central project is not the struggle for autonomy but the generalized instrumentalization of human existence and the *material destruction of human bodies and populations*' (Mbembe, 2003: 14 our emphasis). While he notes that Agamben identified the concentration camp as the site where human beings are reduced to the status of 'bare life', Mbembe's own interest range more broadly to address the role that racism and colonialism have played in developing his necropolitical concept and critique (Mbembe, 2019). Perhaps not surprisingly, the concentration camp and some of its early iterations during the Boer War and in German South West Africa shaped subsequent forms in Europe (e.g. Zimmerer, 2008). The obvious connections included genocide, the role of medical anatomists in collecting scientific 'samples' and the more conventional theme of European atrocities mattering more in Europe than in the colonial territories.

The focus on specific populations is a profound one in that, as we have noted elsewhere, categories of social worth and worthlessness developed across the nineteenth century in ways that have remained with us up to the present day (Robertson & Travaglia, 2015). Many of these were instantiated through the social and medical sciences mediated via prevailing prejudices in nascent nation states including racism more generally and anti-Semitism in particular (Chelouche, 2021). Mbembe's contribution offers an extension of events often seen as distinct from each other and helps us in elaborating a critique of modernity that shows both an intellectual traffic between these conceptual 'domains' and their often-appalling consequences for the populations found lacking. In addition, healthcare and public health more specifically have a parallel history of envisioning the state as a healthy body from which unhealthy elements could be helpfully removed or (after Foucault) institutionalised in controlling environments separated out from those where the state's rules of citizenship more generally applied.

The necropolitical idea, whether taken narrowly and theoretically as political philosophy, or more broadly and practically as applied social critique, can be seen to operate across many domains in which life and death are mediated via social worth. This has additional value in that it not only provides an explanatory mode of how we got to where we currently are, and the discourses we continue to see expressed, but it also helps connect past and current forms of critical analysis, such as zemiology. We have seen and continue to see societal harms unevenly distributed on the basis of social position and categorisation. We continue to see very similar groups devalued on the basis of historically enacted forms of exploitation (e.g. Black Lives Matter). The consequences include reduced opportunities in health, education, access to justice and, ultimately, in the conditions of life and death. The present pandemic continues to illustrate these necropolitical conditions in a variety of ways. COVID-19 represents as risk to the healthy body of the state and a justification for a variety of necropolitical responses and decisions which we elaborate in the next section.

The Necropolitics of COVID-19

The necropolitics of COVID-19 have unfolded in two distinct ways. Firstly, decisions relating to who must die were often couched and justified, as Colombo (2021) argues, ultimately under the argument of economic governmentality with little consideration of the human rights of those (notably including young people with disabilities) who it was deemed must be allowed to die or even, in some cases, encouraged to choose death (as in the case of 'elderly' people pressured to sign 'do not resuscitate' orders) through discourses of differential clinical benefit, for example. This discourse was often hidden, however, behind discourses relating not to medical rationing but to the presumed futility of treatments for these vulnerable individuals and groups.

COVID-19 has sharpened pre-existing socio-economic and health inequalities and inequities both within and across countries (Eyawo & Viens, 2020). As a result the pandemic has had the greatest impacts, in terms of mortality, morbidity and economics, on the most vulnerable individuals and groups in countries across the globe, including, for example, women in India (Chakraborty, 2020a); ethnic 'minorities' in Brazil (Dos Santos et al., 2020); refugees in Europe (Davies et al., 2017); and African-American communities (Kullar et al., 2020). Even within the health and social care professions, social inequalities have been marked in who is more likely to be both infected by and die from COVID-19. Thus, both patients and practitioners may experience socially generated harms through the manifest inequalities and inequalities such systems have at their foundations. These patterns have been observed in the USA and the UK, respectively, but these structurally generated differentials have been observed in other countries as well when we consider who is employed, for example, in aged care facilities and the impact of tenuous employment practices on such workers.

In Australia, the lower-paid, under-trained and highly casualised work experienced by many, often immigrant, aged care workers has contributed to the infections and deaths amongst workers and aged care residents alike (Royal Commission into Aged Care Quality and Safety, 2021). These differentials can be seen not as 'naturally occurring variation' in the system but as consequences of choices made and governance decisions that range from the Federal to state to organisational level. In essence, these decisions impacted markedly on the *capacity* of the health and aged care systems to respond effectively and, therefore, on who was placed at risk and where. Our suggestion here is that the capacity for harms to occur was built into the health and aged care systems at multiple levels. The tolerance for a highly privatised model of both employment and care, focused around very vulnerable people (workers and residents in aged care) was a governance decision in and of itself with profound necropolitical consequences. In Australia, hardly unique in this respect, a consequence of COVID-19 has been that some two-thirds of deaths have been older people, many of them in care facilities.

A necropolitical dimension of this can be observed in that there was an early winningness to tolerate deaths in these vulnerable groups. While we believe these consequences and their outcomes are quite self-evident at this stage in the pandemic, this is far from being the end of the narrative or the pandemic itself. There are already indications that COVID-19 is not 'simply' a short-term pandemic to be resolved by vaccination itself and new or modified vaccines for COVID-19 variants. Rather, we are seeing people with long-term consequences of their COVID-19 infection including both a chronic state in which full recovery is slowed or possibly becomes a permanent scenario. In addition, we know that some survivors are likely to have significant health effects for the long term including respiratory, small vessel and even neurological effects (Heneka et al., 2020). The question here, in societies tolerant of harms and systems that effectively produce such outcomes or casualties, is how will they be treated if and when the pandemic fully recedes? Many of our systems are poor at acknowledging their failures or inadequacies and these people will be living reminders of where things did not go to plan even as vaccinations roll out and levels of protection rise. How will they be treated across the health, ageing, disability and broader social care and welfare environments with which they likely have to contend? The capacity for harms is, therefore, both short and longer term in scope.

COVID-19 and Vulnerability to Risk of Harm

COVID-19 rapidly brought to the fore of international attention not only the risk of harm for vulnerable groups from the virus itself, but also the risks associated with the attitudes, positions and practices of healthcare services and professionals. The rapid spread of the virus, and its virulence, quickly threw up questions about the distribution of various resources in health, aged and disability care, or more accurately, their rationing (Andrews et al., 2020).

It is at this point that the risks of harm for vulnerable individuals and groups from the healthcare system itself began to emerge. As healthcare services became swamped and resources were clearly not able to meet the demand (for either preventative measures or life prolonging 'treatments' like ventilators), decisions were made about the allocation (and re-allocation) of resources, either in real time or in anticipation of the anticipated 'deluge' of patients into acute healthcare systems (White & Lo, 2020).

It is also important to consider and acknowledge the intersectional nature of such harms. As Wilson et al. (2019: 9) note '*Intersectionality shows that paying particular attention to the ways that axes of identity and structural inequality converge can yield unexpected results*'. These axes in COVID-19 illustrated a convergence of age, ethnicity, disability and socio-economic background (Chakraborty, 2020b; Finch & Hernández Finch, 2020; Pareek et al., 2020). People in each of these groups are more likely to have worse health and more co-morbidities than the general population. They are also part of groups that are stereotyped by both society in general and healthcare professionals. The combination of these factors meant that people from particularly vulnerable groups were both more likely to contract and need healthcare assistance for COVID-19, while at the same time being in groups that were not considered 'worth' the resources expended on them. The reasons for withholding care were 'rational', but as Genevieve Bell argues (in relation to technology) 'every piece of technology has a worldview built into it' (Dourish & Bell, 2011). In this case, the technology is not physical but the decision-making process for deciding who or who does not receive treatment and its associated protocols and processes.

It is tempting to assume that almost 30 years into the era of evidence-based medicine (Evidence-Based Medicine Working Group, 1992), the playing field for such decision-making is at the very least rational and at best equitable. The reality, however, does not support this assumption. Firstly, in terms of the 'evidence' many individuals and groups are still not equally represented in the scientific research which forms the base for the evidence upon which decisions are made, including the broad category of women (Nowogrodzki, 2017). Vulnerable groups are harmed in two distinct ways: first through their often systematic exclusion from the research that underpins treatment and or secondly, from their unethical inclusion in research without their consent e.g. in the case of the Tuskegee syphilis 'study' in the USA and the 'unfortunate experiment' with women's cervical cancer in New Zealand (Paul & Brookes, 2015). This is equally true in the case of COVID-19, where there has already been discussion about the exclusion of groups from COVID-19 research (Gogoi et al., 2020; Lackland et al., 2020). Secondly, value judgements about who is (or isn't) worth expending resources on are made in the context of neoliberal and capitalist arguments that have little to do with the potential clinical success or failure of treatments and more, we would argue, to do with the necropolitical arguments surrounding the state's right to decide who may live and who must die (Mbembe, 2019). Thirdly, withholding resources from vulnerable individuals and groups reinforces a cycle of inequities that begins not just at birth, but includes historic multigenerational patterns. These can be seen to continue during the pandemic which has itself both exacerbated and thrown light on these sustained inequities (Abbasi, 2020; Ambrose, 2020; Baptiste et al., 2020; Chakraborty, 2020b; Chen & Bougie, 2020).

Lastly, there is nothing about the COVID-19 pandemic, as a pandemic, that is unusual or could be argued to be unexpected (Inayatullah, 2020). Health systems as services are not putting people at additional risk because of COVID-19 but doing so because of the way those services are structured and operate (and have operated for centuries) and the attitudes of health professionals and organisations, who despite protestations to the contrary, reflect societal attitudes towards vulnerable individuals and groups. In other words, the necropolitical frame lets us see how these and other vulnerabilities are produced in society and through the operation of social systems and practices. This generativity is fundamental to our improve understanding and analysis since the social sciences deal with persistent 'wicked problems' that are not natural but socially produced. A key strategy for this process can be seen in the production and demarcation of particular kinds of space, on the one hand, and the manipulation of existing spaces into necropolitical ones (e.g. aged care facilities). COVID-19 has shown very clearly that these processes on concentration can be beneficial, such as when staff locked themselves in with their residents, or deeply necropolitical, as in the experience of aged care residents in many countries.

Necropolitics and Space

One of the more useful analyses we can perhaps make on the basis of these intersectional events, and their critique, is that the state, its agencies and actions actually serve to produce particular kinds on *necropolitical spaces*. There are the more permanent manifestations of state power and violence, such as the prison, the workhouse, the asylum and the leper colony (after Foucault and see also Crampton and Elden [2006]). In these spaces many practices and procedures (technologies) are well-structured and regulated, including the acceptable forms of violence that take place and their consequences for the morbidity and mortality of individuals contained within them. However, under conditions of crisis, the state and its agents may produce new or even temporary necropolitical spaces that have their own consequences in that they and their occupants are functioning under more liminal conditions—neither permanent nor formalised, although they may become so (e.g. Agamben's concentration camp or refugee camps that may be framed as 'safe zones' but are frequently not very safe at all). A useful example in this specific context was the rush to set up 'overflow' sites for the capture and treatment of COVID affected patients, including in the UK and USA the establishment of 'Nightingale wards', often in parks and other large open spaces which lent themselves to rapid 'deployment' to use the militarised jargon we increasingly see as part of our necropolitical analysis.

These necropolitical spaces functioned in some cases as an implicit acknowledgement of the failed systems in place and the lack of adequate 'surge' capacity to deal with genuine public health crises. The underlying assumption was that deaths would mount rapidly and conventional systems would be overwhelmed leading to many 'sacrifices', especially amongst the vulnerable. In New York state, the discharge of infected patients to residential care facilities produced unnecessary deaths in those care homes which in many, but not all, cases were poorly prepared for the resulting infections amongst residents and staff. Here too, the seemingly expedient actions of the state and its agencies led to more deaths than necessary and a huge impact on the conditions of death as isolation procedures kicked in and families could not visit their sick and dying relatives.

In addition, places such as intensive care units (ICU) that were originally designed to try and keep people alive who had complex injuries and infections can, under these conditions, become necropolitical environments where decisions about the 'survivability' of particular patients are made, often under duress for staff, patients and families. Anecdotal evidence from the United Kingdom around the institutionalisation of 'do not resuscitate' (DNR) orders and their like (e.g. not for resuscitation—NFR) have produced the effect of some places *becoming* necropolitical through the technology of the DNR in that rather than treatment and care, staff have stood by while the patient with a DNR died. These suggest an ongoing spatialisation of necropolitical events and a deeply intersectional and often generative relationship between spaces and necropolitical actions and outcomes. Indeed, even as we write the full scope of these events has yet to be fully analysed. As with the present volume, our expectation is that these forms of analysis will be ongoing for some time to come even as we, eventually, emerge from the present COVID-19 scenario and hopefully begin improved planning for the next pandemic event.

Conclusion

There has been much discussion during the pandemic that isolation has provided a time for reflection. Our argument is that 'simple' reflection, especially for health services, is an insufficient response. What is required, we propose, is critical reflection of both the small and capital c kinds. 'Small c' critical reflection includes techniques such as after action reviews (Allen et al., 2010; Cook & Kautz, 2016) of what occurred before, during and (hopefully) after the pandemic. Equally, if not more important, is the 'capital C' critical reflection which is to say reflection that focuses on emancipatory theories and practices (such as feminism, anti-racism, anti-discrimination). For health services management, this approach aligns with a critical management studies approach, that is to say approaches that either actively argue against, or at the very least do not continue to privilege, functionalist management discourses about the distribution of resources and management of care (Kitchener & Thomas, 2016).

In this chapter, we have inquired on the inequalities, inequities and outright harms that occur within a variety of health and health-related systems when we have business as usual conditions. The developing COVID-19 pandemic and responses to it have destabilised those established, 'taken-for-granted' conditions. While the price has been high, this also represents an opportunity to inquire critically on how contemporary policy and practice domains, including healthcare, present an expansive set of necropolitical assumptions, circumstances and consequences. Contemporary conditions are not a given, they are constructed and maintained through forces which include a significant necropolitical dimension. We know these systems have and continue to produce harms at the societal, systemic and individual levels. Such harms occur in unequal measure to variety of social categories of person. Our position here is that the kinds of harms that fall unequally on vulnerable groups should be carefully examined through a variety of lenses. Here, we have explicitly considered the zemiological and necropolitical perspectives as two scaffolding approaches to such examination and inquiry. It is not that accidental harms can occur that we take issue with here but that patterns of harms occur over time and often to the same categories of person regardless of the specificities of time and place.

References

Abbasi, J. (2020). Taking a closer look at COVID-19, health inequities, and racism. *JAMA, 324*(5), 427–429.

Allen, J. A., Baran, B. E., & Scott, C. W. (2010). After-action reviews: A venue for the promotion of safety climate. *Accident Analysis and Prevention, 42*(2), 750–757.

Ambrose, A. J. H. (2020). Inequities during COVID-19. *Pediatrics, 146*(2), .

Andrews, E. E., Ayers, K. B., Brown, K. S., Dunn, D. S., & Pilarski, C. R. (2020). No body is expendable: Medical rationing and disability justice during the COVID-19 pandemic. *American Psychologist*. https://doi.org/10.1037/amp0000709

Archard, D., & Caplan, A. (2020). Is it wrong to prioritise younger patients with COVID-19? *BMJ, 369*. https://doi.org/10.1136/bmj.m1509

Argulian, E. (2020). Anticipating the 'second wave' of health care strain in COVID-19 pandemic. *JACC: Case Reports*. https://doi.org/10.1016/j.jaccas.2020.04.005

Bambrough, R. (1960). Socratic paradox. *The Philosophical Quarterly, 10*(41), 289–300.

Baptiste, D. L., Commodore-Mensah, Y., Alexander, K. A., Jacques, K., Wilson, P. R., Akomah, J., et al. (2020). COVID-19: Shedding light on racial and health inequities in the USA. *Journal of Clinical Nursing, 29*(15–16), 2734–2736.

Bergeron, S. (2016). Formal, informal, and care economies. *The Oxford handbook of feminist theory* (pp. 179–206). Oxford: Oxford University Press.

Booth, R. (2020, April 2). UK healthcare regulator brands resuscitation strategy unacceptable. *The Guardian (Australian Edition)*. https://www.theguardian.com/world/2020/apr/01/uk-healthcare-regulator-brands-resuscitation-strategy-unacceptable

Chakraborty, D. (2020a). The "living dead" within "death-worlds": Gender crisis and COVID-19 in India. *Gender, Work & Organization, 28*, 330–339.

Chakraborty, J. (2020b). Social inequities in the distribution of COVID-19: An intra-categorical analysis of people with disabilities in the U.S. *Disability and Health Journal, 14*, 101007.

Chelouche, T. (2021). Teaching hard truths about medicine and the holocaust. *AMA Journal of Ethics, 23*(1), 59–63.

Chen, I., & Bougie, O. (2020). Women's issues in pandemic times: How COVID-19 has exacerbated gender inequities for women in Canada and around the world. *Journal of Obstetrics and Gynaecology Canada, 42*, 1458–1459.

Colombo, E. (2021, in press). Human rights-inspired governmentality: COVID-19 through a human dignity perspective. *Critical Sociology, 47*(4–5), 571–581.

Cook, J. A., & Kautz, D. D. (2016). After action reviews in the emergency department: The positives of real-time feedback. *Journal of Emergency Nursing, 42*(2), 146–149.

Crampton, J. W., & Elden, S. (2006). Space, politics, calculation: An introduction. *Social & Cultural Geography, 7*(5), 681–685.

Cutter, S. L., Boruff, B. J., & Shirley, W. L. (2003). Social vulnerability to environmental hazards. *Social Science Quarterly, 84*(2), 242–261.

Davies, T. (2018). Toxic space and time: Slow violence, necropolitics, and petrochemical pollution. *Annals of the American Association of Geographers, 108*(6), 1537–1553.

Davies, T., Isakjee, A., & Dhesi, S. (2017). Violent inaction: The necropolitical experience of refugees in Europe. *Antipode, 49*(5), 1263–1284.

Dodds, S. (2007). Depending on care: Recognition of vulnerability and the social contribution of care provision. *Bioethics, 21*(9), 500–510.

Dos Santos, H. L. P. C., Maciel, F. B. M., Santos, K. R., da Conceição, C. D. V. S., de Oliveira, R. S., da Silva, N. R. F., et al. (2020). Necropolitics and the impact of COVID-19 on the black community in Brazil: A literature review and a document analysis. *Ciencia e Saude Coletiva, 25*, 4211–4224.

Dourish, P., & Bell, G. (2011). *Divining a digital future: Mess and mythology in ubiquitous computing*. MIT Press.

Evidence-Based Medicine Working Group. (1992). Evidence-based medicine. A new approach to teaching the practice of medicine. *JAMA, 268*(17), 2420.

Eyawo, O., & Viens, A. M. (2020). Rethinking the central role of equity in the global governance of pandemic response. *Journal of Bioethical Inquiry, 17*(4), 549–553.

Finch, W. H., & Hernández Finch, M. E. (2020). Poverty and COVID-19: Rates of incidence and deaths in the United States during the first 10 weeks of the pandemic. *Frontiers in Sociology, 5*, 1–10.

Fink, S. (2013). *Five days at memorial: Life and death in a storm-ravaged hospital*. Atlantic Books.

Gogoi, M., Armitage, R., Brown, G., Ryan, B., Eborall, H., Qureshi, N., et al. (2020, in press). Putting the voices and insights of migrants and diverse ethnic groups at the centre of our response to COVID-19. *Public Health*.

Gulliford, M., Figueroa-Munoz, J., Morgan, M., Hughes, D., Gibson, B., Beech, R., et al. (2002). What does 'access to health care' mean? *Journal of Health Services Research & Policy, 7*(3), 186–188.

Heneka, M. T., Golenbock, D., Latz, E., Morgan, D., & Brown, R. (2020). Immediate and long-term consequences of COVID-19 infections for the development of neurological disease. *Alzheimer's Research & Therapy, 12*(1), 1–3.

Hide, L., & Bourke, J. (2018). Cultures of harm in institutions of care: Introduction. *Social History of Medicine, 31*(4), 679–687.

Hilgartner, S. (2007). Overflow and containment in the aftermath of disaster. *Social Studies of Science, 37*(1), 153–158.

Hillyard, P. (2004). *Beyond criminology: Taking harm seriously*. Pluto Press.

Hillyard, P., & Tombs, S. (2017). Social harm and zemiology. In A. Liebling, S. Maruna, & L. McAra (Eds.), *The Oxford handbook of criminology* (6th ed., pp. 284–305). Oxford University Press.

Hulsman, L. H. (1986). Critical criminology and the concept of crime. *Contemporary Crises, 10*(1), 63–80.

Hunter, D. J. (2018). *Desperately seeking solutions: Rationing health care*. Routledge.

Inayatullah, S. (2020). Neither a black swan nor a zombie apocalypse: The futures of a world with the COVID-19 coronavirus. *Journal of Futures Studies, 18*.

Kitchener, M., & Thomas, R. (2016). The critical health care management domain. In E. Ferlie, K. Montgomery, & A. R. Pedersen (Eds.), *The Oxford handbook of health care management* (pp. 117–140). Oxford University Press.

Kotzé, J. (2018). Criminology or zemiology? Yes, please! On the refusal of choice between false alternatives. In *Zemiology* (pp. 85–106). Springer.

Kullar, R., Marcelin, J. R., Swartz, T. H., Piggott, D. A., Macias Gil, R., Mathew, T. A., et al. (2020). Racial disparity of coronavirus disease 2019 in African American communities. *The Journal of Infectious Diseases, 222*(6), 890–893.

Lackland, D. T., Sims-Robinson, C., Buie, J. N. J., & Voeks, J. H. (2020). Impact of COVID-19 on clinical research and inclusion of diverse populations. *Ethnicity & Disease, 30*(3), 429–432.

Lanoix, M. (2007). The citizen in question. *Hypatia, 22*(4), 113–129.

Lugosi, C. I. (2007). Natural disaster, unnatural deaths: The killings on the life care floors at Tenet's Memorial Medical Center after Hurricane Katrina. *Issues in Law and Medicine, 23*(1), 71–85.

Lund, E. M., & Ayers, K. B. (2020). Raising awareness of disabled lives and health care rationing during the COVID-19 pandemic. *Psychological Trauma: THeory, Research, Practice and Policy, 12*(S1), S210–S211.

Marmot, M., & Allen, J. J. (2014). Social determinants of health equity. *American Journal of Public Health, 104*(S4), S517–S519.

Mbembe, A. (2001). *On the postcolony*. University of California Press.

Mbembe, A. (2003). Necropolitics. *Public Culture, 15*(1), 11–40.

Mbembe, A. (2019). *Necropolitics*. Duke University Press.

McEntire, D. A. (2004). Tenets of vulnerability: An assessment of a fundamental disaster concept. *Journal of Emergency Management, 2*(2), 23–29.

Mileski, M., Lee, K., Bourquard, C., Cavazos, B., Dusek, K., Kimbrough, K., et al. (2019). Preventing the abuse of residents with dementia or Alzheimer's disease in the long-term care setting: A systematic review. *Clinical Interventions in Aging, 14*, 1797.

Müller, B. (2019). The careless society—Dependency and care work in capitalist societies. *Frontiers in Sociology, 3*, 44.

National Institute for Health and Care Excellence. (2020). *NICE updates rapid COVID-19 guideline on critical care*. https://www.nice.org.uk/news/article/nice-updates-rapid-covid-19-guideline-on-critical-care

Nowogrodzki, A. (2017). Inequality in medicine. *Nature, 550*(7674), S18–S19.

Outka, E., & Saint-Amour, P. (2019). *Viral modernism*. New York: Columbia University Press.

Pareek, M., Bangash, M. N., Pareek, N., Pan, D., Sze, S., Minhas, J. S., et al. (2020). Ethnicity and COVID-19: An urgent public health research priority. *The Lancet, 395*(10234), 1421–1422.

Paul, C., & Brookes, B. (2015). The rationalization of unethical research: Revisionist accounts of the Tuskegee syphilis study and the New Zealand "unfortunate experiment". *American Journal of Public Health, 105*(10), e12–e19.

Pemberton, S. A. (2016). *Harmful societies: Understanding social harm*. Policy Press.

Rijke, J., Brown, R., Zevenbergen, C., Ashley, R., Farrelly, M., Morison, P., et al. (2012). Fit-for-purpose governance: A framework to make adaptive governance operational. *Environmental Science & Policy, 22*, 73–84.

Robertson, H., & Travaglia, J. (2015). Big data problems we face today can be traced to the social ordering practices of the 19th century. *Impact of Social Sciences Blog*. https://blogs.lse.ac.uk/impactofsocialsciences/2015/10/13/ideological-inheritances-in-the-data-revolution/

Rosenberger, R. (2020). On hostile design: Theoretical and empirical prospects. *Urban Studies, 57*(4), 883–893.

Royal Commission into Aged Care Quality and Safety. (2020). The Royal Commission into Aged Care Quality and Safety. https://agedcare.royalcommission.gov.au/

Royal Commission into Aged Care Quality and Safety. (2021). *Aged care and COVID-19: A special report*. Royal Commission into Aged Care Quality and Safety.

Royal Commission into Violence Abuse Neglect and Exploitation of People with Disability. (2020). Royal Commission into Violence, Abuse, Neglect and Exploitation of People with Disability. https://disability.royalcommission.gov.au/

Scully, J. L. (2020). Disability, disablism, and COVID-19 pandemic triage. *Journal of Bioethical Inquiry, 17*(4), 601–605.

Shea, F. K. (2010). Hurricane Katrina and the legal and bioethical implications of involuntary euthanasia as a component of disaster management in extreme emergency situations. *Annals of Health Law, 19*(1 Spec No), 133–139.

Tierney, K. (2012). Disaster governance: Social, political, and economic dimensions. *Annual Review of Environment Resources, 37*, 341–363.

Todd, P. (2020). *NICE amends COVID-19 critical care guideline after judicial review challenge*. https://www.hja.net/press-releases/nice-amends-covid-19-critical-care-guideline-after-judicial-review-challenge/

Valencia, S., & Zhuravleva, O. A. (2019). Necropolitics, post-mortem/transmortem politics, and transfeminisms in the sexual economies of death. *Transgender Studies Quarterly, 6*(2), 180–193.

van Dorn, A., Cooney, R. E., & Sabin, M. L. (2020). COVID-19 exacerbating inequalities in the US. *Lancet, 395*(10232), 1243.

Vernall, L. (2012). *Social harm and the structure of societies: Interview with Simon Pemberton*. https://www.birmingham.ac.uk/accessibility/transcripts/dr-simon-pemberton-social-harm.aspx

Waring, J., & Bishop, S. (2020). Health states of exception: Unsafe non-care and the (inadvertent) production of 'bare life' in complex care transitions. *Sociology of Health & Illness, 42*(1), 171–190.

White, C., Holland, E., Marsland, D., & Oakes, P. (2003). The identification of environments and cultures that promote the abuse of people with intellectual disabilities: A review of the literature. *Journal of Applied Research in Intellectual Disabilities, 16*(1), 1–9.

White, D. B., & Lo, B. (2020). A framework for rationing ventilators and critical care beds during the COVID-19 pandemic. *JAMA, 323*(18), 1773–1774.

Wilson, Y., White, A., Jefferson, A., & Danis, M. (2019). Intersectionality in clinical medicine: The need for a conceptual framework. *The American Journal of Bioethics, 19*(2), 8–19.

Zimmerer, J. (2008). Colonial genocide: The Herero and Nama War (1904–8) in German south west Africa and its significance. In D. Stone (Ed.), *The historiography of genocide* (pp. 323–343). Palgrave Macmillan.

CHAPTER 14

Rapid Impact Organisation Behaviour (RIOB) Research for Responses by Healthcare Organisations to Evolving Crises (SARS COV-2 Pandemic): Examples of a New OB Specialty

John Øvretveit

Introduction

The subject of this chapter is behaviour change by healthcare staff and changes to the organisation of service delivery and systems. There is considerable organisational behaviour (OB) literature about this subject, but a limited amount of empirically-based evidence or concepts about rapid changes of this type. During 2020 and 2021, managers and practitioners made more rapid changes of this type than they had done in the last ten years, and sometimes over a period of days. The purpose of this

J. Øvretveit (✉)
Medical Management Center, Dept LIME, Karolinska Institute, Stockholm, Sweden

Stockholm Healthcare System, Stockholm, Sweden

J. Waring et al. (eds.), *Organising Care in a Time of Covid-19*, Organizational Behaviour in Healthcare,
https://doi.org/10.1007/978-3-030-82696-3_14

chapter is to encourage and enable organisation behaviour researchers to contribute to more effective health service responses to infectious disease outbreaks and emergency management. It does this by describing and illustrating rapid impact organisation behaviour (RIOB) research, where the customers for the research are managers and other researchers. Using examples of research relevant to the COVID-19 pandemic response, it illustrates different features of RIOB research. It summarises the strengths and weaknesses of this type of research and its relevance to rapid response by health service staff to future emergencies or crises in health service provision.

OB is a wide-ranging area of academic and applied research and theory, inclusive of many theoretical and management traditions. Many prominent concepts from the broad field of OB are useful for conceptualising changes. These included OB research into motivation and incentives, in sustaining behaviour change and sustaining staff health behaviours over a long period of time, as well as the value of narratives told by people that staff respected and trusted, and ideas about evolving and emergent change. Other OB concepts we found of value in this research were stratified systems theory and decentralisation and decision making, as well as system interdependencies and coordination structures and processes: the chapter returns to these when considering the implications for the future of OB. As this is just the beginning of the development of this sub-field of OB research, we expect many other concepts from other parts of the OB will be deployed to understand and contribute to change in evolving and fast-moving healthcare crises.

The rapid research approach described is part of a growing trend that is blurring the boundaries between rapid pragmatic learning and more rigorous traditional research approaches. This trend can be seen in the idea of learning health system, in quality improvement practice research and in partnership research approaches (Etheredge, 2007; Forrest et al., 2018; Øvretveit et al., 2014; Rubenstein et al., 2006, 2014). In the case example considered in this chapter, this approach was natural and necessary for the fast research response required to provide valid information to inform decision making.

Fast Health Service Response to Emergencies and Crises

Most healthcare services have an emergency response plan and have practised how to operate in the event of a disaster such as a fire, flood, earthquake or terrorist attack. These responses are informed by best practice guidance based on research and practice from previous disasters. In contrast to these single-event emergencies there are infectious disease outbreaks such as influenza, TB and common sexually transmitted disease. These are known infections and can be planned for. For these, health services are able to make changes to manage their response but also maintain ordinary services, unless they have no spare capacity, as is common in the UK NHS winter influenza "emergencies".

However, rather than known single-event or time-limited emergencies, healthcare services are less well prepared and able to respond to evolving crises, such as AIDS and new infectious diseases, where knowledge of the nature of the disease, transmission and care is built over time. COVID-19 was one such disease and there will be more.

There is a large body of research into disaster management and related subjects, including public health and population responses. However, the two most often cited texts in the field give little attention to behaviour change and organisation change and then only in relation to communication with the public (Koenig & Schultz, 2016; McEntire, 2006). It is notable that little of this knowledge draws on organisation behaviour research and that little such research has been carried out in, or describes, changes by service delivery organisations in response to emergencies, especially outside of hospitals.

The SARS COV-2 virus became a pandemic, with an infectious disease about which little was known, especially about the practice and organisational changes needed to respond and how to make these changes quickly, and often at scale. Leaders and staff at different levels of the health system often had to make and implement decisions about change in practice and organisation quickly with little information. Can organisation behaviour knowledge and researchers contribute to how health services plan and respond to such "evolving outbreaks"?

To address this question, the paper reports the RIOB approach used in study of Stockholm healthcare response to the pandemic, as well as two other examples that blurred the boundaries between pragmatic data gathering and analysis and rigorous research. The paper defines organisation behaviour research (OBR) as the systematic study of the behaviour of individuals, groups and organisations. Although concentrating on observable behaviour and performance, OBR also investigates perceptions, emotions and cultures which may explain behaviour (Øvretveit, 2001). The RIOB research used in the Stockholm healthcare response to the pandemic was research designed to enable change to behaviour or organisation to be accomplished in less than 12 months, as well as to contribute to OB science, using methods suited to these dual objectives.

The RIOB research for purpose required a partnered research approach where "researchers, practitioners, patients or others work together, with different roles, to use research both to solve practical problems and to contribute to science". Throughout this paper, the term "practitioner" is used to refer to clinicians and managers alike (Øvretveit et al., 2014).

The chapter suggests that a sub-specialty of organisation behaviour research into emergency response management and organisation is urgently needed to use OBR to understand and assist the organisation, and management of the resources and responsibilities, and implementation of changes for providing health care in response to an emergency event or episode (preparedness, response, mitigation and recovery). This includes responses to the specific emergency event or episode, as well as prioritising and providing routine pre-event health care. It includes managing the balance of resources and responses between the emergency and routine care at different phases of the emergency episode.

To address this question, the chapter first presents three organisation behaviour studies relevant to responding to the Covid pandemic, with different objectives and designs. It then discusses features of rapid impact organisation behaviour research using illustrations from the three examples. It closes by describing the opportunities for RIOB research for this and future infectious disease outbreaks and emergencies, and how to develop the science of emergency management using OB theory, findings and methods.

Examples of Relevant Research

Implementing Rapid Adherence to Hand Hygiene Practices

The objective of this study was to examine the impact of the COVID-19 pandemic on hand hygiene performance (HHP) rates in acute care hospitals. HHP rates were estimated using an automated hand hygiene monitoring system installed in in 7 general hospitals and 10 paediatric inpatient units in 2 children's hospitals. A segmented regression model was used to estimate the trajectory of HHP rates in 10 weeks leading up to a COVID-19-related milestone event (e.g. school closures) and for 10 weeks after.

The study found three effects, all of which were significant. Average HHP rates increased from 46 to 56% in the months preceding pandemic-related school closures. This was followed by a 6% upward shift at the time school closures occurred. HHP rates remained over 60% for 4 weeks before declining to 54% at the end of the study period. The report discussed possible reasons why HHP first increased as the pandemic began and then decreased as it progressed (Moore et al., 2020).

One feature of this research is the innovative use of digital technology to provide evidence rapidly to enable data-informed decisions. The study used an automated hand hygiene monitoring system for data collection and fast analysis using software. This was able to provide detailed tracking of changes in behaviour that could be analysed quickly in different ways. A second feature was the use of behavioural science to consider different explanations of the changes in HHP rates at different times, and referenced in the 9 studies supporting these explanations (Moore et al., 2020). This study thus contributes methodological, empirical and theoretical knowledge to developing an OBR science of emergency response management and organisation. It is an interesting question as to the advantages, disadvantages and feasibility of reporting these data about performance to managers and infection control specialists during the data gathering.

Hand-Hygiene Compliance: An Organizational Approach

In this study, the Veterans Health Administration Center for Organization, Leadership and Management Research worked closely with one veterans health system on an intervention, "based on the premise that although hand hygiene is an individual act, achieving high rates of compliance requires interdependent organizational action". The study found that four medical centres "demonstrated statistically significant hand-hygiene improvement over the course of the project" and three did not. The analysis found that "consistent with our hypotheses, we found that hand-hygiene compliance was strengthened by the presence of three interacting organizational components that medical center managers and clinicians can affect: 1. robust clinical process redesign to engage staff and incorporate evidence-based practices in routine operations; 2. active top leadership commitment to the redesign effort; and 3. links to management structures and processes to support, align, and integrate redesign" (VanDeusen Lukas et al., 2010).

One feature that enabled both research and improvement changes was the partnership approach and practical focus of the research unit working within the VA health system. A second was the social and organisational perspective brought to bear on an individual behaviour that is challenging to change and sustain. The study contributed understanding of the organisation and management factors that are critical to hand hygiene and are relevant to more effective change to ensure this behaviour in future disease outbreaks, as well as for infection control in routine care.

A Rapid Impact Organisation Behaviour (RIOB) Partnership Study

The objective of this study was to describe, evaluate and give feedback to management about the emergency response to COVID-19 made by the public primary and community healthcare division within the Region Stockholm health system.

The data collection was through a weekly survey of all management heads of the primary and community healthcare services ($n = 110$), and from minutes of management meetings, interviews with the emergency management team and documentation from the emergency management system and emergency planning documents, as well as service data from digital databases (Ohrling et al., 2020b).

An analysis of the weekly surveys was reported to the emergency management team to give an overall understanding of the organisation and practice challenges that the heads of service delivery units were facing, their solutions and their needs. Over the longer term, the study was able to describe the evolving response over 9 months and important organisation and managements lessons for the future. These include changes that were needed in ordinary operations as well as changes for improved responses to infectious disease outbreaks. The latter were reported as findings about changes in service utilisation, about effectiveness of organisational changes, matching demand to supply in an evolving crisis, system understanding of interdependencies, and health deterioration amongst non-Covid patients, follow-up and outreach, and use of data and rapid research.

Features of Rapid Impact Organisation Behaviour research

These three examples show different types of RIOB research. Table 14.1 summarises features of this type of research, many of which are exemplified in each of the examples. Some are further discussed below to show an approach that could be developed to build a sub-specialty of organisation behaviour research into emergency response management and organisation.

Manager Customer-Participants

The "customer" for the first hand hygiene study was not specified but, from the information by the journal in which it was published (American Journal of Infection Control), the primary customers appear to be infection control specialists, healthcare managers and researchers. The "customers" for the second hand hygiene study were managers of the medical centres and region for the VA health system, as well as OB researchers. For the third example study, the "customers" were the top level emergency management team of the primary and community healthcare organisation and the service delivery unit managers.

One feature of rapid impact organisation behaviour (RIOB) research is the explicit dual aim of contributing to practical improvement to organisation and to the science of organisation behaviour. Each of the three studies contributed to both, but the proportion of timely assistance to practising managers compared to the scientific contribution with academics as customers was different in each study.

Defining Objectives, Deliverables and Time Targets (Parameters)

A key feature of all research is to define objectives, but the approach to doing so was different in the third RIOB research study compared to the first two studies.

Traditional OB research typically defines objectives after reviewing previous empirical and theoretical research to identify gaps in scientific knowledge and possible methods and theoretical frameworks that might be used in a study. The first study was not an OB study and the previous research reviewed was of hand hygiene compliance. "A literature search did not reveal any studies reporting on hand hygiene compliance of

Table 14.1 Features of rapid impact organisation behaviour (RIOB) research and illustrations

Features	*Illustration*
Manager or clinician customer-participants	These types of partners are participants in the research at all stages. They decide some questions they need answering in a timely way, and provide access to these data. They provide some data during the research and help to interpret findings and share publication
Defining objectives, deliverables and time targets (parameters)	Practice-based or patient-customers for the research shape the objectives in terms of the information they need and by when. Researchers suggest or negotiate information to be collected in terms of research they have reviewed and gaps in OB knowledge
Research and practice partners	The primary partners are the customers for the research. Other important partners are people that provide access and guidance to already collected data and its validity and timeliness for the research questions/objectives
Investigation Design and methods	RIOB research does not have time for full randomised controlled trials, but may use stepped wedge prospective designs. More often, observational designs are used, sometimes involving one or more comparative study sites, and sometimes time-series designs. Often the design uses already collected data, which can be qualitative data
Multidisciplinary perspective and project management	Much OB research is multidisciplinary and RIOB research especially so. Customer-participants often benefit from information or solutions that is shaped by a number of disciplinary theories or methods. This often requires a multidisciplinary project team or advisory group and more complex project management

(continued)

Table 14.1 (continued)

Features	*Illustration*
Digital research	To meet the time targets, already collected digital data and technologies to analyse or collect primary data quickly are necessary. Examples are software to analyse digital data in databases and Internet or automatic monitoring collection systems

health care workers in hospitals during the first pandemic of the twenty-first century (influenza A/H1N1) or the current COVID-19 pandemic". However, the empirical contribution to knowledge about this behaviour in an organisation during a pandemic was important.

The second study was a practical OB study, and the previous research reviewed to help define objectives was research into key factors in organisational change for the type of intervention studied. The researchers described building a "consolidated version of the organizational transformation model (OTM) based research on complex organizational change, microsystem effectiveness, and organizational diffusion of innovation" (VanDeusen Lukas et al., 2010).

The third study defined objectives in terms of the information that managers needed rapidly to make better informed decisions about organisation and behaviour changes. It also drew on OB and implementation research concepts to decide which data was important to collect (e.g. inner and outer context, from the consolidated framework for implementation research, Damschroder et al., 2009), with a view to contributing to scientific understanding in a later analysis.

Research and Practice Partners

"Research partners" describes many different stakeholders with different levels of involvement at different times in the research process. Studies can be classified at one end of a continuum from entirely researcher directed to, at the other end, entirely directed by non-researchers. In between, researchers and other partners jointly decide or consult about different aspects of the research. For example, research funders may fund particular questions or subjects rather than those of the researcher as is the case in researcher initiated proposals.

In considering emergency responses by healthcare organisations, one important partner for research is the service delivery staff who implement changes and change their practices and organisation to respond to the emergency. In some research, they are the research-customers. In the first study, the partners were nine hospitals who enabled access to the data. In the second study, the primary partners were managers and clinicians at the study sites who contributed to formulating the research questions, as well as providing data and contributing to interpretation of the findings and subsequently using the research to make changes. In the third study, there was a strong and continuing partnership between researchers and practitioners at each stage of the research. Indeed, the principle investigator (and author of this paper) was employed 50% by the healthcare organisation and 50% by the medical university, and most researchers on the team had joint appointments.

Investigation Design and Methods

For OB research into responses by healthcare organisations to emergencies, there are designs that include experimental and observational designs, and qualitative, quantitative and mixed methods for data collection (Ryan et al., 2013). Design often includes hypotheses or theoretical frameworks to shape the data that will be collected.

The first study used an observational time-series design, with data from an automated hand sanitiser to compare hand hygiene from 10 weeks leading up to a COVID-19-related milestone event and for 10 weeks after. Differences were found but explanations about the cause of this organisational behaviour finding were speculative. The scientific contribution was empirical but not theoretical.

The second study used a mixed-methods longitudinal comparative case study design, informed by OB concepts. The organisational model for implementing and investigating evidence-based clinical practices for hand hygiene was based on OB research that discovered three interacting organisational conditions critical for success: active top leadership commitment; clinical process redesign; and links to senior management structures and processes.

The third study was an OB action research observational design, using mixed methods of data collection. It was different from the first two mainly in reporting some data analyses made during the study to the emergency response management team. Like the second study, it used OB concepts to frame data collection and analysis at the levels of individual clinicians, heads of service delivery units and the top level team managing the service delivery units.

Multidisciplinary Research Perspective

OB is a scientific multidiscipline: OB research uses different scientific disciplinary perspectives to frame study data collection and/or interpret findings. One study may use one perspective, for example economics, or socio-technical systems theory, and another may use multiple perspectives, especially if considering changes at a number of organisational levels.

The disciplinary perspectives used in study 1 were public health, statistics and hygiene sciences. In study 2, researchers were from a Center for Organization, Leadership and Management Research and the larger team included wider range of disciplinary perspectives that were brought to bear in the study: health services research, statistics, health informatics, organisation and management studies, implementation science and public health. The disciplinary perspectives used to design and conduct the third study included statistics, health informatics, implementation science, organisation and management studies, policy analysis and health services research.

These studies were performed by project teams with members from different scientific and professional disciplines. The project management process is more complex than for projects where all share the same disciplinary concepts and values. Effective project management to integrate the different understandings of the team members is needed with attention to precise and efficient communication and explanations of concepts with examples that are unfamiliar to others when used by one member: team science provides useful tools to help RIOB research (Cooke et al., 2015; Guise et al., 2017; Stokols et al., 2008).

Digital Research

Most OB researchers now use digital technology to source, collect and analyse data. The first study used data collected from automatic monitoring of use of sanitisers and software to estimate changes in use of sanitisers over time and as a proxy for hand hygiene compliance. The second study sourced data from the health systems databases and also used digital technology extensively to communicate and collect and compare data directly from their study sites. The third study used the internal secure health system Internet to administer and analyse the weekly survey of 110 managers of service delivery units, as well as data from regional, national and local service databases and open source prediction modelling software. To develop RIOB research, it may be necessary for researchers to become more familiar with which databases might provide timely and valid data for their studies, and to access and analyse these data. In addition, knowing technical experts who can quickly be recruited to the team is important.

Implications for OB Research into Emergency Management in Healthcare Organisations

Research and experience of the emergency response of healthcare service delivery organisations of COVID-19 suggest that there is limited use of evidence-based knowledge about behaviour and organisational change. Emergency preparation and planning for these organisations might be improved by using evidence-based OB knowledge that has been produced by OB researchers using conventional experimental and observational designs. The third study demonstrated that RIOB research could contribute to both improved response during the pandemic and scientific understanding of emergency organisation and management in non-hospital health care. The implications of the studies and the discussion in this paper are that OB researchers could contribute more to planning and response to future emergencies and to the science of emergency management. But to do so OB researchers would need to develop skills, research practices and research systems in certain ways, and especially to undertake RIOB research.

One development needed is in understanding about, and motivation to, contributing to emergency planning and response management. The motivation is helped by recognising the contribution that knowledge about OB could make, and the value and importance of making this contribution. Understanding involves knowing more about the terms, literature and guidance use by those involved in emergency management (Koenig & Schultz, 2016; McEntire, 2006). Many researchers trained in traditional methods regard the best way to make a difference for patients as being through using these methods, and that research-to-practice implementation is a separate issue and not their responsibility. Designs and methods to integrate implementation into the research or to carry out rapid impact or action research are unfamiliar to many. The skills and research practices to use these methods would require development.

Another development area is for skills to work more closely in partnership with non-academic customers of OB research. This includes communication skills, for example to simplify and frame research for customers without being simplistic or misleading. In addition, negotiation skills are needed to ensure access to data and data collection that might not provide immediate and direct benefit to customers but which is important for theory development and scientific contribution.

A fourth area is the development and use of research systems, and especially for RIOB research where rapid access, collection, analysis and reporting of data are necessary. The development of these systems is a specialist task that requires close cooperation with health systems or national data systems and health informatics skills and is considered in the literature on learning health systems (Etheredge, 2007). But OB researchers need to influence the development of these systems for research purposes. To do this, and to access and analyse the data, OB researchers will need further to develop their knowledge of which data is available, the validity of the data from different databases and skills in health informatics (Forrest et al., 2018).

A fifth area is in concepts more suited to emergencies such as some infectious disease outbreaks that unfold and take different directions over time, in part because knowledge about the infectious disease develops. One OB concept that we found useful to describe and understand the response of the Stockholm healthcare organisation to the pandemic was as an "evolving response", where decisions and actions built on emerging knowledge and previous actions. One OB theory that helped to explain how fast locally tailored responses made by service delivery units did not have negative impacts on other services and cause system sub-optimisation was a theory of management decentralisation. This theory combined the concepts of delegated authority, management capability and accountability in a theory of management decentralisation (Ohrling et al., 2020a).

For research into the evolving response of healthcare organisations to emergencies and ongoing crises, other OB concepts and theories are useful before data gathering. For example building on OB features that previous research suggests are important for appropriate, effective and fast organisation change to respond to the changing situation. These can be used for deductive observational or hypothesis testing or experimental OB studies. The concepts can be used after data collection to interpret, understand or explain the documented organisational changes made to respond to the emergency or evolving situation and to build theory.

The last area considered here is researcher rewards and incentives, especially for those employed full-time in academic institutions. These typically promote in terms of publications in high-impact scientific journals that are sometimes less able to assess the quality of non-experimental quantitative research. In addition, career incentives involve the number of competitive research grants won, where reviewers may be less able to assess the quality of rapid impact or action research designs and methods. A number of non-governmental foundation funders are increasingly including social impact in and stakeholder involvement in assessing research, and are more prepared to consider rapid impact or action research proposals.

Conclusion

This chapter set out to answer the question, can organisation behaviour knowledge and researchers contribute to how health services plan and respond to emergencies and "evolving outbreaks"? The first study gave empirical knowledge about changes to hand hygiene performance before and later in the pandemic emergency. This study showed how an automated data collection system of the use of hand sanitisers was a low cost method to collect data about changes to an important behaviour of organisational members during the pandemic. It did not use behavioural or organisational research or concepts before data gathering or later in the analysis to interpret the findings, so the contribution to OB knowledge was limited apart from illustrating opportunities to use digital technologies for OB research.

The second study on the same subject did use OB knowledge to frame data gathering and analyse the findings, and showed how OB research could contribute to how health services increase hand hygiene performance. The third study shows methods and features of RIOB research that can directly help health services to respond during different phases of evolving outbreaks and also contribute to scientific knowledge about organisation and behaviour in emergencies.

As regards the implications for OB as a field, undertaking more of this type of research requires the development of OB researchers' competencies, research practices and systems. The need for these skills has been highlighted by the Covid pandemic. Building these capabilities and research could help to increase the use of OB knowledge within the field of emergency management and form a new sub-discipline within the field.

Appendix: Definitions of Terms Used in This Paper

Organisation Behaviour Research (OBR) is the systematic study of the behaviour of individuals, groups and organisations. Although concentrating on observable behaviour and performance, OBR also investigates perceptions, emotions and cultures which may explain behaviour (Øvretveit, 2001).

Emergency management by a healthcare service delivery organisation (EM by HSDOs): Emergency management by a healthcare organisation is the organisation and management of the resources and responsibilities, and implementation of changes for providing health care in response to an emergency event or episode (preparedness, response, mitigation and recovery). It includes responses to the specific emergency event or episode, as well as prioritising and providing routine pre-event health care. It includes managing the balance of resources and responses between the emergency and routine care at different phases of the emergency episode.

Partnered research "an activity where researchers, practitioners, patients or others work together, with different roles, to use research both to solve practical problems and to contribute to science". Throughout this paper, the term "practitioner" is used to refer to clinicians and managers alike (Øvretveit et al., 2014).

Rapid impact organisation behaviour (RIOB) research: research designed to enable change to behaviour or organisation to be accomplished in less than 12 months, as well as to contribute to OB science, using methods suited to these dual objectives.

References

Cooke, N. J., et al. (2015). *Enhancing the effectiveness of team science*. National Academies Press.

Damschroder, L. J., Aron, D. C., Keith, R. E., Kirsh, S. R., Alexander, J. A., & Lowery, J. C. (2009). Fostering implementation of health services research findings into practice: a consolidated framework for advancing implementation science. *Implementation Science, 4*(1), 50. https://doi.org/10.1186/1748-5908-4-50.

Etheredge, L. M. (2007). A rapid-learning health system. *Health Affairs (Millwood), 26*(2), w107–w118. https://doi.org/10.1377/hlthaff.26.2.w107

Forrest, C. B., Chesley, F. D., Jr., Tregear, M. L., & Mistry, K. B. (2018, August). Development of the learning health system researcher core competencies. *Health Services Research, 53*(4), 2615–2632. https://doi.org/10.1111/1475-6773.12751. Epub 2017 August 4. PMID: 28777456; PMCID: PMC6051975.

Guise, J. M., et al. (2017). 2017 Organizational and training factors that promote team science: A qualitative analysis and application of theory to the National Institutes of Health's BIRCWH career development program. *Journal of Clinical and Translational Science, 1*(2), 101–107.

Koenig, K., & Schultz, C. (Eds.). (2016). *Disaster medicine: Comprehensive principles and practice* (2nd ed.). Cambridge University Press.

McEntire, D. (Ed.). (2006, Spring). *Disciplines, disasters and emergency management: The convergence and divergence of concepts, issues and trends from the research literature* (Electronic Textbook). Federal Emergency Management Agency, Emergency Management Institute.

Moore, L. D., Robbins, G., Quinn, J., & Arbogast, J. W. (2020). The impact of COVID-19 pandemic on hand hygiene performance in hospitals. *American Journal of Infection Control.* S0196-6553(20)30805-1. https://doi.org/10.1016/j.ajic.2020.08.021

Ohrling, M., Øvretveit, J., & Brommels, M. (2020a). Can management decentralisation resolve challenges faced by healthcare service delivery organisations? Findings for managers and researchers from a scoping review. *International Journal of Health Planning and Management*. https://doi.org/10.1002/hpm.3058.

Ohrling, M., Øvretveit, J., Lockowandt, U., Brommels, M., & Sparring, V. (2020b). Management of emergency response to SARS COV-2 outbreak in Stockholm and winter preparations. *Journal of Primary Healthcare, 12*(3), 207–214. https://doi.org/10.1071/HC20082

Øvretveit, J. (2001). Organisational behaviour research in health care: An overview. In L. Ashburner (Ed.), *Organisational behaviour and organisation studies in health care: Reflections on the future* (Chapter 1, p. 9). Palgrave Macmillan.

Øvretveit, J., Hempel, S., Magnabosco, J., Mittman, B., Rubenstein, L., & Ganz, D. (2014). Guidance for research-practice partnerships (R-PPs) and collaborative research. *Journal of Health Organisation and Management, 28*(1), 115–126.

Rubenstein, L., Meredith, L., Parker, P., Gordon, N., Hickey, S., Oken, K., & Lee, M. (2006). Impacts of evidence-based quality improvement on depression in primary care: A randomized experiment. *Journal of General Internal Medicine, 21*, 1027–1035. https://doi.org/10.1111/j.1525-1497.2006.00549.x

Rubenstein, L. V., Stockdale, S. E., Sapir, N., et al. (2014). A patient-centered primary care practice approach using evidence-based quality improvement: Rationale, methods, and early assessment of implementation. *Journal of General Internal Medicine, 29*, 589–597. https://doi.org/10.1007/s11606-013-2703-y

Ryan, R., Hill, S., Broclain, D., Horey, D., Oliver, S., & Prictor, M. (2013, June). *Cochrane consumers and communication review group*. Study Design Guide. http://cccrg.cochrane.org/author-resources. Accessed 5 October 2020.

Stokols, D., et al. (2008). The science of team science: Overview of the field and introduction to the supplement. *American Journal of Preventive Medicine, 35*(2), S77–S89.

VanDeusen Lukas, C., Engle, R., Holmes, S., Parker, V., Petzel, R., Nealon-Seibert, R., Shwartz, M., & Sullivan, J. (2010). Strengthening organizations to implement evidence-based clinical practices. *Health Care Manage Review, 35*(3), 235-245.

CHAPTER 15

Will the "New" Become the "Normal"? Exploring Sustainability of Rapid Health System Transformations

Carolyn Steele Gray, G. Ross Baker, Mylaine Breton, Karin Kee, Mirella Minkman, James Shaw, Maike V. Tietschert, Paul Wankah, Walter P. Wodchis, Nick Zonneveld, and Henk Nies

Introduction

Health, social, and community care agencies are undergoing rapid changes in response to the COVID-19 pandemic. Arguably we are facing a "window of opportunity" in which "there is a heightened probability that efforts to alter a system state will be more likely to succeed"

C. Steele Gray (✉)
Bridgepoint Collaboratory for Research and Innovation, Lunenfeld-Tanenbaum Research Institute, Toronto, ON, Canada
e-mail: Carolyn.SteeleGray@sinaihealth.ca

C. Steele Gray · G. R. Baker · J. Shaw · W. P. Wodchis
Institute of Health Policy, Management and Evaluation, University of Toronto, Toronto, ON, Canada

J. Waring et al. (eds.), *Organising Care in a Time of Covid-19*, Organizational Behaviour in Healthcare,
https://doi.org/10.1007/978-3-030-82696-3_15

(Brundiers & Eakin, 2018: 2). These "windows" occur because disasters can disrupt or destroy institutions and infrastructure while revealing political processes that can more easily become subject for review by the public and social actors (Brundiers & Eakin, 2018). For national, regional, or network-based health systems that have struggled for years to carry out major transformations, this window could heighten system readiness for innovation, one of several components that drives health system transformation (Greenhalgh et al., 2004). However, some disaster literature cautions that in time pressured environments the emphasis is often on short-term needs, rather than longer-term goals (Brundiers, 2018), which can have lasting long-term institutional impacts (Olshansky et al., 2012). In addition, a major crisis like the pandemic creates economic and social disruptions which can limit the ability of systems to respond effectively. Thus, despite efforts of systems to respond rapidly and secure needed change, questions remain regarding how these changes will impact the trajectory of healthcare systems transformation over the long term.

Answering these questions requires theoretical guidance, derived from theories and studies that have explored and explained sustainability of health system transformation alongside those that seek to understand transformation in the context of a local or worldwide disaster. In this chapter, we propose a theoretical framework that brings together theories from the disaster response and sustainability literatures to propose a way to explore the long-term impact of rapid health system changes related to COVID-19. This framework is applied to three case examples from three different jurisdictions to offer preliminary content validation and suggest how the framework could guide future inquiry.

The presented theoretical framework links work focusing on understanding sustainable innovation in health care with core concepts from relevant disaster response theories. The synthesized framework is designed to inform inquiry that assesses *whether rapid changesmade in response to*

M. Breton
Faculty of Medicine and Health Science, University of Sherbrooke, Sherbrooke, QC, Canada

K. Kee · M. V. Tietschert
Vrije Universiteit Amsterdam, Amsterdam, The Netherlands

M. Minkman · N. Zonneveld
TIAS Business School, Tilburg University, Tilburg, The Netherlands

health system shocks are likely to be sustained and help to transform systems of care over the longer term. Responses to COVID-19 in three jurisdictions are used to explore the utility of the framework to inform research and practice.

We engaged in a single phenomenon approach to theory integration, in which two theoretical perspectives exploring a common dependent variable (in this case sustainability) are brought together to better understand the concepts that influence that variable (Mayer & Sparrowe, 2013). The Dynamic Sustainability Framework (DSF) was used as the starting point as it has been widely applied in studies exploring the driving mechanisms behind sustainability of health system change across a variety of contexts. Relevant disaster response literature was purposively selected to identify frameworks and studies that: (1) adopt a complexity science lens like the DSF; and (2) have been applied to healthcare contexts. This was not an exhaustive search of this literature but rather a focused inquiry into how components of the DSF may need to be modified when being applied to a disaster response environment, like the COVID-19 pandemic. Tables that demonstrate where theories converge and diverge were generated, discussed, and agreed upon by co-authors. Concepts that were deemed similar were combined, and relationships between concepts were discussed considering the theoretical frameworks. A sub-group of the author team next worked to iteratively generate a visual representation of all relevant theorized constructs and connections. The visual framework was presented to the larger team for review and refinement.

As a preliminary test of the framework, we applied it to three cases, presented here as short case reports overviewing rapid changes occurring in response to COVID-19. Reports come from three jurisdictions across two countries, one case in The Netherlands and two cases in Canada (Ontario and Quebec) where there have been ongoing efforts to improve

P. Wankah
Department of Gerontology, University of Sherbrooke, Sherbrooke, QC, Canada

H. Nies
Vilans, Utrecht, The Netherlands

J. Shaw
Department of Physical Therapy, University of Toronto, Toronto, ON, Canada

health system delivery prior to the pandemic. Co-authors on this paper have been studying models of care in these jurisdictions for many years and drew on their research and knowledge of their jurisdictions to identify relevant cases to fit this purpose. Case examples were thus selected purposively (supporting exploration of multiple components of the framework), and with an aim to vary to types of responses being explored. Each case offers examples of responses that act upon different levels of the health system thus demonstrating the utility of the framework for macro-, meso-, and micro-level transformations. The Netherlands case focuses on changes occurring at the national level (macro-level example), the Quebec case focuses on a particular healthcare sector (long-term care, meso-level example), and finally, the Ontario case focuses on a particular care delivery model (virtual care delivery, micro-level example). Selection was also based on both criterion and convenience sampling, as these were cases fit our criteria for examples of innovation in a non-stable situation like the pandemic and were already well known to co-authors. As such, these cases were conducive to rapid exploration. Case reports are generated from publicly available information, informal key informant conversations, as well as ongoing case study research conducted by co-authors.

Theoretical Foundations

Sustainability in Health System Transformation

Studies and reviews exploring sustainability as an important component of health system transformation are increasingly prevalent in the health systems literature. Sustainability in health care can be viewed as a branch of the implementation process, defined as "what happens when an innovation becomes routinized within an organization or other setting" (Côté-Boileau et al., 2019: 6). Sustainability does not require a rigid adherence to a particular set of actions or activities. Instead, the innovation in question can (and arguably should) be continuously adapted and improved over time (Lennox, 2020). Côté-Boileau and colleagues published a scoping review of sustainability, scale, and spread in 2019 that suggests understanding what drives these processes requires attention to: (1) the innovation or change; (2) the processes through which it is adopted; (3) the people involved in that adoption; and (4) the context in which adoption occurs (Côté-Boileau et al., 2019). Importantly, this review found that context should be understood as being "an active social ingredient" in the sustainability of an innovation within a health system. The right context can enable alignment between an innovation and existing needs and capacities in societies, allowing key stakeholders to view the innovation as credible, valuable, and feasible. In other words, the right context can create a *window of opportunity* for change to occur.

Researchers have emphasized different components of sustainability, some focusing on the sustainability of specific activities or programs, employing an *intervention-focused* approach, and others taking a wider view to determine whether changes continue to move a system in a desired direction, adopting a *system-dynamic* approach. The latter approach is more applicable when dealing with complex interventions in complex systems, allowing for the identification of interrelated, shifting components occurring in systems as they move quickly to respond to a changing environment (Greenhalgh et al., 2012). The system-dynamic approach is similar to complex adaptive system-oriented approach, which suggests the need to recognize not just the components of the implementation or sustainability process, but also the relationships between those components (Braithwaite et al., 2018). The value of applying this type of complexity, or dynamic, lens to understand and drive system transformation has been supported by the Institute of Medicine (2001) as well as in the broader literature on health system transformation (Best et al., 2012).

Several frameworks that have adopted this system-dynamic view of sustainability are available, including the Dynamic Sustainability Framework (DSF) (Braithwaite et al., 2018; Chambers et al., 2013; Lennox, 2020). The DSF attends to the components of sustainability identified in the literature (Lennox, 2020) as well as in the Côté-Boileau scoping review (Côté-Boileau et al., 2019), and emphasizes a process-oriented view in which "sustainability is the process of managing and supporting the evolution of an intervention within a changing context" (Chambers et al., 2013: 8). Core to this framework is that an intervention needs to "fit" to the practice setting and environment in which it is placed, and that fit will need to adapt over time as individuals, teams, organizations, and systems evolve. The DSF includes seven tenets that suggests what characteristics of interventions, settings, and environments are likely to enable fit, and thus sustainability, of the intervention over time, for example that interventions require ongoing optimization and organizations require a continuous learning ethos. Studies exploring sustainability of evidence-based initiatives have demonstrated the importance of adaptation, and the ongoing organizational learning required to support that adaptation (Fleiszer et al., 2015). Adopting a dynamic approach that attends to multiple components has also been argued to be important to studying sustainability of whole-system change efforts (Greenhalgh et al., 2012).

Lessons from Disaster Response Research

While the DSF offers a useful framework to explore sustainability of healthcare systems changes, it is clear responses to the COVID-19 shock to the health system are developing rapidly to meet urgent needs. This unstable environment could challenge two assumptions of the DSF. First, that ongoing measurement across domains can be used to ensure fit between an intervention, the organization, and wider ecological system. During COVID it has been argued that what data is relevant to collect, for whom, at what time and for what purpose is not always clear, and often these data may be difficult, or impossible, to collect (Austin & Kachalia, 2020). Second, the DSF does not assign a weight to any level of fit, meaning fit of an intervention to an organization may be just as important as fit to an ecological system. However, political drivers may overrun other considerations and drive change decisions, as has been argued to be the case during the COVID pandemic (Pulejo & Querubín, 2020). Disaster response literature offers insights that help in understanding sustainability in this more volatile context improving the application of the DSF framework.

The *Post-Disasters Windows of Opportunities Framework* (Brundiers & Eakin, 2018) is an analytic framework developed to facilitate the documentation and analysis of case studies of sustainability transitions following disasters. Like DSF, this framework rests on the assumption that change occurs with a complex adaptive system and focuses on organizational and system level change as the unit of analysis. Both frameworks also suggest adaptation, continuous learning, and enabling mechanisms (e.g., change agents, aligned incentives) are necessary for sustained change. For example, Quarshie and Leuschner (2018) argue that natural disasters can catalyze change when continuous learning processes are adopted; activating social mechanisms for actors, organizations, and institutions over time.

The Windows of Opportunity framework suggests that disasters create the conditions, input and resources that open a window of opportunity needed to catalyze change; identifying three unique phases as part of this change process:

1. *The pre-disaster context*: Environmental and organizational contexts (including policies and activities) that relate to the change event of interest.
2. *The period of disaster*: Includes changes triggered by the disaster that impact all dimensions of society (environment, health, social, economic), through formal and informal mechanisms. In this period change agents (key actors and networks) can capitalize on windows of opportunity to mobilize change.
3. *The post-disaster period*: Stabilization of changes occurs within a new system, including stabilized changes to operational and strategic activities, as well as organizational structure and culture.

The Rapid and Sustainable Transformation (RAST) Framework for Health Systems

Figure 15.1 offers a visual representation of the proposed Rapid and Sustainable Transformation (or RAST) framework that builds on the elements presented in the theoretical foundations section. The framework identifies components in the pre-disaster and during-disaster contexts that can drive change within a system. As suggested by the theoretical foundations influencing this model, mechanisms that enable continuous adaptation are identified as likely drivers of sustainable change. Note we include an "other" category as we anticipate additional mechanisms could be identified through testing the framework. While chronological time is depicted across the bottom of the framework, we recognize that interventions, responses, and subsequent events can occur at varying paces depicted by the curved arrows that change shape and size over time. We do not include the post-disaster context in this version as we are far from a post COVID-19 world and, as such, cannot explore this phase of transformation empirically. Future work should include attention to recovery and resilience processes (see Norris et al., 2008; Sword-Daniels et al., 2016) as part of a fulsome longitudinal analysis. Each component of the framework is defined (with identified sources) in Table 15.1.

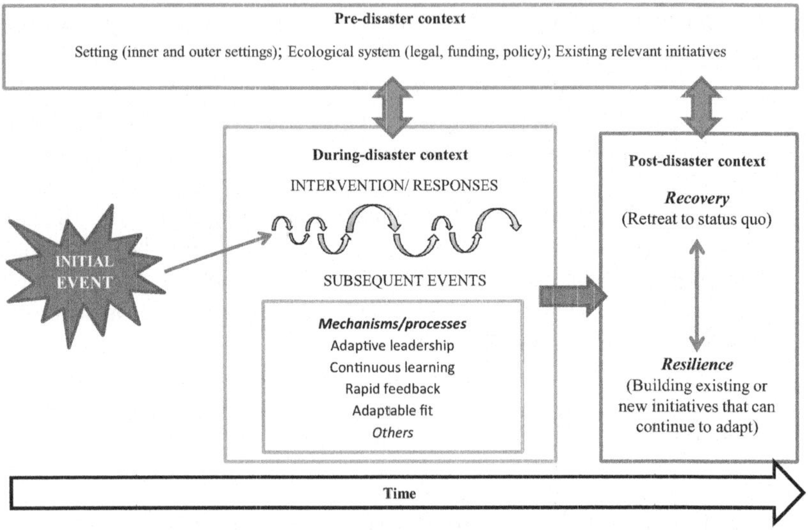

Fig. 15.1 Generic RAST

Case Reports

The intention of the case reports is to demonstrate the feasibility and applicability of applying RAST to help understand rapid changes occurring in the context of a pandemic and provide initial assessment of content and face validity of the model. Table 15.2 offers a summary of each of the three cases, aligning components of the case to constructs of the RAST framework. The case reports in Table 15.2 offer more detailed discussion, with an emphasis on the nature of the responses and supportive conditions.

Interplay Between Centralization and Decentralization: Awakening "Slumbering" Structures in The Netherlands

This case report overviews the national level policy responses to the COVID-19 pandemic in The Netherlands, emphasizing the interplay between a centralized response and regional adaptation of that response. The case represents an exploration of macro-level change.

Table 15.1 RAST concept definitions [REVISED]

Concept	*Definition*
PRE-DISASTER CONTEXT[a]	Policies and activities related to the change event of interest. For operational clarity this is defined as the context before regions began rolling out COVID-19 related policies and regulations, and before the first "state of emergency" in relation to COVID-19 was declared
Setting (inner and outer)[b,c]	Human and capital resources, organizational culture, climate and structure, process for training and supervision
Ecological system[b]	Consists of multiple practice settings influencing those working around the intervention in question, legislative and regulatory environment, local, regional and national level markets, and characteristics of the population
Existing care initiatives	New or ongoing initiatives intended to move a network or region toward health system transformation
INITIAL EVENT	When regions began responding to COVID-19 or first declared "state of emergency," triggering the first wave of significant intervention and change
DURING-DISASTER CONTEXT[a]	Policies and activities related to the change event after its initial occurrence. Includes changes triggered by disaster affecting all dimensions of society (environments, social, economic), through both formal and informal mechanisms
Intervention/response[b,c]	Includes components that are expected to affect behavior or change, to be delivered by a specified individuals who have a set of characteristics (e.g., practitioners), which is supposed to lead to a particular set of outcomes, through a delivery platform (e.g., clinic visits, virtual care, health apps, etc.)

(continued)

Table 15.1 (continued)

Concept	*Definition*
	Characteristics of the innovation/response—requires balancing fidelity to the initial objective of the intervention and adaptability to meet local contextual needs Types of responses[d]: Response actions for risk reduction; resources and services; policies; training; relocation and structural
Supportive conditions[b,c] (mechanisms to drive sustainability)	Conditions that enable the intervention to become sustained over time ***Support conditions:*** (1) Adaptable innovation (perceived value of innovation); (2) distributed leadership; (3) reciprocal accountability; (4) absorptive context; (5) iterative timing and pace of change; (6) empowering management support; (7) decentralized governance ***Seven tenets of DSF*** 1. Interventions require ongoing optimization, enabled through adopting quality improvement approaches 2. Through continuous improvement, ongoing learning by all stakeholders (developers, interventionists, researchers, patients) can be achieved 3. Ongoing feedback (measurement) should be practical and relevant 4. Effectiveness can be maintained (and improved) through each subsequent iteration 5. Strong fit is necessary, but "fit" likely changes over time due to changes in how interventions are delivered, characteristics of patients, providers and settings, and the broader environment 6. Organizational learning must be a core value to support continuous adaptation 7. Ongoing stakeholder involvement is necessary to maintain fit over time

(continued)

Table 15.1 (continued)

Concept	*Definition*
Subsequent event(s)	Other events related (or un-related) to the pandemic may trigger additional interventions/responses throughout the process (e.g., BLM movement, union strikes in QC)

[a]Brundiers and Eakin (2018), [b]Chambers et al. (2013), [c]Côté-Boileau et al. (2019), [d]Sword-Daniels et al. (2016)

Pre-COVID-19 Context

The Dutch healthcare system is organized as a regulated competitive market. Different sectors and services are governed by specific legislation, including the Social Support Act (support at home, day activities, temporary respite), the Health Insurance Act (GP care, hospital care, rehabilitation, medication), and the Long-term care Act (nursing home care, care for people with disabilities, long lasting 24/7 care). The national government is responsible for ensuring population health, through frameworks for care provision. The Ministry of Health, Welfare and Sport holds primary responsibility for health and health care, but increasingly that responsibility is centralized to local authorities Korneman et al. (2016). The Ministry acts through intermediate bodies such as local authorities, Health Care Insurers, National Health Authorities, Inspectorates, and research institutes such as the National Institute for Public Health and the Environment (NIPHE). Research institutes provide regular reports on the health of the population and state of healthcare systems and services to the central government. The vast majority of health and social care providers are private not-for-profit organizations working based on mostly yearly contract with healthcare insurers or with municipalities and professionals, clients, and insurers who are organized in national umbrella organizations. There are many different stakeholders and actors who attempt to influence the health system, and the government receives expert advice from advisory bodies and research institutes.

Table 15.2 International case examples describe using the RAST Framework

RAST framework concept	*The Netherlands case*	*Québec case*	*Ontario case*
PRE-DISASTER CONTEXT			
Ecological system	The national government holds "system responsibility," acting through intermediary bodies to deliver health and social care services. In this way, The Netherlands follows both a bottom-up and top-down approach to health system transformation, in which intermediaries, which include Advisory Boards and research institutes provide scientific, societal, or funding advice to support evidence prior to establishing policies	The healthcare system in Québec is structured on 34 health organizations across the province. The governance is based on a top-down approach, in which government bodies (in particular the Ministry of Health and Social Services) provides central guidance for how policies are implemented and funded. Long-term care is regulated by the provincial Ministry of Health and Social services who regularly inspects these organizations	The governance and delivery of healthcare services in Ontario is largely a bottom-up approach, in which government bodies like the Ministry of Health set a general agenda but allow organizations to determine how best to meet the objectives of that agenda. With regard to virtual care, prior to COVID-19 there had not been a strong central mandate for adoption of virtual care, as such most existing policies and regulatory frameworks were in place to address data privacy and security needs, with very limited funding and infrastructure in place to enable organizations to adopt virtual visits

RAST framework concept	*The Netherlands case*	*Québec case*	*Ontario case*
Setting (inner and outer)	Health and social care services are delivered by largely private not-for-profit organizations. Professionals, clients, and insurers are organized under umbrella organizations. Labor market shortages are a serious concern and are occasionally a reason for temporarily shutting down services	Long-term care services are delivered through public and privately-owned organizations that have mixed funding models. Most of these organizations operate under tight budgets and often experience staffing shortages	As of early 2020, few healthcare providers and organizations were delivering much care virtually. Key stakeholders, including professional associations, identified a lack of supports and resources to support virtual care
Existing relevant care initiatives	The Netherlands has established 25 regional networks, notably "Safety Regions," already established to mobilize multiple actors in response to large disasters and crises. Moreover, there are 11 acute care networks in order to organize timely and appropriate admission of patients according to the existing quality standards	Health system reforms put in place in 2015 exacerbated staffing challenges in Long-term Care centers, creating instability in available of staff and structure of teams	Initiatives were underway to update privacy legislation, introduce funding for virtual visits, and provide supportive technologies in response to professional association's call for reform. Government agencies were leading this work in collaboration with the Ontario Telemedicine Network

(continued)

Table 15.2 (continued)

RAST framework concept	*The Netherlands case*	*Québec case*	*Ontario case*
INITIAL EVENT	The COVID-19 pandemic prompted a response from the national government to fight the pandemic beginning in March 2020. Numerous non-urgent health and long-term care services were scaled down or closed. Moreover, non-acute patients were initially reluctant to use the existing services	Due to a delayed response from the government, the COVID-19 pandemic disproportionately impacted on long-term care homes requiring targeted strategies	The COVID-19 pandemic resulted in the closing of all but essential healthcare services in mid-March 2020 making virtual visits a more urgent option for those seeking care
DURING DISASTER CONTEXT			
Intervention/responses	Central leaders, including the Prime Minister, King, and Ministers from other policy domains, quickly took leadership to develop a central response strategy. Responses included policies, resources, and services to mitigate spread and meet needs of those infected with COVID-19. Much of the strategy enabled existing networks to mobilize and meet needs more effectively as partners. In particular the acute care networks were extended by long-term care services. In some regions non-acute care networks were established	Due to the severe COVID-19 outbreak in Long-term care homes, many staff had to undergo 14 day quarantine, exacerbating the existing staffing shortage. The government engaged in a policy and resource response by: 1. Mobilizing frontline providers from other sectors to move to long-term care facilities 2. Developing a fast-track hiring and training program for 10,000 orderlies	Ontario's responses to provide greater access to virtual care were largely through new regulations and funding allocation. These responses included: 1. Release of temporary virtual care billing codes for physicians 2. Passing of new legislation to amend laws regarding collection and sharing of personal health information that enabled more virtual care delivery

RAST framework concept	*The Netherlands case*	*Québec case*	*Ontario case*
Supportive conditions (mechanisms that could drive sustainability)	The Netherlands embraced ***adaptive leadership*** approaches which enabled continues iterative changes to the strategy, which involves many stakeholders from across health and social care organizations and Ministries. The nation also used ***continuous learning*** in which data was continuously collected and experts were consulted to adapt the strategy	Responses in Quebec were largely centralized and targeted to meet this specific need. However, government and senior executives did engaged in some ***adaptable innovation*** work to develop creative solutions to the emerging and rapid problem	The Ontario approach enabled ***adaptable innovation*** as healthcare organizations were given permission to experiment with different platforms and approaches to see what best fit their needs and local contexts
Subsequent event(s)	After a national evaluation with some 100 experts the strategies were adjusted: more local/regional testing, targeted responses and strategies. Regional and local dashboards, more test capacity and supply of protective means. Also attention for societal persistence as well as sustaining in the healthcare sector. Thirdly, to provide perspectives for people with long-standing needs		Later in June 2020, the province established the Ontario Health Data platform to enable information sharing across organizations to support planning and delivery of care for COVID-19 patients
POTENTIAL IMPLICATIONS			

(continued)

Table 15.2 (continued)

RAST framework concept	*The Netherlands case*	*Québec case*	*Ontario case*
Potential implications of the during disaster activities	The adaptive response informed by continuous feedback in the Dutch system suggests that changes being made are more likely to fit local needs. Responses aligned with several support conditions and tenets of the DSF including: adaptable innovation and continuous learning to support ongoing optimization. According to the DSF this approach can create a supportive condition for ongoing sustainability of the new partnerships. Decision-making was also challenged by key values (such as cost containment and market-mechanisms) that have driven the Dutch system since before the pandemic. Alignment to normative foundations such as solidarity among the population, equality in quality of care, and access to all citizens may also support longer-term sustainability of changes	While the fast-tracked hiring process put in place could constitute an adaptable innovation to address a longer-term issue of staffing, this targeted response may not be sustainable given ongoing funding challenges. Specifically, the remuneration and financial incentives put in place for new staff may create conflict between different providers. There are additional ongoing legislative barriers and poor working conditions that can lead to continued staffing challenges in Quebec	In Ontario many of the changes seem to be largely centralized. While this could impede sustainability of changes, the low rules environment of these changes allows for organizations to adapt them to their local needs. The creation of new supportive infrastructures that were previously identified as barriers (such as funding models) could lead to sustained change should these continue to be supported. However, it remains to be seen whether providers will continue to want to work with patients remotely

During-COVID-19 Context: Policy, Resource and Services Responses Through Adaptive Leadership and Continuous Learning

The Dutch response to COVID-19 was characterized by ***system level and adaptive leadership*** that initiated multiple types of responses (in policies, resources, services, and other areas) with the national government taking a central role in organizing the "fight" against the pandemic. System leadership was executed in a joint effort between the Dutch national government, the national Outbreak Management Team (OMT) and regional network organizations. The Prime Minister (PM) led all communication on relevant policy measures. From March to June 2020, 34 press conferences were held, in which the PM appeared 31 times, alongside one or two other healthcare ministers. Depending on the policy decision, the PM was also joined by ministers of different departments, such as the Minister of Education after schools were closed.

As time progressed, leadership became more distributed and expertise based. The Minister of Health actively invested in ***continuous learning*** by analyzing lessons learned from the crisis with multidisciplinary experts. Ministers from other policy domains partook in press conferences and drafted White Papers for Parliament on how the COVID-19 crisis affected their fields, including economic affairs, social security, and culture. The content of white papers and press conferences gradually changed from updates on the current state of the health system to measures that were being taken to address societal consequences. Traditional differences between political parties blurred and became permeable. For example, when the Minister of Medical Affairs collapsed while addressing Parliament, he was replaced by an interim Minister from an opposing political party. The expertise of OMT members was also expanded from virology and epidemiology to economy, family medicine, microbiology, and other areas of expertise. These actions prompted greater intersectoral integration.

The adoption of an adaptive leadership approach resulted in continuous changes in the composition of responsible institutes, organizations, experts, and policies made. Various temporary regulations were issued addressing, for example, the need for isolation and quarantine. Initially, these measures were guided predominantly by scientific evidence and recommendations made by the OMT, led by the director of the NIPHE.

As part of this adaptive strategy, pre-existing "slumbering" structures were activated to iteratively address challenges. For example, when the number of patients in need for intensive care increased rapidly between

March and May 2020, existing Regional Acute Care Networks were positioned to allocate patients, protective resources, and staff in regions and across the country, adding COVID-19 care to their acute care portfolio. The networks organized services across national boundaries, supported by representatives of rehabilitation centers, nursing homes, among others, who were added to these networks. Assisted by regional public health authorities, directors of the 25 "Safety Regions" (networks of municipalities installed for disaster management) led public efforts at the regional and local level and collected population level data to inform an "intelligent" lock down. However, the functioning of these regional networks differed in their responsiveness and effectiveness and the need for more central coordination resulted in development of a national coordination center.

Multidisciplinary Team Challenges in Long-Term Care in Quebec, Canada

The COVID-19 crisis in Québec was particularly felt in the delivery of multidisciplinary care for older adults in long-term care (LTC) facilities. In fact, 75% of reported mortality due to COVID-19 in Québec occurred in LTC facilities (Coulibaly & Fortin, 2020). This case report offers a meso-level exploration, examining governance challenges in the organization and delivery of inter-professional care in LTC facilities of Québec.

Pre-COVID-19 Context

In Québec, the responsibility of governing and funding health service delivery falls to the Ministry of Health and Social Services. Delivery is managed through regional bodies responsible for delivery of different types of services. Generally, the province has taken a top-down approach to health system delivery and reform with strongly centralized decision-making. In LTC, there are several ownership and funding models. Publicly funded and governed LTC facilities (*Centres d'Hébergement de Soins de Longue Durée*—CHSLD) are embedded in larger governance structures called Integrated Health and Social Service Centres (IHSSC) (Wankah et al., 2018) created through vertical mergers with hospitals, local community health centers, and rehabilitation centers. CHSLDs employ a broad range of health and social care providers such as physicians, nurses, social workers, occupational therapists, physiotherapists, and orderlies. Privately owned LTC facilities are entrepreneurship initiatives with mixed funding from government and direct contributions from patients. Private facilities employ a similar range of health and social care providers as public facilities. Both public and private LTC facilities must adhere to provincial regulations for care and are regularly inspected by their regional health authorities and the Ministry of Health and Social Services. In Québec, as of March 31, 2018, around 33,500 people aged 65 and above were living in public or private LTC.

Like all healthcare organizations, LTC facilities in Québec have been operating on tight budgets and limited staff for the past two decades. Gagnon et al. (2017) reported staff shortages, high turnover of staff and reliance on private staffing agencies as problematic issues in delivering multidisciplinary care in LTC. This challenging organizational setting has meant physicians, nurses, and orderlies often face difficult situations. For example, the recent 2015 health system reforms prevented family physicians from enrolling LTC patients in their patient panels, leading to their growing disinterest in practicing in LTC homes. Nurses working in LTC often had huge patient loads leading to burnout and orderlies experienced poor working conditions (Da Silva, 2020). These factors have contributed to instability in inter-professional LTC teams in Québec.

During-COVID-19 Context: Rapid Human Resource Policy and Funding Changes to Address Workforce Shortages in Long-Term Care

Initially, the Québec government delayed announcing strict measures to control the spread of COVID-19 in LTC homes. Although visits to nursing homes were restricted on March 14, 2020, residents of these homes were still allowed to visit their families in the community (Da Silva, 2020). Furthermore, LTC staff often worked in several facilities. These conditions may have contributed to a massive spread of the infection among this vulnerable population with dramatic consequences. On May 18th, at the first peak of the epidemic, Québec was reporting 1,091 active cases across 180 facilities, affecting nearly half of the publicly funded LTC homes (Shingler & Montpetit, 2020). As of mid-June 2020, 3,642 of 5,300 of COVID-related deaths occurred in LTC (Luft, 2020). In addition, the COVID-19 crisis exerted extra pressure on the already strained LTC workforce. Nurses and orderlies who were exposed to the infection were quarantined for 14 days, and other frontline personnel did not report to work to avoid infection, leading to an acute workforce shortage.

The government reacted to this shortage largely through new human resource policies and additional funding. The first stage of disaster response consisted of mobilizing frontline providers from different sectors (hospitals, rehabilitation centers, etc.) to work in LTC homes along with external support from the military and the Red Cross. Second, a medium to long-term strategy included fast-track hiring and training program for 10,000 orderlies across the province to support LTC facilities. The government provided very attractive financial incentives to recruit persons onto LTC staff. More than 60,000 people had applied to the fast track for orderlies program at the time of writing. These responses were largely centralized to quickly meet a specific need. Arguably, the novel nature of this response represents an ***adaptable innovation***, that required ongoing iteration and tailoring to meet local needs. However, the new program raised several additional challenges concerning remuneration and financial incentives for other types of health system providers. Moreover, system leaders may have to improve work conditions so LTC facilities are more attractive working environments for all providers in these facilities. And government still needs to address the legislative barriers to the enrollment of LTC patients in the panels of family physicians and improve the working conditions of nurses and orderlies.

Rapid Virtualization of Care in Ontario, Canada

In Ontario, adoption of virtual care delivery remained limited in early 2020, with only 10% of care delivered virtually in the province prior to the COVID-19 pandemic (Bryski, 2020). This case report takes a micro (or service)-level focus, exploring how Ontario responded to healthcare access service needs though broader adoption of virtual care services.

Pre-COVID-19 Context

The Ontario Ministry of Health (previously the Ministry of Health and Long-term Care) holds responsibility for leadership and strategic planning of healthcare service delivery. Similar to The Netherlands and Québec examples, local delivery, planning, and funding are managed on a regional basis. In general, the government has taken a bottom-up approach to transformation, in which the central government sets high-level strategic aims, but allows local regions and organizations to determine how best to achieve those aims consistent with provincial legislation and policy.

Virtual care delivery in Ontario has been a challenge for some time. The College of Physicians and Surgeons of Ontario had established expectations for clinicians delivering virtual care or telemedicine in 2007 (updated 2014) suggesting a move in this direction (Council, 2014). However, just prior to the COVID-19 pandemic, it was generally acknowledged that Ontario lagged behind other jurisdictions, in particular the United States, in terms of delivery of virtual care (Women's College Hospital Institute for Health Systems Solutions and Virtual Care [WHIV], 2019). Recognizing this shortcoming, the Canadian Medical Association, a national organization representing physicians, released a white paper identifying 3 barriers to virtual care adoption: (1) insufficient payment mechanisms to compensate physicians for virtual care visits; (2) varying licensure requirements for delivering care virtually; and (3) lack of interoperability between systems and related issues around privacy and security of personal health information (Canadian Medical Association, 2019). Despite these barriers, some organizations had adopted virtual care practices more widely to improve access and coordination of care delivery. For example, some team-based primary care practices used virtual home visits with homebound patients to deliver both one-on-one and team-based care (Steele Gray et al., 2018).

While these examples were the exceptions rather than the norm, there were some efforts to address barriers to adoption underway before the COVID-19 pandemic hit. Notably the Ontario Ministry of Health established a Virtual Care Program, which, among other things, had been working with the government and Ontario Medical Association to address barriers by establishing compensation schedules (Ontario Ministry of Health Claims Services Branch, 2019). There were also efforts to update the Personal Health Information Protection Act, 2004 (PHIPA), the legislation responsible for protecting the collection and sharing of personal health information.

During-COVID-19 Context: Rapid Regulatory and Funding Changes

In Ontario, the COVID-19 epidemic led to the closing of all but essential healthcare services in mid-March 2020. Two rapid and fairly major regulatory and funding shifts occurred which drastically accelerated virtual care becoming a "mainstream delivery channel for healthcare services" (Ontario Telemedicine Network, 2020a). The first shift occurred on

March 19th, and then on March 21, 2020 with the release of temporary billing codes to allow physicians to be compensated for providing routine care via telephone or video conferencing (Ontairo Ministry of Health, 2020). Billing for virtual care became possible using either the Ministry approved Ontario Telemedicine Network (OTN) platform (the only method previously allowed), *or* any other non-approved solutions. OTN then offered a series of recommendations on how organizations could select appropriate platforms, considering such aspects as image quality, privacy and security, clinical workflow, and available technical support. Organizations and clinicians were thus set free to experiment with whichever platform best suited their needs, a flexibility that had not been available prior to COVID-19.

The second shift occurred on March 25, 2020, with the passing of an Omnibus Bill (Bill 188, 2020), which included a number of amendments to existing legislation including to the PHIPA as well as the Freedom of Information and Protection of Privacy Act. With regard to PHIPA, over a dozen sections were amended, expanding the ability to link data across platforms (through loosening of rules around collecting and storing of patient health numbers), allowing individuals to access their personal health information electronically. While the Bill includes loosening of some rules, there was some additional restrictions put in place, requiring vendors to adhere more strongly to PHIPA. These protections allowed for more vendors to enter this market so long as they can demonstrate patient data is safe and secure.

While legislative change is typically slow and inflexible, the Ontario virtual care case suggests rapid adaptation of policy and regulation is possible. For example, early in the process additional billing codes got added as they became needed, and organizations were encouraged to use any virtual platform available to them, with additional guidance provided as organizations learned about technology vulnerabilities (Ontario Telemedicine Network, 2020b). Creating an adaptable policy environment enabled some organizations to rapidly adopt and adapt this innovation to move a large portion of their care delivery to virtual access overnight. One example is St. Joseph's Healthcare in Hamilton, Ontario which responded to the LTC crisis, as well as the more fluid rules around adoption of virtual care platforms to offer virtual hospital visits to LTC residents (Hamilton Health Sciences, 2020; Pierson et al., 2020), quickly adopting the Pointclickcare platform to support bi-directional flow of information as patients transferred between sites (PointClikcCare, 2020).

While St. Joseph's was already working toward establishing improved digitally enabled care delivery prior to COVID-19 (St. Joseph's Healthcare Hamilton, 2020), they appeared to have adapted their strategy to align with the rapidly changing environment.

Discussion

The Netherlands, Québec, and Ontario cases all illustrate how in regulatory, policy and funding changes can address challenges occurring at macro-, meso-, and micro-levels. However, the pre-disaster environments and mechanisms used to enable those responses differed across the cases potentially influencing sustainability of these changes. In this discussion we compare environments and mechanisms across cases and offer a theoretically guided reflection on the implications for the sustainability of these changes over time.

The Pre-disaster Context: Setting the Stage

The three cases illustrate how the pre-disaster context can set the stage for the types of responses that decision-makers and other stakeholders in government and healthcare organizations will enact. The DSF suggests that we need to understand this context in order to assess how to "enable beneficial adaptation of the intervention and improve sustainability" (Chambers et al., 2013: 3). The examples presented support this contention, particularly in the Dutch and Ontario examples which have demonstrated that local tailoring of response was beneficial in meeting local needs. The ecological contexts of Ontario and The Netherlands set the stage for this local tailoring, as both jurisdictions have a history of a bottom-up or middle-out approaches to transformation. Québec, by contrast, has relied more on a top-down approach in which the Ministry of Health and Social Services provides more rigid guidelines for how policies are to be operationalized. In Ontario, having the freedom to select a virtual care platform that suited the needs of their providers and patients meant St. Joseph's could quickly implement changes that would fit their context. By contrast, in Québec, centralized planning for the fast-track hiring process could not attend to varying local challenges (such as working conditions within long-term care) which could reduce likely sustainability of that approach. The relatively rigid, centralized response may not be sustainable over time, as hospital personnel, the military, and Red Cross workers return to their respective duties.

The cases also demonstrate that local organizational contexts (the inner and outer setting) may also influence the types of responses selected. In disasters, key relevant contextual issues that influence responses can include previously established prevention and mitigations activities (Brundiers & Eakin, 2018). Our cases also demonstrate that existing health policies, funding models, and partnerships may influence how jurisdictions respond. In Québec, for example, the pre-COVID LTC setting played a crucial role in shaping how the province responded to the sudden and widespread outbreaks in these institutions. Notably, COVID-19 exposed the history of staffing shortages and little budget flexibility to address these needs, and these factors were thus the target of policy changes. While many regions around the world also experienced spikes in LTC, not all responses focused on a targeted human resource strategy (Hsu & Lane, 2020), suggesting the organizational setting may have driven the type of response selected. The Dutch case illustrates how pre-existing structures (the acute care networks) could be enlarged and accelerated to become a rapid response structure that operates at regional level. Previously established processes for central coordination could also be leveraged to support collaboration across regions and national borders.

The During-Disaster Context: Supportive Conditions for Sustainability

Across all cases, COVID-19 exposed existing gaps and problems that required greater attention. While each case adopted similar types of responses (regulation, policy, and funding) the ways in which they were operationalized creates different conditions that can either support or hinder sustainable change. Although the cases don't offer an exhaustive list of the types of processes, or change mechanisms, that are being adopted by healthcare systems globally to address COVID-19, they do illustrate some of the supportive conditions for sustainability (Côté-Boileau et al., 2019; Lennox, 2020).

In the Dutch case adaptive leadership approaches were leveraged as part of central and regional policy, regulatory, and funding responses. Furthermore, the Dutch PM worked with different Ministry leaders as new issues arose, a strategy that supported coordinated government responses as well as local adaptation. The inclusion of a continuous learning approach enabled a better fit between intervention and context, a factor suggested by the DSF to support ongoing sustainability. However, coordination occurred centrally on a national or regional level resulting in some challenges for tailoring this top-down approach to local contexts. According to RAST the continuous learning approaches that support ongoing adaption to improve the fit of policies to local contexts will facilitate sustained change.

The Ontario case similarly illustrates how flexibility in adopting innovation allows organizations to optimize their approaches to regulatory and funding changes. For example the shift toward virtual visits for LTC residents could be a change that will remain for the longer term. While it is still too early to assess whether these tactics are acting as mechanisms to enable sustainability of these interventions, the theory informing the RAST framework suggests that the strategies being adopted in the Dutch and Ontario example are promising.

The Québec case offers a centralized, or top-down, strategy in which government decision-makers acted quickly to deal with an acute problem. While the response was innovative in the way it addressed the emerging human resource shortage, this approach may lead to "secondary events" that will require further response. Specifically, the new incentives put in place for LTC staff alters the established broader sector compensation structure which may require further changes to address perceived inequities or lead to staff turnover for those who feel the changes are unjust. More broadly, the large number of deaths in the Québec LTC sector could also lead to important reforms in quality standards and governance, requiring further adjustment to the human resources strategy. These potential subsequent events or unintended consequences of the first response could occur rapidly or more slowly over time.

Implications for Sustainability

While some environmental disasters like a fire, flood, or earthquake may occur relatively quickly over a matter of days or weeks, often post-disaster contexts will last longer. For instance, the recovery process for the island of Montserrat in the West Indies following a volcanic eruption spanned a decade (Sword-Daniels et al., 2016). At this time of writing, the world remains a far distance from a "post-COVID" context, which requires that we start with examining the trajectories set by the responses and use theory to help predict where current changes may leave us when entering a post-disaster context down the road. Both the sustainability and disaster response theories discussed in the background section of this paper suggest that adaptability is a driver of sustainable change. Also important may be the use of multiple mechanisms as a means to reinforce sustainability. A 20-year retrospective study of the sustainability of the integrated health and social care model in Sweden demonstrated that multiple mechanisms identified in the DSF worked together to create a dynamic culture and structure that could continuously adapt to changing needs (Klinga et al., 2018). While actors in all three case examples presented here engaged in some level of rapid adaptation to a new or evolving need, the question remains whether there are enough embedded structural changes to maintain a dynamic and adaptive approach, as was the case in Sweden.

Another consideration not fully explored here is the role of shared values to drive sustainability. Decision-making often underpinned by certain values. For example, while cost containment is usually a dominant issue in the Dutch and Québec systems, it seemed to be less important during the first period of the COVID-19 crisis, especially in the early months. Later, it became an issue but often implicit when discussions about restarting usual care were not only health based but also had important consequences for the financial situation of healthcare organizations. Similarly, while Ontario had restricted the development of virtual care in part due to concerns about threats to privacy, these issues were downplayed in the changes to funding and privacy legislation. Although these values implicitly guided decision-making, they were not discussed explicitly, being systematically weighed against each other. For sustainability, examining the alignment between these types of normative foundations and the efforts of the many institutions and domains involved is crucial (Côté-Boileau et al., 2019). A broader perspective, addresses the ethical aspects and underlying values in policy decisions, would enrich our understanding of how norms and values informed change in each case.

Finally, while not captured in these case reports, it may be important to determine the influence of public responses to health system changes and reforms. Public emotions and attitudes have been shown in the policy literature to play an important role in the policymaking process. Weible et al. (2020) argue that during COVID-19, governments have appealed to public emotions such as trust, fear, and anxiety to legitimize policy choices. Also, the acceptance of the public to conform to measures by the government develops over time. Additionally, they suggest governments have used culturally relevant "charged language" to appeal to shared values like nationalism, pride, and shared responsibilities ("only together we can fight COVID-19") to frame and legitimize policy decisions.

Future Work

While it is too early to determine if the RAST framework presented here can explain or predict the sustainability of rapid system responses to COVID-19, our illustrative cases suggest the framework is able to identify key components that require attention when studying sustainability in rapid changing environments. The disaster response literature outlines how emergencies such as the pandemic create a window of opportunity that enables rapid changes to address pre-existing system shortcomings. Sustainability theory, specifically the DSF, helps us attend to the many components and iterative changes that are occurring in these complex systems. Importantly, the framework also aligns to identified "simple rules" of large system transformation, emphasizing the need to understand history and context, establishing rapid feedback to support iterative learning, and encouraging distributive leadership and engagement with key stakeholders like physicians, patients, and families (Best et al., 2012). A number of these rules are being applied in the presented cases, but time will tell whether these changes can be sustained.

This paper offers a theoretical contribution by bringing together selected health services and organizational behavior literatures on sustainability with the literature on disaster response. The RAST framework helps advance organizational research around health system transformation through the demonstration of how the components of sustainability are interrelated and how these components may be weighed differently. The framework highlights, in particular the importance of history (the pre-context) and time as crucial contexts. Applying this framework and asking ourselves "what didn't change", even in time sensitive environments, reveals system foundations that will take more time and targeted effort to shift in future system transformation. In the presented cases, for example, the traditional values of cost containment and centralized decision-making proved to be deeply anchored and shaped how the systems responded. The pandemic simply shook the dust from these histories and social norms; revealing them as deeply rooted guiding forces in these health systems.

The framework is not comprehensive nor based on a systematic review of the literature. Rather, targeted searches for systematic reviews and relevant frameworks and models that would apply to the aims of this project were used to identify key constructs. Thus, some important constructs may have been overlooked or could have received more attention, such as the public reactions, moral considerations, and conflicting views within each society. The brief case reports illustrate the proposed relationships between components of the framework and offer an early exploration of how rapid responses during a pandemic may, or may not, have lasting impact on systems. These cases were purposely selected, and we may have missed contradictory cases that would support modifications to the framework. Finally, not all potential supportive conditions or tenets of sustainability suggested in the DSF (as identified in Table 15.1) were represented in these cases, and future work would be required to determine whether these conditions or mechanisms occur in disaster responses.

To address these limitations, further tests of this proposed framework via prospective and retrospective case studies should follow a range of case examples across jurisdictions. This research can determine whether any constructs are missed, and to identify which mechanisms are enabling sustainable responses. The theoretical grounding of this work supports broad applications to guide explorations of health system shocks such as COVID-19 pandemic and health system responses. We present this framework as a beginning approach and encourage those working in complex health systems test this framework in their own jurisdictions, across a variety of forms of health system transformation.

References

Austin, J. M., & Kachalia, A. (2020). The state of health care quality measurement in the era of COVID-19: The importance of doing better. *JAMA, 324*(4), 333–334.

Best, A., et al. (2012). Large-system transformation in health care: A realist review. *Milbank Quarterly, 90*(3), 421–456.

Bill 188, Economic and Fiscal Update Act, 2020. (2020).

Braithwaite, J., et al. (2018). When complexity science meets implementation science: A theoretical and empirical analysis of systems change. *BMC Medicine, 16*(1), 63.

Brundiers, K. (2018). Disasters as opportunities for sustainability: the case of Christchurch, Aotearoa New Zealand. *Sustainability Science, 13*(4), 1075–1091.

Brundiers, K., & Eakin, H. (2018). Leveraging post-disaster windows of opportunities for change towards sustainability: A framework. *Sustainability, 10*, 1–5.

Bryski, K. (2020, August 18). *Virtual beats viral*. https://infoway-inforoute.ca/en/what-we-do/blog/access-to-care/8585-virtual-beats-viral

Canadian Medical Association. (2019). *Virtual care in Canada* (Discussion Paper). Canadian Medical Association, Ottawa, ON.

Chambers, D. A., Glasgow, R. E., & Stange, K. C. (2013). The dynamic sustainability framework: Addressing the paradox of sustainment amid ongoing change. *Implementation Science, 8*(1), 117.

Côté-Boileau, É., et al. (2019). The unpredictable journeys of spreading, sustaining and scaling healthcare innovations: A scoping review. *Health Research Policy and Systems, 17*(1), 84.

Council, C. (2014). *Telemedicine* (C.o.P.a.S.o, Ed.). Toronto, ON.

Coulibaly, S., & Fortin, B. (2020). *COVID-19 et maintien à domicile des aînés* (CIRANO Papers).

Da Silva, R.B. (2020, July 30). *Portrait des CHSLD et enjeux en contexte de pandémie*. https://policyoptions.irpp.org/magazines/april-2020/portrait-des-chsld-et-enjeux-en-contexte-de-pandemie/

Fleiszer, A. R., et al. (2015). An organizational perspective on the long-term sustainability of a nursing best practice guidelines program: A case study. *BMC Health Services Research, 15*(1), 535.

Gagnon, É., Clément, M., & Bordeleau, L. (2017). Speaking out and being heard residents' committees in Quebec's residential long-term care centre. *Health Care Analysis, 25*(4), 308–322.

Greenhalgh, T., et al. (2004). Diffusion of innovations in service organizations: Systematic review and recommendations. *The Milbank Quarterly, 82*(4), 581–629.

Greenhalgh, T., et al. (2012). "If we build it, will it stay?" A case study of the sustainability of whole-system change in London. *The Milbank Quarterly, 90*(3), 516–547.

Hamilton Health Sciences. (2020). *Virtual care for long-term care*. Hamilton, ON.

Hsu, A. T., & Lane, N. (2020). *Impact of COVID-19 on residents of Canada's long-term care homes—Ongoing challenges and policy response* (p. 15; I.L.T.C.P. Network, Ed.). Report in LTCcovid.org.

Institute of Medicine Committee on Quality of Health Care in America. (2001). *Crossing the quality chasm: A new health system for the 21st century*. Washington, DC: National Academies Press (US) Copyright 2001 by the National Academy of Sciences. All rights reserved.

Klinga, C., et al. (2018). Understanding the dynamics of sustainable change: A 20-year case study of integrated health and social care. *BMC Health Services Research, 18*(1), 400.

Kroneman, M., Boerma, W., van den Berg, M., Groenewegen, P., de Jong, J., & van Ginneken, E. (2016). The Netherlands: Health system review. *Health Systems in Transition, 18*(2), 1–239.

Lennox, L. (2020). Sustainability. In P. Nielsen & S. Birken (Eds.), *Handbook on implementation science* (pp. 333–367). Edward Elgar Publishing.

Luft, A. (2020, September 17). *Quebec coroner orders public inquiry into COVID-19 deaths in long-term care residences.* https://montreal.ctvnews.ca/quebec-coroner-orders-public-inquiry-into-covid-19-deaths-in-long-term-care-residences-1.4988171

Mayer, K. J., & Sparrowe, R. T. (2013). Integrating theories in AMJ Articles. *Academy of Management Journal, 56*(4), 917–922.

Norris, F. H., et al. (2008). Community resilience as a metaphor, theory, set of capacities, and strategy for disaster readiness. *American Journal of Community Psychology, 41*(1–2), 127–150.

Olshansky, R., Hopkins, L. D., & Johnson, L. A. (2012). Disaster and recovery: Processes compressed in time. *Natural Hazards Review, 13*, 173–178.

Ontairo Ministry of Health. (2020).*Billing for virtual physician services and technical guidance.* Info Bulletin. Ontairo Ministry of Health, Toronto, ON.

Ontario Ministry of Health Claims Services Branch. (2019). *Virtual care program—Billing amendments to enable direct-to-patient video visits and modernize virtual care compensation.* Info Bulletin, Toronto, ON.

Ontario Telemedicine Network. (2020a, August 10). *Important COVID-19 information and updates.*

Ontario Telemedicine Network. (2020b). *Cyber security advisory—Zoom.* Ontario Telemedicine Network, ON.

Pierson, S., et al. (2020). *Virtual care for long term care—Launching Monday!* (S.J.s.H. Hamilton, Ed.). Hamilton, ON.

PointClikcCare. (2020). *Better collaboration means better care for long-term care residents.* Hamilton, ON.

Pulejo, M., & Querubín, P. (2020). *Electoral concerns reduce restrictive measures during the COVID-19 pandemic* (National Bureau of Economic Research Working Paper Series, 2020. No. 27498).

Quarshie, A. M., & Leuschner, R. (2018). Cross-sector social interactions and systemic change in disaster response: A qualitative study. *Journal of Business Ethics, 150*(2), 357–384.

Shingler, B., & Montpetit, J. (2020). *Quebec finally gets a handle on COVID outbreaks in long-term care, but is it ready for a 2nd wave?* CBC News, Montreal.

Steele Gray, C., et al. (2018). Using information communication technology in models of integrated community-based primary health care: Learning from the iCOACH case studies. *Implementation Science, 13*(1), 87.

St. Joseph's Healthcare Hamilton. (2020, August 1). *Integrated Comprehensive Care (ICC).* https://www.stjoes.ca/hospital-services/integrated-comprehensive-care-icc

Sword-Daniels, V. L., et al. (2016). Unpacking long-term disaster recovery processes: A case study of the healthcare system in Montserrat, West Indies. *International Journal of Mass Emergencies and Disasters, 34*(1), 113–142.

Wankah, P., et al. (2018). Reorganising health and social care in Québec: A journey towards integrating care through mergers. *London Journal of Primary Care, 10*(3), 48–53.

Weible, C. M., et al. (2020). COVID-19 and the policy sciences: Initial reactions and perspectives. *Policy Sciences, 53*(2), 225–241.

Women's College Hospital Institute for Health Systems Solutions and Virtual Care (WHIV). (2019). *Enhanced access to primary care: Project evaluation final report* (p. 59). Women's College Hospital Institute for Health Systems Solutions and Virtual Care (WHIV), Toronto, ON.

Index

J. Waring et al. (eds.), *Organising Care in a Time of Covid-19*, Organizational Behaviour in Healthcare,
https://doi.org/10.1007/978-3-030-82696-3

P

The manufacturer's authorised representative in the EU is Springer Nature Customer Service Centre GmbH, Europaplatz 3, 69115 Heidelberg, Germany. If you have any concerns regarding our products, please contact ProductSafety@springernature.com

Printed and bound by CPI Group (UK) Ltd, Croydon, CR0 4YY
30/09/2026
02225459-0018